Concepts of Person

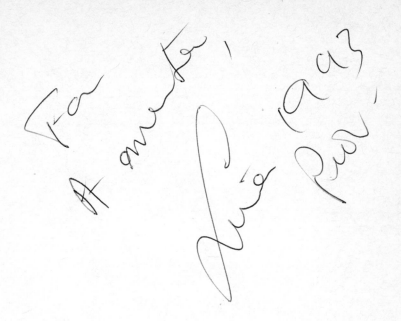

CONCEPTS OF PERSON

KINSHIP, CASTE, AND MARRIAGE IN INDIA

Edited by Ákos Östör,
Lina Fruzzetti,
and Steve Barnett

Contributors

Ákos Östör
Lina Fruzzetti
Steve Barnett
Sylvia Vatuk
T. N. Madan
Anthony T. Carter
R. S. Khare
Pauline Kolenda

DELHI
OXFORD UNIVERSITY PRESS
BOMBAY CALCUTTA MADRAS
1992

Oxford University Press, Walton Street, Oxford OX2 6DP

New York Toronto
Delhi Bombay Calcutta Madras Karachi
Kuala Lumpur Singapore Hong Kong Tokyo
Nairobi Dar es Salaam
Melbourne Auckland

and associates in
Berlin Ibadan

Originally published by
Harvard University Press 1982

Printed at Rekha Printers Pvt. Ltd., New Delhi 110020
and published by S. K. Mookerjee, Oxford University Press
YMCA Library Building, Jai Singh Road, New Delhi 110001

For Leila, Katya, and Amy

Foreword

by David Maybury-Lewis

THE STUDY OF KINSHIP, broadly defined, has traditionally occupied a central place in anthropology. This is not only because anthropologists regularly studied peoples who carried out the bulk of their social interactions in terms of kinship, but also because the very study of kinship held out the promise that it would one day enable anthropology to emerge as a true science of society. Ever since Lewis Henry Morgan first discovered the regularities in kinship systems and tried to account for their occurrence in different parts of the world, anthropologists have been lured by the prospect of using kinship analysis to link the necessary with the contingent in human affairs, to establish the scientific bridge between nature and culture. It was clearly in this spirit that Lévi-Strauss wrote *Les structures élémentaires de la parenté* over thirty years ago, but since then the dream has faded. Some Marxists still claim that kinship analysis has a central place in a proper (Marxist) science of anthropology, and some sociobiologists seem to believe that scientific kinship analysis will render anthropology obsolete. I find both claims unconvincing. Yet it is clear that anthropologists in general have lost faith in the traditional approaches to kinship.

This malaise was well summed up by Rodney Needham, who noted that when British social anthropologists decided in 1969 to get back to firm anthropological ground, they proposed a conference on kinship and marriage. Needham was invited to convene the conference, but the publication resulting from it was skeptically entitled *Rethinking Kinship and Marriage.* In it Needham himself wrote that "there is no such thing as kinship and it follows that there can be no such thing as kinship theory" (p. 5). By this he meant that kinship was too poorly defined for there to be a theory of it and, furthermore, that mere redefinition of it would not help. There were epistemological problems in the conceptualization of kinship whose solution would render conventional analysis obsolete.

The problem is that all societies recognize, and many attach huge importance to, the relationships anthropologists have loosely called kinship. Yet these relationships are so embedded in their cultural context that they cannot usefully be analyzed separately from that context. There is thus no such thing as kinship theory as distinct from cultural (or social) theory. This is what David Schneider too has been insisting on, and it is this insistence which serves as the point of departure for the present volume.

Concepts of Person is a major contribution to the trend in anthropological studies which treats the classic topics of traditional kinship analysis in a wider frame of reference. The essays in this volume present a series of interconnected arguments around a central theme, relating cultural categories and social behavior to ideas about the person in Indian society. The approach builds on the work of Louis Dumont to show the connection (as opposed to the conventional contrast) between the social theory and practice of north India and the corresponding ideology and action of south India. In so doing, the volume sheds new light on the topics of caste, kinship, and marriage in India, but it also has a wider significance, transcending its considerable contribution to Indian studies.

It is one of a number of parallel investigations in different parts of the world which seek to analyze cultural categories systematically and to relate them to social action. These studies do not focus directly on kinship and have, for this reason, succeeded in resolving some of the traditional problems of kinship analysis. Instead they show how a people's cosmological ideas and social theories are linked to their notions of the person, the self, and the individual. They also show the connections between social theory and social action in such a way as to make possible a comparative study of ideologies and their operation.

Such an approach has worked well for the small-scale tribal societies of Australia and South America. It has proved illuminating as applied to the larger politics of Indonesia and Southeast Asia. This volume shows how fruitful it is when applied to a huge society with a civilization as ancient and complex as that of India. These investigations are thus fulfilling an old anthropological dream. It is not the dream of creating a science of society out of kinship studies, which proved to be a will-o'-the-wisp. It is instead the realization of the old anthropological ambition to deal with a wide range of human societies in a single, comprehensive frame of reference; to link, in the words of Lévi-Strauss, the elementary with the complex. This is being accomplished not, as Lévi-Strauss predicted, by a breakthrough in our understanding of Crow and Omaha systems (which turned out to be a false problem) but rather through the development of a new style of cultural anthropology.

Concepts of Person marks an important stage in this development, for it extends the approach to one of the most complex of all civilizations. Its publication is also significant in another sense. With the appearance of this volume, Harvard Studies in Cultural Anthropology has published arguments from different regions of the world—from South America (in *Dialectical Societies*), Indonesia (in *The Flow of Life*) and now India—all converging on a number of common central themes. In this way the series has provided, and hopes to continue to provide, the materials for a new comparative anthropology which will be inspired by the old anthropological virtue of illuminating the general through the intensive study of the particular.

Preface

THIS VOLUME ORIGINATED in the discussions between Louis Dumont, Lina Fruzzetti, Ákos Östör, and Steve Barnett in Princeton during the fall and winter of 1973. We planned to hold a small international conference around themes we found to be central to an anthropology of South Asia. The first phase of the work was carried out while Östör was a member of the Institute for Advanced Study, Fruzzetti was a Foreign Area Fellow, and Barnett was on the faculty of Princeton University. This conference was organized in 1976, and the final revisions of the papers were completed in 1980. We are grateful to three institutions and many people for making our work possible. The Wenner-Gren Foundation and the Association for Asian Studies provided grants, Harvard University made a financial contribution and gave us the use of several facilities. Professors of the Anthropology Department provided hospitality to the participants. We would like to thank all the sponsoring institutions for their warm support, the Department of Anthropology and Harvard University for hosting the conference, the National Humanities Center, where Ákos Östör held a fellowship while preparing the volume for publication, the faculty and families of the department for helping with the arrangements in every way, and the participants for putting up with several years of delays and changes.

Ákos Östör
Lina Fruzzetti
Steve Barnett

Contents

*Concepts of Person: Fifteen Years Later**

Ákos Östör
Lina Fruzzetti

CONCEPTS OF PERSON (1982) has taken its place among anthropological works of the early 1980s which attempted to develop new interpretive approaches and categories for the analysis of South Asian societies. Renewed interest in indigenous cultural concepts and the cultural construction of the person now encompasses all areas of the world and several distinct approaches which have failed, as yet, to engage in any significant dialogue with each other. Witness the appearance, a few years later, of a collection entitled *Category of the Person* (ed. Carrithers 1985) which inexplicably made no reference to our earlier volume. For this new edition (published by the Oxford University Press), we cannot survey the entire field; rather we select a number of studies directly concerned with the kind of work *Concepts of Person* represents.

I

Contributors to the original Harvard University Press edition have continued to extend and refine the approaches they announced in their articles.

Sylvia Vatuk writes:

At the time I wrote 'Forms of Address. . .' I had already begun doing research and publishing in two related areas: gender and ageing. In studying both women and the elderly in India I was centrally concerned with cultural meanings and constructions. For example, a 1982 paper deals with differing interpretations (as between Hindus and Muslims) of the cultural meaning of female veiling. In a 1984 publication I was able to combine my interests in both gender and ageing in an exploration of South Asian cultural constructions of female sexuality through the life course. Here I focused specifically upon the question of what is thought to happen to her sexual identity as a woman ages. Again, in a 1987 publication I discussed the issue of Indian women's ability to exercise authority and power over others, and autonomy in terms of her own activities, and how this changes as she grows older. My most recent work on ageing (1990) describes the anxieties expressed by the old people I studied in the Delhi area about becoming physically helpless and dependent in old age, and tries to situate the meaning of these anxieties within the Indian cultural context, distinguishing them from the fears of Americans who also express a wish to avoid dependency in later life.

In 1984, having worked among Hindus in India for my entire career, I began a project whose initial goal was to formulate a cultural account of Muslim kinship and marriage. For various serendipitous reasons, however, this has developed into a study of the past two hundred years through the eyes and experiences of a large Muslim descent group whose members are located mainly in Madras and Hyderabad. In this study I am particularly interested in the way that a 'family culture' and a family is contrasted with a personal identity as constructed and maintained over a number of generations, helping to mold and direct the responses of members of the family to the hardships and opportunities presented to them in a society experiencing dramatic social transformation. A forthcoming article on the cultural construction of shared identity (in press) presents some of my thinking on this, and a book is under preparation.

T. N. Madan writes:

The essay on 'the Ideology of the Householder . . .' was first written in 1976–7, rather hesitantly, at the invitation of the editors of the volume who were also the organizers of the Harvard conference on the concepts of the person (December 1976). The hesitancy reflected a process of rethinking that was going on in my mind regarding the scope of anthropological studies (including those of kinship)—whether and to what extent values should be included in them. I had written a paper two years earlier drawing attention to these questionings in a very general way (see Madan 1975).

This essay was further revised, though not extensively, and published in Madan, ed., 1982. The 1982 text has been reproduced in Madan 1987a, 1989. It should be obvious that I believe this essay to be useful not only in rounding off my earlier structural–functional study of Pandit kinship and marriage but also as a contribution to providing a corrective to the view that sees renunciation as the central motif of Hindu life at the cost of the values of auspiciousness and well-being associated with domestic—the latter being the central theme of *Non-Renunciation*. Incidentally, *Non-Renunciation* includes an essay, 'Living and dying,' written in 1982–3, which continues to reflect what I hope is a broadening of my theoretical approach to the study of society, acknowledging the importance of people's own ideas about their life, their 'lifeworld', though not espousing a wholly phenomenological perspective. This same attentiveness informs my current studies of religion, politics and society (see Madan 1987b).

Anthony Carter writes:
In a tradition deriving from Mauss through Fortes, my contribution to *Concepts of Person* was concerned with personhood as a kind of office, a capacity to act in society that is culturally defined and conferred by society. I have not written more on personhood in Maharashtra, but I have used the concepts involved and some of the material in a very different context.

Much of my research since the conference on which *Concepts of Person* was based has been concerned with problems in demography. As this research has developed I have become increasingly aware that available theoretical perspectives are based on or lead to a series of impasses. Among these are wholly unsatisfactory, even if widely accepted, concepts of agency and culture. In both the classic macro-sociological and the newer economic accounts of fertility change, culture is conceived of as a set of residual norms distinct from and external to action. This separation of culture repeatedly insists on breaking out of the place assigned to it while at the same time failing to perform the functions demanded of it.

I am now working, therefore, on a more adequate theory of agency, joining the company of Bourdieu, Giddens, Lave and others, but concentrating particularly on fertility. In general terms, I am looking at the ways in which what Lave calls 'activity-in-setting, seamlessly stretched across persons-acting and setting often turns the latter into a calculating device.' More specifically, I am interested in how features of domestic space and activities, including talk, the body, and personhood enter into flows of conduct involved in family formation as aids in problem solving. With regard to personhood in particular, I am pursuing insights developed by Kristin Luker in her work on abortion, insights suggesting that culturally variable decision points constituted in the course of family formation are shaped in part by concepts of personhood as these are deployed in the management of relations with sexual partners and family.

I had a first shot at these questions in a brief essay (1988). I will pursue them further in a forthcoming book on population problems tentatively titled *Vital Events: The Anthropology of Family Formation*.

R. S. Khare writes:
My work on Indian notions of personhood has proceeded mainly in three contexts—the Untouchable, the eater, and the saint. The three examples underscore different interrelationships Hindus pose between body (or bodies) and soul for conjuring up the notion of personhood. These exercises allow me to pursue the questions of extension (and alienation) between Hindus' learned and popular notions of body and soul. For Hindus, can there be a body or a person without a soul?

Pauline Kolenda writes:
Since the article on widowhood among 'Untouchable' Chuhras, I have published several papers on aspects of Chuhra life (see e.g. Kolenda 1987a

and b). Other caste communities have been the focus of some of my writings—a village of Brahmans in southern Tamilnadu, as well as Nadars and other castes of that region (e.g. Kolenda 1984), and Rajputs of Khalapur, the dominant caste community in the north Indian village where Khalapur, the dominant caste community in the north Indian village where the Chuhras were the lowest caste (ibid.). I have written more generally on caste in India (e.g. Kolenda 1986) and on family structure in one state, Rajasthan (1989), and on changes in caste attitudes in village Khalapur over a thirty-year period. Within cultural anthropology more generally, I have taken interest in the developing anthropology of women and have written commentary on various issues and works, as well as editing a book (1988). Currently I am analyzing a south Indian marriage network, an effective form of caste community, that of the low-caste Nattatti Nadars of southern Tamilnadu.

II

The separate treatment of gender, as an important aspect of Indian societies, began in the late 1960s and early 1970s. Gender studies were able to build on new approaches to kinship, caste, marriage, and hierarchy. Drawing on Schneider, Dumont, and Marriott's cultural, structural, and symbolic studies, recent analyses of the cultural construction of gender utilize indigenous conceptions and meanings of *woman* and *person* (Das 1982; Dhruvarajan 1988; Fruzzetti 1981, 1982; Krygier 1982; Madan 1983, 1987; Marglin 1985; Stutchbury 1982; Wadley 1975, 1986).

Constructions of gender involve the domains of ritual, caste hierarchy and power, purity and pollution, and the system of relationships and exchanges among groups in the formation of marriage alliances. Interpreting the notion of womanhood and of women as persons in South Asian culture necessitates the separation of gender from caste, kinship and marriage. At present newer, feminist perspectives are enriching the anthropology of gender in India. Concerns with subjugation, exploitation, and the decline of women's position began to problematize the study of gender. One direction, which looks at the position of women from a national and international perspective, tends to ignore cultural specificity and utilizes more abstract universal constructions.

Other recent research, not necessarily on gender but critical of our approach, has evolved along two divergent lines. One, represented by McKim Marriott and his disciples, has termed itself the ethnosociology of India. The other, more traditional, is still concerned with issues of hierarchy, caste, kinship, hypergamy and the like (Scheffler 1980; Parry 1979; Gray 1980; Good 1982).

Marriott has developed a distinctive and influential approach to, among other things, the person in India (or variably, Hindus in India, although neither category is *constituted* in analysis). Marriott refers to an indigenous system of thought while proceeding in terms of a transactional, dyadic, sociological theory of exchange. The theory depends on the designation of units, substances, and strategies of exchange. Marriott's approach, announced about fifteen years ago in a series of mostly co-authored works (Marriott 1976; Marriott and Inden 1974, 1977; Inden and Nicholas 1977), has been followed with a new contribution by Marriott himself and essays by scholars close, and others not so close to his style of work (ed. Marriott 1990). The earlier series were strongly criticized by the editors (see Barnett, Fruzzetti, and Östör 1976—and their contributions to this volume) on philosophical, epistemological, and ethnographic grounds. In defense of his work, Marriott composed a thoughtful and significant rejoinder (1976) which occasioned further critical remarks by us (Barnett, Fruzzetti and Östör 1977). These remain unanswered. After a gap of fifteen years come refinements of the original theory. Astonishingly neither Marriott nor the other contributors refer to the earlier exchange. We have noted some fundamental stumbling blocks to the progress of a particular ethnosociology and until those are removed any further refinement is fraught with difficulties. The strictures we raised are still applicable, even though Marriott's theory has undergone a degree of transformation.

Dirks (1987, 1989), while not directly concerned with concepts of person, argues in principle against the separation of status and power, and hierarchy in terms of purity and pollution. In elevating royal power to superiority he has trouble formulating a theory of hierarchy. Further problems arise with his attempt to deal with kinship/marriage in terms of power. Power as concept and strategy cannot account for kinship relations and choices of partners to alliance. Nor can it, in a superior position, constitute persons, relatives, codes of conduct, gender, and descent lines.

In a similar vein Raheja, one of Marriott's disciples, restages the battles of the 1960s and 1970s in attempting to demolish Louis Dumont's contribution to anthropology. In an article purporting to be a review of the literature Raheja (1988a) makes an indiscriminate attack on Dumont's work only to vindicate her mentor, while failing to make a reference to the one critical exchange in which Marriott himself participated. So much for scholarship.

Raheja follows Dirks in the matter of power but criticizes the residual argument of hierarchy which would merely reverse the positions of Brahman and Kṣatriya. Raheja's problems start and end with gift exchanges, the core of her contribution. *Dān* is given inter- and intra-caste, in the appropriate ritual context, to 'move away inauspiciousness'. Receiving *dān* is inauspicious, the 'poison in the gift', while giving *dān* is auspiciousness itself. Raheja abstracts exchanges out of the larger cultural universe and conflates *saṃskāras* with exchanges in general. With an air of making a major discovery Raheja wonders why others have not recognized the significance of *dān*. But then she fails to consider the one full-scale work on marriage gifts (Fruzzetti 1982) which *does* consider the larger cultural universe. Raheja's restricted gift matrix does not deal with, among other things, purity, hierarchy, and marriage alliances. Not surprisingly, caste for Raheja is none of the above, rather it is the daily, contextualized center-periphery of exchange on specific terms. What happened to the sacred, ritual, and Hindu ideologies and practices in general?

The crucial question for anthropological theory is why Brahmans, superior in status, accept a gift when the act of receiving is polluting, inauspicious, and inferior? If the giver may well ignore this question the taker (and the anthropologist) cannot. After all we have to consider the entire universe of discourse: merely reproducing the ideology of the giver is not enough. Comparisons must be made, empirical observations can be put together with collective and historical categories, including the realm of the Shastras. Anthropologists cannot convert the particular ideologies of particular informants directly into cultural theories without any further mediation.

Parry's and Raheja's arguments are curiously hierarchical, succeeding merely in reversing the direction of encompassment. Now it appears that giving and inauspiciousness are the encompassing elements, but on what theory (and warrant of cultural facts in support) does the argument rest?

For Marriott, Raheja, Dirks and others the task is, in Appadurai's words, to 'put hierarchy in its place', which for these anthropologists seems to be no place at all. In our view, the shared endeavor should no longer be for or against Dumont (although we stand by our formulations of 1976 and 1977 [Barnett, Östör and Fruzzetti 1976, 1977]). Rather, it should be the comparative understanding of societies to which Dumont has made a secure, unimpeachable contribution. We have been critical of Dumont's work, he has criticized us, we recognize his profound achievements, and yet we are able to take a different direction.[1] Dirks, and especially Raheja reduce Dumont's complex and difficult work to a parody of structuralism, with single-minded absolutes of religion *or* politics, purity *or* power, high *or* low, and further reifications of Western ideology, while they leave the cornerstone of *Homo Hierarchicus* undisturbed, the relational and comparative analysis of India *and* the West, indigenous *and* analytic categories, and the changes occasioned by two centuries of colonial and independent regimes.

More specifically our work has come under fire from several directions: kinship terminology (Scheffler 1980) alliance and hypergamy (Gray 1980; Good 1982).[2] Going beyond these instances, in a more positive way, is the attempt of Milner (1988) to embrace all rival approaches, cultural and sociological, and construct an ambitious comparison of marriage systems in South Asia in the shape of grand theory. Milner argues that while there is a degree of 'status homogeneity and endogamy in marriage alliances', departures are also institutionalized and can be accounted for, among other factors, by the structural and ideological 'encapsulation' of variant patterns. While successfully assimilating data from diverse theoretical contexts Milner's remains an external, sociological grid made up of seemingly universal social-science categories where variation and deviation are accommodated in sub-systems and sub-theories.

We are in sympathy with Milner's synthesis because he made an effort to accommodate an approach different from his own, call it what you will, cultural, symbolic, or interpretive. Major differences with his sociological account remain, but it is important to examine just what general theories and cultural accounts accomplish, how and where they converge and diverge.

Another reason for our sympathy is that Milner's article rekindles interest in a style of analysis that has been somewhat neglected. Our studies of Bengali kinship and marriage have been taken up in the literature more in the ways they contribute new ethnographic data, and less as a promising theoretical departure. In terms of theory, our work was assimilated to 'Chicago ethnosociology', whatever that is, a strange circumstance since we have criticized several accounts emanating from Chicago (see Introduction, Chapter 2, and Conclusion). Be that as it may, we hoped and still hope to expand the universe of kinship-marriage both in terms of ethnography and interpretation.

The concept of 'alliance' came into our comparison of Bengal and Tamilnadu through the debate concerning the way descent and marriage theories order areas of social relationships (see Chapter 1). Lévi-Strauss has opposed generalized to restricted exchange (FZD vs. MBD marriages) establishing alliance as a principle of social structure. More specific is Dumont's reformulation of cross-cousin marriage as alliance between brothers-in-law, to which, eventually, even Lévi-Strauss deferred. Dumont's subsequent studies of terminology and marriage in North and South India set the stage for all subsequent discussions of the question. Accounts of alliance today range from Dumont's restricted version to a broad notion of marriage involving a relationship between the relatives of bride and groom. For Dumont, alliance meant a terminological marriage rule which designates marriageable partners and is passed down the generations.

What was exciting and original about Dumont's work was the recognition that alliance was not 'cross-cousin marriage', in the language of consanguinity, but a cultural distinction between various categories of kin wrought by the dominance of affinity. The designated marriage categories were not 'cousins' but 'brothers-in-law'. Later on Barnett (1976) elaborated the argument by adding the cultural logic of *utampu* (male aspect of blood) and *uyir* (female aspect). Marriage assures a 'maximum exchange of *utampu* and *uyir* within [the] kindred. South Indians marry precisely those persons of equivalent purity with whom they share the least' (p. 14). So-called cross-cousins share the least *utampu* and *uyir*.

Nothing like the Tamil situation obtains in North India—not in the case of terminological rules, not in the inheritance of marriageable categories, not in the creation of endogamous groups. Yet there are similarities in kinship/marriage practices, north and south, and not surprisingly there are concomitant ideologies and categories. For these reasons we spoke of 'alliance' in Bengal. Dumont and Vatuk on the other hand looked to a restricted universe of kinship terminologies to reveal the ideology and the needed categories, but could not come up with an elegant system to parallel the clarity of the South Indian case.[3]

What is to be done in such a situation? One can limit the universe of social relations and find the rules therein. Some regularities and patterns will emerge even from partial segments of social systems. This is what seems to have been accomplished by componential analysis, and the search for terminological and generative rules—Scheffler, Lounsbury and others have written in this vein. Or one can explore whether or not kinship (or relationship) categories 'express' something else, to wit, the vexed problems of marriage practices may be cleared up by rules of kinship terminology. Dumont, Vatuk and others wrote critical variations on this theme. Quite different are attempts to find, in kinship-marriage ideologies and practices, the production and reproduction of economic and social systems, for which of course the above approaches are entirely beside the point.

Scheffler outdoes all others when he claims to perceive enough 'internal inconsistencies' in our criticism of terminological studies to 'discard' our data. But wait, it turns out that a few rewrite-rules take care of both 'inconsistencies' and data. One may well ask just what is achieved by this sort of kinship algebra? Scheffler's view of the genealogical kinship grid is so secure that he can legislate, from 6000 miles away, what is valid data and what is not. His procedure is to tinker with the elements till they fit the theory.

Scheffler objects to our way of establishing categories such as *bhai*. In his eagerness to refute us he mistakes Dumont's and Vatuk's work for ours. Reproaching us for not pursuing the cultural categories where they may lead, he claims that we conflate the meaning of kinship terms with their vocative use, an absurd accusation. Conceivably Scheffler did not read the careful exposition of *bhai* in our essays, having confined himself to the introductory parts of our account where we indicate the range of usages concerning *bhai*. He ignores the evidence for marriageable and non-marriageable *bhai*, the hierarchical aspect of the category, and is not aware of the direction (marriage and death rituals) in which the cultural logic is taking us. Nor does he seem to have noted the arguments for defining relatives and for constituting persons, blood, marriage, line, seed and earth, and the like as cultural categories. All this is not surprising since we explicitly argue that terminology (in Scheffler's sense) does not deliver the system and that we have to leave his kind of restricted universe if we hope to make sense of what is going on in Bengal. Ritual, hierarchy, encompassment and not terminological rules set apart the meanings of *bhai*.

Alternatively one can go on, as we did, to a more general universe of kinship derived from any or all of the above, and work our way over to an indigenous system or domain of kinship, marriage, ritual, sacred, and exchange ideologies and practices— exhibiting properties of regularity, order, or pattern, apprehended through a dialectic of both social science and Bengali cultural categories.

Finally one can, as Milner did, look for a general theory that would account for some variations, incorporating parts of the above approaches, and end up with, admittedly, low-level generalizations, which if they do not deal with all exceptions and details, at least sum up the shared features. The shared features, however, may not be the significant ones. What is to become of differences? What is the purpose of such theories? Are variations peripheral to a general theory of marriage? A failure to recognize the differences among these approaches leads to reproaching one or another for failing to do what it does not set out to deal with and is incapable of doing.

It seems to us that in social science 'kinship' is never complete in itself, analytically speaking, since in one case it expresses marriage or some other domain, while in others it is duly accounted for by economic, jural, or political facts. Is that which expresses or that which is being expressed something else? What then are all these 'things'? Mere epiphenomena of each other? Are we to disassemble kinship into economic, political, social (stratificatory) and ideological components? Is there nothing that sets kinship apart on a level with other domains of social relationships?[4]

III

How and where do we start making sense of kinship/marriage practices? Where do we bring in and when do we leave the 'native' ideologies? Everyone answers these questions somehow but we all differ in the terms and extent to which we try to make sense of what we see and hear. Should we continue to contrast northern confusion to southern clarity? Is it not misleading to set up structural elegance as a contrast? Can't we make sense of Bengali practices, starting with whatever stimulus, be it general theory or particular ideology, and proceed comparatively or parallel to other work on Tamilnadu, Maharashtra, or Kashmir? We are convinced that it is possible to do both, but we have to be aware of what we are doing and where we are being led.

What is alliance? If we draw the boundaries very strictly then alliance may only apply to a few groups in the South. What kind of universe should we include? What do the practices and the ideas/terms attached to them mean? Either we do what Dumont and some others practice, and start with consanguinity and affinity, genealogical terminology, and proceed to lay this grid on some local domain of practices, or we pursue the indigenous cultural logic to wherever it may lead. Dumont in fact did a partial job of both, breaking off the latter perhaps too soon so that he could rescue a semblance of the former. But neither approach takes refuge in statistics or quantification: the problems of terminology, category, logic and rules will not be solved by piling up incidence of marriage, especially when the job of what is to be quantified has yet to be attended to.

Gray (1980) reproaches us for reducing hierarchy to inequality in marriage relationships. He avers that the wife-giving/wife-taking relation is hierarchical, while in our essays it is merely an unequal gift-giving relationship. Not so, Dumont could be as easily accused of reducing alliance to *equality* in the South. Within particular limits hierarchy can not prevail since endogamy calls for a level and measure of equality. At that stage hierarchy is reasserted through ritual. We have argued that hypergamy is subsumed by the ideology of marriage alliance. Marriages are entered through negotiated equivalence. The superiority of wife-taker endures after the ritual only in the marriage concerned. Hence the continued and unequal gift-giving relationship *and* the possibility of a reversal in the direction of subsequent marriages.

In Bengal we do not find a hard and fast hierarchy in the shape of ranked groups giving and receiving brides. But does wife-giving *define* any group anywhere in the North?[5] Hierarchy comes about in the marriage ritual and in the situation brought about by marriages. This does not involve groups: the central hierarchical act in the ritual (other than the linking of bride and groom) is the bride's father touching the groom's knee, as if the whole bride-giving line or side were englobed by the line about to be established. But this is only momentarily so in the act of *kanyādān* itself, since the bride alone is assumed into the line of the groom, and is then separated in other ways (through *baṇgsa*, *sapiṇḍa*, and *śrāddha*) from her father's line.

Anthropological accounts of hypergamy are also suspect: they cannot accommodate exchange marriages within the same endogamous group. If they do, then 'hypergamy' can only be regarded as a partial and selective, not a completely ranked system that exhausts an entire social universe. Saraswati's data from Mithila and ours from Bengal routinely refer to exchange marriages (see Figures 1–9). Hence 'hypergamy' is, at best, a status and exchange ideology artificially separated by social scientists from the wider domain of marriage and ritual.

Parry (1986) and Raheja (1988b, 1989) argue along similar lines about the nature of gift-giving. In the *dāna* exchange the impurity and inauspiciousness of the gift-givers are removed. When given in a ritual context, to 'a Brahman, Barber, Sweeper, or a wife-taking affine, . . . the gift will bring misfortune unless the correct ritual precautions are taken' (Parry,

Exchange Marriages in Bengal and Mithila

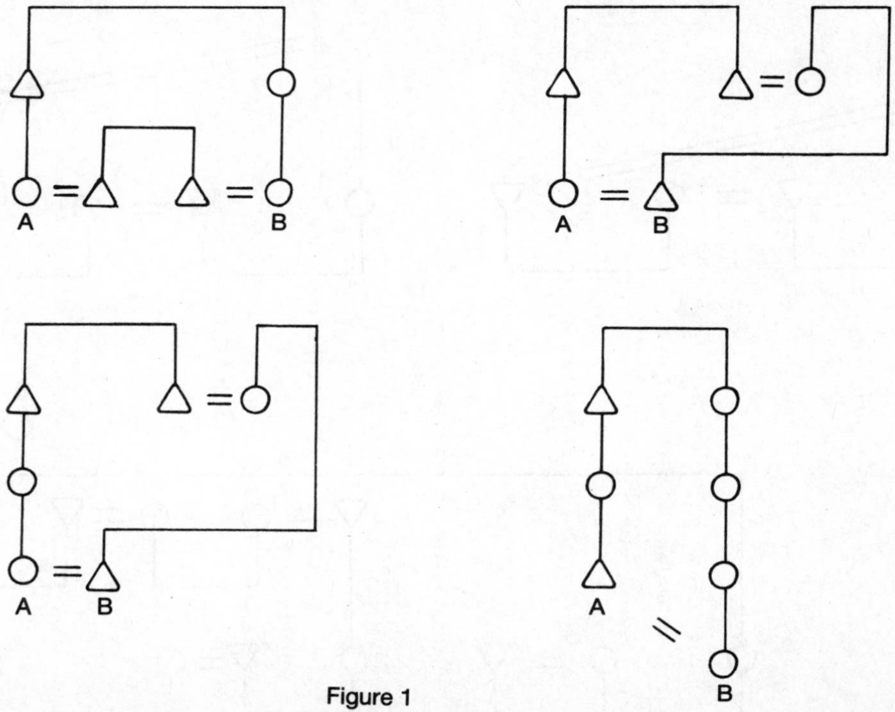

Figure 1

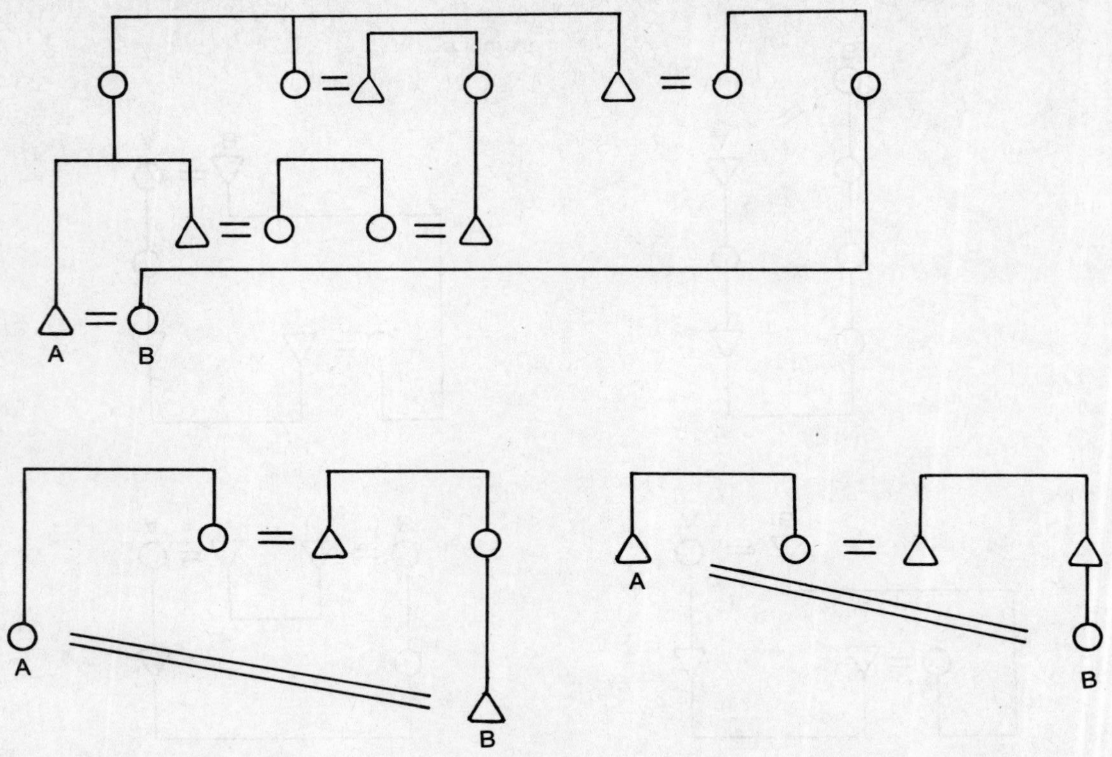

Figure 2

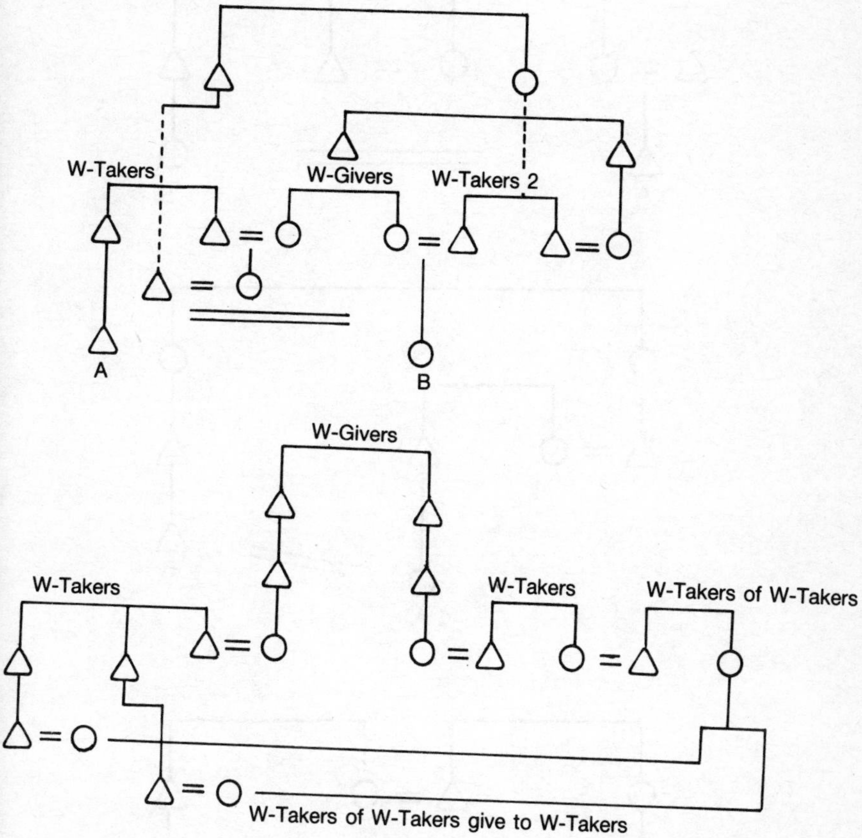
W-Takers
W-Givers
W-Takers 2
A
B
W-Givers
W-Takers
W-Takers
W-Takers of W-Takers
W-Takers of W-Takers give to W-Takers

Figure 3

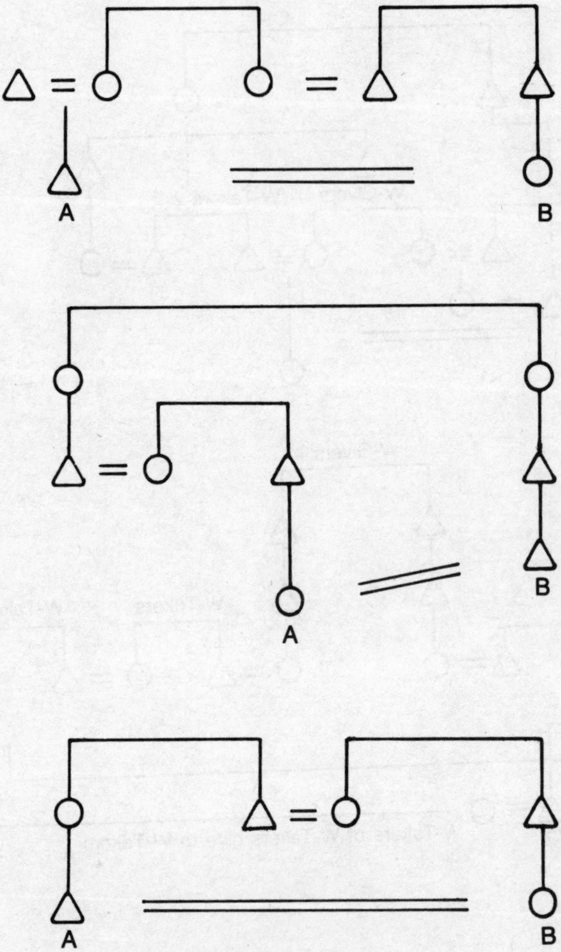

Figure 4

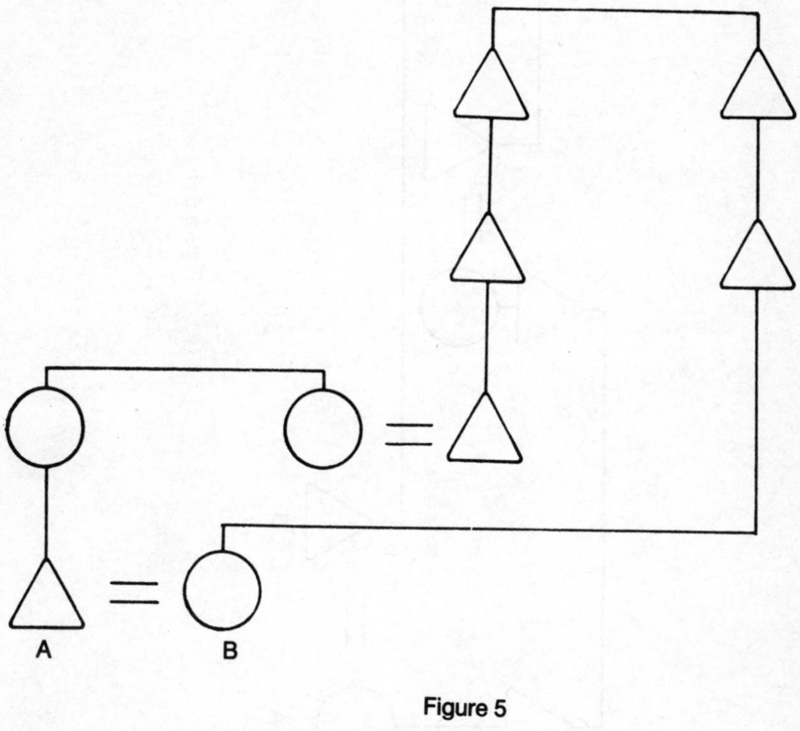

Figure 5

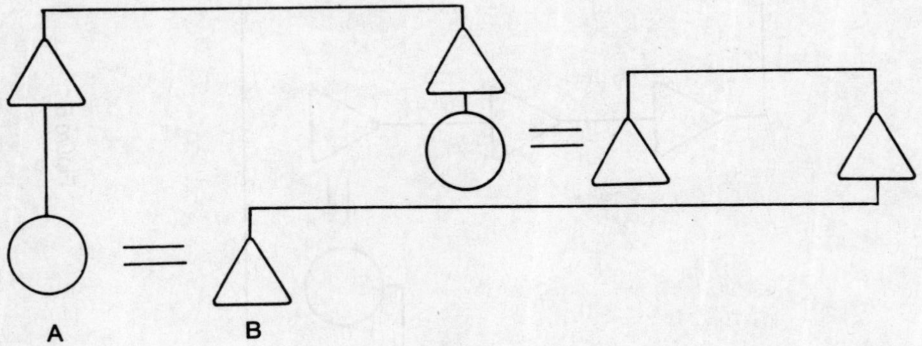

Figure 6

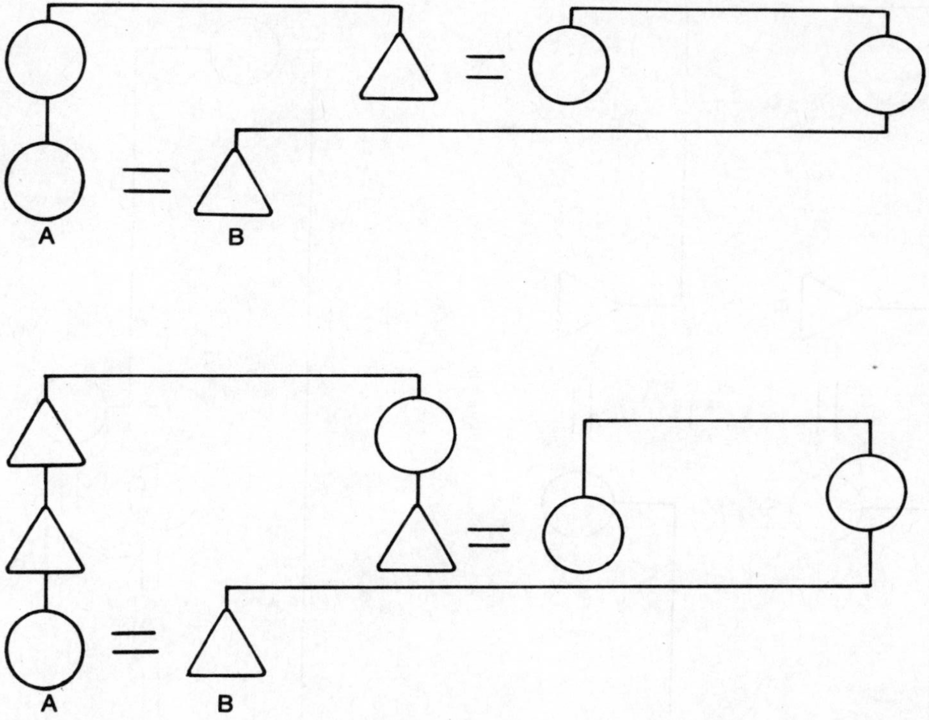

Figure 7

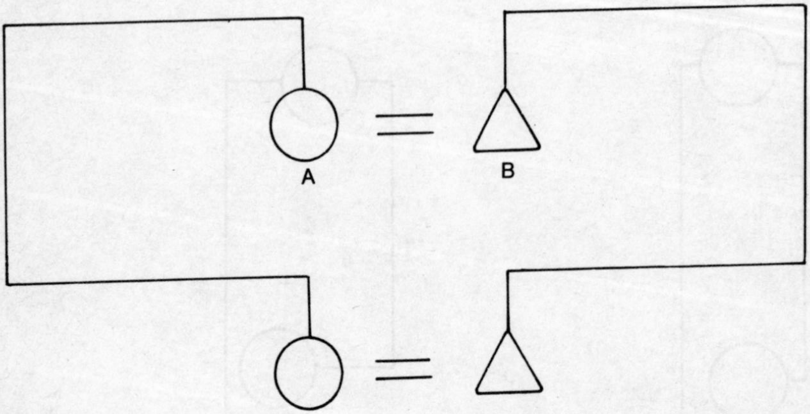

Figure 8

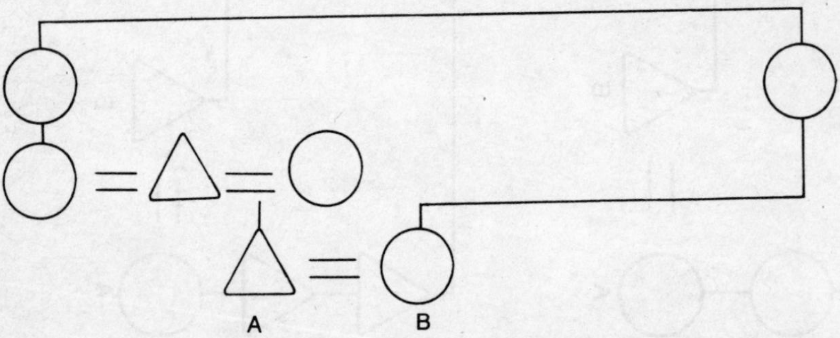

Figure 9

1986:460). Parry follows up this narrow description of the *dāna* gifts by drawing a clear parallel between the way the gift of the bride, *kanyādān*, and all other *dānas* affect the wife-takers as a group, arguing that the inauspiciousness they receive places the wife-takers in a permanently inferior position. Yet *kanyādān*, the gift of a virgin, is the most sacred, pure, and auspicious gift, a *dāna* given once in the woman's lifetime. Accepting the bride is auspicious in itself, without any poison or impurity. This circumstance jeopardizes both the narrow, undifferentiated exchange view of Raheja and Parry, and Parry's detaching of hypergamy from the wider universe of kinship/marriage/caste and ritual. Marriage as a sacred rite removes the possibility of any impurity occurring in the descent line of the bride's father. It is the bride-givers who are, at the time of *kanyādān* and by extension subsequently, obligated and subordinated to the bride-takers. However this is an encompassing, hierarchical, rather than stratified, status relationship, the direction of which can be, and in some contexts such as Bengal, Mithila and elsewhere, is reversed.

Parry's detailed account of caste and marriage in Kangra (1979) suggests that there are no hard and fast boundaries to groups, that it is difficult if not impossible to arrange 'clans' in a hierarchy, that there are exceptions everywhere—yet he insists on 'hypergamous hierarchy' with inferiors giving to superiors (or equals) immediately above them in a neat ladder-like arrangement. It appears further that 'groups' of givers and takers are hard to define, marriages are negotiated case by case, ranking and precedence are contested, alliance-like practices are recognizable, and hierarchy is everywhere.

In 1979 Parry still argues that the high value of *kanyādān* makes it fit for equals or superiors alone, hence the subsequent and paradoxical, one-sided gift-giving to the bride-takers. Later, in reconsidering the 'Indian gift', and in part accepting Raheja's suggestions, Parry (1986) claims that the gift inferiorizes the receiver. What happens now to hierarchy let alone 'hypergamous hierarchy'? The proffered answer would reverse the direction of superiority, elevate episodic, behavioral, and dyadic transactions to the level of cultural principles. Raheja devalues hierarchy, making centrality and mutuality superior in exchange, englobing both (á la Dirks) in (royal) power. In making such a *hierarchical* argument, she offers neither warrant nor theory. What happens to the *encompassed* element (to put it in Dumont's terms)? Could not Raheja's narrow, one-dimensional, 'dominant' giving itself be encompassed in yet another direction?

The classical version of hypergamy represents a rationalized system that is extended out of individual marriage relationships to a ladder-like progression up and down a scale. Is there a bottom pool and top scarcity of brides in a system of hypergamous practices other than the purely abstract, hypothetical demands of the model? Are brides recruited at the bottom and expendable at the top? De these (external) sociological generalizations exhaust an entire universe or are they mere tendencies alongside other practices? We surmise that these questions are open to construction from data in actual marriage cycles. The rationality of hypergamy is too rarified to be true of actual ideology and practice. We can see such recruitment happening in each particular case, depending on changes in valuation, so that a higher status family would bring in a daughter-in-law, not just directly below themselves, but from *anywhere*, especially when the marriage is concluded by negotiation, and not by the ladder-like succession of hypergamous groups giving and taking brides. For hypergamy to convince there should be a kinship domain separate from marriage and both to be separate from caste. The entire society in question would have to be divided and ranked into groups with firm boundaries, arranged on a vertical ladder and exchanging brides without exception in strict precedence up and down the line.

The problem with the concepts of hypergamy/hypogamy/isogamy is that they are predefined as social science systems and then illustrated from Indian materials. Less problematic than hypergamy is the case of the alliance system where terminology and practice point to the repetition of intermarriages in endogamous groups, especially in the South. The repetition is possible in parts of the North; neither prescribed nor forbidden by terminology, nor demonstrated by the orderly progression of marriage cycles, it is ruled out by some groups (by other means) and allowed by other groups. Hence there is no alliance of brothers-in-law in an ordered and predictable system, rather an alliance-like scheme which challenges us to generalize, compare and interpret all the contrasts and similarities between North and South.

Is hierarchy, not the watered-down version of hypergamy, a central feature of alliance? We have to distinguish several senses. The key element of a hypothesis issuing from a theory of hypergamy—the existence of ranked endogamous groups— does not prove to be a significant empirical feature. Were the case otherwise, what would happen to equality? How would the system establish equivalence between marriageable lines or categories? Hierarchy *and* equality are linked in kinship and marriage. The husband/wife tie is explicitly hierarchical, the wife being *arddhangini*, a part of her husband with other, linked cultural categories of conduct such as *bhakti/sneha* (devotion/affection) which further extend the universe to be considered.

Arguments of the kind we have advanced in 'Seed and Earth' (Fruzzetti and Östör 1976b), Dumont (1980, Introduction to the complete English edition) now regards as ideas detached from their institutional/behavioral basis, which shows to what extent he is adhering to a predefined, sociological universe of kinship. For Dumont, we seem to get rid of the kinship/caste distinction not on the basis of ethnography but on that of 'word usages'. He claims to stay close to 'behavior' while our 'cultural analysis' does not reach the 'ground'. Yet what else is anthropological analysis but the elucidation of words in relation to practices? Only the 'words' we look at are not consanguinity, patriliny, cross-cousins, and the like, but seed and earth, marriage exchange, blood, and line, all indigenous terms. We do not see what Dumont's objection has to do with the cultural categories we discussed, related to actual practices as they are and not to disembodied thought experiments. We are engaged in transforming 'native' categories into social science ones in analysis. We agree with Dumont that in 'kinship' there is a 'scientific category in the making' but we do not exclude from it the system of relationships ordered by sets of indigenous categories. The crucial issue is how kinship categories are to be defined.

Our discussion of alliance in Bengal issues from actual practice, actual ideology, linked pairs in action and category yielding ideas and relationships in the Bengali universe of kinship and marriage. How else would one study these phenomena? This is what Dumont set out to do in teasing out the logic of alliance between brothers-in-law: dealing as much with concepts and 'native' terms as with 'behavior'. Our argument has never been that there is no Bengali kinship, marriage, or even alliance, rather we argued, and still argue, that there are no genealogical kinship, no sociological system of hypergamy, no South Indian-type alliance, and no positive science-like rules. *Adan-pradan* (giving and taking brides in marriage) is a cultural principle, not a sociological marriage rule emanating from scientific categories, which are presumably demanded by predetermined terminologies, statistical frequencies and the like. The least we can do is consider the implications of Bengali practice for a comparative, cultural study of India as a whole. This is in fact what we attempted with our comparison between West Bengal and Tamilnadu.

Finally, we genuinely wonder what general theories, such as Milner's (1988) add to our understanding of Indian kinship and marriage. Certainly his does what he asks of it: a partial inclusion of regional variants into a general theory of marriage as a device of ordering status relationships among social groups. Milner does an admirable job of fitting in the recalcitrant pieces, but at the expense of cutting the outlines to very gentle curves. One of the problems is that an acquaintance with the particular case will have already given us more than the general theory can possibly deliver. To this extent, the general is already situated within the particular. Milner concludes that 'cultural accounts' do not exclude a general language of status groups and stratification. It may be comforting to know, for the purposes of one kind of science, that such translation is possible. What do we gain in terms of kinship, marriage, alliance and the like in India? Have not cultural analyses taken much of that translation already in their stride?[6]

Milner's analysis achieves the goals it sets: some patterns emerge and status relations get ordered across Indian societies. However, unlike the case of other sciences, for anthropology the construction of such low-level generalizations may not be so enlightening. Once we know the general outline we want to go deeper in quest of distinguishing characteristics, from stratification to hierarchy, from principles of status groups to purity, pollution and power. The particulars in this case already imply the general.

Thus the contribution of a general theory lies chiefly in its *a priori* value: if for the reasons already mentioned we deem the pursuit significant, then the possibility of gathering regional Indian data under such headings as 'status maintenance', 'structural encapsulation', and the like is valuable. Milner's theory summarizes the general features of marriage practices in different parts of India and attempts to incorporate various ideological and practical features by adjusting the theory and developing subtheories. So far so good, but in terms of prediction this seems to be telling us what we already know. Rather than revealing something new, the procedure orders general data in a conventional way, reassuring us rather than extending our intellectual reach. This is a translation of the third or fourth order since even a cultural account can only pretend to second-order status. After all we have already translated from Tamil/Hindi/Bengali to gain our data.

Fundamental questions remain: in what terms shall we discuss kinship, *jāti*, and marriage alliance in north, south, east and west India? What kinds of relationships are we concerned with in the different, given cases? We are all looking for links, patterns, and regularities but what universe of relationships, what kind of categories, and what interpretive and theoretical ends, in narrower or wider compass?

Introduction

Ákos Östör
Lina Fruzzetti
Steve Barnett

THE CHAPTERS of this volume represent the final version of papers discussed at a conference on new approaches to South Asian caste, kinship, and marriage held at Harvard University, December 10–13, 1976. Our aim was to advance the problem of comparison in anthropological research by exploring, with scholars expert in various subregions of South Asia, the extent to which new models of caste, marriage, and kinship, based on extended analyses of indigenous categories, articulate into regional South Asian models of the construct of the person. The deliberations provided the first comprehensive review of new developments in symbolic, cultural, and structural anthropology applied to that area rich in history and social diversity. The conference was small and well focused. The debates, discussions, and papers that emerged yield a volume that synthesizes regional studies into new approaches to South Asian kinship and caste.

The discussions allowed scholars an opportunity to work toward elaborating the underlying common themes. A number of anthropologists have been working independently along similar lines for the past few years. The problem of the unity of South Asian culture can be approached through the analysis of the anthropologist's apperception of indigenous symbolic forms, rather than through abstract domains of analysis posited before any investigation. These forms share surprising similarities that illuminate what has been described in the literature as regional differences.

The need for such a conference became apparent to us in the course of completing a monograph consisting of several papers on Bengali and Tamil kinship and caste. It occurred to us that several scholars had been working in this area of studies for some time, using structural, symbolic, and cultural approaches to the same set of problems.[1] We were struck by the common concern for combining regional and all-India models of kinship and caste. These scholars—some established figures in the field, others younger but building on their senior colleagues' work—had not been in sustained contact with each other. The papers and discussions served to provide a general discourse on several regions of South Asia as a step toward formulating both a comparative theory and an epistemology of social anthropology.

Papers were contributed by a number of scholars. Sylvia Vatuk has written extensively and critically on the problems of north Indian kinship. T. N. Madan has written on Kashmiri kinship and family and participated in the controversy surrounding the issue of marriage relations. Anthony Carter has contributed to the debates about terminology and marriage rules. Ravindra Khare has published numerous papers on the problematic aspects of hierarchy, affinity, and household relations. Pauline Kolenda has written many studies of family and caste in south India. Ralph Nicholas is the coauthor of the controversial *Kinship in Bengali Culture.* Among those who commented on the papers were David Schneider and Louis Dumont. S. J. Tambiah published many influential works on *varna,* caste and kinship, dowry, and hierarchy. Nur Yalman has made numerous contributions in the field of Sri Lanka systems of kinship and marriage as well as hierarchy. David Maybury-Lewis participated in several related debates; his contributions to alliance theory, relationship terminology, and the like are sufficient justification for his presence among Indianist anthropologists. Indeed, the very full participation of Schneider and Maybury-Lewis helped transcend the territorial boundaries so often established in our discipline. Their work represented the contribution of South Asian studies to anthropology in general. It is no coincidence that the theoretical point of departure of the conference and of our separate and collaborative studies was provided by the profoundly significant works of Louis Dumont and David Schneider. Though initially anchored in traditional kinship studies, both these sets of contributions transcend those limitations and speak to a general science of humankind.[2]

Placing himself firmly in the tradition of studying society through the sociological apperception of man, Dumont recognized the difference between anthropological systems of genealogical kinship and the south Indian system of alliance. The fallacy of cross-cousin marriage was found to mask the equivalence of brothers-in-law and the transmission of affinal ties through generations, resulting in the repetition of past marriages. The theory issuing from this discovery gave Dumont an indication of the relationship between *we* and *they*—between Western and Indian societies—for comparative social theory as well as for the understanding of social facts in terms of ideologies.

Dumont's south Indian study reveals a domain where affinity reformulates an assumed consanguinity, designates wife-givers and wife-takers, and provides rules for marriage through subsequent generations. In this sense terms taken to be kin terms yield a universe, systematic and similarly structured throughout the different levels, and express parsimonious relationships between wife-givers and wife-takers. In addition they point to the replication of these relationships in later generations by classifying the categories of agnates and affines into those people one can and those one cannot marry. To the question, "In view of this, what happens in north India?" Dumont suggests that although terminology does not express a similar system in the north, marriage practice does, and a caste principle—hypergamous marriage achieving a system similar to that achieved by alliance in the south—invades the domain of kinship through a system of prestations and asymmetrical relations between wife-givers and wife-takers. Though the analysis is inspired by alliance theory, Dumont finds consanguinity in the north Indian nomenclature but no marriage rules, whereas in the south the logic of the nomenclature expresses the rules for the system of marriage (Dumont 1966, 1961, 1964). The categories that are abstracted out of the terminology configure with each other in a system, but they are descriptive of elementary relationships starting from Ego, whereas in south India the terms oppose each other in a structure. For this reason Dumont (1966, 1970) rightly refuses to speak of a "structure" in the north Indian case: no opposition of wife-givers and wife-takers and no "kinship" rules for marriage. But he found enough similarities of practice to suggest that the terminology does not express the domain of kinship; rather it obscures an underlying south Indian practice. Dumont noted that the north Indian nomenclature does at least emphasize marriage, which is one item significantly shared with the south. Affinity, in the sense of alliance, is thus no stranger to the north, but the nomenclature is not clear. Dumont's conclusion is that a south Indian practice is obscured in the north by the terminology. Hence, Dumont advises us that if the terminology does not express the system, then we must look for the regularities elsewhere.

Starting from a different point of departure, Schneider's cultural study of kinship in society achieved convergent though even more explicit results. Until recently it was generally assumed that kinship deals with basic social problems such as incest, the allocation of rights over the reproductive process and its results, and the division and classification of people, groups, lineages, and so on resulting from these prohibitions and allocations. It was also held that different societies solve the same basic problems in different ways and that this diversity can be analyzed genealogically—if not universally in the same manner, at least in the particular social equivalents of genealogy. This near unanimity, here characterized in outrageously general terms, has been under fire for some time from various directions. Schneider's is the most radical of current attempts to come to grips with kinship as something other than the most exact, measurable, concrete, and quantifiable field in anthropology. Lest it be thought that we are making another plea for cultural relativity, we hasten to add that Schneider's work is particularly well suited to cross-cultural application. In a number of well-argued contributions Schneider challenged the assumption that something called kinship exists in every society as a way of classifying people and groups through consanguinity, affinity, descent, filiation, and the like (Schneider 1968, 1970, 1972). Kinship in these terms is the creation of the investigator, not the property of native social systems.

There may be domains of kinship relations in different societies, but this is a question for research and analysis in cultural terms. It is evident that *kinship* is used in two senses here. The first—which assumes kinship to be a substance of social relation through descent, filiation, and genealogy—we reject, with Schneider, as a fallacious imposition of an assumed substantive system on culturally diverse societies. The second—which refers to a domain of culturally defined social relations—assumes, for analytical purposes alone, that there are domains of relationships among persons in different societies that are susceptible to analysis in cultural terms. Mindful of Schneider's warning that there may be no kinship in the genealogical sense in any society and that kinship studies are exercises in anthropological fallacy, we retain a use of the term in the second sense. This is indeed an important lesson of Schneider's work: a particular concept need not carry substantivist implications unless we make it do so. In view of Schneider's contribution, however, we can no longer attribute genealogical or any other content to the study of kinship if we are serious about retaining a general anthropological language without the requirement that it describe kinds of relationships obtaining in particular domains of Western or any other cultures. The burden of the proof in each case is on the anthropologist to give as full an account of a cultural domain as possible and to present an analysis in cultural terms using symbols that differentiate domains and express concepts underlying relationships among the units of indigenous domains.

A striking example of the application of Schneider's work comes in a previous study (Barnett 1976). It is clear that in the West we view substance apart from code; we stress individual autonomy and consistency of personal action. For the south Indians of this study, since substance enjoins code, personal action is segmentary, with different modes of relating and motivation among and within hierarchical levels. Since substance enjoins code, the person is encompassed within a holistic ideology; there is no personal substance prior to and apart from placement in the whole or apart from a relational understanding of identity. Here we can extend David Schneider's understanding of substance and code in American kinship to the case of south India. Schneider sees two sorts of kin relationships in the United States: those of natural relatives, persons related through blood, who follow certain codes among themselves, and those of in-laws, who are relations only through code. Significantly, natural relations remain so even if they do not follow acceptable codes. In the American case, substance is ultimately distinct from code; it does not enjoin a code because it remains unchanged (that is, altered code does not result in altered substance).

Both the Indian and American examples illustrate the basic features of any ideology. An ideology expresses a double distortion: it has a natural ground, outside symbolic constructs, and its limits are real, bounding the scope and range of human activity. This is why Schneider's approach has such powerful cross-cultural validity. Natural substance is just that: it is ideologically believed to be given in nature, to be the way things are. And code for conduct characterizes the scope of activity, given a particular view of natural substance.

In light of the discussions that emerged from the conference, we now feel that not only is terminology a poor guide to kinship but that we do not even know what constitutes kinship in India in these terms. What we do know is that students of Indian kinship assume a universalistic genealogical model that would identify a kin domain and a set of terms within it in accordance with a priori assumptions. In this respect Schneider's cultural and Dumont's structural approaches are complementary, the former stating explicitly that we must find a system in the given configurations of cultural domains, the latter insisting, in the case of north India, that there is no structure and no domain to the traditionally identified kinship terminology.

The idea and the focus of the conference were supplied by a series of our articles that were published in *Contributions to Indian Sociology*. These essays were circulated to participants before they wrote their own papers. Our papers, written for different reasons over the course of three years, nonetheless contained a common theoretical orientation and provided the basis for a new kind of structural comparison founded on indigenous categories, here the cultural construction of the person in Tamilnadu and Bengal.

Two separate papers on Bengal by Lina Fruzzetti and Ákos Östör, "Is There a Structure to North Indian Kinship Terminology?" and "Seed and Earth," developed as a continuation of recent attempts to delineate a north Indian terminological system. The former discusses recent writings by Louis Dumont and Sylvia Vatuk in the light of Bengali usage. It is an extended analysis of the possibilities and limitations of formal kinship theory in the light of a specific body of evidence. The inability of formal kinship theory, artificially bounded by something called a domain of kinship, to provide a coherent ordering of Bengali usage gave the impetus for the second paper, which grounds these usages in Bengali ideas about the nature of the person in groups and relationships. These two papers pass from a formal discussion of kinship to a recognition of its limitations to the significance of indigenous categories that crosscut the boundaries of kinship and caste. In a series of other publications Fruzzetti and Östör elaborate a cultural and structural approach to several interrelated domains of society in Bengal. (See Fruzzetti 1979, 1981, 1982; Östör 1979, 1980, n.d.; Fruzzetti and Östör n.d.)

The paper on Tamilnadu, "Coconuts and Gold," by Steve Barnett, benefited from previous work on south Indian kinship. It starts with the problem of the encompassed person in holistic caste society. As the author feels that an understanding of caste apart from kinship is inadequate, he elaborates on the indigenous south Indian categories that underlie both. Barnett sees south Indian culture as providing ways of looking simultaneously as what anthropologists separate as caste and kinship. In other words, principles of hierarchy and encompassed equivalence provide a single way of moving from alliance to subcaste to caste. These principles also allow for much flexibility and provide the possibility of new approaches to change and continuity in recent south Indian history. In other publications Barnett has elaborated an overall approach to recent changes in south Indian culture. And in a book written with Martin Silverman (1979), Barnett extends this perspective on south Indian change to encompass aspects of Western ideology. The papers on Bengal started with kinship and moved to structures that are basic to kinship and caste, while the paper on Tamilnadu started with caste and also moved to structures that are basic to kinship and caste.

This independent convergence stimulated our initial discussion and informs the paper entitled "The Cultural Construction of the Person in Bengal and Tamilnadu," by Fruzzetti, Östör, and Barnett, reproduced in this volume. It is a collaborative effort drawing data from the first three papers. We found surprising similarities in the Bengali and Tamil cultural construction of the person despite apparent radical differences in marriage rules in each region. Yet, we were ultimately concerned with matters that rarely surface in that form in anthropology: the epistemological basis of the possibility of social inquiry. To further that aim, the effort was exploratory to the point of being risky. It can be argued that until more is known, our synthesis is premature. Yet, at certain moments, discussion is advanced through venturesomeness. We think we have contributed to a comparative approach to Indian anthropology, and we invite further steps that will supplant our initial discussion.

The conference was attended by Louis Dumont, David Maybury-Lewis, David M. Schneider, Stanley Tambiah, and Nur Yalman, who acted as discussants. Papers were contributed by Steve Barnett on person and blood, Anthony T. Carter on person and hierarchy, T. N. Madan on person and household, R. S. Khare on the cultural language of kinship, Pauline Kolenda on low-caste widows, Sylvia Vatuk on terms of address and kinship, Ralph Nicholas on the nonexistence of the incest taboo in India, and Lina Fruzzetti and Ákos Östör on blood and ritual. Much of our deliberations concerned the person in social relations: who, what, where, when, and how a person is a person; whose construct this is; how the construction of the person is related to kinship studies in general. Yet no one forwarded a theory of the person—for good reason, since we did not aim to replace the universality of genealogy with that of the substantive person. Several papers (Fruzzetti and Östör, Barnett, Carter, Madan) dealt with Indian notions of the person as a basis for understanding problems of kinship, caste, and marriage rather than as a way of arriving at psychological or phenomenological theory. The approaches of these papers differed, and indeed they occasioned lively discussions. Yet they informed the discussion of the other papers by Khare, Vatuk, Kolenda, and Nicholas, which did not have the same explicit focus on the person and still succeeded in raising similar issues; and they were closely related to the other papers as well as to the central trend of the discussions.

Each paper was discussed in a separate session with all participants in attendance, hence the extraordinary level of intensity attained by the discussions. Papers were subsequently and extensively revised. For these reasons the volume strives for an unusual degree of internal dialogue, both within the arguments of individual papers and in the encounter among the set of papers as a whole. As a result some element of redundancy may be detected by the reader. All contributors refer to Dumont and Schneider and may appear to restate positions already outlined elsewhere in the volume. Although the essays start from a similar base, each develops its position from a different formulation of a broad initial consensus. Thus, the contributors give their own account of structural and cultural approaches. The results are different, and the varying views of the basic matter itself are valuable. Finally, we regret that the papers by Barnett and Nicholas could not be included in this volume.

1

The Cultural Construction of the Person in Bengal and Tamilnadu

Lina Fruzzetti
Ákos Östör
Steve Barnett

THE IDEA OF comparing Bengali and Tamil ideas about kinship developed as we examined our data in light of the existing literature.[1] We discovered similarities that seemed to agree with the basic intent of previous studies attempting to construct an all-India framework for thinking about these matters, yet these similarities were submerged by an emphasis on regional differences (Dumont 1961, 1964, 1966; Kapadia 1947, 1958; Karve 1965).

Comparison presupposes that we know what we are comparing; that we have an idea of domains and boundaries. Yet this is what is at issue: What is the domain of kinship in Bengal and Tamilnadu, and how is that construction of kinship related to caste? Differences between the two regions are all too apparent and have been stressed in the literature: Tamil MBD and FZD marriages and their prohibition in Bengal, clear structural overlap of terminology and marriage classes in the south, and the illusive problem of terminology as a system in Bengal. The Tamil system appears to be an alliance system generated through cross-cousin marriage and guaranteed terminologically. While it is difficult to perceive the systemic nature of Bengali kinship and terminology, by contrast Tamil kinship becomes a domain apart from caste because of the equivalence of brothers-in-law (Dumont 1957).

The hierarchy between brothers-in-law generally observed in north India gives Dumont warrant for saying caste and kinship participate in the same construction of holistic hierarchy. These pathbreaking statements by Dumont both undergird our efforts and provide a critical foil for our theoretical elaborations.

Dumont puts the problem thus: the ideology of caste encompasses and thereby situates all aspects of Indian culture. Caste ideology is holistic:

the ultimate focus of value falls on the society, not on particular, abstract individuals as in Euro-American society. Castes are ranked not as autonomous units but as dependent parts of an independent whole (for Dumont the analogy is parts of the body, each necessary, none sufficient). The principle of ranking is ultimately the opposition of pure and impure, seen unambiguously in the opposition of Brahman and untouchable, so that castes are ordered along a scale of relative purity (Dumont 1970).

Since we take these points as our baseline, it is necessary to say that we are aware of the storm of comment and criticism that followed *Contributions* (old series) and more especially *Homo Hierarchicus.* Oddly, the criticism that has gained the most currency seems the weakest: that Dumont's constructions represent Brahman (read oppressor) notions and so cannot be generalized as Indian culture. In this view lower castes see through the Brahman mystification and reject those views that make them inferior. However, those same lower castes replicate the caste system among themselves and participate in local life. As Lukács wrote: "The organs of authority harmonize to such an extent with the [economic] laws governing men's lives, or seem so overwhelmingly superior that men experience them as natural forces, as the necessary environment for their existence. As a result, they submit to them freely, which is not to say they approve of them" (Lukács 1971:257).

For Dumont domains can be characterized and bounded by reference to their underlying structural features. A distinct kinship structure emerges in the south, where cross-cousin marriage reciprocally defines the equivalence of brothers-in-law and, in turn, generates a system of marriage alliance among a number of families over some generations. Where brother-in-law equivalence is not apparent, Dumont suggests we are once again in the world of caste. And so, for much of north India, marriage relations and kinship terminologies do not emerge apart from caste. Put another way, the ideology of caste in the north Indian case directly encompasses kin relations; both caste and kinship take on significance through the underlying structural features of holism, hierarchy, and purity-impurity. In the south we need additional principles—alliance, equivalence—to account for kin relations. In the south we can discretely bound kinship apart from caste.

Dumont's caution, despite his overriding concern with an understanding of the structure of an all-India culture, seems amply warranted by the difficulties encountered in previous efforts to construct a model of kinship applicable throughout the subcontinent. These models, given an inadequate comparative ethnographic base, tend to rely on textual constructions of marriage rules and seem wide of the mark where good information of daily life exists. Still, Dumont's approach, while solving major questions about Indian forms of kinship, raises at another level many of the problems he disposed of at the level of a genealogical construction of the universe of kin. The basic problem is the articulation of kin and caste in the south: What are the structual features that underlie equivalence and hierarchy, alliance and rank? The question of bounding thus reappears, this time with an important feedback effect. If we say equivalence complements hierarchy (one cannot have one without the other), then the southern distinction between caste and kinship loses strength to the extent that kinship becomes, despite and through the initial separation, an aspect of caste. In addition, we are directed to look for forms of equivalence in the north rather than see a structure of pure hierarchy.

Our present comparative effort both builds upon Dumont's work (his construction of Indian culture, his discussion of alliance systems, and his concern to develop frameworks applicable to the entire subcontinent) and recognizes the continuing problem of how to analytically create and bound subsystems of meaning within a given cultural universe. We compared two regions (Bengal and Tamilnadu) for which we have detailed ethnographic knowledge. In no way should this effort be generalized to other regions without incorporating equivalent ethnographic detail for those regions. Our argument is programmatic rather than inclusive or exhaustive, recognizing that any genuine all-India comparative effort must be the work of many scholars in reasonably close collaboration. Just pointing this out suggests the increasing tension between present forms of research and publication and the advancement of the anthropological perspective. This effort developed and took shape as we discussed Bengali and Tamil forms of marriage and descent, trying to understand these not as instances of a genealogically based pattern but as aspects of the possibilities of the cultural construction of the person, in relations and groups, in India.

This concern led us to focus on what is passed from parent to child, on what each parent contributes to the child, and how this affects the child's place within family and caste. Here we were struck by Bengali and Tamil similarities, variations on a theme, despite clear differences in marriage rules.[2] We began to see that in Bengal and Tamilnadu the same kinds of things passed between parent and child, although these were ordered differently in each case. And further, these parent-child relations also ordered the potential marriage partners of the child (again, different partners in each case). We unfolded a complex structure of hierarchy encompassing equivalence both in Tamilnadu and Bengal. We may initially state the central point of similarity as a common stress and emphasis on alliance, here characterized not as the logical outcome of the genealogical construction of MBD and FZD marriage but as the ideological concern that a particular marriage reestablish or reinvent antecedent ties between groups. Following this, our strategy for comparison is to ask why alliance is so crucial despite the disparity over whom one can marry.[3] In this light, we see a similar ideology of hierarchy in both Bengal and

Tamilnadu, an ideology based on shared notions of parent-child relations.

This view of course does not solve the paradoxes of contemporary kinship theory, but it does suggest where impasses lie and where inquiry may be redirected. David Schneider's rejection of the genealogical assumption in kinship studies (1968, 1972), based primarily on his work in the United States, opens a significant line of thought in Indian research. For Schneider an understanding of kinship built up from genealogical assumptions (affinal and consanguine relations, kinship terms illustrating genealogical positions, and so on) imposes, in a more or less obvious way, our notions of kinshp on vastly different social functions. The question of what *we* impose on *them* raises the entire matter of how anthropologists construct boundaries, of how they divide up the initial whole they confront and are confronted with. For too long we have avoided the epistemological issues of how anthropologists know by paraphrasing Radcliffe-Brown (who paraphrased Durkheim and Weber): we know through experience. Field work is justified as a kind of anthropological baptism because the field work experience allows us to confront difference directly by juxtaposing our ways of life and their ways of life. However, the hidden lemma of the anthropologist's tabula rasa gives this position a kind of feigned innocence. After Kant we can hardly say we confront anything directly; rather we construct difference, we have antecedent ideas about what will appear different. As anthropologists we can study the appearance of difference alone (naïve empiricism) or try to understand our antecedent ideas through the appearance of difference, thus penetrating to a deeper level of difference, one not so innocently attached to our own ideological proclivities.

Anthropologists may respond that they, in fact, attempt to do just this. A particular approach in anthropology typically begins by classifying; those not so attracted to that approach expose problems in the classification (forcing the data, embarrassing overlap), and eventually the approach is recognized as inadequate by all but a few whose reputation and professional ego are at stake. This occurs under the mantle of scientific activity when in fact it represents a particular historical and ideological pose. Science here becomes a metaphor, taken over from the natural sciences, whose power lies in the fact that it itself cannot be suspended. The central task of any anthropological sudy of symbolic forms is to show the ideological underpinnings of those systems of classification that claim to be scientific and neutral.

These are difficult matters, made more problematic by our studied avoidance of them. Here we want to stress that Schneider raises questions that go to the heart of founding an anthropology that does not, once again, merely reflect our imbeddedness in a particular historical moment. And his methodological prescription is basically simple: question every proposition that our own ideology places outside itself as "natural" (as concrete, material reality, the nuts and bolts of society). Anthropologists have seen the domain of kinship as analytically isolable because affinal and consanguineal ties appeared as natural, biological givens.

Tamilnadu

This outline of aspects of Tamil kinship benefits directly from Dumont's writings on basic patterns of marriage and alliance and his structural analysis of Tamil (Dravidian) kin terms. Since we are in essential agreement with his construction of the argument for south India, we can immediately move to other matters, taking as our starting point the fit between kin terms and marriage rules as well as the principle of marriage alliance in its most general form.

The basic question is: What is the relation of units of equivalence to units of hierarchy? Units of equivalence are initially encompassed by units of hierarchy; hierarchical units are culturally prior constructs out of which forms of equivalence derive. The basic unit of equivalence in Tamilnadu society (and the reader should keep in mind that much of the following material is based on extensive field work with one caste, KVs, plus corroborative data from other non-Brahman castes), the *vakaiyara,* or kindred, is our primary concern, for it is the unit within which relations usually called kinship relations occur. By starting with the problem of the intersection of hierarchy and equivalence, we put the question in the most general form: How is south Indian society constructed? What are the cultural features that structure the whole and order its various subdivisions?

The whole of south Indian case society is ordered along a continuum of purity-impurity. Relative purity orders caste rank as well as subcaste distinctions. These subcaste distinctions take the form of units within which marriage can be arranged. Many castes refer to these units as *vakaiyaras. Vakaiyaras* are the smallest units of equivalence (of equivalent purity for intracaste action) in south Indian caste society. This needs explication since, on the one hand, persons can differ in purity and on the other, units are relational, emerging in sets of relations with other units. *Vakaiyaras* are not directly significant for intercaste relations since the range of purity of the caste as a whole counts, not the narrower range of purity of ranked *vakaiyaras* within the caste. However, *vakaiyaras* ultimately bound the range of purity of the entire caste by regulating forms of marriage and, therefore, controlling the transmission of blood purity from generation to generation. They are the smallest unit of action in caste society, since personal purity, as long as that person does not exceed limits set by kindred and caste, does not affect relations between hierarchical units.

Principles of caste hierarchy are well known, but the principles of action within units of equivalence in caste society remain obscure. Difference in hierarchical action amounts to a difference in relative purity, while difference within *vakaiyaras* cannot be based on distinctions of purity. By focusing, on south Indian ideas about the transmission of purity from parent to child within a *vakaiyara* (the cultural construction of the person), we will also develop criteria where there is no purity difference.

Caste purity is situated in a person's blood (*irattam*), *blood* here not simply expressing a biological quality, for it is a term with multiple connotations in Tamil. The movement of blood in the body and its transformations to other body substances is the basis of much south Indian indigenous medicine and is a rich metaphor in daily speech. The form of transmission of this blood purity from parent to child underlies the entire ideology of south Indian caste society. South Indians say condensed blood can become semen, a repository of purity and power, given its accumulation at the base of the brain through sexual abstinence. In a woman condensed blood can become breast milk. The child is formed from these aspects of condensed blood, as well as from mother's blood directly transferred in the womb. The child, then, is formed from his parents' blood and inherits the purity contained in that blood.

Blood purity itself can be divided into two aspects—*utampu,* here roughly glossed as body or matter, and *uyir,* spirit or motion. *Utampu* is a male aspect of blood (ultimately linking a line of men and unmarried women to a particular caste ancestor) and *uyir* a female aspect. When a woman marries, her *utampu* becomes identical to that of her husband, while her *uyir* remains unchanged. As south Indians say, a wife takes her husband's *kotiram* (his line), or really his *kulam,* a segment of that line within one *vakaiyara.* The terms *line* and *lineage* should not convey the orthodox anthropological meaning here, since that definition, deriving primarily from African material, does not allow the possibility of women changing their lineages.

Within a particular *vakaiyara* there are two rules of marriage that together divide the *vakaiyara* into an unmarriageable segment and a marriageable segment. Marriage, say south Indians, must unite two people (to avoid incest there must be something to unite), but their unity cannot be total (to avoid incest some difference must remain). These rules, along with south Indian ideas about blood purity and the difference in forms of transubstantiation of *utampu* and *uyir,* result in marriage with MB and FZ children (and terminological extensions) and proscribe marriage to MZ and FB children. MB and FZ children have different *utampu* and *uyir,* so that there is *utampu* to unite (the woman can take her husband's *kotiram*) while difference in *uyir* persists after marriage. MZ children share *uyir,* so their marriage would be incestuous since, given the *utampu* change, no difference would remain between them. FB children share *utampu,* so their marriage would be incestuous since there would be nothing to unite (*uyir* does not transubstantiate).

Thinking about marriage from a south Indian perspective stresses maximizing difference and the potential for exchange within the *vakaiyara,* or kindred. Given south Indian ideas about the transmission of blood purity within the kindred, their form of marriage provides for the maximum exchange of *utampu* and *uyir* within that kindred. South Indians marry precisely those persons of equivalent purity with whom they share the least. But we must be wary of too quickly interpreting this on our own model of the importance of difference in selecting a marriage partner, as in the marriage rule: Do not marry a relative. For us that difference, taking on significance in an individualistic ideology, preserves our personal autonomy by maintaining the boundaries of self: we marry another monad like us. For south Indians, difference, taking on significance in a holistic ideology, generates a particular whole, the kindred, within which persons are partial components. It is in part a matter of (ideo)logical priority: for us the person is prior to any particular social formation; for south Indians the construction of the person derives from a hierarchical conception of society.

We can now see that south Indian forms of alliance, though representable in conventional anthropological categories, appear to them in a somewhat different light. Rather than a given alliance generating overwhelming obligations for continuation so that a small number of families ally over many generations, south Indians arrange marriages with many families for many reasons within a kindred, which may include 150 families. In a sense, we are suggesting that an old anthropological dispute, the relationship of prescribed to preferred marriage, is in this case not so much a distinction of statistics versus structure as a matter of the way an ideological system is understood. Following south Indian ideas, we can understand their form of marriage as ideologically consistent, not as a disjunction between what people say they do and what they in fact do. In Tamilnadu alliance occurs precisely through marrying those with whom one shares the least, and to that extent, Tamilians see particular alliances as arenas for manipulating other qualities (landholdings, occupational prestige, education, political influence, as well as, of course, good relations through a number of generations).

We can now order the cross-cutting complexity of south Indian units of family, kindred, line, and caste in terms of the basic ideology underlying the construction of the person. Blood purity shared by all caste members situates a caste in the hierarchy of all castes. The person is created from a particular combination of caste blood purity (*utampu* and *uyir*) within the smallest hierarchical subdivision, the kindred. Since a person's blood purity alters, given the way he acts in the world, the kindred emerges as that unit of action that guarantees a particular code for conduct (ultimately through the threat of outcasting). Units of hierarchy (caste, subcaste, kindred) act as wholes toward each other with the behavior of any member of the relevant unit redounding to the rank of that unit as a whole (blood purity alters given different codes for conduct, and in extreme cases, this altered purity can be passed from generation to generation). Within kindreds, given south Indian notions about the transmission of blood purity, there is a maximum flow of substance within the unit. The idea of the *kotiram* reflects the crucial role of the kindred in south Indian life, for the *kotiram* (*utampu* passed from a caste ancestor to present generations of men and unmarried women) can and does cross kindred boundaries: the same *kotiram* can reappear in different kindreds. Thus, the *kotiram*, though basic to aspects of south Indian ritual (especially death rites), is not significant for understanding marriage or alliance, for the kindred, not the line, bounds a unit of equivalent purity. Given south Indian ideas, purity must be a combination of *utampu* and *uyir* (found in the kindred) and is not an aspect of *utampu* alone. The kindred bounds a particular range of blood purity and provides a mechanism for passing that range of blood purity from both parents to children. Any change in *utampu* plus *uyir* is a change in purity, potentially affecting a person's caste and kindred membership. In addition, *utampu* alone can change, as when a woman marries, but this change is not one of levels of purity; the woman remains a member of the same kindred. In short, in Tamilnadu the notion of line is subordinated to the notion of kindred. Within kindreds, segments of line (*kulams*) become basic to maximizing the flow of substance, since one must marry a person of different *utampu*. But here the hierarchical point returns, since the *kulam* is encompassed; its boundaries are those of the kindred.

Bengal

Persons are culturally constructed as relatives (*āttiya kuṭum*) in groups, and groups in alliance. What constitutes the person? What makes persons equal as well as different within and without groups? How are differences constituted and matched in alliance?[4] A brief account of the cultural construction of the person through relationships, blood and marriage leads us to units of equivalence created by blood ties in a line and marriage ties among sets of lines.

Relatives

Who is a relative (*āttiya*) in Bengal, and how does a person become an *āttiya?* The first question presents us kinds of *āttiya*, those by blood (*rakta*) and those by marriage (*biye*), relatives through shared locality (*pāṛā āttiya*), and so on. The second question leads us to analyze Bengali cultural constructs, the notions of conception and transmission of similarities and differences among groups of people, the idea of relatedness, the concept of the person as *āttiya.* Furthermore, the complementary male-female constructs as originators of an issue, contributors to the formation of a child, emphasize the significance of *āttiya* as a person and as a member of various units, more or less inclusive, in a system of hierarchical action.

Āttiya is a person with whom one shares something—a relationship in blood (*rakta āttiya*) or a relationship established through marriage. These relationships do not exhaust the Bengali notion of relative. There are other sets of relationships: *samparka* and *sammandha,* relationship in general and a specific marriage link, expressed through codes for conduct such as *pāṛā āttiya* or *emni āttiya* (just-as-you-please relative), *charachari āttiya,* and so forth. *Āttiya* can be both *nikaṭ* (near) or *dūr* (distant). One who is in a *rakta āttiya samparka* (blood relationship) alone is contrasted to the above kinds of *āttiya* with whom one shares something other than blood, the former being a specific and the latter a general kind of *āttiya,* both being characterized by the same codes for conduct. One can have an *āttiya* relationship with a person who shares the same village, *pāṛā* (neighborhood), work area, or *guru* (religious preceptor), in which case the person concerned is an *āttiya* in sentiment and attitude (in other words a code of conduct enjoined by the *āttiya* tie), in part structured by the symbols of blood relationship and a certain kind of action.

Āttiyas share something, and a group of such persons is one's *āttiya svajan* (one's own people). An *āttiya* with whom one shares blood cannot be a *kuṭum* (relative in marriage). One gives daughters in marriage to persons with whom one shares no blood tie, in which case the marriage itself establishes a person as an *āttiya* through the ritual, *biye,* creating *kuṭum āttiya. Kuṭums* are persons to whom one can give to or from whom one can take daughters—the giving and the taking establishing new sets of relationships. The *kuṭum āttiya* group is opposed to one's relatives by blood (*rakta āttiya*), who are in turn split into different classes of relatives in some way or another. One's own *rakta āttiya* are also one's *jñāti* (roughly defined as relatives in and through the male line) and one's *bhāiyat* (those related through the brother tie), *sātpuruṣ* (the seven generations of men), and finally the wider group of one's *gotra*-linked people. These groups include the women married into one's own or one's father's *baṇgśa* (line). A *jñāti,* a member of one's *bhāiyat,* or a person with the same *gotra* cannot become one's *kuṭum* because to be a *kuṭum* one cannot share any of the above, neither *gotra* nor blood. *Kuṭum āttiya* are an ego-based group, and groups of such persons are also conceptualized as people in a locality: *kuṭum ghar* and *kuṭum bāṛi* (residence of *kuṭum*). A married woman refers to her husband's *ghar* as her *śvaśur ghar* (in-laws' house)—the same *ghar* being a *kuṭum ghar* to her father and her father's *jñāti.* A man's *kuṭum ghar* becomes his children's *māmā ghar* (MB's house), the *kuṭum āttiya* of one generation becoming the *rakta āttiya* of the next. In this way one does share blood with one's *māmā* (MB), even though a MB is outside one's *jñāti.* In Bengal the *sapiṇḍa* (the male-line ancestors to whom funerary offerings are given) exogamy does not refer to the blood *āttiya* on the mother's side, yet one's *mayer bāper ghar* (MF's house) also constitutes a group of blood *āttiya.* In addition to the *sapiṇḍa* in the classical sense the blood relatives on one's mother's side are also excluded from marriage. *Āttiya* are also conceptualized as people in a locality—the *śvaśur bāṛi* of a male person becomes his children's *māmā bāṛi,* and for a female person her *śvaśur ghar* becomes her children's *bāper bāṛi.* The reference to locality changes with each succeeding generation of *āttiya.* Locality is here encompassed by ties among groups of relatives.

Āttiya is a general term for a relative, where the relationship is established either through *biye, rakta,* or a code for conduct (*sammandha-samparka*). *Āttiya* also means relatives in the male line, blood being passed in the male line, but in addition *biye* (marriage) is the major complementary construct that has to be considered in this context. Blood is something shared among persons in a *baṇgśa, bhāiyat,* and a group of *jñāti,* because these persons are related to each other in the male line. *Baṇgśa* being an ego-based group, *kula* refers to a succession of ancestors stretching beyond memory to a founding ancestor figure whose line is being perpetuated. The term *kul* refers to blood purity, quality, highness, and nobility, that which must be preserved as it is handed down from one generation (*puruṣ*) to the next. The deity of the *kula,* the *kula debatā,* and its worship is a responsibility shared equally by the male members of the line. The term *kula* has a double meaning: it is both an attribute and a group. Like *kula,* the *baṇgśa* (the ego-based line) is traced in the male line and includes unmarried daughters as well as in-marrying women. A specific ancestor of the *kula* may be designated as the starter of a specific *baṇgśa.* Males establish their own and continue their father's *baṇgśa,* this being accomplished by marriage. The wife (*strī*) of a man is a vehicle through which he establishes (*pratiśṭhā*) his *baṇgśa,* transmitting his blood to the children through his wife. In this sense blood creates and maintains the difference among male lines of different generations. *Rakta* (blood) is a Bengali construct referring to a substance, enduring and persistent, a permanent attribute that is recognized and transmitted in the male line through women. Here blood is a symbol for a relationship among persons and groups of persons. Blood classifies and equalizes, differentiates and hierarchizes relationships among persons in groups.

A person shares with one's *bhāiyat* the blood passed in the male line, but at the same time a person shares blood with one's mother's side (*mayer stor*), one's MB, MZ, MM, MF, and so on, though these are outside the *sātpuruṣ* group of one's father's side. The *bhāiyat* also share each other's rituals of purity and pollution, the latter being caused mainly by the death of a person in the *bhāiyat* or of an *āttiya* in the male line. Blood (*rakta*) being shared by the *bhāiyat* and *jñāti* classes of relatives includes the segmented *sātpuruṣ* groups as well. The *rakta* tie defines one's *bhāiyat* and in the same way are defined by male linkedness. *Jñāti* share the same *gotra,* and sharing the same *gotra* disqualifies *jñāti* for marriage. *Gotra,* like blood, is transmitted in the male line. *Gotra* implies a common ancestral figure, a label attached to those sharing a hypothetical common origin. Beyond the *sātpuruṣ* the *gotra* is the only differentiating index between all possible and non-*jñāti* persons for the determination of marriage.

Lines are created in and through marriage: blood and marriage establish a unit of equivalence in a segmentary, hierarchical way, which is extensible from a single person, the originator of a line, to a series of lines linked by marriages, with an equally extensible locality component. Blood and marriage, together with the code of conduct they imply for the persons related in lines and through marriages, also establish differences among lines and sets of lines linked by marriages, sufficient to allow a hierarchical separation into smaller units of equivalence.

What does marriage do to bride and groom? The bride changes her *gotra* from that of her father to that of her husband, but she does not change her own blood, nor is her father's blood changed to that of the husband. A married woman still retains her blood tie with her father. Her father's *sapiṇḍa* will stop with her, since she will pass her husband's blood to her children, not her father's. Nonetheless she maintains *sapiṇḍa* ties with her father and mother, but these ties she retains only with her parents. Women as wives pass their husbands' blood to the children, and in this way in-marrying women transmit the *baṇgśa's* blood and carry, preserve, and save the male line. Blood is thus connected to the idea of *baṇgśa,* the continuation of the male line, allowing the passage of blood from male to male through females. Here the relation of marriage and line to *āttiya* becomes clear. *Rakta* is shared by all blood relatives—these being one's *jñāti, bhāiyat,* and *baṇgśa* people, all one's male-linked relatives. Shared *rakta* defines close (*nikaṭ*) relatives and forbids marriage with such *āttiya. Gotra* also helps keep the male lines separate. A daughter's daughter is already outside the *sātpuruṣ;* thus a *jñāti's* DD can come into the original line as an in-marrying wife. A *nikaṭ āttiya,* however, cannot be a wife to a male member of the same line, so a FFBD cannot be regarded as a *kuṭum.*

Biye is entered into so that the male line can be continued through the creation of male children. The *adikar* (responsibility and reason) of marriage is to establish a new *baṇgśa* and to continue a previous *baṇgśa.* We said earlier that women do not establish *baṇgśas* and do not transmit their fathers' blood to their children. Women categorize themselves as the field (*khettra*) and men as the cultivators of the field, the providers of the seed. Husband and wife, *svāmī* and *strī*, are cultivator and field. Men sow the seed and the field accepts the seed, nourishing and increasing it as blood of the child. Blood creates semen and semen creates blood. The mother contributes her *mātri śakti* to the offspring. In the creation of the child, the mother complements the father. The mother's blood and milk strengthen the child's bones and increase his flesh. The child is born through the father (*bāp diye janma*) and is given by the mother, the latter being the *janma dātā*. The child is born out of a male line and is introduced to the world (*paricay karā*) by the father. The *paricay* is through the father and not the mother, since women cannot pass their fathers' blood to the children. It is the father's prerogative to give *paricay* to the child. The mother is the giver of birth, but the child is born of the father (*pitrir janma*). The mother, like a vessel, accepts the seed and keeps, contains, nourishes the seed as does the earth. As a result, the line (*baṇgśa*) is given by the father, a recognition given to the male line, through the passage of male blood. Women as mothers pass their *mātri śakti* to the children, that which they share with their brothers, sisters, mother, and the rest of the people on the maternal side. Thus the married woman still retains blood ties with her *bāper bāṛi* (father's house) even after her marriage and change of *gotra*. The married woman's tie with her father and his *jñāti* is an enduring one even though she will not pass their blood to her children. Relationships encompassing locality (a woman's *bāper bāṛi*) forbid the marriage of a woman's children with people of her *bāper bāṛi*, but this does not exclude marriage with the *baper bāṛi kuṭum lok* (relatives by marriage).

Marriage Alliance

Since the problem of alliance has been amply discussed in the context of south India, we need to situate the problem in the light of our data, as an ideological feature in north India. Such an approach proceeds of necessity from local systems to a comparison of various regional configurations at the level of structure. As a result no attempt is made to translate the alliance system of anthropological theory into Bengali terms. Rather, we take the marriage exchange ideology of Bengali practice as our point of departure. Before we take up the question of what should be meant by alliance in both Bengal and Tamilnadu, let us outline the *ādān pradān* ideology and practice of marriage in Bengal.

Ādān pradān in Bengal is a language of alliance and a practice of exchanges in marriage: daughters and gifts of many kinds (including respect, honor, status, quality, and so forth). To conclude a marriage the *baṇgśas* of the bride and groom have to be matched. The units linked by marriage are *kulas, baṇgśas, ghars,* and *paribārs* (the line encompassing locality). *Ādān pradān* refers to the gift of the bride and to the continuing reciprocal, though unbalanced, relationship between the two sides as well as the marriage links among *baṇgśas* and the reversals of repetitions of marriages through previous and subsequent generations.

The alliance language of *ādān pradān* means to give women to and take women from *ghars* and lines in a form of exchange that may constitute a system extending over generations and wider localities. The difference between this kind of exchange and classical hypergamy is the absence of concrete enduring groups to whom one either gives women or from whom one takes women in marriage. In Bengal the structuring of subsequent marriages may alter with each exchange, with each giving or taking of a woman. There seems to be no set rule or terminological principle for the giving of a daughter in marriage over and above the marriage rules of *gotra* and blood exogamy and *jāti* endogamy. Subsequent marriages may or may not be contracted with the same *baṇgśa* (and *ghar*) to whom one gave or from whom one took a son or daughter in marriage, the second or third exchanges further strengthening the ties between the *ghars*. On the other hand, marriage links may end with the initial exchange, *sampradān* (the gift of a bride) ending the *ādān pradān* cycle without any further exchanges between the two *ghars*. There are also cases where marriages contracted two or three generations ago are replicated. In short there are no strictly pure and simple rules as to whom one can give or from whom one can take women within the *jāti* (subcaste). The choices are open-ended, and they set up new patterns, considerations, and manipulations with each exchange.

Bengali *ādān pradān* has an added feature that makes it different from the rest of north Indian practice. The possibility of reversals in the direction of marriage is very much a part of the Bengali system, and often it is the preferred arrangement. To this we must add that in most cases the reversal in the direction of marriage is not repeated in the continued giving of daughters or sons. Such reverse marriages when contracted usually end with the exchange of a daughter and a son. Repeating the reversal or even giving further daughters to the same *ghar* is not desired. It is in the case of a single giving of a daughter or a son to a certain line that a *ghar* attempts to give again in the same or subsequent generations. *Ādān pradān* does not limit the exchange of marriages to only certain lines, allowing marriages within a larger unit of equivalence consisting of marriage-linked lines.

The case for Tamilnadu is different. There the system of alliance is concerned with maintaining the purity and the ordering of the *vakaiyaras* irrespective of the line, since the male line expressed in the *kulam* is within the *vakaiyara* as a whole. Though the notion of a male line is important in Tamilnadu, marriages are contracted within the *vakaiyara,* and in doing so the purity of the *vakaiyara* is secured. Because of the absence of such groups from whom one can take and to whom one can give a daughter in Bengali marriage, Bengalis must match lines so as to maintain the quality and status of their line. Matching lines and marrying within the *vakaiyara* serve the same purpose. In the end it is the purity and quality of the male line, the purity of blood, that is maintained. This is the aim of marriages: a careful calculation of the proper marriage through the matching of *baṇgśas.*

Unlike the *vakaiyara* case, in Bengal it is lines that are matched, not a group of *ghars.* In this case the system of alliance in Bengal is different, more flexible and open-ended, though no less structured in terms of who can be matched, when, and how. The Bengali case posits a difference between lines and persons in terms of blood, quality, and purity. Negotiation and calculation are new for each case. Thus, in Bengal one matches one's own line to another by marrying with an equal or a better *ghar,* and in this way the quality, purity, and status of the line is maintained. In Tamilnadu marriages take place within the kindred to maintain the purity of the *vakaiyara* (and indirectly of the *kutumpam* as well).

What maintains the quality, status, and purity of line in Bengal? What is a high (*ucca*) line and a low (*nicu*) line? How is one *baṇgśa* ordered in relation to others? What are the criteria used in the matching of the *baṇgśas?* When they are matched, are the same criteria used for different generations of the same *baṇgśa,* and if not, how diverse can the system be in this regard? Matching *baṇgśas,* brings into consideration smaller units of *ghar* and *paribār* as well as relationships within larger units, all of which are encompassed within the male line. To some extent even the *kuṭum* of the line are involved as potential *ādān pradān* parties. Thus *baṇgśa* considerations introduce questions that link the *bhāiyat, ghar, paribār,* and *jñāti.* In these cases the *kuṭum* are also questioned: To whom did this particular line give women in the past? Are the *ghars* to whom they gave women of the same status? In Bengal, then, the unit of equivalence is the set of actual and potential lines and houses parties to *ādān pradān. Baṇgśa* considerations go beyond the immediate *ghar* (house). They concern the *jñāti,* relationships beyond the *bhāiyat,* beyond even the *sātpuruṣ* of one's relations. Actions deemed to be impure that may have occurred in one's *bhāiyat,* such as a FFFBSS's contracting an intercaste or otherwise improper marriage, are held as impure for the male line, affecting the whole line. In this sense the activities of the *bhāiyat* are accountable and affect one's eligibility for marriage with a good *ghar.* When a daughter is to be given to a *ghar* as a wife, the father of the *kanyā* does not concern himself with the smallest unit, the *paribār* and the *ghar* of the line alone, but with the whole line, segmenting over several generations. Similarly those who will accept the *kanyā* will also look at and raise questions about the line of the girl's father.[5] By *baṇgśa* actions we mean the actions of living members of the same line and in extreme cases also the past actions of past members of the same, more distantly segmented line. Thus the *bhāiyat* code for conduct is examined: the quality of the line is affected by action, and the effect is shared in the line as well as the *paribār*. Past actions are also counted: To whom were the line's daughters given in marriage? What is the standing of those *ghars* and lines in relation to one's own? In general what is the relative position of all these lines in one's *jātir sāmaj* (caste society)? A *baṇgśa* that always gave its daughters to equal or better *ghars* will have no trouble finding husbands for its unmarried daughters in the future in equal or higher-status *ghars* and lines.

Lines that give daughters to and take women from each other form a unit of equivalence that includes in theory the *jāti* as a whole. Several other factors such as land ownership, wealth and past connection, and past position limit the choice. Having established the potential boundaries of a unit of equivalence, a line gives daughters in marriage to another line, the unit being different for each exchange. Lines and houses in such an exchange relation are then within one unit of equivalence in opposition to other such units (even though within these units differences may be retained in a segmentary fashion down to construction of a single person in terms of blood purity, quality and status of the line, and so on). The line that is considered for a possible exchange is matched to one's own: Do other lines and houses of one's own *jāti* in the same locality dine with them? What other houses have contracted marriages with them in the past and/or invited them to their rituals and festivals? Did they have any improper marriages in the past, such as intercaste marriage, widow remarriage, marriages contracted with blood relatives, or even interreligious (Hindu with Muslim or Christian) marriages? Other considerations have to do with codes for conduct: Did they break their personal, *baṇgśa,* or *jāti* codes of action? Did they obey caste and kinship rules, and so forth. The evaluation extends to yet other matters before a marriage agreement is contracted with a line. The matter of wealth and accumulation of wealth is of concern to both *ghars:* Has the *ghar* in question acquired "bad" wealth in the past? Have there been any scandals or inferior marriages? Have the men maintained sexual relations with low-caste women? Was there serious disease in the *ghar* and line? All these may affect the quality and the purity of the line in question. Having matched the lines, one can approach the head of the *ghar* for the consideration and discussion of marriage.

In Tamilnadu the *vakaiyara* as a whole maintains relative purity so that each *kutumpam* (family) within it is equivalent. In Bengal the male lines have to be matched, since units of equivalence are calculated and created for each case of alliance. In Tamilnadu the *vakaiyara* removes the need for matching lines. In this sense then in Bengal the stress is placed on the male line's purity and quality. The crucial way of maintaining this is by contracting marriages between equal and matched lines.

The quality (*guṇ*) of the line—blood, purity, aristocracy, high status—is transmitted by generations of males in the *baṇgśa*. On the surface, then, alliance in Tamilnadu is constituted horizontally, the stress being on the *vakaiyara,* the kindred, and the *kutumpam* within the kindred. In Bengal alliance is determined vertically, since one has to match one's *baṇgśa,* with another, *baṇgśas* being the male lines of each *ghar* (house), wider *paribār,* and non–ego-based ancestral line, the *kula.* Tamilnadu alliance stresses the *vakaiyara* purity in contrast to another *vakaiyara,* keeping marriage within the kindred by cross-cousin marriages. Bengali alliance stresses the *baṇgśa, ghar, bhāiyat,* and *jñāti* relationships, since all of these involve persons related in the male line. In Tamilnadu alliance is perceived as reestablishing previous marriage ties, and in Bengal each marriage exchange in itself establishes alliance, opening the possibilities for a new set of exchanges. There are differences among lines and sets of lines, parties to an alliance, but we should add that this differs from hypergamy in that *ādān pradān* may change with each exchange in the same *ghar* and line. The same *ghar* may set up a marriage link with *ghar* X and give a daughter in marriage to that *ghar;* the next *ādān* may be entered into with a different *ghar,* and a newly bounded unit of equivalence is thus set up with *ghar* Y, even though *ghars* X and Y may or may not themselves exchange daughters in marriage. In this sense *ādān pradān* in Bengal differs from the classical theories of hypergamous marriage. *Baṇgśas* are ideally ordered high and low, but not all lines in a *jāti* are thus arranged, nor is there a mechanism of alliance within the *jāti* as a whole that would show rank transactionally for all exchanges of daughters. A daughter is given in marriage to a *ghar,* while a second daughter may be given to the same *ghar* or to an entirely different *ghar* and line, provided that the unit of equivalence with the new *ghar* has been determined by the matching of the two *baṇgśas.* The criteria are recalculated for each *baṇgśa* in each case, and in these considerations one or another criterion may predominate over the others. Lines are primarily compared to each other in terms of quality, but other factors such as wealth, locality, connections, and prospects are also considered. In this way even though two lines may be regarded as equal within the *jāti* in terms of blood purity and *baṇgśa* status, there are other factors that may influence the alliance.

We have suggested two ways of looking at the high or the low status of a *ghar. Ghars* and lines more or less equal to each other are further distinguished by factors other than the purity of the male line. These factors, as we stated earlier, are the economic standing and influence, political and occupational, of the potentially allying houses and lines. Levels of education and employment pose further questions for the *kartā* (head of household) about to give his daughter in marriage.

Unlike the south Indian case where cross-cousin marriages are possible and terminology does spell out marriageable categories, in Bengal the terminology does not refer to any specific marriage rules. Furthermore, Bengali terminology transforms affinal groups of one generation into consanguines in the next, thus rendering a concrete grouping of those one can marry difficult, even impossible to attain. In Bengal the question of marriage is the equivalence and matching of *baṇgśas,* the standing of *ghars* in terms of quality and codes for conduct. It is in the questions of blood quality and purity, male line and position of women in the line, coupled with what happens to women in marriage that the construction of the person and theories of conception make sense in the ordering of *baṇgśas* in relation to each other. In short, alliance in Bengal and Tamilnadu can be stated comparatively: alliance depends upon two constructions of difference—difference among hierarchical units, which operates through their separation, and difference within units of equivalence, which operates through exchange and combination. In Tamilnadu these units are given prior to a particular alliance (which is within the *vakaiyara*), whereas in Bengal a particular alliance determines these units. Without elaborating it, we can see this in the system of gift giving in both regions: equal gifts are exchanged in Tamilnadu, while detailed sequences of unequal gifts are exchanged in Bengal.

Bengal and Tamilnadu Compared

The various essays on Bengal in this volume are no more a traditional anthropological study of kinship than the essay on Tamilnadu is one of caste. The Bengali and Tamil studies examine the cultural construction of the person in different domains, yet in spite or because of this seeming limitation there is no difficulty in discussing, among other things, kinship and caste, alliance, and hypergamy. Though regarding Bengal hardly any mention is made of caste, hierarchy and *jāti* are not far away from the core of the discussion; and although hardly any mention is made of kinship regarding Tamilnadu, alliance and equivalence are central to the discussion. Nevertheless we did not set out to do separate kinship and caste studies in these two regions. On the contrary the person-in-kinship approach to Bengal complements the person-in-caste approach in Tamilnadu; and despite our different points of departure, we encounter no barrier to a comparison between Bengal and Tamilnadu in terms of the person, the ideas of relatedness, blood, line, and alliance. The only impediment to our comparative approach is given by anthropological orthodoxy, which would, in some cases, too rigidly oppose the sociological constructs of caste and kinship, hypergamy and alliance, transaction and ranking, north India and south India. So without any further deliberation we dissolve the artificial boundaries of kinship and caste and discuss aspects of both as indigenous cultural constructs of the person in a domain of thought and action. Our comparison is, therefore, meant as a new departure in the study of Indian society based on underlying structural principles for the construction of the person in two regions of India. As such the comparison is meant to stimulate further discussion of the person, hierarchy, *jāti,* and alliance.[6]

The most immediate difference between Bengal and Tamilnadu is the relative emphasis on line and kindred in the two regions. In Tamilnadu the line is stressed less than in Bengal, marriages taking place within the *vakaiyara.* By contrast the nobility and purity of the line (*baṇgśa*) is fundamental in Bengal, marriages taking place within a larger unit of matched and matchable lines. Thus marriage in Bengal is determined by principles defining lines in vertical relationships, whereas in Tamilnadu the analogous principles define lines within the *vakaiyara* in horizontal relationships. If we can speak of such marriages as an alliance between two units within a wider unit in both cases, then alliance in Tamilnadu (*sampanti*) means the reestablishment of previous ties in new marriages, while in Bengal alliance (*biyer ādān pradān*) means the creation of new marriage ties in the image and principles of past ones—a matter close enough to merit detailed examination.

In both Bengal and Tamilnadu a marriage tie cannot link blood relatives, blood being a category that is constituted differently for the two regions. Speaking within a universe of equivalence (alliance units within *jāti*), marrying nonblood relatives signifies the establishment of maximum differences for exchange, which in turn creates equivalence. In both regions marriage has to recreate or establish some previous tie or image of a tie, the definition of these ties and the ways of bringing them about being different in Bengal and Tamilnadu. In addition there is a terminological rule for marriage in Tamilnadu, while there is none in Bengal. This circumstance immediately raises two related questions. First, given the similarities of alliance in the limited sense given to the term above, why should there be a terminological rule in the one case and not in the other? Second, if there are underlying similarities between Bengal and Tamilnadu, then are the defining principles of the domain within which we find variations on a theme limited to expression through the terminology? On the contrary they may be expected to emerge in and through the cultural constitution of the domain. A corollary of these questions is the dual puzzle that if the genealogically constituted terminology does not yield a marriage rule in Bengal, then where are we to look for the rule of alliance practice; and if among others such a rule is also terminological in Tamilnadu, is there not a way of arriving at the same rule of alliance other than through the terminology for cross-cousins or brothers-in-law?[7] In speaking of alliance in Bengal and Tamilnadu, we are not looking for rules at the level of nomenclature, which should make it necessary to posit an inverted caste-kinship relationship and a differential mixture of domains for the two regions. Rather we attempt to discover the meaning of relevant categories for analysis from ideology and practice as given separately in the two regions. In attempting an analysis of how the indigenous domain is constituted in Bengal and Tamilnadu, we also alter the terms of comparison. As we pointed out above, the result is that the very notion of alliance takes on a different meaning.

Alliance, in our sense of the term, is incomprehensible without a system of hierarchy.[8] But units engaging in hierarchical action are within themselves also units of equivalence—a complementarity extending through all levels of vertical and horizontal relationships in Indian society. In our case the unit of equivalence is the *vakaiyara* in Tamilnadu and a set of *baṇgśas* in marriage links in Bengal. In Tamilnadu equivalence is assumed within the *vakaiyara,* a bounded whole within which marriages take place, the process determining marriages going on to establish differences sufficient to allow the conclusion of a marriage alliance. On the other hand, in Bengal the set of lines forming a unit of equivalence is theoretically extensible to the *jāti* as a whole. Since we are dealing with a relational, segmentary, and oppositional system in a hierarchy, we note that the smallest unit of equivalence, *baṇgśa,* is also the unit of alliance, the marriage link among lines in a wider locality establishing the unit of equivalence within which lines are matched to establish equivalence.[9] Matching an entirely separate, outside line to a set of lines linked by marriages involves bringing two previously unrelated units of equivalence into a new, larger unit, which of necessity has to conform to the image of previous ties in both units.

Since the unit of equivalence is bounded in Tamilnadu and open in Bengal, the limitation to the total set of lines available for marriage is set by *vakaiyara* boundaries in Tamilnadu and by *jāti* boundaries in Bengal, while in the latter case *jāti* equivalence is also segmented into smaller units of equivalence, a circumstance unparalleled from the Tamil example. The difference is a function of the constitution of persons in line and kindred and of the relative position of line and kindred in Bengal and Tamilnadu. Thus the principle of alliance is valid for both regions, but the form it takes is different. This is in part due to the differences between the ways in which units to the alliance are constituted and between units of equivalence based on a concept of line in Bengal and a concept of kindred in Tamilnadu.

The differences between the two regions are apparent in the ideas of sharing blood. If we do not share blood, a condition of marriage, then how do we determine equivalence? In Tamilnadu the unit of equivalence is one that includes the combination of blood differences necessary for marriage, while in Bengal the line represents shared blood, and one must go outside the line to establish equivalence through the necessary blood differences. In both cases there are principles to unite and equalize the units linked in a marriage. Marriage requires different *gotras, kotirams,* and different blood (a different blood line in Bengal and different *uyir* and *utampu* in Tamilnadu). This requirement allows the creation of equality by marriages expressing differences. Thus, there are principles dividing and separating the units of the alliance. These are given by the separation of the parties to the alliance into different *uyir* and different *utampu* in Tamilnadu and into different *baṇgśas, jñāti,* and *māltri śakti* in Bengal. A differentiation through the female element is necessary in both cases.

The rules for convergence and divergence in the two regions follow from the indigenous understanding of conception. In Tamilnadu the father's semen is the source of the child's *utampu* and gives body to the child. *Uyir,* the mother's contribution of the female element, is unchangeable, whereas the *utampu* of a woman changes in marriage to that of her husband. Hence the marriage link has to be created out of different *uyir* and different *utampu.* Implicit in the Tamil constructs of *uyir* and *utampu* is the idea of maleness (*purusa*) and male line (*kotiram*), neither of which structures marriage within the *vakaiyara.* By contrast, in Bengal the father is the source of the child's blood (semen, *bīj,* into *rakta,* blood), which is augmented and increased by the mother's blood and milk and her *mātri śakti* (power), which is her unique complementary contribution. *Mātri śakti,* as the female element and the mother's contribution, complements *puruṣa,* the male element, transmitted through the male line (*baṇgśa*), which is also the blood line in Bengal.

A theory of alliance applicable to both Bengal and Tamilnadu follows from underlying structural similarities in the construction of relatedness, which in turn derives from indigenous theories of conception and the cultural construction of the person. Alliance in Tamilnadu repeats previous marriage ties, while in Bengal it creates or recreates marriage ties through principles for matching and excluding lines that may or may not have been previously linked by actual marriages. The local ideology emphasizes alliance in both cases through maximizing differences within the unit of equivalence. The possibility of alliance demonstrates the equivalence within these units, which are themselves established by hierarchical action.

The difference between Bengal and Tamilnadu is evident in the composition of blood, a complex multivocal symbol. In Bengal blood expresses maleness, male line, *gotra, mātri śakti,* and male-female complementarity. But these are not concrete entities substantively aggregated as particles in a general flow of blood. Rather they are constructs symbolically expressed by blood, the latter itself being a construct for a substance passed in a male line through females. Blood is then a symbol referring to a substance as a vehicle for the expression of several related concepts (Geertz 1974). The same process of construction is true of Tamilnadu. There blood is constituted of two aspects that enjoin and are affected by a code of conduct. *Utampu* and *uyir* are the male and female elements of blood, which are inherited by a newborn from its father and mother respectively. *Uyir* is permanently fixed, while *utampu* is transformed in women upon marriage. Men as well as women have *uyir* and *utampu,* and marriages are structured by the combination of different *uyir* and different *utampu* in the selection of prospective marriage partners. Needless to add, however, the actual choice of a bride or a groom has to do with a long process in which the above principles form a limitation and a boundary in a realm of possibilities, the final selection depending on additional considerations such as employment, education, wealth, connections, future prospects, locality, politics, and so forth.

In both Bengal and Tamilnadu blood symbolically expresses pairs of opposing but complementary principles.

change/permanence
male/female
utampu/uyir
puruṣa/mātri śakti
Śiva/Durgā
seed/earth

The combination of active and passive elements defines the units of equivalence—lines in Bengal and kindreds in Tamilnadu. In both cases the complementarity of the male and female elements acts to structure units on the level of principles.

The *uyir/utampu* aspects of blood in Tamilnadu make MBD and FZD nonblood relatives and therefore ideal marriage partners. The lack of such separation in Bengal makes MBD and FZD blood relatives, and consequently such marriages are proscribed. Here blood is conceptualized as male in the construction of the person with the female contribution encompassed in the male line.

Upon marriage women change their *utampu* and *gotra* in Tamilnadu and their *gotra* alone in Bengal. But in neither case are a married woman's ties to her father's side completely severed. These remaining links are much clearer in Bengal, for obvious reasons, but even in Tamilnadu a married woman observes her father's death pollution, and her *uyir* remains that of her mother. In Bengal the married woman does not change her blood, merely her *gotra* (one of the constructs expressed by and transmitted through blood in the male line). She observes her father's death pollution because she shares the same blood. For a woman the blood line is cut in relation to her siblings, but even in this case a blood relationship remains. In Tamilnadu marriage means losing one line and gaining another one, while in Bengal both lines remain but only one is transmitted—that of the husband. These circumstances neatly differentiate the meaning of *baṇgśa, gotra,* father's, in-laws', and husband's lines in Bengal. The different ways of constructing blood in Bengal and Tamilnadu also account for the difference in funerary rites (*śraddha*) as these affect a married woman.

The *vakaiyara* is the unit within which marriage alliance takes place in Tamilnadu. Relative blood purity defines *vakaiyaras* in hierarchical relation to each other. The principle underlying the caste system as a relational, holistic system does not stop at the boundaries of kin groups but reaches all divisions till the smallest unit of hierarchical action is reached (Dumont 1957). *Vakaiyaras* are differentiated by relative purity and codes of conduct that may alter that purity. The unit holding relative purity is the *vakaiyara* in Tamilnadu and the line, or a set of lines, in Bengal. Purity and hierarchy are defined by *uyir* and *utampu* together. *Utampu* alone constitutes *kotiram,* and since *kotirams* cross-cut *vakaiyaras,* the same *kotiram* within the *vakaiyara* yields the *kulam. Kulam* and *kotiram* provide the line emphasis in Tamilnadu. Lines are thus a significant feature, but they do not structure marriages. In Bengal *gotra* and *baṇgśa* are almost identical features, but they do structure marriages. The contrast is clear in the relative importance of the kindred in Tamilnadu and the line in Bengal. Kindred and line are in turn structured by the differential construction of the person, blood, and conception in the two regions. The bilateral kindred is present in Bengal but in different form. The functional equivalent of the *vakaiyara* emerges in Bengal through the indigenous theory of conception, the mother's contribution to the child, the mother's continuing link to her father's side, the children's continuing links to their mother's side, and finally through the position of the married woman between her natal lines and her in-laws' lines, with the concomitant relations between these two sets of lines. The code of conduct aspect of these relationships (exchange, gift giving, ritual duties, shared purity and pollution, commensality, and so forth) also highlight the structuring of equivalence through lines in Bengal and kindred in Tamilnadu, together with the complementary though subordinate position of the kindred in Bengal and of the line in Tamilnadu on the level of structural principles.[10]

The principle of hierarchy in Indian society explaining vertical relations among units is complemented by equivalence within each unit. The cultural construction of the person and the indigenous theories of conception act to constitute hierarchy as well as equality within and without the units of action. Purity and quality of blood (in kindred and line) oppose units of equivalence (of greater or lesser inclusiveness) to each other in a system of hierarchy (castes, lines, kindreds). The units of hierarchical action are created and defined in relation to each other through indigenous principles entering into the construction of the person, blood, marriage, and conception, yielding units of equivalence in a hierarchically ordered whole. Thus there is no warrant for opposing caste to kinship on the level of structure, since as we showed for Bengal and Tamilnadu the indigenous system allows us to consider kinship and caste together, without any internal impediment, as units of hierarchy and equivalence in a single whole.

Alliance, then, creates units of equivalence in Bengal and Tamilnadu. Its significance in both cases is that the units are for hierarchical action. In Tamilnadu previous ties within the units are replicated by uniting categories bearing different *uyir* and different *utampu.* In Bengal previous ties may be replicated so long as the blood and *mātri śakti* components differ. Alliance in Bengal creates further equivalence out of differentially ordered lines by matching selected lines out of an indefinite number of other lines, representing previous alliances linking larger segments.[11] In both Bengal and Tamilnadu the system turns on marriage. Beyond the ideological similarities there are striking parallels on the level of concepts. Alliance, in our sense of the term, is *sampanti* in Tamilnadu, while *sammandhī* is a specific relative by marriage and *sammandha* is a link by marriage in Bengal. The Tamil *kutumpam* comprises relatives in a locality (family), while the *kutumba* in Bengal are relatives by marriage in general. The Bengali *paribār* comprises a group of relatives encompassing a locality. The inversion could not be clearer: one's closest relatives in a locality are relatives by marriage in Tamilnadu and by blood in Bengal—the Tamil *kutumpam* is the functional equivalent of the Bengali *paribār,* with kindred and line respectively dominating the constructs. Consequently persons of the Tamil *kutumpam* are *rakta āttiya* (blood relatives) in Bengal, while relatives by marriage (*kutumba*) are further distinguished from blood relatives.

We can now see that having started with attempts to develop a framework applicable to India as a whole, we cannot recast Bengal in the structural image of Tamilnadu, nor can we recast Tamilnadu in the structural image of Bengal. Yet a comparative approach starting with the differences between the two regions allowed us to arrive at a statement of similarities on the level of structural principles. Proceeding from an analysis of *vakaiyaras* and *baṇgśas* as the limits of hierarchy, we developed a principle of alliance applicable to both regions in terms of the indigenous construction of the person, allowing us to establish units of equivalence for hierarchical action.

2

Bad Blood in Bengal: Category and Affect in the Study of Kinship, Caste, and Marriage

Lina Fruzzetti
Ákos Östör

LEVI-STRAUSS has written that affectivity is the most obscure side of man and for this reason we should concentrate on logic, classification, and categorization in the study of social relationships.[1] Affectivity or the affective element in this sense pertains to the emotions, feelings, dispositions and states of being. In a sense Lévi-Strauss is right: the subjective intuition of universal mental states and the a priori attribution of meaning to sentiments and emotions in actions and practices across societies would indeed be an exercise in obscurantism. But in a different sense he is wrong.

Whatever anthropologists, sociologists, and behavioral scientists may think of universal dispositions, moods, and feelings, societies may and do categorize attitudes and dispositions in terms of their own traditions, history, and culture. Despite markedly scientific biases, students of kinship also characterize attitudes as a significant or component part of terminological systems. There is no agreement about how this characterization should be done, yet while attitudes are deemed to be legitimate, feelings, sentiments, and dispositions are not. These questions usually surface in our discipline in discussions of what kind of data belong or do not belong to a kinship universe, whether terms of address, attitudes, and so forth are a legitimate part of kinship studies. From our point of view the question is moot because it ignores the indigenous cultural construction of categories for relationships among persons, which may be affective or terminological or structured or even affinal and consanguineal, or they may point beyond any and all of these analytical, functional, and sociological conceptions of our discipline. Ignoring the logic of indigenous categories, no matter in which direction it chooses to take us, is the surest way of sinking into the quicksand of the question: what is kinship? Is it an expression of some other reality, a representation of fundamental economic, political, or jural determinants? The usual results of such discussions in abstraction are the future refining and reifying of terminologies, typologies, and functional or structural universals without attaining the least degree of understanding.

Our own discussion of what in kinship discourse would constitute the affective element is cautious and exploratory to a fault. We set out at least to extend the universe of discourse to a wider domain of culturally categorized social relations; at most we hope to demonstrate that the cultural construction of affectivity, or what approximates anthropological views of affect, is in fact a part of relationships among persons and groups in society with significant tasks of ordering, defining, and interpreting these relationships. Furthermore, we may find that genealogical kinship terminologies and analytically perceived marriage rules discussed in these terms do not and cannot accomplish the tasks performed by cultural categories of affect even in regard to the resolution of problems besetting orthodox kinship studies.

In the first of three previous studies devoted to the problems of kinship, marriage, and caste in Bengal, we discussed the recent writings of Louis Dumont (1957, 1966, 1975) and Sylvia Vatuk (1969, 1972) in the light of Bengali kinship terminology.[2] We asked whether or not the Bengali kinship terminological grid has a structure, and we indicated the general problems inherent in studying nomenclature as guide to a "kinship" domain. One of the major obstacles in the formal approach to Indian kinship theory is the a priori assumption that we know what constitutes kinship terms or a kinship universe (Schneider 1970, 1972). Dumont's structural study of south Indian terminology, marriage practices, and alliance concluded that in the Dravidian case there is a system and a structure in the terminology. South Indian marriage alliance practices fully accord with the affinal relationships of the terminology. Thus, in the crystal clear Dravidian system of kin terms is yielded a kinship universe systemic and similarly structured throughout the different levels (Fruzzetti and Östör 1976a). This universe divides relationships into those between wife-givers and wife-receivers, relations that replicate themselves in later generations by classifying the categories of agnates and affines into those who can and those who cannot give women in marriage. Dumont's venture into the study of north Indian kinship yields different results from the south Indian case. Despite some similarities and differences between the two systems, Dumont found that north Indian terminology had no structure, no opposition of wife-givers and wife-receivers, no kinship rules that could be applied to marriage practices. He concluded that in north India an underlying Dravidian practice is obscured by the terminology and that one can elucidate the system from caste rather than kinship principles. In a subsequent study Vatuk briefly challenged these conclusions, stating that north Indian terminology has a structure and a logic whereby some sorts of marriage rules can be deduced from kinship terms. Vatuk confronts similar problems and difficulties in defining the fundamental categories of kinship and in delivering a structural analysis. Thus, genealogical schemata or genealogical terminological systems prove to be an unreliable guide to understanding categories of persons, marriage rules, concepts of relationships in line and marriage, affinity, and consanguinity. Dumont's clear Dravidian kinship structure cannot be found in north India. Nevertheless, the attempted analysis of the Bengali terminological system led us to a wider and more meaningful consideration of other questions pertaining to marriage rules, the conception and indigenous construction of the person, the many and varied meanings of *blood,* the notions of relatives, and kind of relations.

Our second essay, written about the same time, differs in approach and method of analysis, since in the first essay we chose to work in terms of an a priori assumption of what constitutes a kinship domain. In the second essay we sought to extend the boundaries of our investigation to work with the cultural categories of what constitutes a person, a relative, types of relationships, and so forth. Working independently on marriage rituals, household worship, *pūjās,* ancestral worship, and so on, we became aware of the close relationship between caste, marriage, kinship, and belief. To understand specific life-cycle rituals we were led to investigate a domain of relationship among persons, relatives, and groups of people. To questions as to what constitutes a kinship universe, a distant or a near relative, blood, *gotra, jñāti, kuṭum,* and non-*kuṭum,* or briefly what is generally lumped together as consanguinity and affinity in the kinship literature, we found no solution, answer, or coherence in traditional approaches to kinship in elucidating indigenous meanings from terminological studies. For this reason in the second essay we attempted to understand the meaning of Bengali marriages, the rules of marriage rituals, and prohibitions and exchanges as well as the relationships between male and female, women and lines, lines and lines, and lines and persons in and out of marriage, and so forth. We approached the study of Bengali kinship culturally and structurally. We did not posit a genealogical grid for an assumed kinship system. We followed the meaning of indigenous terms for relationships, practices, and usages to arrive at the system in which these terms participate. Thus, our concern in the second essay was to find meaning in the cultural constructs and concepts applied to behavior, attitude, and sentiments as codes for conduct and the way cultural constructs define and interpret social reality for people.

Bengalis have several ways of distinguishing relatives—blood relatives, relatives in marriage, relationship relatives, as well as male-line-carrying relatives and female-line-carrying relatives. They discriminate between *āttiya, kuṭum,* and *jñāti* through other intertwining cultural constructs of *rakta, gotra, baṇgśa, biye,* and *sammandha.* Opposition of consanguinity to affinity does not deliver a meaningful system in this case. To give an example, *baṇgśa* (line) and *gotra* are passed in the male line through *rakta* (blood), but they are also acquired by in-marrying women. "*Baṇgśa* and *gotra* are not genealogically based on blood, rather they are cultural constructs which refer to the Bengali notion of marriage as the 'establishment of a line' and they do so in different ways" (Fruzzetti and Östör 1976b: 129). *Gotras* are important for marriage just as *jñātis* are necessary for the recognition of blood and pollution in a line. Persons are *āttiya, kuṭum, jñāti,* and they share *baṇgśa, rakta, kula,* and *gotra.* The central issues are the notions of conception and transmission of similarities and differences among groups of people, the ideal of relatedness, and the formation of a relative. Questions of male and female complementarity in the origination of an issue and who contributes what to the formation of the child further highlight the multilevel and varied meanings of the Bengali constructs of blood. The male seed is accepted by the earth, where femaleness (womb) encompasses the seed, while in turn earth, seed, and issue are encompassed by the male line, owing to the nature of Bengali marriage, birth, and transmissions of lines, *gotra,* and so on.

Marriage and birth are clearly intertwined in Bengal. Women are exchanged between lines, for women are either daughters of a line (*gotrer meye*) or wives of a line (*baṇgśer bou*). The language of alliance, to give and to take women to and from lines (*āḍān pradān*) extended our study to comparison between Bengal and Tamilnadu. Along with Barnett we reexamined notions of conception and birth in relation to the question of alliance. In our joint comparative paper (1976, reprinted in this volume) marriage, blood, and line became central to our understanding of the person as well as the matching of lines for marriage, quality of blood and line, and purity and pollution rules for relatives. Though the comparison of north and south India may be bold and even hasty, we feel that it serves its purpose first, in the comparison of kinship domains, and second, in the applicability of a method of analysis, giving fuller consideration to indigenous categories and concepts as yielded, conceived, and formulated by the people in action. The three essays serve as a background for the subject of this essay concerning the question of affectivity in Bengal.

Ties of affectivity are categorized as such, and these kinds of relationships affect ritual performances surrounding marriage, birth, and death. Again, ritual and kinship considerations enter into the orderings of relatives and kinds of relationships.

We take the Bengali conception of relative as given and proceed to analyze what might seem to be a puzzle: the problem of what the Bengalis call "bad blood." Why is this expression cast in the metaphor of blood, and why are one's relatives by marriage divided into two opposing groups? What we want to emphasize is that in Bengal affectivity is cast in terms of blood. Given our exposition of the multivocal and multilevel indigenous explanation of blood, here is one more case in point, which adds to further understanding of the Bengali conceptions of blood, relative, person, and so forth.

In Bengali society the preliminaries and negotiations of marriage raise a number of issues regarding who can marry whom and, as a result, what distinguishes one relative from another, *jāti* endogamy being observed in all sacred Hindu marriages. Our discussion is occasioned by a particular saying one often hears among women during marriage negotiations. The saying itself serves as a rule for one of the marriage prohibitions in Bengali Hindu marriage. In these situations two sets of female relatives are opposed to each other, the opposition and the contrast between the *baṇgśa* (line) or *bāṛi* (household, also signifying a line in this context) of these two sets leading to the problem of bad blood. The saying, *Māsīr bāṛi nasi, pisīr bāṛi basi,* asserts that the line or house of one's MZ is inauspicious while that of the FZ's is auspicious, using the females (MZ, FZ) as the connecting links of a newly created alliance. Auspiciousness and inauspiciousness refer to blood (*rakta*) defined in symbolic terms, since in neither case are blood relatives married to each other. In the first case (MZ's house) the blood does not mix well, and in the other (FZ) it mixes well. The symbolic meaning of the term *blood* becomes clear when we realize that the inauspicious effect manifests itself during the marriage rituals or soon after. Here, then, through the two females who are connecting relatives to two different lines different problems are posed regarding the further giving of women into the same line, resulting in a preference for giving daughters twice to the same line.

The question here is not the direction of giving women in marriage alliance or the giving of women to the same line one has given to in the past or the giving to alternative lines. The problem of bad blood is not phrased or defined in relation to the hypergamous unions, the ensuing direction of women at marriage, or the dowry itself. Why, then, is there a concern with bad blood in one marriage and not in the other? Can we deduce a solution to this puzzle merely from the positioning of the person in the system of kinship, marriage, and caste or in other domains as well, such as the rituals of marriage, death, and birth and the cultural field of affectivity in relation to both maternal and paternal sides? Recall that in this case one's MZ's *bāṛi,* or house, is not the same as one's MB's, since a MZ after marriage joins her new relations in her husband's house. Therefore, one's married MZ in this case is treated differently from one's unmarried MZ, who lives in her father's and brother's house (the male or female Ego's maternal house).

What constitutes bad blood? When does blood not mix well? In both cases a marriage of a woman to her FZ's line or to her MZ's line will not involve marrying *nijer āttiya* (one's own relative). Nor are the similarities of *gotra,* or membership to the same *baṇgśa,* in question here.[3] Fear of the inauspicious effect caused or brought about by marrying a girl into her MZ's line is a major concern for Bengali women, even more so than for men. There is a preference to give further to the line to which one gave a daughter before (to the FZ's *bāṛi,* again stressing that the woman is not married to her FZS but to a male member of that line). In elucidating the incursion of bad blood we have to analyze first the relationship of a female Ego to her MZ before and after marriage and second the case of the incoming wife, who as a member of her husband's line and house adopts the code of conduct of that line. In Bengali Hindu marriages women undergo a change of status through the change of their *gotra* to that of their husband. Though some accounts of Bengali kinship and marriage claim that women undergo a bodily transubstantiation, we argue to the contrary that women in marriage are adopted through the ritual into their husband's line, where their status changes directly from that of daughter of a line to wife of a line.

In Bengal a distinction is made between different women in the household (*ghar*). Bengali men and women differentiate between one's own daughters and the incoming wifes of the line. The crucial feature is the *gotra,* and here again the differentiation between the two categories of women is simple—it depends on whether one is born or adopted into a *gotra. Por gotra* (after *gotra,* that is, came into, adopted into the *gotra*) and *gotrer meye* (daughter of the *gotra*) are the two terms that clearly distinguish between the two sets of women in a house as daughters or wives. For Bengali women birth and marriage rituals enter into the ordering of their position in a *gotra* as daughter; marriage reverses the act and makes it possible for a woman to be adopted into a different line as a wife. The adoption process makes it possible for women to carry a man's seed in their womb, the seed which itself is male. The new wife will always share her father's and brother's blood, and the sharing of blood makes it impossible for her children to marry into that line, precisely because complete transubstantiation does not take place at marriage.[4] In Bengal blood is passed and carried in the male line. *Blood* here and throughout our essay refers to a category of a substance that is permanent, enduring, transmitted through the male members of the line, the incoming women or wives of the line acting as its carrier.

Bengali women acquire a new set of relatives at marriage, though they retain ties with their father's side. Nonetheless, the incoming wife, a new member of the husband's line, ends her membership in her father's *sapiṇḍa* (ancestors to whom offerings are made). Though she has been adopted into a new *gotra* through the marriage ritual, her children cannot be given in marriage to her brother's children because complete bodily transubstantiation does not take place.

There are many stories exemplifying what can happen to an inauspicious marriage, most culminating in the death of the bride (never the husband), a circumstance further complicating the puzzle of bad blood. To understand the problem of why a marriage into a MZ's line is inauspicious, one may contrast the relationships of a woman to her MZ's line with the auspicious effect of the preferred marriage to the FZ's line. The relationship between a woman and her *māsī* poses no problems before marriage. It is the change of status that the woman goes through during the marriage rituals that complicates the question. Here we emphasize the change of conduct, since the marriage in itself should be possible because it does not involve blood (*rakta*) relation nor *gotra* or *sapiṇḍa* membership. If the problem lies somewhere else, we may then move from the consideration of marriage rituals to other rituals that might involve *gotra* and *kuṭum* (relatives by marriage) in the ordering of social relations. Here we have to ascertain who is present at the death rituals and anniversaries or the mortuary rites, who gives what to whom, and what are the duties of the various *nijer āttiya* (one's relatives) and *kuṭum* (relatives by marriage). We are not suggesting that we oppose universal affinity to consanguinity, nor are we stating that we wish to remain within specified genealogical considerations or particular categories of people. We are recommending that we try to understand the changes marriage rituals bring about and the relationship of these changes to codes of conduct and to other rituals in society. We propose to oppose two specific relatives to a female Ego: her MZ and FZ. When the MZ's house is the point of reference, we are not alluding to a specific person but the category of person in that house. For Ego to consider marriage in her MZ's line means considering her MZHBS or any of her MZH's classificatory brothers, excluding her own MZS, because they would share the same *mātri śakti* (mother power or ability). We are thus considering a married MZ, a woman to whom a female Ego is related through her mother, her own as against her in-marrying *śvaśur lok* (in-laws).

The problem of giving a woman to her MZ's line lies not in the similarities of *gotra, baṇgśa,* or *sapiṇḍa* but in the creation of *kuṭum* and in the obligations of these *kuṭum* to each other. We stated earlier that marriage is central to the understanding of social relations culturally constructed in Bengal. The consequences of marrying a girl into her MZ's line is clearest in the marriage rituals, where the act of giving a woman to another line places that line below the giver. The giving and taking of women in marriage again manifests itself at the mortuary rituals, where the difference between high and low statuses is expressed again through gift giving to specific persons within a group. In a previous study we stated that exchange marriages and reversals in the direction of marriages are possible in Bengal and that one can give more than one woman to the same line. Thus, no sociological rules of hypergamy apply. Yet to give a woman to her MZ's line would not mean giving to the same line but to the *kuṭum* of *kuṭum;* thus, three lines would be involved in that particular relationship.

Certain kinds of filial and maternal relationships are established between two lines through marriage and birth. Here enters the question of affectivity: behavior and codes of conduct among persons are not explained directly by blood (*rakta*) relatedness but indirectly by death pollution, mortuary rites, or change of *gotra,* along with the creation of hierarchies and inequalities of giving and taking women in marriage. Those relatives in one's male line who observe one's *śraddha* (mortuary rites) should coincide with the set of relatives who observe a marriage prohibition among each other. Thus we agree with Kapadia when she states that the "concept of *sapiṇḍa* relationship is unilateral in the rules of impurities to be observed on birth as well as death" (1949: 271–272). Offering water libations (*jal deoyā*) to the dead was, and still is, prescribed in terms of membership in a set of male lines—the *sapiṇḍa āttiya.* Thus, death and birth impurities stress the *sapiṇḍa* ties in the male line, whereas marriage prohibitions among *āttiya* introduce the maternal line as well as one's male line. Impurities caused by death affect the members of the male line only, and not the maternal side. Kapadia argues that the "stress is in the [agnatic] family" rather than in associating rules of impurity with the performance of *samaṣkāras.* Again it is the significance of both the father's and the father-in-law's sides that accounts for observing the rules of impurity in relation to the married woman's father and mother. Bengalis are even more specific and stress that though marriage separates the two sides (father's and husband's lines), the link continues through affect and continuing ties of blood relatedness. In the first case the link by affect is demonstrated through visitations and gift giving at various life-cycle rituals and some more specific duties to one's *kuṭum.* Link by blood relatedness is maintained by marriage prohibitions with each other. Those *āttiya* who sit on the same *ghāt* (open water's edge, where ritual performances take place) to offer water libations to the dead, to one's ancestors, are thus prohibited from marrying each other. We hope by exploring a female Ego's relationship to her paternal, husband's, and maternal sides to elucidate similarities or differences in expressed culturally constructed affectivity to each side and ways in which to throw some light on the puzzle of bad blood.

The Paternal Side—*Bāper Bāṛi*

Males born into a *baṇgśa,* or line, remain and retain membership in that line until death, unless they are adopted through a ritual into a different line within the same caste. Daughters of a line are expected to treat residence in their paternal household as temporary. Women are not meant to remain permanently in their father's house: it is expected that all women will marry and leave for their husband's place. In Bengal there are two models for women to follow, one for young unmarried girls and the other for married women, who are expected to model their lives on those of their own mother or mother-in-law. There are neither aspirations nor models for spinsterhood in this society. Marriage thus becomes central in the lives of Bengali women.

The young *kumārī* (unmarried girl in her prepuberty years) roams about freely in her father's house, running in and out without being punished for her movements. Her relationship to her father and brothers is open, affable, and easy without any kind of shyness or reserve. But she will have to leave her father's house one day, and this she is made aware of at an early age. Mothers always try to delay the marriage of their young daughters, but the male members fear the prolonged unmarried state and insist on an early marriage, if at all possible. Many marriage songs portray the father of a young bride as being determined to marry his daughter early, while the mother cries and pleads for one more year's delay. Nonetheless, though fathers are soft and warm toward their daughters, they know that the daughters leave one day. Daughters are given away in marriage if there is a good—not just any—opportunity available. The elaborate marriage negotiations and the initial search by the father for an appropriate groom exemplifies the father's concern for his daughter. Fathers are known to be gentle to the very young, though they may change suddenly as the girl comes of age and must be married. Young, unmarried girls are affectionately called "little mother," Goddess Durga, or Laksmi by their fathers. The relationship between them is a very special one.

Though the father is generous and kind, at the same time he has to be harsh in the treatment of his sons; he is a disciplinarian, a figure of authority. He demands respect in the house from his own *paribār* (wife, family world). Seniority is respected in a Bengali household. Elders are given the respect (*sammān*) due to age, and the younger generation receive *adar, sneha* (affection, love) from the elders. The kind and quality of affection from one set to the other differs on the basis of seniority. The father, or his elder brother if he has one in the house, is the head *(kartā)* of the house. In matters of the house both private and public, all decisions stem from him. The position of the *ginnī* (the eldest, most respected lady in the house) differs from that of the *kartā.* She is in charge of the activities of the *saṇgsār,* those actions that are of concern within the house. Both males and females in the house share the responsibilities of bringing up the children. Two women who are both wives of the same line, though they themselves are from two other lines, may bring up their children together in the same house. The children will receive direction together, without any differentiation among them. The children in return will offer *bhakti* (devotional love) to their parents, a kind of love that parallels that offered to a deity.

A wife, on the other hand, offers *bhakti* to her husband not because of the age difference but because the husband is a deity to her, a Śiva or a Kṛṣṇa. Husbands are persons sacred to their wives. They are respected at all times, obeyed no matter what degree of equality is established between their previous households. It is inauspicious for a woman to be in an unmarried state, and being married completes the cultural expectations for and of a woman in Bengal. To her husband she owes all her future. As long as he is alive, she enjoys the full life of a married woman. His death cuts her off from the life of the living. She changes her life style into that of a widow, an inauspicious status among women.

The Maternal Side—*Māmā Bāṛi*

The mother's brother's house is one where both females and males are free from inhibitions, from the need to adhere to certain codes of conduct, or specified behavioral preferences. Toward one's *māmā* (MB) and his wife, *māmī mā,* the expressed feeling is one of *adar, bhālo bāsā.* The children reciprocate the same feeling. One shows respect to a *māmā* but in a way different than to one's father and FB. The *māmā* is the one to whom the males go for help with specific complaints. Males and females may have problems that only a MB can help to solve. At any rate they still visit the *māmā's* house because of the freedom and ease one can enjoy there. This specialized relationship is initiated soon after the birth of the sister's daughter or son: the MB ritual duties begin as early as that. At certain life-cycle rituals the MB is responsible for specific tasks. At death or marriage rituals he has duties to perform for the children of his married sister and for his sister and her husband as well. The B-Z relation does not end with the marriage of a sister. The bond is strong and reappears on the various ritual occasions that a brother has to observe toward his married sister and members of her husband's house. The brother takes over the duties of his father toward his married sisters. As the father gives away his daughter in marriage, his son continues to give the line of the married daughter gifts and services because of the established alliance relationship. The gifting and the obligations extend from his side to that of his sister, but the reverse is never the case, except at the death of a woman's father or mother, when married women must observe the death rituals with expenses provided by their husband.

What are the relations between the MZ, her married sisters, and the children of her sisters? Relations with the mother's sister, whether married or unmarried, are not very elaborate. Once a sister is married, she moves to a different house. Her brother will, however, observe the same ritual obligations to her and to her children, but the relationship between the two married sisters remains weak. The two sisters are married to two different lines, two lines that are in a wife-taking relationship with their brother. A married woman has more occasion to visit her HBW's house than her own married sister's house. Yet the two married sisters remain related through a blood tie. Again we draw on Kapadia's excellent study to illustrate this point: "The stream of feeling of union naturally diminishes with the remoteness of the degree of kinship. The further two persons are apart from each other in generation and household, the less powerful will be the bond of union between them" (Kapadia 1947: 273). The relationship will be more or less intense according to whether or not the duties and rights expressed toward each other are ritually necessary. A brother and a married sister are more bound to each other than two married sisters. Thus, two married sisters may or may not keep up their relationship, their brother's house being the only place where they can meet from time to time. Married women are constrained in their movements to other households. A married woman may go to her *jā's* (HBW's) house more easily than to her own married sister's house. She and the *jā* are brought into the same line and live under the same roof. She and her married sister are separated and live in different households or even distant towns. Yet, though the married sister is tied to a different and remote line, sisters may not give their daughters in marriage to each other's husbands' lines. Why?

A woman (or for that matter a man) has little to do with her *māsī* unless the occasions of marriage and festivals bring them together. Yet the relationship between the two is sweet, warm, and free, without any expressed ritual prohibitions: a mother's sister is likened to one's mother. After her marriage, the MZ is a rare visitor to her own paternal household (Ego's MB's house). The only occasion that might bring her to her own paternal house are the festivals, marriages, and deaths when she is invited along with her husband, since she is in point an affine of an affine, while at the same time she is a blood relative even if she now belongs to a new line. Intimate advice regarding sex may be given by a MZ to a new bride, whereas it is not a common phenomenon for a mother to advise her daughter about to be married in matters of sex. The MZ attends to her ZD during such occasions. She will not visit her ZD often after marriage. Perhaps marriage is the one occasion when she is in such close contact with her ZD. Visitations become fewer than before the marriage, since the new bride has to take on new duties and adapt to the line's code of conduct, which may not favor freedom of movement. Nonetheless, the MZ remains attached to her ZD, more so than the FZ to her BD.

The relationship between Ego and her FZ is not as close as that between a MZ and ZD. A woman may live in the same house as her FZ, especially before marriage, but after marriage the constant visitation of a woman to her father's or brother's house brings the two women in close contact. The relationship between both female and male Ego and the FZ is tense and serious; it is one that demands more respect and obedience than the rlationship to one's mother. A FZ is very critical of her brother's children, often finding a way to criticize her *boudi* (BW). The incoming wives to any line do not always get along with their husband's sister, married or unmarried. The women vie with each other and watch for faults to criticize. The question of dowry, how much or how little was given, is crucial to understanding such animosity and distance between the women. The mother-in-law takes sides with her married daughters on such occasions. The new wife is criticized for having brought very little wealth into the house. Nevertheless, as far as marriage is concerned, the preferred form of giving is to give twice to the same house.For a female Ego to be given to the same house as that of her FZ is considered to be very auspicious. The question here is not that the giver give less of a dowry. On the contrary, he might have to give more than he expected to previously because he is giving a daughter to an alredy known house, to his allies. The direction in which both goods and virgib pass is one, and two females, FZ and her BD, become *jās* to each other, a relationship marked by equality.

Bad Blood

The relationshipbetween an unmarried girl and her married and unmarried MZ and FZ can help elucidate the meaning of bad blood, since affectivity in Bengal is also expressed in terms of blood symbolism, and vice versa. Now it becomes clear that the problem posed is not to be understaaod in ters of the type of marriage or the direction of past or present marriage alliances. One reason why a particular form of marriage is not favoted has to do with mortuary rites and the presence of certain *attiya* at rituals of purification.

Since the problem of bad blood does not occur in marriages involving the FZ's side, we now move to the consideration of other possible areas of solution. Women, having finally exhausted the numerous stories about the results of such marriages, claim that the negative results of the marriage of a woman to her MZ's line becomes clear at the mortuary rites. The marriage rituals create new relationships and ties along with obligations that each new relative is bound to follow because of the sacred nature of the tie brought about by marriage.

In Figure 2.1, for E_2 the ZH is *bhagnīpati,* and the latter's brother is a brother to Ego as well. A ZH is shown respect at all times, especially on certain ritual occasions. In this particular marriage E_3 was prevailed upon by E_2 and the other males of the line to accept the gift of a virgin, E_1. It is this act, in the ritual of marriage, which makes and differentiates the relations between the brothers-in-law (*bhagnīpati* and *śālā*). In marriage the *kanyadān* or *sampradān* (gift of the virgin) creates two kinds of

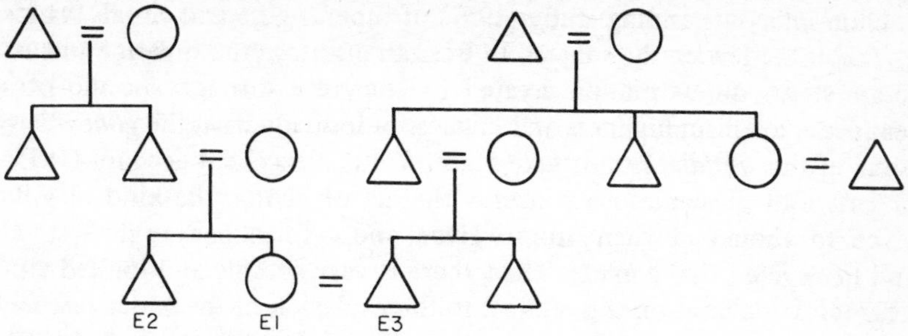

Fig. 2.1. Relationships with the ZH's line upon marriage.

relationships through the exchange of women.[5] Intimately related to marriage rituals and gift exchanges are mortuary rites, when similar exchanges take place so that the two sets have to be understood in terms of each other.

In case of a death in E_2's married sister's line (that is, in her husband's *baṇgśa*), all persons in the line become polluted, provided that the death occurs within the *sātpuruṣ* (male linkedness up to the seventh generation). At that time E_2 himself (or his father or any other male of the line) has a significant role in the *śraddha* rituals as an obligation toward the *kuṭum.* A male from the married woman's father's line has to be at the *ghāt* (the edge of an open body of water) where some of the mourning rites take place. At the same time gifts have to be made by those who gave the woman in marriage in the first place. Thus, further gifts have to be made by wife-givers at *śraddha* (mourning) ceremonies of wife-takers.

Along with the gift of a virgin in marriage, gifts and prestations are also given to the same group. Marriage is one of the life-cycle rites in which, unlike birth and death, no pollution concern is manifested. Birth creates pollution, though it is a happy occasion. Death and the subsequent mortuary rites are performed with the utmost care and precaution. Pollution caused by the departed relative is removed with the aid of a Braham. One's *sapiṇḍa* relations (up to the seventh generation) are affected by the death pollution (*aśauc*). Though *kuṭum* (relatives by marriage) are not polluted, nonetheless they are also affected by death—in their role as providers of gifts to their married daughters and their children. Here, the distinction of and the differences between the quality of gifts are marked in that at mortuary rites the gifts are given because those who gave a woman in marriage must now reenact their lower status (as wife-givers) and help her remove the pollution caused by death. Throughout the annual festival cycle gifts are presented to one's married daughters and sisters, but the obligation to give is not prescribed by the *pūjās* and festivals. In the mortuary rites *kuṭum* are obligated to give specific ritual items and clothing to a married daughter.

Dumont's outstanding study (1957) of funeral gifts and rituals stands as one of the few on the subject. In Bengali marriage the superior and inferior status differentiation created by marriage through specific rites reappears to affirm highness and lowness of individuals at the *ghāt* where some of the *śraddha* rituals take place. Vatuk's excellent account (1975) of gifts and presentations concerns the act of giving, the kind of gifts given, to whom and when gifts are given, and so forth, but not the festival and life-cycle ritual context. Thus, there is very specific and limited ethnographic material on this subject to the exclusion of the wider picture.

Here we are not specifically concerned with the ethnography of mortuary rites but with the way the ritual includes a number of *āttiya* in its organization of removing death pollution. First there are the activities at the *ghāt*. At the *ghāt* the males of a married woman's father's line have to "lift" the married daughter or sister (*ghāt tula*). A married woman has to be brought home from the *ghāt* by her F, FB, B, or other men of the line. Thus the death pollution is "lifted" from the woman through the gifts her original line makes to her new *baṇgśa.* The wife-givers give *tulsi mālā* (sacred basil-bead necklaces), *lal gumsi* (red string waistbands), and new, pure clothes to be worn after the final bath of the *śraddha,* when the period of pollution is completely over. The gifts are bestowed first on the married woman, her husband, and her other children, and then on other persons of the line. The performance of this ritual varies according to the *jāti* concerned, the period of pollution varying between ten and thirty days, but it usually takes place a day before the final rituals facilitating the passage of the departed spirit from ghost (*preta*) to ancestor (*pitri puruṣ*).

The *śraddha* gifts flow from wife-givers to wife-takers, as do the *dān* (gifts) in marriage rituals. The gift of the virgin is thus related to the gifts given at *śraddha.* The direction of giving is maintained throughout on ritual occasions, festivals, and the like. Thus, the mourning rites bring out the continued imbalance of the relationship between wife-givers and wife-takers (gift giving being accompanied by respect for those who accept the gift). Also the original line has to lift the pollution of the allied line in relation to the crucial and dual position of the married woman; in a sense the givers are made to share, in relative terms, the pollution of wife-takers.

Although *beyan-beyay* are in egalitarian, reciprocal relationship to each other, the rituals of marriage and death emphasize the deference and respect the giver must show the taker. This respect relationship is created by the *dān,* and here the hierarchy is unmistakable; the same difference of giver and taker is again expressed in *śraddha* relationships.

For a woman to marry into a previously unrelated line creates no problems for the gift-giving relationships of marriage and *śraddha.* At the *ghāt* the people of the two lines meet in the only relationship created by the ritual itself. No one need avoid anyone else, and no reversals of role, attitude, and respect are required. In the case of a woman marrying into her FZ's male line, a preferred form of marriage, the situation alters considerably although the relationship itself is an auspicious one.

In Figure 2.2. Ego is eligible to marry X, Y, or Z, all of whom belong to lines previously unrelated to Ego. Regardless which of the three she marries her *pisī* (FZ) will also become her *jā,* since the three men belong to the same *kul* and *baṇgśa.* It is common to give women in marriage to one's FZH's brothers. Kinship terminology does not differentiate here between eligible and noneligible marriages.

By marrying his daughter to his ZH's line, Ego's father's line has given women twice to the same group. (Not only is this practice quite common in Bengal, but its subsequent reversal is permitted also.) When a *śraddha* takes place in this situation (with Ego married to X, Y, or Z), then Ego's B, F, FF may all be present at the *ghāt* to lift Ego's death-pollution. Ego's FF, F, B are her FZ's F, B, BS, respectively. So again we can state that the repeated giving of women to the FZH's line creates no new contradictory or opposing relationships that may cause problems at the *ghāt* in the *śraddha* rituals. Such problems do, however, arise in our third case.

That a married woman's father's line retains a number of significant duties such as the *ghāt tula* need not surprise us. Marriage rituals have not ended the F-D tie. Women are brought into a line so that the line can continue through the birth of male children. Likewise, Kapadia (1947) likens male adoption to the reason for which marriages are contracted: to continue the line. In this sense it can be argued that marriage is a form of adoption, or adoption a form of marriage.[6] Here we must briefly touch on an earlier point regarding the transubstantiation of women at marriage into their husband's body—the two-person argument. *Ek deha* (one body) and its relation to *piṇḍa* (funerary offering to the ancestors) be-

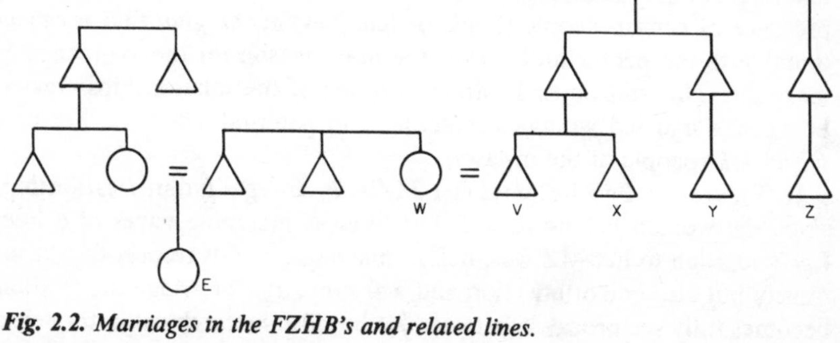

Fig. 2.2. Marriages in the FZHB's and related lines.

comes problematic when one has to explain why the *piṇḍa* (ball of rice) is offered to one's male *pitris* and not one's female-linked ancestors.[7] Women are not mentioned in a husband's *śradda*. As a matter of fact, *sapiṇḍa* as it has been described by Inden and Nicholas (1977:3, 13) does not mean only one body because of the "particles" shared by the people of a line. Kapadia (1947:61) states that the term has had a wide variety of meanings and interpretations, two of which refer to sharing particles of the same body directly or immediately, which would accommodate women as daughters and as wives born or adopted into two different lines. Secondly, again drawing on Kapadia, we note that at *śraddha* the officiating Brahman cannot be of the same *gotra* (relationship) as the people for whom he is performing the mortuary rites. Another important consideration is that the priest cannot officiate for his *yani āttiya* (relatives on his maternal side). The maternal side is just as important at *śraddha* rites as one's own *sapiṇḍa* side. A married woman observes the same number of days of pollution for her dead parents as an adopted son would for his own genitors.

Married women do keep their ties with their father's line after marriage even though the two lines are in a *kuṭum* relation to each other. No change takes place in the relation of a woman to her MF's line upon her marriage. Her MB attends her marriage not as an affine to a new group of *kuṭum* but as a *māmā* to the bride. But the MB shows respect in his relations with his ZDH's people, just as a *kuṭum* should.

In Figure 2.3, were Ego to marry her MZHB, immediate or extended (X, Y, or Z), she would make an inauspicious marriage, one of bad blood. Although no blood rule would be infringed by such a marriage, such a union is impossible because the blood does not mix well (*rakta mise jāy na; rakta khārāp haye jāy*). Inauspiciousness results from the sacredness of marriage, the ritual that transforms the words into what they state. Since the union is sanctified by the gods, the problems created for the two sets of relatives are particularly significant. These problems come to a head at the *ghāt* in the *śraddha* rituals. The newly established relations of marriage would create confusion at the *ghāt* and would constitute a bad omen, eventually resulting in the death of the bride. It is the inevitable presence of certain people (kinds of relatives) at the *ghāt* that is objectionable to the people and is thus the main reason for the avoidance of marriage. This can be understood in terms of the relationships created between a married woman's maternal and paternal sides and her new *śvaśur lok* (people of the in-laws).

In Figure 2.3 Ego becomes her MZ's *jā*, an egalitarian relationship, since the women belong to different lines as incoming wives of a line. Ego's relation to her MZ was, before marriage, one of respect due to seniority but also one of affection and warmth. After marriage the relation becomes fully reciprocal as between *jās* but also hierarchical in the sense

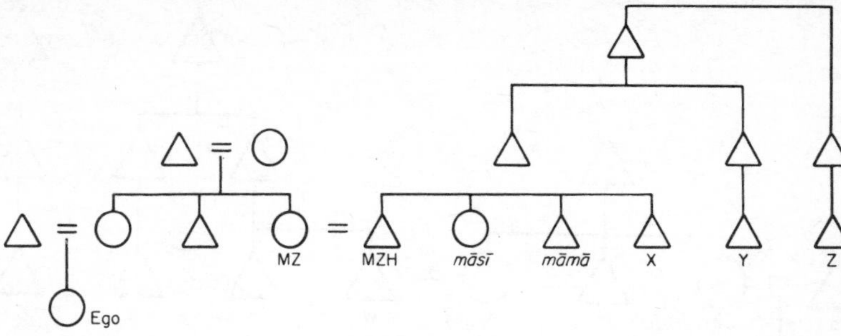

Fig. 2.3. Marriages involving bad blood.

that seniority among wives of the line is strictly observed in relation to *saṇgśar,* the world of everyday life. Matters come to a head at the *ghāt* in the mourning rites. In the case of marriage to a FZH's line ("brothers" by extension), no matter who comes to the *ghāt* from the father's line, the representation is correct.

In the case of Figure 2.3, however, the group of relatives present at the *ghāt* would include persons from the mother's as well as the father's side, thus mixing different categories of *āttiya* in a cross-cutting fashion. Here Ego's F or B would have to appear at the *ghāt* as an obligation toward *kuṭum lok.* However, Ego's MZF or MZB would also be present at the same time for the same purpose. In addition to Ego's F her MB would have to be present also: one on his daughter's behalf, the other on his sister's behalf, both men being in a deferential relationship to Ego's husband's people (in this case both the F's and the MB's lines are on the same side in a giving relationship to the same group through Ego). Yet through his marriage, having received a woman from E's MB, E's F is a *kuṭum*—specifically *baṛo kuṭum* to E's MB. However, through the new situation brought about by E's marriage to, say, X, the *baṛo kuṭum* and his *śālā* (a hierarchical relation) are both placed in a respect-deference relationship to the new *kuṭum,* thus being effectively collapsed in the same category. Thus hierarchy, avoidance, respect, and separation in a specific relationship are all merged in an attitude of deference toward a new group of *kuṭum* (*jāmāi babu* and *śālā*) thus sharing a lower status vis-à-vis their overlapping *kuṭum.* E's husband's *kuṭum* are her own *kuṭum* as well, with the exception of her own parents, in that relationship. E's *jā* (her MZ) and the *ja's āttiya* become E's *āttiya* by extension. E's *māmā* (MB) thus becomes a "brother" after marriage and E_3's *śālā* (E's MB) also becomes a "brother" to E upon her marriage to X (see Figure 2.4). Furthermore, E's *māsī* (MZ) becomes a "sister" and a *jā.* Similarly, for E_2 her *bonai* (or *bhagnīpati*) becomes, upon the marriage of E to X, her "brother." E's MZH becomes a *bhāśur* (HeB), a relationship marked by extreme respect and avoidance, tinged with a sexual overtone, thus giving

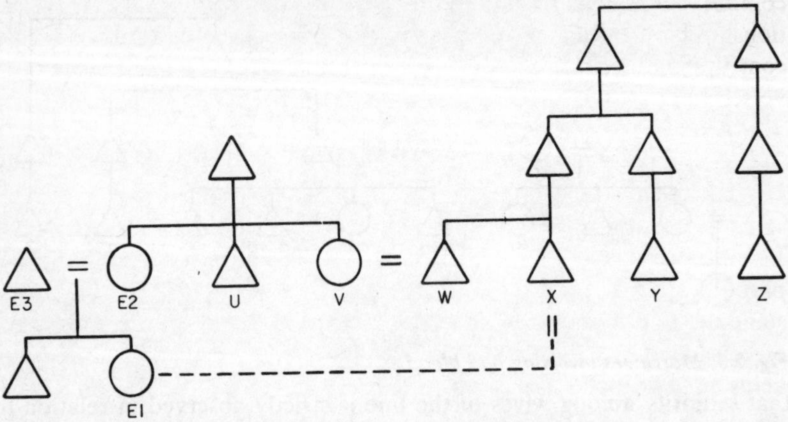

Fig. 2.4. Relationships attending marriages of bad blood: for E_2 *before [after] the marriages U is bhāi [bhāi] V is bon [boudi] W is bhagnipati [bhāi] X is bhāi [jāmāi] Y is bhāi [jāmāi] Z is bhāi [jāmāi]; for* E_1 *before [after] the marriages U is māmā [bhāi] V is māsī [jā] W is mesa [bhāśur] X is māmā [bhāi or husband] Y is māmā [bhāi or husband] Z is māmā [bhāi or husband]; for* E_3 *before [after] the marriages U is śālā [bhāi] V is śāli [bon] W is śālpati bhāi [jāmāi or address by name] X is bhāi [jāmāi] Y is bhāi [jāmāi] Z is bhāi [jāmāi].*

rise to an untenable situation.[8] A married woman is in an easy, affectionate relationship with her *jā's* brothers, who are in turn in a MB relation to her children. In Figure 2.4, however, E's own MB becomes, by extension, her children's MB.

Marriages involving three lines in this fashion (those of MB and MZ) are to be avoided. The changes in relationships brought about by marriage would create a series of incompatible links in terms of respect, affection, and category of person for the relatives involved. The consanguineal and affinal codes of conduct would be, in some cases, reversed and contradicted, especially in the position of MB, the MZ-HBW relation, and so forth. Yet, despite such difficulties, the problems at this level could be avoided were it not that such marriage alliances are very rare and that the main concern is not with the possibility of confusion in terms of blood relations, culturally defined and understood, or indigenous categories of relatives with appropriate codes for conduct. The main objection to this form of marriage comes more immediately from the emphasis on the mother's side (*māyer stor*) of one's relationships, on the maternal line, and on the continued significance of relationships with the mother's side, even though this link, like all others, is encompassed by the male line in a wider context. In Bengal the relation to the mother's side is strong: *māyer jinis* (mother's "thing") like *māyer dudh* (mother's milk) enters into the indigenous construction of the person. The pull (*ṭān*) of the maternal side continues despite marriage and the move to a different locality. This relationship is often characterized as a free, open, easy, and soft one, thus contributing the equivalence aspect of alliance within a hierarchical universe.

Beyond Kinship

What social scientists would classify as affect or affectivity is also, to some degree, culturally categorized and constructed. As such it is not, as Lévi-Strauss would have it, the "most obscure side of man"; rather it is a part of a system of relationships that is susceptible to analysis and understanding. The genealogical approach to kinship would rule these data out of consideration, and yet, as we saw, the inclusion of these categories helps us understand and resolve the problems of orthodox kinship studies. Thus, the extension of our investigation to the construction of the person, to the indigenous notions of conception and birth, to the rituals of marriage, birth, and death, make it possible for us to discuss the relations between wife-givers and wife-takers, the complexity of marriage rules, the categorization of persons in relationships, and the indigenous system of alliances—results that the study of kinship terminologies has consistently failed to provide.

The method of procedure we followed was one of systematic and gradual extension of the universe of discourse from sociological categories of kinship through the indigenous construction of relationships to the rituals of *biye* and *śraddha*. These rituals in themselves establish a new line or mark the passage of the soul from the state of being a ghost to that of an ancestor; they also clarify the questions of alliance, marriage exchange, and the separation of wife-givers and wife-takers. Furthermore, the relationships between father's side, mother's side, and marriage sides conceptualized in terms of soft and hard and other categories elucidate the position of the married woman between these sides, explain the multiple meanings of blood (*rakta*) as a way of classifying relationships, and rescue affectivity from vague sentimentality, universal emotionalism, and weak psychologizing. The affective (soft, warm, sweet) relationship to a *māmā* (MB) and *māsī* (MZ) extends the blood symbolism to the MZHB's line in prohibiting marriage, while it does not do so on the father's side, where relationships are hard and respectful.

The set of categories we discussed in this essay should now take their place alongside the more generally accepted kinship terminology as a part of a domain culturally and locally constituted. There is a logic to the continued extension of this universe of discourse. While trying to find the structure of Bengali kinship terminology, we realized that some of the most intriguing questions cannot be answered from within the a priori boundaries of genealogical kin terms. Yet even in this restricted domain, we found configurations and patterns suggesting the wisdom of considering a different set of data rather than forcing the terminology to deliver rules. Rather than press the configuration of terms toward conventional results, we chose to follow the indigenous logic of relationships among persons and thus came upon more illuminating findings than strictly functional and structural studies would have allowed. In discussing the notions of relatives by marriage, blood, and line, we are able to clarify the terminological anomalies of "brothers," of marriageable and unmarriageable categories, and the divergence of marriage practices and terminological rules. Thus, we saw no reason to oppose caste to kinship, since the Bengali version of marriage alliance makes it possible to create the hierarchy and equivalence of lines, sets of lines in practicing marriage exchanges, and of *jātis* as wholes. In dealing with terms such as *seed, earth, blood, line, ādān pradān,* and so forth in the light of actual practices, we extended the domain under investigation far beyond sets of genealogically linked terms. The next step was, not surprisingly, a comparison of north and south Indian practices and categories in the light of data from Bengal and Tamilnadu. Through this comparison we were able to narrow the previously posited gap between south and north India and to report the marriage practices of two regions as variations on indigenous themes of alliance rather than treating them as completely different fields of alliance versus hypergamy. Once again we found no need to oppose kinship to caste principles to resolve the differences between the two systems.

The necessity of including new and novel sets of data in our account was already foreshadowed in our earlier study of the terminology. The alliance feature of Bengali marriages, the repetition of marriages, the reversals in the direction of marriages, the position of women as daughters and wives of a line, the nonlineage nature of Bengali *baṇgśas,* the significance of conception, birth, and death in the construction of relationships, the many meanings of blood as a symbol, the importance of mother's side, father's side, and the categories of affect in the constitution of relationships led us from terminology to relatives and relatedness, marriage and death rituals, and a whole set of practices and categories hitherto excluded from the study of kinship. Yet it is also clear that there is a continuity to these endeavors and that each additional study speaks to the problems of the previous ones.

In considering marriage and death rituals we have succeeded in extending the domain of relationships we set out to analyze and understand. The *sapiṇḍa* calculations at the time of marriage and the *śraddha* rite within the actual marriage ceremonies demonstrate the close link between *biye* (marriage) and *baṇgśa* (line)—the passage of women into and out of *baṇgśas*—as well as *śraddha,* the transformation of ghost into ancestor, and the commemoration and feeding of ancestors. The ancestral rites performed at marriage are also called *śraddha* or *piṇḍa* (the offering of balls of cooked rice to the ancestors) or *nāndīmukh* (literally the facing of the ancestors). These rites render the continuity of the line visible from the departed through the marriage partners to the promise of an issue (*phol,* fruit). They also bring the blessings of the ancestors to the auspicious start of yet another *baṇgśa,* the segmentation of yet another line.

This *śraddha* and *biye* are explicitly related. In the *śraddha* rites themselves marriage relationships play a crucial part: the duties of *kuṭum* to each other are so important that when a death occurs in the house, the husband immediately informs his *kuṭum ghar* (his wife's people). The *kuṭum,* in their turn, have responsibilities to their once *jñāti* and daughter of the line, who now shares the death pollution of her new *jñāti,* her husband's people.

Śraddha and *biye* rather than birth and death are the significant cultural parallels here: these are therefore among the most elaborate and most carefully observed rituals. Marriage brings a new person into the line, with the promise of births and the continuity of the line. *Śraddha* transforms a person from a wandering spirit into a deity, an ancestor. The life-cycle rituals in between these serve to build and bind the person into his or her position in society (*samāj*), caste (*jāti*), and so on according to *dharma* (duty) and *karma* (performed works).

Biye and *śraddha* are concerned with both one line and many lines. Marriage articulates the relationships among *jāti* units, bringing about hierarchy and equivalence through the linking of partners within *vakaiyaras* in Tamilnadu and across *baṇgśas* in Bengal. From a wider perspective these variations are different sides of the same totality: in a society where lines are the central value, marriage in the local cultural sense will perform the task of constructing and allying lines, establishing proper exchanges among lines, and creating values from the maintenance of hierarchy and equivalence among and within the units. In a case, however, where the horizontal units of purity are valued and where a whole unit practicing marriage exchange is hierarchically related to other similar units, but where no marriages take place across these units, there marriage will order all relationships without separating lines for the consideration of marriage and will transmit the marriageable or nonmarriageable relations from generation and generation.

In the Bengali case *rakta* (blood) in the *baṇgśa* (line) is the supreme value, since it extends throughout the society. Yet because of its importance *rakta* does not in itself structure marriage relations. Rather *biye* mediates between lines and makes possible the continuation of lines. Hence the simultaneous duality of *kuṭum-jñāti* relations of the same persons linked by marriages: one can be a *jñāti* and a *kuṭum* at the same time. Thus, *rakta* need not mean "blood" in the biological or genealogical sense; rather it is among other things a category used to exclude persons from the circle of marriageable partners.

Hierarchy in marriage can also be understood in these terms, especially in the often vexing problem of women in and of *baṇgśas.* A married woman is able to carry on the line of her husband to those of her sons not because she shares her husband's body in substance or blood (an item of anthropological belief demonstrating a fallacy of misplaced concreteness) but because they are one in the hierarchical sense of relationships: separation and encompassment. A wife is *arddhaṅginī* (literally half part) of her husband, because in intercourse she contains a part of his body. This is an encompassing relationship and a dramatic assertion of hierarchy. Similarly bride and groom are *patri* and *patra,* both meaning vessel. This is not an either-or question: husband encompasses wife and wife encompasses husband in a dual, hierarchical relationship. The wife's encompassing relationship is set within the dominance of the line in the wider universe; thus, one hierarchical relation is placed and reversed within another. Because of the *svāmī-strī* (H-W) relationship the woman contains a part of the man, and at a higher level of segmentation the husband's line encompasses the wife.

Attendant on this relationship is the categorization of the H-W relation as one of *bhakti* (devotion) and *sṇeha* (affection). These are also hierarchical and relational terms appropriate to the link between higher and lower units in a segmentary system. Thus *bhakti* and *sneha* characterize the relationships between husband and wife, parents and children, superior and inferior. Common to all these ties is the orientation of *bhakti* toward the hierarchically lower.

It is in the consideration of mourning rituals that we come to a full realization of the cultural construction of the affective element, even in relation to marriage roles. *Śraddha* rituals are particularly enlightening in the categorization of relationships among persons. Just as the marriage ritual itself establishes hierarchical relations, which do not carry over into closed, concrete, hypergamous circles of wife-givers and wife-takers forever preserving the directions of marriage, so too the *śraddha* rituals create the same imbalance among marriage-linked relatives in addition to further separating nonmarriageable categories of persons, as in the case of bad blood in the *māsī's* line. Thus, relationships are grouped, bunched, telescoped, or extended into wider or narrower categories, but not as a result of contemplating a priori sets of kinship terms for fundamental relationships marked with some grammatical device or another. Rather, the rituals themselves hold the answer to the puzzle, *biye* and *śraddha* as a reality in themselves and not as an expression or representation of something else.

In *śraddha* it is the direction of giving the matters, not the algebra of who gets what, except where the increasing distance of a relationship causes the giving of lesser gifts—but then the result is obvious enough. To our knowledge the variation in the amount or kind of giving has not been linked to distinguishing fundamental categories of kinship in whatever sense. On the other hand, the *kuṭum* of a deceased are not merely givers of gifts. They also offer water (*jal deoyā*) in the *śraddha* rites, which duty they share with the *jñāti*. This is a consistent feature of all *śraddha,* whether it be that of the high Brahman or the low Bauri.

Śraddha rituals, and especially *ghāt tula,* also serve to separate wife-givers and wife-takers and to forbid marriages where no rule, blood or otherwise, would accomplish the task of prohibition. Nevertheless *rakta* and *baṇgśa* predominate with an effort to extend *jñāti* and/or *rakta* relationships into the immediate circle of *kuṭum*. With the birth of a child all *kuṭum* relations of GO become *rakta* relations for the new issue on G + 1. Thus, in a wider universe marriage is encompassed by the relationships of blood and line while structuring rather than being structured by those relationships. Here we come close to Tamil practice, where marriage relations structure blood relations, albeit in a quite different way. In Bengal the ideology of blood and line (*rakta* and *baṇgśa*) has to cope with *biye* and *kuṭum* relations lineally, whereas in Tamilnadu categories within the *vakaiyara* order both marriage and blood without causing problems for lineal relations.

Bad blood, *māyer stor* (mother's side), *koṭho* versus *modhur samparka* (hard versus sweet relations) are attitudes and feelings, the affective element culturally constructed. As such they are not vague expressions of some other more real domain, but they play a part in the structuring and articulation of relationships among persons, between wife-givers and wife-takers, *kuṭum* and *jñāti,* and among *āttiya* in general. Yet the consideration of these categories and practices does not come from kinship terminologies or from rules of consanguinity and affinity but from the cultural construction of relationships even when these appear to be mere affectivity. On closer examination the affective element turns out to be indigenously structured and categorized as a part of the same domain we tried to understand in our previous studies.

The question can no longer be what the terminology is or does. Rather the crucial problem concerns the links among terms, categories, practices, and usages established by the indigenous logic of relationships. In both marriage and mourning rites we find the same double articulation of *kuṭum* and *māmā* (MB) relationships. *Kuṭum* and *māmā* serve as points articulating the relations of two groups of persons. *Māmā* is *kuṭum* in one direction and blood relative (*rakta āttiya*) in another for two distinct groups, being *māmā* and *kuṭum* at the same time rather than just one or the other. Thus, two lines of *kuṭum* articulate around *jñāti* (*āttiya*) figures—remembering that *māmā* being *śālā* (WB) to a ZH itself stands for a *jñāti-kuṭum* relationship and not just a *kuṭum* or just a *jñāti* category.

The link through bad blood would transform the MB into a wife-giver when he should be free of marriage exchange giving and taking (implying respect and deference) in relation to his ZD. Furthermore, the *śālā-jāmāi babu* relationship would also be wiped out by such an alliance vis-à-vis the *māmā.* There would be no hierarchy either, since both MB and MZH's line and house would stand in a wife-giving relationship to the new line and *śālā* and *jāmāi babu* would be collapsed in an exclusively *kuṭum* relationship toward this hypothetical third group in the alliance.

Kinship terminologies in the orthodox sense do not order the seemingly incompatible relations between *biye, kuṭum, baṇgśa,* and *jñāti.* Nor do they express marriage rules; hence, we have to pursue the logic of relationships from restricted to wider and wider domains. There is also a double articulation of *baṇgśa* and *biye* in the assumption of a person into the line through marriage. But this transformation does not annul the ties of a married woman to her father's house. Rather it renders visible the position of women in, of, and between lines. It also accounts for cases in which line-related persons come into a marriage relationship (for example, a *pīsīmā* may also be a *jā* to her BD).

Categories of relationships in a line transform *biye* and *kuṭum* links into *baṇgśa* and *jñāti* ties. The significant discrimination here is between *jñāti* and *kuṭum,* since *āttiya* overlaps both kinds of relationships. Not surprisingly, invitations to wedding and mourning rituals are sent to *jñāti* and *kuṭum,* not to *āttiya, rakta* or otherwise, suggesting that the occasion and the categorization of relatives complement each other and are possible only in this kind of context.

The ideology of line also provides a value, yet because of its importance it has to submit to articulation and structuring through marriage. The two are part of the same universe without the necessity to oppose kinship to marriage, consanguinity to affinity. Ultimately *biye* itself serves the tasks set by lineality. Lines must be preserved (*baṇgśa rakkha*), but they must also be brought together. Thus, hierarchy and equivalence are a part of the same totality. *Śraddha* and *biye* order and articulate the links among lines, and in accomplishing this task the question is not only how hierarchical and unequal relations are established between wife-givers and wife-takers, distinctions that need not carry over into other domains of everyday life, but also what is the reality and significance of ritual—marriage, birth, and death. Ritual also creates, defines, and interprets hierarchy while it remains something in itself: the service and bringing of the gods to witness, the passage of the soul from ghost to divinity, the creation and maintenance of the universe in terms of proper order (*dharma*). Among other things *śraddha* and *biye* also order relations among persons, but we would not be able to understand all the tasks and meanings of rituals if we were to restrict their symbolism and purposes to the mere expression of social structure and social relationships. To a great extent rituals are the relationships we try to analyze and understand, being something in themselves and being related to and expressing other domains at the same time.

3

Forms of Address in the North Indian Family: An Exploration of the Cultural Meaning of Kin Terms

Sylvia Vatuk

THE DESCRIPTION and analysis of kinship terminologies have traditionally assumed a central place in anthropological studies of kinship. But throughout there has been an ongoing debate about the nature of the relationship between terminology and other behavioral, social-structural, and cultural phenomena of a kinship system and about the value of terminological analysis for understanding kinship in any broader sense. In recent years these issues have increasingly been phrased in terms of the need to properly establish the meaning of the kin terms with which one is dealing; especially controversial has been the question of the relevance of biological relatedness to the terminological classification of kinsmen and to patterns of kin-term usage. Thus, the standard analytical procedure of mapping a selected—and necessarily finite—set of kin terms onto a genealogical grid has been called seriously into question, even as the techniques that rely upon such an initial procedure have been undergoing increasingly sophisticated refinement at the hands of enthusiastic practitioners.[1]

One of the most serious barriers to a successful elucidation of the meaning of kinship terms through the more generally accepted analytical approaches arises as a direct consequence of the practice of being overly selective in the choice of data. In order to make the terminological material manageable, and in order to impose a certain amount of regularity and consistency—however artificial—upon it, much of the wide variety of kin term use recorded in the field is set aside and considered, if at all, only in passing references. The result is often to exclude from the analysis much of the more significant and revealing evidence that the anthropologist has gathered about the actual use of kinship terminology.[2] Schneider, of course, began some time ago to call attention to this kind of problem in his discussions of American kinship terms (1955, and 1968:83–106), and he has elaborated his critique in a more recent essay aimed specifically at practitioners of the techniques of componential analysis (1969). While in the course of his discussion Schneider makes a number of valuable observations, what I am especially concerned with here is his attack on the generally accepted dictum that modes of reference and address not only differ from one another in a number of respects in all societies but actually make up two distinct systems that may be understood independently of one another (1969:29–34). The unfortunate practical consequence of such a conception of the reference/address distinction has been that the analysis of address has been sorely neglected. The resulting emphasis on terms of reference has been justified by some (see, for example, Murdock 1949:97–98, 106–107) on the grounds that reference terms alone accurately denote kinship status or category, while the address system is related to role behavior or, as Goodenough puts it, is affected by "personal considerations" (1965a:262). It is interesting that those few analysts who have actually dealt with the intricacies of address terminology take a somewhat different view. Conant, for example, says in the conclusion to his analysis of Jarawa terms of reference and address, that "in comparison to the system of reference, the system of address more precisely segments the 'social environment' . . . and provides a matrix or guide for the recognition of 'social structural reality' " (1961:29). And McCoy, while agreeing that the Chinese reference system is a more complete classificatory device than is the address system, stresses that "for analysing the data of a single culture, where completeness more than general applicability is the prime concern, it would be unwise to neglect either system" (1970:224).

There is clearly some practical difficulty in handling address forms analytically, and we can discern an element of rationalization in some of the arguments for its neglect. Murdock points out that "terms of reference are usually more complete than terms of address . . . Furthermore, terms of address tend to reveal more duplication and overlapping than do terms of reference" (1949:98). But Schneider convincingly attacks the assumption that even within the domain of reference terminology a complete list of terms can be made that excludes overlap, redundancies, alternate terms, and variant usages. The appearance of doing so is typically accomplished only by the use of such devices as explicit or implicit "elicitation frames," such as Goodenough has recommended for the collection of kinship terms (1965a:262).

Whatever the reasons, it remains the case that until very recently only a small number of kin terminological studies have dealt in any way, other than in passing, with address forms. The very thorough early study of

Chao (1956) is still an almost unique example: in it the whole range of varying uses of Chinese kin terms in a wide variety of contexts is laid out in a systematic manner. Schneider has done this more discursively for American kinship. It is perhaps indicative of some problems to be encountered in such a venture, not only in the analysis but, more important, in the collection of data, that both of these scholars are native speakers of the languages they describe and are themselves members of the cultures concerned.

In a number of more recent kinship studies Schneider's strictures about the inclusion of forms of address appear to have been taken to heart, as evidenced in the increasing attention being given them in discussions of kin terminology. For example, Basso (1975) deals with address as well as reference for affines among the Kalapalo of central Brazil and Drummond (1978) with address terms for *mother* and *mother surrogate* among English speakers in Britain and the New World. In both cases the material on forms of address is presented in the context of a more general cultural account of kinship (Schneider 1968), and no attempt is made at completeness—understandably so, since the author's focus is not on terminology per se but on cultural meanings of kinship in a broad sense. Within the camp of those committed to formal techniques of terminological analysis, the work of Casson (1975) and Casson and Özertuğ (1974, 1976) on Turkish kin terms is also noteworthy for its inclusion of deliberately elicited data on address.

There is also a fairly extensive and growing body of sociolinguistic literature on modes of address in general, including, but not limited to, the use of kin terms in address (see, for example, Evans-Pritchard 1948, Brown and Ford 1961, Goodenough 1965b, Ervin-Tripp 1972, Bean 1978). A closely related literature examines pronominal usages in address in languages that make a distinction between intimacy and respect in the second-person (see, for example, Friedrich 1960 for Russian, and Jain 1969 for Hindi). Typically in this literature, however, in discussions of the issue of choice in the selection of a mode of address, that of address by a kinship term is treated as a unitary alternative, requiring no further analysis or specification. An exception is to be found in Bean's important recent monograph, where, in the course of an extended analysis of all forms of address in Kannada, the issue of choice and variation among kin terms is examined in detail (1978).

Contextual Variability

If we observe and record the actual use of kinship terms in ongoing, natural conversation, we may note their occurrence in two main kinds of contexts: first, in speaking about oneself or another person to a third party (the referential context), and second, in speaking directly to another person or persons (the vocative context). In any language there are usually certain kin terms that may be observed to be used only in a referential context, or that are used only rarely and in unusual circumstances to address someone directly. Schneider gives as an example the English term *second cousin* (1955:1196). Most terms, however, are used both vocatively and referentially, though possibly with distinctive grammatical inflections. With some terms, in the referential context the social identity of the third party—the addressee—limits their use. For example, in speaking about my mother to one of my sisters I would refer to her as Mama, which I would not do in speaking about her to a stranger. Terms also vary in their range of inclusiveness, in that some denote a single kin type, while others cover a number of distinct kin types or an entire category or class of kin for individual members of which there may in some cases also exist alternate terms of greater specificity. For certain kin types there may be a number of different terms, some synonymous or nearly so, others varying in connotation along dimensions of affectivity, respect, and so on. Examining context more precisely than the gross distinction between reference and address allows for, we may observe that some terms occur only in certain limited and special settings or at particular times. The use of other terms may be observed to vary with attributes of the speaker such as stage of life (child as opposed to adult, for example) or sex. All of these complexities of context of kin term usage present difficulties of analysis that are time consuming but nevertheless entirely amenable to systematic treatment once one has been able to disentangle the rules that govern the choice of a term in any given situation (see, for example, Tyler 1966).

Quite another kind of analytical complexity is created by the kind of behavioral strategies or tactics to which Swartz (1960) and Bloch (1971) have drawn attention, namely the employment of terms situationally, as part of a process of "defining a role relation between speaker and hearer" or of creating "a transformation in the social situation" (Bloch 1971:80). Schneider has given a good example of this kind of variability in the choice of terms for particular occasions or circumstances when he cites an American informant, who usually calls his father Pop but addresses him as Dad when he asks to borrow the car (1955:1206). In this same general category would fall the use of the brother term in Hindi (*bhāī*) to address a stranger from whom one wishes to solicit assistance or the use of the son term (*betā*) to mollify a sulking daughter. Khare, in this volume, and Das, in a recent paper (1976), give other perceptive examples of the way that moral constraints determine the tactics of kin term usage in Hindi and Punjabi. It is clearly much more difficult to handle this kind of variability within the context of any kind of traditional terminological analysis. The question of tactics indeed brings to the fore the necessity to examine at a profound level a culture's concepts of kinship relatedness and the cultural meaning of exclusion from the inclusion in the overall category of kin as well as the subcategories of kinds of kin. To do so requires far more familiarity with the culture's shared assumptions about the moral meanings of the kin terms themselves and of kinship in general than is typically manifested in terminological analyses that depend upon the genealogical model.

Another somewhat related problem in the analysis of ongoing kin term usage is presented by the phenomenon of the regular and customary (as distinct from the occasional and immediately strategic) use of genealogically inappropriate kin terms in reference or in address.[3] An example in American English would be the habitual use of the term *Mom* to refer to and address one's wife. If such a usage were purely idiosyncratic within a given culture it would not be of particular interest, but to the extent that it is a common practice among men of a certain segment of American society to so address one's wife, it is potentially revealing of certain features of structure and meaning in the American family. Drummond has provided other examples of such a phenomenon in English, referring to the pattern in matrifocally structured Creole families in Guyana, in which the maternal grandmother is called Mummy and the genealogical mother Auntie. He points out that this pattern may be extended to the male members of the family circle, for example by addressing the father as Brother or Buddy (1978:36). In his view this employment of genealogically inappropriate terms of reference and address—in a situation in which the true genealogical relationships among the actors are known and explicitly acknowledged by all concerned—is revealing of the cultural construction of motherhood in English-speaking societies in the Old and New Worlds.

In very different cultural settings similar phenomena have been reported. Fortes has observed, for example, the practice among the Tallensi of addressing the daughter-in-law as *ma* (mother), and he relates it to the structural tension between parents- and daughters-in-law in the patrilocal extended family (1949:93–96, 96n). In the case of address patterns within the Japanese family, the consistent use of terms that do not reflect true genealogical relationships has also been described by a number of authors (Fischer 1964; Beardsley, Hall, and Ward 1959; Kitaoji 1971; and Lee 1976), and, as we shall see, has usually been explained in terms of the structural dynamics of the patrilocal stem family. Although it has not previously been described in any detail for northern India, such a pattern of using genealogically inappropriate terms of address within the family and close kindred is a very typical feature of kin term usage in the Hindi-speaking region. In looking more closely at this seemingly aberrant mode of interacting with kinsmen, we shall see how an examination of the patterns and regularities in actual verbal use of kinship terms, in natural contexts, may elucidate some central moral and symbolic themes in the cultural meaning of kinship relationships in this society.

Kinship Terminology in North India

It is only during the past ten years that the Indo-Aryan kinship terminologies of northern India have begun to be subjected to detailed analysis by anthropologists. We may trace the initial impetus for such studies somewhat further back, to Dumont's 1962 publication of a comprehensive descriptive account of Hindi terminology in the context of a discussion of kinship and marriage among Brahmans of eastern Uttar Pradesh. But we began only in the seventies to see the growth of a significant body of literature to which one might turn for extended data and analytical interpretations of kinship structure and terminological systems in what Karve, delineating the regional distribution of kinship patterns in India (1965), has designated as the Northern Zone. Particularly worth noting in this connection are a number of empirical studies, based on original field research, of kinship in Punjab, at the western edge of this zone (Das 1976; Leaf 1971, 1972), in the Hindi-speaking north-central belt (Dumont 1962, 1966, 1975; Vatuk 1969a, 1972, 1975), in Gujarat to the southwest (van der Veen 1972, Pocock 1972), and in Bengal to the east (Chatterjee 1972, Fruzzetti and Östör 1976, Inden and Nicholas 1977). In addition, there have been attempts by others, working with secondary data, to subject north Indian terminologies to formal semantic analysis (for example Carter 1973, Turner 1975, Scheffler 1977, 1980).

Beyond presenting new data of a descriptive kind on systems hitherto understood only in broad, general outline, the new literature on north Indian kinship has been characterized by a common search for indigenous Indian cultural meaning in the realm of kinship, whether pursued in the explicitly Schneiderian mode (as, for example, by Inden and Nicholas 1977) or otherwise (Das 1976). The route to this kind of understanding has been largely through explication of such basic Indian theories as those of the nature of sexual union, conception, birth, the person—concepts and ideas fundamental to an overall theory of kinship.

I prefer to approach the search for such cultural conceptions through an examination of address usage, a critical form of communicative behavior among kin.

Modes of address within the family and kinship network have been considered in the literature on north Indian kinship and kinship terminologies only sparingly and almost incidentally. In an earlier publication (1969b) I dealt with some aspects of the use of Hindi modes of reference and address among neighbors in an urban community, including the use of kin terms between persons not related by actual biogenetic or genealogical ties. There, in the context of what is generally called fictive kinship, I attempted to delineate a number of social and cultural characteristics of persons that seem to determine the selection of appropriate kin terms among neighbors who are in regular and intimate social contact. The extent to which similar, or other, considerations might also help to govern the selection of kin terms of address and reference among persons mutually acknowledging genealogical relatedness was not investigated at that time, nor has it been investigated by me or by others in respect to north Indian kinship terminologies since then.[4] I would not, of course, recommend ignoring genealogy in a search for the meaning of kin terms in Hindi, if for no other reason than that it is explicitly recognized by members of the culture as one of the key criteria according to which one chooses an appropriate form of reference of address toward a person with whom such a relationship can be traced. But knowing the genealogy does not enable one to predict all instances of actual kin term usage, nor can one always correctly deduce the existing genealogical relationship from observed forms of reference or address. Interestingly, this is so not only when Hindi speakers talk to or about persons at the periphery of their kinship networks but most particularly when they do so within the nuclear and extended family or household.

My data on this issue come from composite sources: from field research in Meerut City, Uttar Pradesh, in 1966–1967, in a mixed-caste, middle-class urban neighborhood; from an investigation of kinship and marriage among Gaur Brahmans in Uttar Pradesh and the Delhi area in 1969–1970; and from field research on aging and the family in an urbanized village of the Raya Rajput caste in New Delhi in 1974–1976. For the most part the data consist of observed usages of kin terms in spontaneous address rather than forms elicited by direct questioning of informants. Some direct-question interviewing was undertaken in order to clarify or enlarge upon observed instances of address among kin. However, in this interviewing any attempt to present hypothetical examples was avoided, and even where informants gave information about their habitual mode of addressing particular relatives, every attempt was made to check this information through subsequent observation. Because the data gathered were incidental to investigations whose primary focus was elsewhere, and the findings were at first largely serendipitous, they are unfortunately unsystematic and incomplete. Consequently, there are a number of questions that the research raises but cannot answer. However, the data as they are suggest the nature of the problem and, I hope, point the way toward a more thorough and systematic investigation.

General Principles of Kin Term Address

Indigenous Hindi concepts clearly distinguish the manner in which two persons are related to one another (*lagnā, rishtā honā*) from the manner in which they customarily address one another (*kahnā, pukarnā*). Genealogy is neither a necessary nor the only component in a relationship;

nevertheless, where a clear genealogical link is present, and is known and acknowledged by both parties, it is usually accorded primacy when one responds to the question, "How is X related to you?" (*āp ko kyā lagte hãi?*). Thus, an appropriate response to such a query would be, for example, "He is my MB" (*mere māmā hãi*), or—particularly in the case of a distant (*dūr ke*) uncle, not the mother's true (*sagā*) brother—the more precise, "He is related to me as a MB" (*mere māmā lagte hãi,* or, *rishte mẽ māmā hãi*). The terms used in this type of referential context normally form the basis for the descriptions of the kinship terminology of Hindi and related languages that are available in the literature.

In brief, and to use the standard Kroeber (1909) and Lowie (1929) criteria for kin term classification, Hindi terms, as used in reference, consistently make distinctions of sex of referent, generational level, sex of linking relative, lineality collaterality, and consanguineality affinity. Only in Ego's own generation is there within the immediate kindred any merging of distinctive kin types into a single category, in that sibling and cousin terms follow the so-called Hawaiian pattern. But the sixty-odd terms with primary referents in Ego's immediate kindred are also used to classify more distant relatives with whom some genealogical connection—whether through descent or marriage—can be traced, according to principles of genealogical extension that are logical and unproblematical for any mentally competent adult of the culture, although they present challenging difficulties for formal semantic analysis (see Carter 1973, Turner 1975, Scheffler 1977, 1980).

In the context of direct address a more limited number of terms is utilized; with some exceptions kin terms used in address are either identical to or slight lexical modifications of the terms used in reference. However, many of the terms that are used in reference are seldom or never used in address. It may be useful first to make some general remarks about address among kinsmen in Hindi. A first principle in this regard is that one must always address a person who is senior to oneself (*baṛe*) by a kin term, never by his personal name. To "take the name" of someone (*nām lenā*) is to assume seniority over or to place oneself on an equal footing with him. This is a general principle governing address among unrelated persons as well as among kinsmen: the use of the personal name is appropriate only in addressing junior (*choṭe*) persons or acknowledged equals. Since the hierarchical structure of the Indian family is such that there does not exist a truly equal relationship within it, asymmetry with respect to usual address forms within the family is the rule.

Seniority within the family or kin group is described by informants as being of two kinds: senior in age (*umar mẽ baṛe*) and senior in relationship (*rishte mẽ baṛe*). The former is self-explanatory. The latter is a complex of generational standing and differences in kinship rank, such as exist, for example, between a married woman and her in-laws or bride-givers and those to whom they have given women in marriage. When the person being addressed is senior either in age or in relationship to Ego, the use of the given name should be avoided. In case of any significant discrepancy between Alter's status vis-à-vis Ego in terms of relative age and his status in terms of relative relationship, there is the possibility of ambiguity with respect to the appropriate form of address and the ways in which this is handled vary to some extent from one individual to another.

Given the principle of asymmetry in address, one normally addresses senior consanguineals and their spouses by the genealogically appropriate kin term; this is in most cases the same term that is used for them in referential contexts. To this term may be appended a respect suffix, typically *-jī*.[5] In practice such a suffix appears to be used more consistently when addressing males. While its most obvious function is to express the speaker's respect for the person being addressed or referred to, it may connote a variety of other things as well, such as the formality of an encounter, mocking respect, or emphasis—for example, when the person being addressed does not respond promptly.

For in-laws, on the other hand—and here I use Busch's useful distinction (1972) between kinsman's spouse and spouse's kinsman, or in-law—it is not appropriate to use in address the usual terms of reference. Khare attributes this avoidance of in-law terms in address to a culturally specific consanguineal ethos in Hindi kinship (1975); while there is undoubtedly something to be said for such an interpretation, it is instructive to note how cross-culturally widespread such an avoidance is. As far away as central Brazil, Basso notes the presence of such an address pattern and explains it as resulting from "the cultural ambiguity of, or embarrassment with, affinity, and the concomitant need for avoidance of the topic . . . in most speech situations" (1975:221). In Hindi, then, one's in-laws are generally addressed by the same term that one's spouse uses to address them. However, since married women formally avoid speaking or even showing their faces to senior males of their husband's kindred, there is, for a female speaker, no traditionally accepted way of addressing certain male in-laws, notably the HF and HeB. In the present context of social change, particularly in urban areas and among the educated, many families are relaxing avoidance practices and thus require an acceptable mode of address for those relatives to whom traditionally a woman would not have had occasion to speak. A somewhat similar situation exists in the case of address between spouses, where traditional practice was to avoid any direct contact and communication in the presence of others, at least during the early years of marriage.

Ambiguity in the Application of Address Rules

The principles for address usage summarized here are of course predicated on the assumption that speaker and addressee are related to one another in only one way, or if they can trace more than one relationship, that they agree upon the one that should take precedence for purposes of address. They also rest upon the assumption that the matter of seniority can be unequivocally established, enabling the principle of asymmetry in the use of a kin term in address to be followed. In many actual cases, however—and this is most likely beyond the circle of the immediate family and close kindred—such assumptions do not hold true, and it is not unusual, therefore, for two persons to be presented with more than one possible choice of mode of address. A common instance is one in which there is a discrepancy between relative age and generational level. Such a discrepancy would be created when there is a large age difference between husband and wife, for example in cases of a man's second marriage (where he is likely to be considerably older than his wife) or in cases of leviratic widow inheritance (where the wife may be much older than her late husband's younger brother). They also occur in large extended families, where births have been spaced throughout the reproductive cycle of the women. After a number of generations there are bound to be such discrepancies, often involving as many as three generations, in a widely ramified lineage. Thus, for example, one may occasionally find persons of approximately the same age who are related by known genealogical links as classificatory *dādī* and *potā* (FM/SS). Discrepancies of a single generation are extremely common, as are cases in which junior in-laws are older than a senior of the same generation.

The problem of whether, cross-culturally, kinship status is predominantly determined by genealogical category or relative age, and how this is related to marriage choice, has been discussed at some length by Needham. He concludes, after examining a number of specific instances from societies with a variety of social organizational patterns, that "in a lineal descent system"—as opposed to a cognatic system—"categories will be preponderant" (1966, republished 1974:106). This observation holds true in most instances for the Hindi kinship system, if we limit our attention to the referential use of terms, for when relationships are being specified, care is invariably taken to give the genealogically appropriate category term, regardless of the relative ages of the persons involved. But when we move on as here to a consideration of address usages, we can see a definite tendency for shifts to be made in order to bring relative age and generational rank into accord. A person of a junior generation is expected to be addressed by his given name, as is a younger person; but there is considerable ambiguity about the appropriate form of address for an older person who is of a junior generation or a younger person who is simultaneously one's senior in generation. There is no respectful kinship term of address for those junior in generation, and therefore, in order to give recognition to the age seniority, it is necessary to "raise" such individuals in generation in order to be able to address them with proper deference.

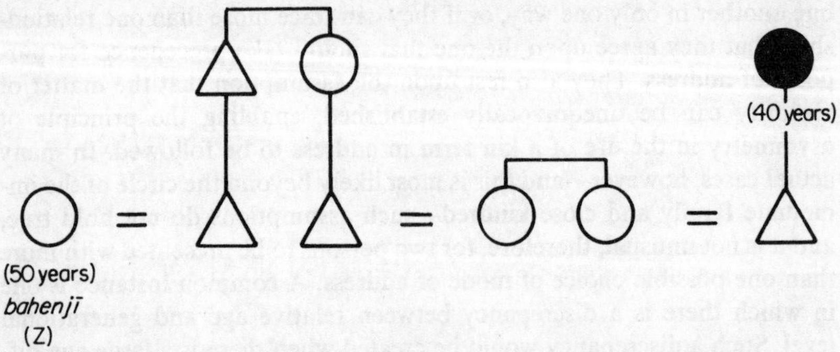

Fig. 3.1. Address forms in a case of age-generation discrepancy. Ego uses own generation kin terms of address for a woman who is older than she, though of a junior generation. Alter is a classificatory SW to Ego and by virtue of the relationship could be addressed by her given name, were their relative ages equivalent or reversed.

Examples may be seen in Figures 3.1, 3.2, and 3.3. In the first, two distant relatives by marriage address one another as sisters, although they are of adjacent generations, the junior kinswoman being older than the senior. The need to take into account both age and generation sometimes results in a situation in which the two partners in a dyad use nonreciprocal terms for one another. For example, in Figure 3.2, Ego uses the term *jījī* (eZ) for her FBSD (classificatory BD, *bhatījī*), while the latter calls her *buā* (FZ, the genealogically appropriate term) in return. Here, in fact, the age dif-

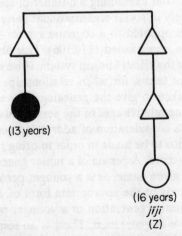

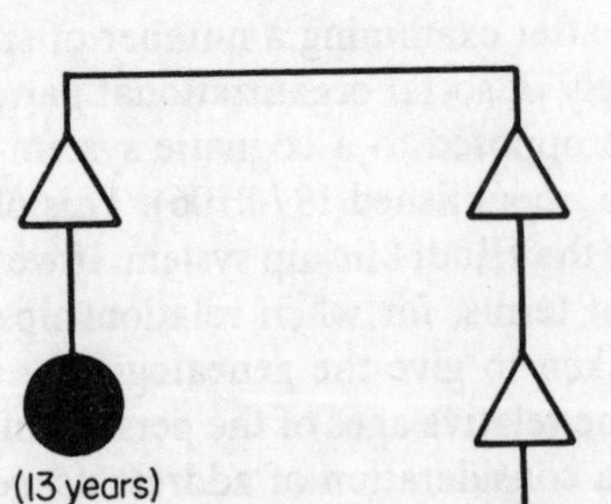

Fig. 3.2. Address form in a case of age-generation discrepancy. Ego uses an own-generation kin term of address for a niece who is a few years older than she. If relative age did not favor Alter, Ego would use her given name in address.

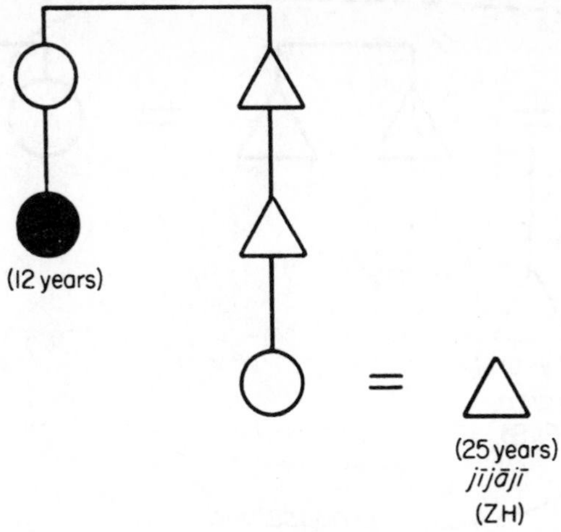

***Fig. 3.3.** Address form in a case of age-generation discrepancy. Ego uses an own-generation kin term of address for an older man who is related by marriage in a junior generation. In terms of generation and relationship alone, Alter, as a classificatory DH to Ego, would be addressed by name.*

ference is not great. In Figure 3.3 a twelve-year-old *phūphas* (classificatory WFZ) was heard to address her twice-as-old MBSDH (classificatory DH) as *jījājī* (ZH), admonishing him at the same time to be careful about joking with her because, *"mãi tumhārī buā lagtī hū!"* ("I am related to you as a FZ!"). The speaker in this instance was making reference to the stereotyped joking relationship between ZH and WZ. By her remark she rejected the possible presumption that she was initiating a joking relationship by addressing her new relative as ZH, and thus reasserted the primacy of the true relationship over the etiquette of the address form. The interchange, made in a bantering tone and appreciated with amusement by the onlookers, illustrates very well the indigenous conceptual distinction between relatedness and mode of address.

In the reverse direction, to address a younger person with a kin term appropriate to his senior generation status seems incongruous, while to ignore seniority in favor of age is to risk offense. The situation is recognized as an amusing one, particularly if the age-generation disparity is significant, and one may observe considerable variation among individuals in their response to it, some being much more punctilious than others in recognizing seniority wherever it is due. Ego in Figure 3.4 is a young man who is always extremely polite, sometimes even overdoing his conformance with good manners. He consistently uses the genealogically appropriate kin term *cācā* (FyB) for his two-year-old FFZHBS and addresses the child's mother, a woman only a few years older than himself, as *dāddījī* (FM, the genealogically appropriate term for her, his

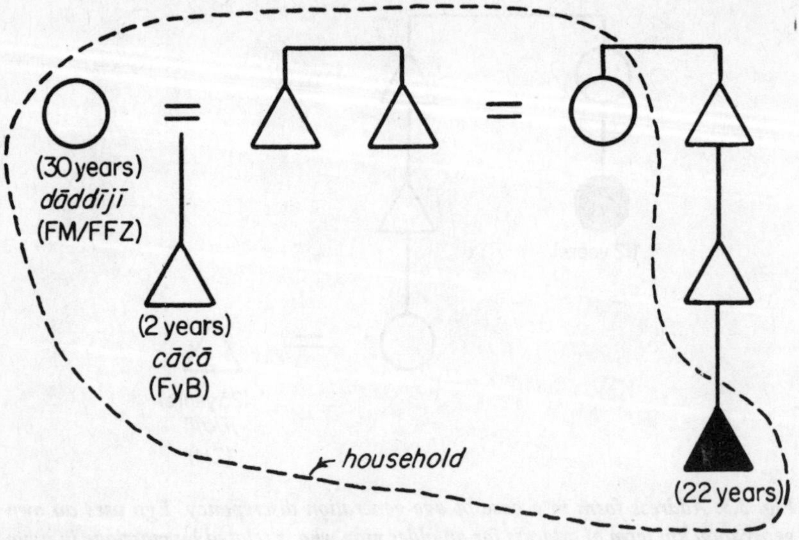

Fig. 3.4. Address form in a case of age-generation discrepancy. Genealogically appropriate address terms are used despite the relative ages of Ego and Alter, giving recognition to generational seniority.

FFZHBW). One can generalize the point illustrated in these examples by saying that discrepancies of relative age and generation are typically brought into accord by the selection of an address term that expresses deference for seniority. In other words, wherever respect ought to be shown, for whatever reason, the choice of address term is usually made accordingly, even if in order to do so the actual generational position of the person being addressed must be altered.

A more complex problem of choice is present when the genealogical links between Ego and Alter are multiple and may be traced in more than one way. In such cases, of course, it is not only the vocative but also the referential usage of kin terms that is problematical. At issue is the definition of the relationship, the assignment of Alter (and, reciprocally, oneself) to the appropriate kin category. In such cases a choice must be made between two alternative interpretations of the nature of the relationship, in order to give terminological priority to one. Needham (1966) and Eder (1975) have both dealt with this problem of the resolution of conflicting kin categories in cognatic societies where close kin marriage is the rule. Such conflicts are not as common in unilineal societies having rules of exogamy as well as bilateral marriage prohibitions. In Hindu north India the strict avoidance of marriage between consanguines and between certain categories of affines as well ensures that cases of overlap of relationships will be fairly rare, at least where close kin are concerned. But one

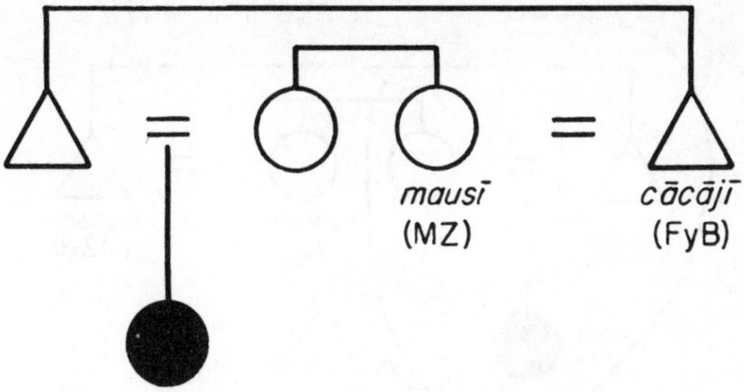

Fig. 3.5. *Address form in a case in which there is a choice of mode of reckoning the relationship. Here the matrilateral term of address is used, recognizing the more direct genealogical link to MZ/FBW.*

type of instance that does occur with some frequency in north India is that of the marriage of two sisters or female cousins to two brothers or male cousins. Here, the relationships, for example between Ego and his parallel uncle and aunt, may be traced through both his father and his mother, as the categories of FB/MZH and MZ/FBW, respectively, coincide in the same individuals (see Figure 3.5). Such marriages are fairly common among certain castes in this region, including the Raya Rajputs, among whom I have most recently carried on research. One would perhaps expect that, consistent with the patrilineal bias of the north Indian system, the matrilateral connection in such a case would be superseded by the patrilateral and that in the terminology of reference and address the categories FB and FBW would prevail for both. However, this does not happen. Rather, precedence is given to closeness of consanguineal connection, and while the husband of the pair is referred to and addressed by the appropriate patrilateral term, *cācā* or *tāū* (depending upon his age relative to that of Ego's father), his wife retains her natal designation as *mausī* or *māsī* (MZ). And in a case in which the patrilateral connection is more distant than the matrilateral, even the relationship to a father's "brother" may be traced through the more direct female link. For example, in Figure 3.6, a man of the same caste and *gotra,* resident of Ego's own father's village, is called *mausājī* (MZH) rather than the expected *tāū* (FeB), as he would be called were he not married to Ego's mother's sister.

Another type of situation, one with more wide-ranging implications for role conflict, occurs when two persons who are already related affinally are later united in marriage or become related again affinally, but in a different way, through the marriage of other persons in their kin networks. Or two persons distantly or fictively related by consanguineal ties may later become affines through a marriage joining two of their respective

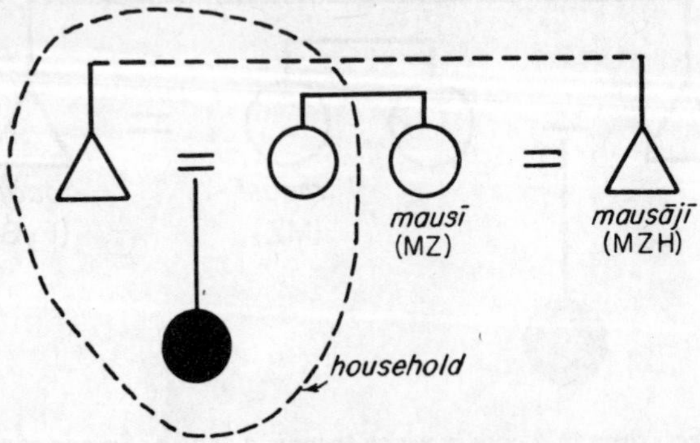

Fig. 3.6. Address form in a case in which there is a choice of mode of reckoning the relationship. Here the matrilateral term is used for the MZH/FB, giving recognition to the more direct, and closer matrilateral link.

kinsmen. In such cases, all other conditions being equal, the preexisting relationship continues to be recognized terminologically. So, for example, a woman marrying into a village where one of her *māmās* (her MFZS, classificatory MB) is resident continues to address and refer to him by this term, and she does not avoid him as she would if she were to trace the relationship through her husband, by which reckoning he is her husband's father's elder brother. A complicating factor in situations of a change in an existing relationship occurs when Ego becomes, as a result of a new marital union, a bride-giver (and hence one who has the obligation to give gifts and refrain from accepting hospitality) in relation to an Alter toward whom he has previously had a neutral (neither giving nor taking) relationship or toward whom he was a bride-taker (see Vatuk 1975 for an explanation of these categories and their implications). Das has discussed cases of this kind of conflict in relationship categories as it affects her Punjabi informants' obligation to give presents at weddings (1976). In general the same principle she enunciates there holds true for the choice of address terminology: that relationship according to which one is a giver takes precedence over others in defining the relationship. Such an example is illustrated in Figure 3.7.

For the most part, forms of address outside the immediate family but within the kin network follow the general principles outlined in the preceding paragraphs. It would be quite possible to present these principles in the form of a formal analysis of Hindi kin terms of address, along the lines of Casson's (1975) or Bean's (1978) analyses of Turkish and Kannada, respectively. Such an analysis, incorporating the rules discussed above, along with other rules for their contextual application, would have a high degree of predictability for actual address behavior outside the household or extended family. But within the latter group, careful obser-

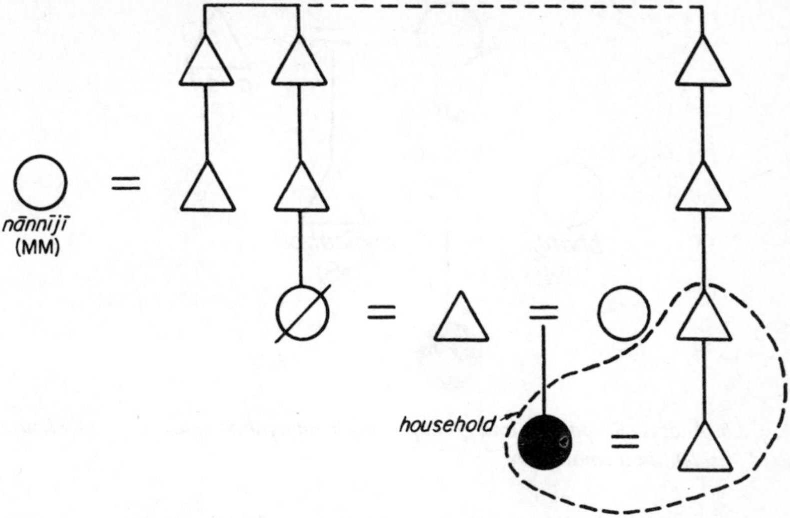

Fig. 3.7. Address for classificatory HFFBW (genealogically appropriate address form is dāddī, FM). In this case there is a choice of mode of reckoning the relationship. That relationship according to which Ego is a classificatory DD prevails over the affinal relationship, and the older woman retains her position as bride-giver vis-à-vis Ego.

vation would reveal considerable variability in actual usage, and the utility of the formal analysis would break down. It is within this primary group that we would come up against a dramatic illustration of the inadequacy of a genealogical model for clarifying actual address behavior in this region of India.

Address Usages within the Family

Parent and child. In addressing parents, children utilize kin terms almost exclusively. The standard reference terms for M and F are *mā̃* and *bāp*, respectively. In address for the mother, the appropriate term, *mā̃* (or one of its variants, *ammā* or *mātājī*), may be used. However, in practice some other kin term is regularly used. Observation showed that one of the following alternatives occurred with at least as much frequency as did any of these genealogically appropriate mother terms:

bhābhī (BW)[6] [Fig. 3.8, 3.9][7]
bobbo, jījī, or *dīdī* (Z) [Fig. 3.10, 3.11, 3.12, 3.13]
bahū (W, SW) [Fig. 3.14]
mammī (M) [Fig. 3.13, 3.15, 3.16, 3.17]

I do not have statistical data on the relative frequencies of these alternatives, but the first two are very common and might even be called the

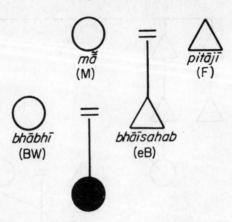

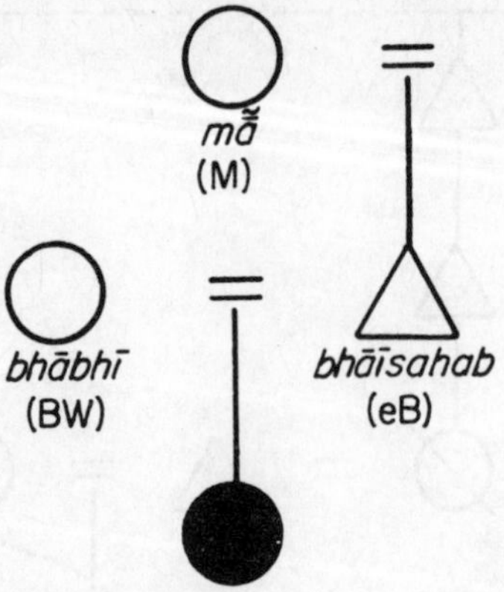

Fig. 3.8. Address for parents and grandparents in an agnatic extended family household, resident in a small town.

usual modes of address for the mother among men and women who are now adults. Among the sister terms, *bobbo* is a rural term, while *jījī* and *dīdī* are used primarily in urban families. The term *mammī* is a loan from the English "Mummy," and in urban areas it is the term generally used today by young children for their mothers. I have also recorded a number of seemingly idiosyncratic usages, such as the use of *cācī* (FyBW) for the mother (see Figure 3.18), which nevertheless fit into a pattern consistent with that which emerges when we analyze the occurrence of the more common alternative terms for the mother in the context of the total complex of address usages within the family.

For a father the educated urban polite form of address is the same as the usual form of reference for him, namely *pitājī*. In many families he is addressed by this term even if the mother is customarily called by terms for *sister* or *brother's wife*. A variant father term, also genealogically appropriate, is *bāpu*, a term that connotes more intimacy and familiarity than *pitājī*. But just as in the case of address for the mother, there are a number of other terms used in practice for the father, each of which enjoys wide currency:

cācā[*jī*] (FyB) [Fig. 3.10, 3.11]
bhāī-sahab, bhaiyyā (B) [Fig. 3.8]
pāppājī (F) [Fig. 3.13, 3.15, 3.16, 3.17]

In rural areas among adults by far the most usual form of address for the father is *cācā* or *cācājī* (FyB). The use of a brother term is also quite frequent in both rural and urban areas, while the modern urban use of the English-derived term *pāppā* (usually with the respect suffix, -*jī*) is gaining ground, along with the use of *mammī* for the mother in younger families.

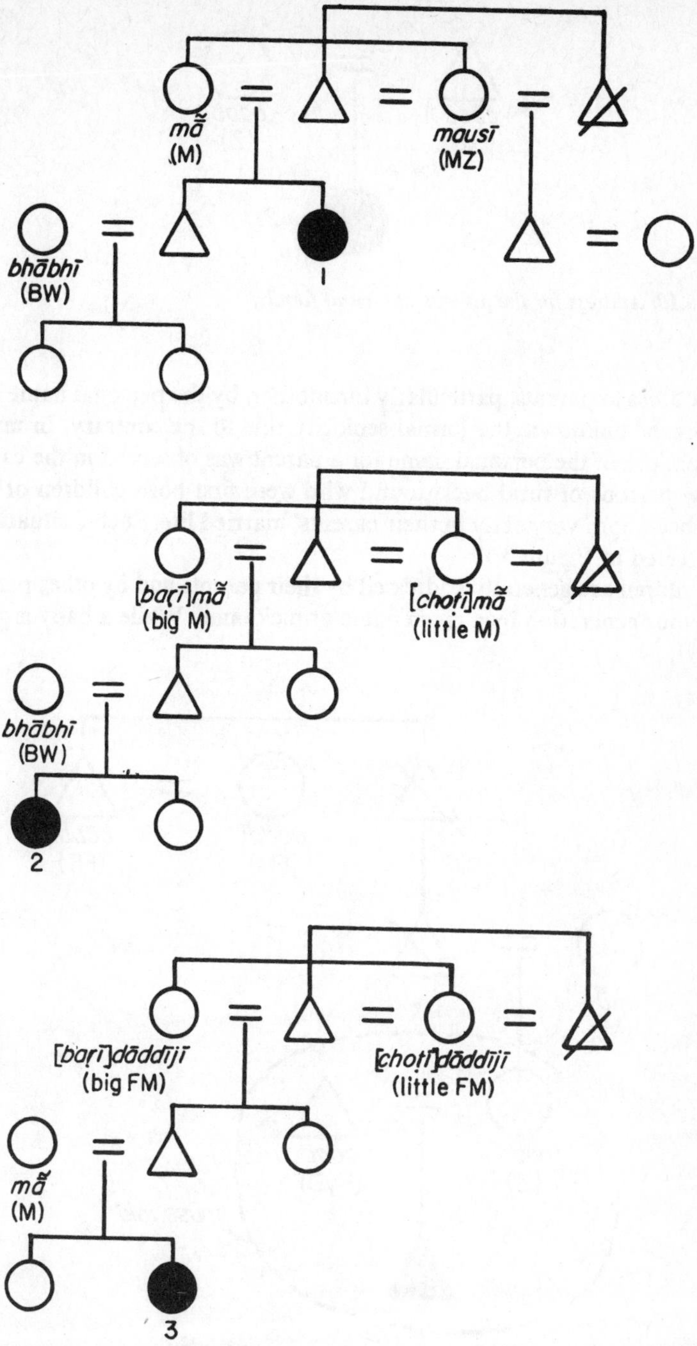

Fig. 3.9. Address for mother and grandmothers by three Egos of different generations and/or ages within the same agnatic extended family household. In the senior generation there has been a case of widow inheritance subsequent to the marriage of two sisters to two brothers.

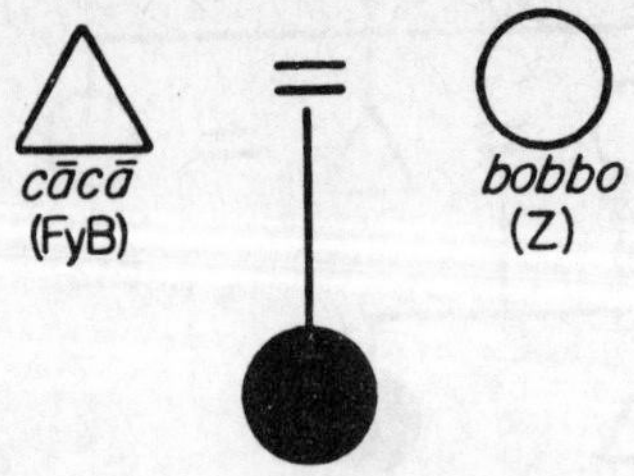

Fig. 3.10. Address for the parents in a rural family.

Address to parents, particularly the mother, by the personal name is by no means unknown, the formal seniority rule to the contrary. In my research, use of the personal name for a parent was observed in the case of a few persons of rural background who were first-born children or who had been born very early in their parents' married life. Such a situation is illustrated in Figure 3.19.

Children are generally addressed by their parents and by other persons of senior generation by a given name or nickname. While a baby is given

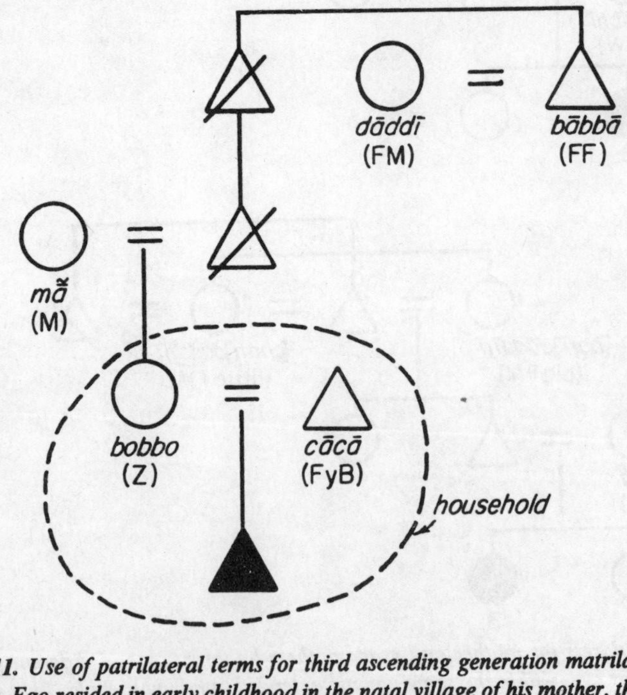

Fig. 3.11. Use of patrilateral terms for third ascending generation matrilateral collaterals. Ego resided in early childhood in the natal village of his mother, though in a nuclear household with his parents and siblings.

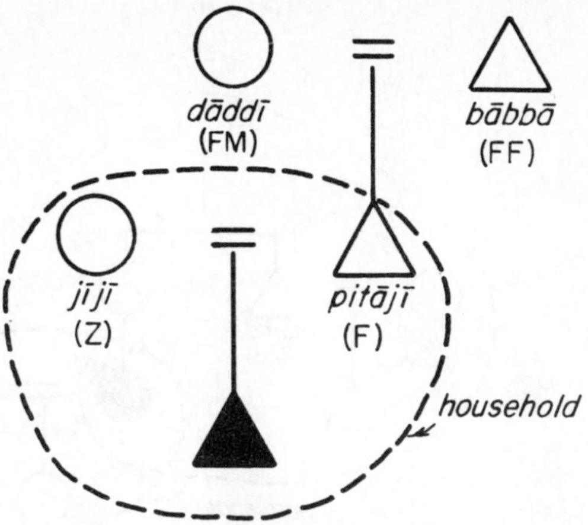

Fig. 3.12. Address for parents and paternal grandparents in a formerly rural family recently migrated to the city. The grandparents of Ego remain in the village home.

a formal, official name in a ceremony shortly after birth, this name is frequently ignored, at least for the early years of his life and is replaced in general use by a nickname or some other more ordinary or popular name, called a house name (*ghar kā nām*). Nicknames are varied: they may have reference to some physical characteristic of the child, such as *kālū* (Blackie), but meaningless or nonsense names that have an endearing or diminutive connotation are also very popular, for example *bablū, pappū, gullū, gaplū.* Also common are nicknames that simply mean "baby" or "child," such as *lāllā* (little boy), or *munnī* (little girl). The latter names may be used by anyone to address any child, whether or not he knows the child's customary personal name, but sometimes they become attached to one particular member of a family and continue to be used into adulthood as that individual's nickname. Modern urban usage seems to favor certain English-derived nicknames, especially for boys, such as *bobī* (Bobby), *pinkī* (Pinky), *dainī* (Danny), or *kitī* (Kitty). These are often taken from the names of film characters or stars, but in many cases the source is uncertain. Like other house names these tend to be replaced by more traditional Hindi names when the child is enrolled in school, either by the original given name that was bestowed shortly after birth or an entirely new name chosen by the child himself, by a parent, or sometimes even by the teacher who is making up the enrollment list. A child typically continues to be addressed and referred to by his *ghar kā nām* at home and by intimates, while school friends and acquaintances not close to his family will use his school name (*skūl kā nām*).[8]

The regular and customary use of a kin term when addressing a child is very rare, but on occasion a parent may use the terms *beṭā* (S), *beṭī* (D), or

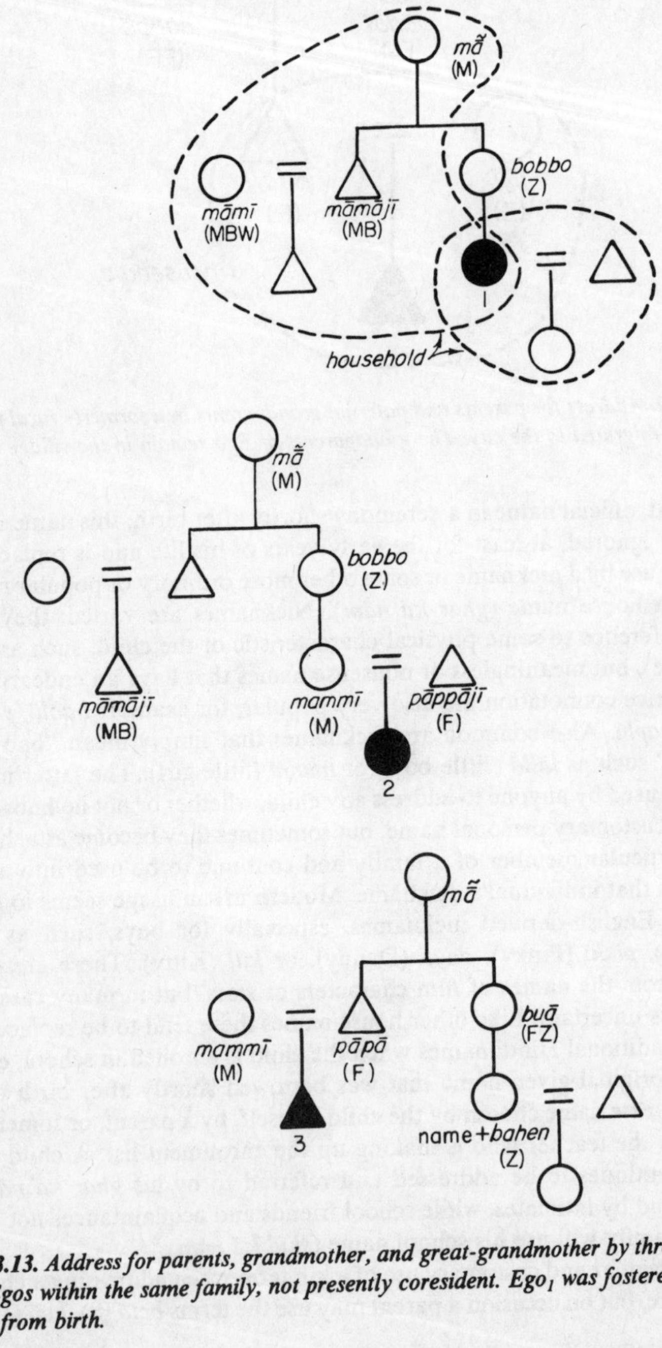

Fig. 3.13. Address for parents, grandmother, and great-grandmother by three different Egos within the same family, not presently coresident. Ego$_1$ was fostered by her MM from birth.

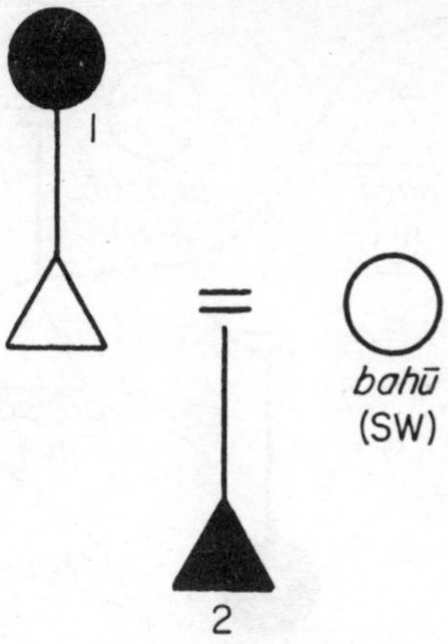

Fig. 3.14. Address term used by two different Egos (Alter's HM and S) in a rural extended family. For the former the term is genealogically appropriate, for the latter it is not.

biṭiyā (D, diminutive), usually as a sign of affection. Particularly interesting is the use of the term *beṭā* to address a daughter, especially lovingly or conciliatorily. On the other hand, a parent may show displeasure with a child who is behaving too independently or is bossing others about by addressing him or her as *tāū* (FeB), *bābbā* (FF), or *dāddī* (FM). Such usages are occasional and situationally determined—"tactical" in Bloch's terminology (1971). They are unlikely to be used on a regular basis for ordinary address.

Brother and sister. For address among siblings, and among cousins of the same generation, relative age is crucial. According to the asymmetric

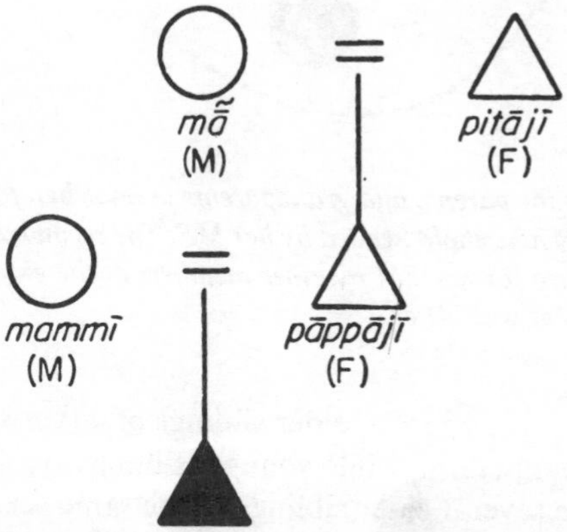

Fig. 3.15. Address forms used by a young, urban child living in an agnatic extended family household.

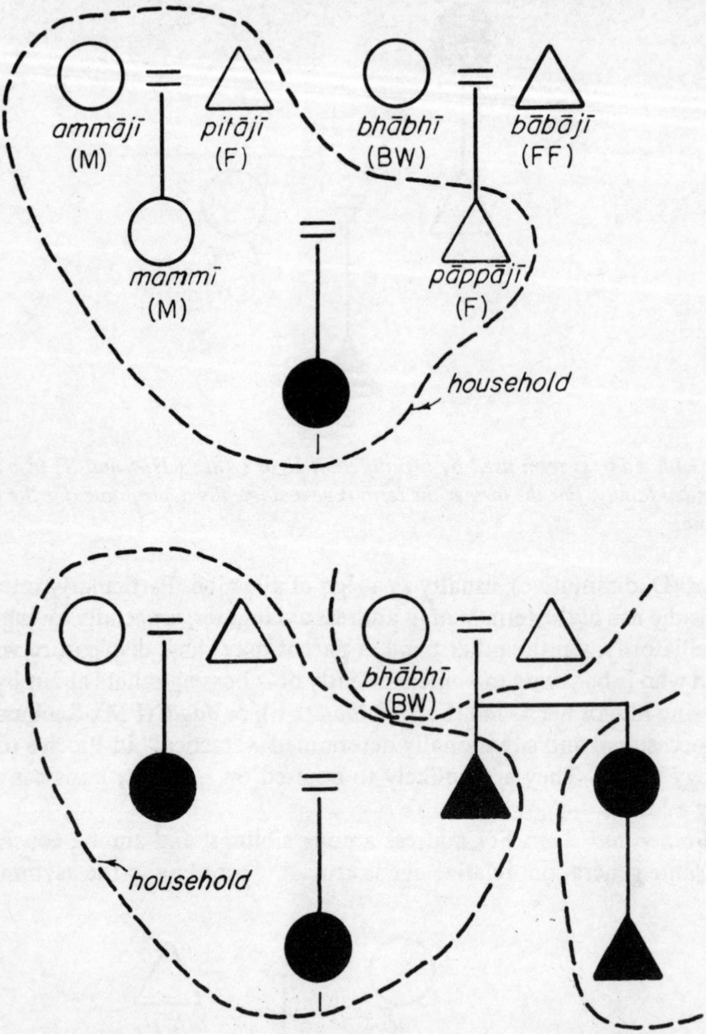

Fig. 3.16. Address for parents and grandparents in an urban family. Ego_1 resides in an extended family household headed by her MF. The second diagram illustrates the use of the same term for her FM by other members of the extended family, none of whom are coresident with Alter.

principle of kin term address, elder siblings of either sex are customarily addressed with a kin term, while younger siblings are addressed by name. Where there are several elder siblings of the same sex, the name may be used in combination with the kin term when it is necessary to distinguish between two or more siblings who are present at the same time. One

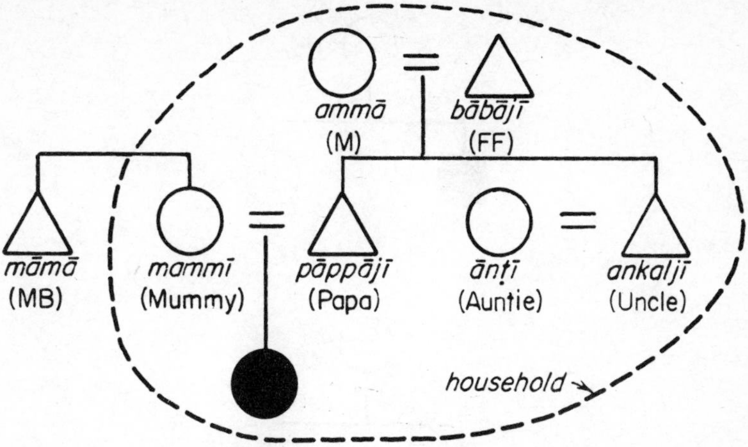

Fig. 3.17. Use of English-derived terms for first ascending generation lineals and collaterals. Ego resides in an agnatic extended family household which includes FB/FBW. Her MB resides separately.

rarely observes the reciprocal use of the given name, even between siblings of the same sex who are close in age, without the accompanying kin term. In the pecking order of a sibling set or a set of cousins, the right to be addressed as *bhāī-sahab* (eB) or *jījījī* (eZ) is jealously and often vociferously guarded, even by young children with only a few months' seniority over the others. For brothers and male cousins the appropriate terms of address are *bhāī-sahab, bhaiyyā,* or the personal name plus *bhāī* (for example, *rām bhāī* or *rām bhāī-sahab*). Sisters and female cousins who

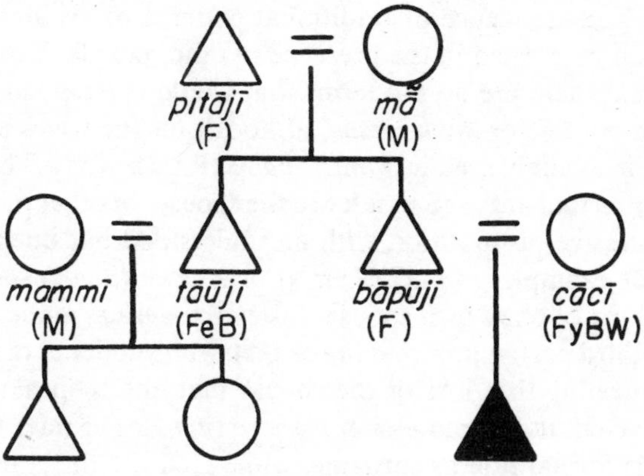

Fig. 3.18. Address forms in an agnatic, extended family household. Ego uses for his M and FeBW the same terms that are used for these individuals by his older cousins, FeBS and FeBD, terms that for them are genealogically appropriate. The two sets of cousins use distinct terms, however, for their respective F and FB.

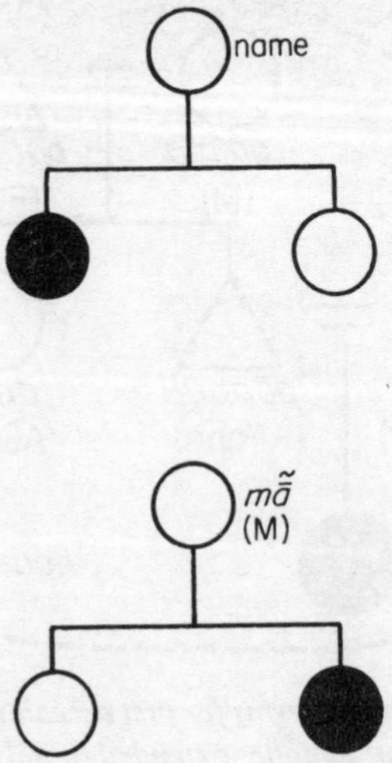

***Fig. 3.19.** Address for the mother by an elder and younger sister, respectively, living in a large, lineally extended household.*

are older than the speaker are addressed as *bobbo* in the rural area, while in the urban setting the terms *jījī* and *dīdī* are preferred. The respect suffix *-jī* may also be added to any of these brother and sister terms (*bhaiyyājī, jījījī*). In contrast to the practice for senior members of the immediate family, genealogically inappropriate terms are never used for siblings. At least, I have no such examples in my data.

Husband and wife. The matter of address between spouses is ambiguous; this is a consequence of traditional patterns of avoidance between husband and wife when in the presence of other people. Even in a referential context there are no kin terms that would correspond precisely to the English *my wife* or *my husband,* although for the wives of others the term *bahū* is available, as in *rām ki bahū* (Ram's wife). The words for *woman* or *man* that are used to refer to the spouses of other persons, or the simple possessive postposition with an understood but unexpressed object—as, for example, *rām kī* (Ram's) or *sītā ke* (Sita's)—are not used when speaking of one's own spouse. Instead, the usual mode of reference is with the third person pronoun (*he* or *she*), with subtleties of emphasis or context indicating that it is of the spouse that one is speaking. Women often use the clarifying expression *mere vo* (my He) or refer to their husband by his formal title or surname, while men use the expression *ghar mẽ* (at home) or *bāl bacce* (the children) when speaking of the health, wishes, or activities of their wives. After children have been born to a couple, the two may resort to teknonymy: thus, *rām kī mā̃* (Ram's mother). The personal name of the spouse is almost never used in reference. Women will not even take the name (*nām lenā*) of their husband in order to identify him to a third person and often avoid it in other contexts as well; thus the joke about the wife of a man named Krishna reciting prayers to *pappū ke cācā* (Pappu's FyB, that is, Pappu's father).

In address there is a similar avoidance of the given name by both parties and in general an avoidance of any form of direct address. The most common device, when it is necessary to make it clear to the spouse that he or she is being spoken to, is to use a Hindi equivalent of *Hey!* or *Listen!* (for example, *suno!*). If this is not sufficient, teknonymy may be used, making reference to one's own child or, failing that, to a nephew or niece.

Father's parents and son's child. The genealogically appropriate terms of address for the paternal grandparents are *bābā* (FF) and *dādī* (FM), or the rural *bābbā* and *dāddī,* with the respect suffix appended more consistently in address to the former than to the latter. It is most common, however, for the father's mother to be addressed regularly as *mā̃* or by some other variant of a Hindi genealogical mother term, such as *ammā* or *mātājī.* This usage for the paternal grandmother almost always coincides with the use of some terms other than these for the genealogical mother, as illustrated in Figures 3.8, 3.9, 3.13, 3.15, 3.17, 3.18, and 3.20. There are even some instances in my data (see Figure 3.16) in which the father's mother is addressed as *bhābhī* (BW), *jījī* (Z), and even *bahū* (SW).

A corresponding practice in the case of the father's father is to address him with a father term (see Figures 3.8, 3.15, and 3.18). This is somewhat less common than the use of a mother term for the paternal grandmother, and it is not at all unusual for the FM to be addressed as *mā̃* or *ammājī* or by some other term appropriate to a woman of a lower generational level, while the FF is accorded the genealogically appropriate term. For examples, see Figure 3.16, in which FM/FF are termed *bhābhī* and *bābājī* (BW, FF), and Figure 3.17, in which they are *ammā* and *bābājī* (M, FF).

Husband's parents and son's wife. The standard rule for the address of in-laws prescribes that with certain exceptions a woman uses her husband's term of address. There are distinct Hindi terms of address for father-in-law and mother-in-law (*susarā* and *susarī* or *sāssū*), but these are extremely abusive in connotation and are generally reserved for addressing opponents in a heated quarrel; they are rarely used to address any person who actually stands in the genealogical relationship of parent-in-law.[9] A woman thus normally addresses her HM by whatever term her husband uses or by any other variant of the mother term. If he uses such a term as *bobbo* (Z) or *bhābhī* (BW) for his mother, she may use this also, or she may instead address her mother as *mā̃* or *aṃmā* (M).

Avoidance prescriptions require that a woman not directly address her HF at all. In case of dire necessity, she may ask another to relay a message or even call out ostensibly to a child, even one too young to speak, a message intended for him. In modern families, where the rules of avoid-

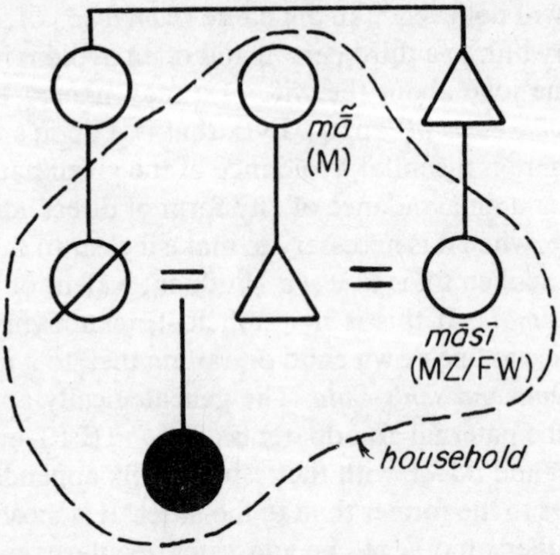

Fig. 3.20. Address for a stepmother and for FM in a rural, agnatic, extended family household. This form of address for the FW other than M is usual even in cases in which she is not a MZ, as she is here.

ance have been relaxed for one reason or another, women usually adopt the husband's own term for his F.

When addressing the SW, parents-in-law either use her given name or address her tekynonymously with their son's name (*rām kī bahū* or simply *rām kī*—Ram's wife) or the name of a grandchild (*pappū kī mā*—Pappu's mother) or with the genealogically appropriate kin term, *bahū* (SW), alone. New brides are often initially referred to and addressed in their conjugal homes by the name of the village from which they have come, and this usage may stick in later years as a personal nickname. In the Delhi village in which I did research, an elderly woman is still addressed by members of her family and by neighbors as Vaziro, recalling her origins in the village of Vazirpur. Another, the most junior of four wives in a large family of brothers, was nicknamed Mandivālī, because of her birth in a district of the city of Delhi known as the Vegetable Market (*sabzī mandī*).

Husband's brother and brother's wife. Just as among siblings, relative age is important in determining address usage between siblings-in-law. The relevant factor, however, in the case of HB and BW is the relative ages of the husband and his brother rather than the ages of the opposite-sex siblings-in-law themselves. Only in certain situations where there is a considerable age gap between H and W and where, therefore, a HyB may be markedly older than his eBW, do the relative ages of HB and BW become significant. The HeB is in any case a relative to be strictly avoided; just as with the HF, there is no traditionally acceptable way of addressing him. Since other in-laws of Ego's own generation are in most instances

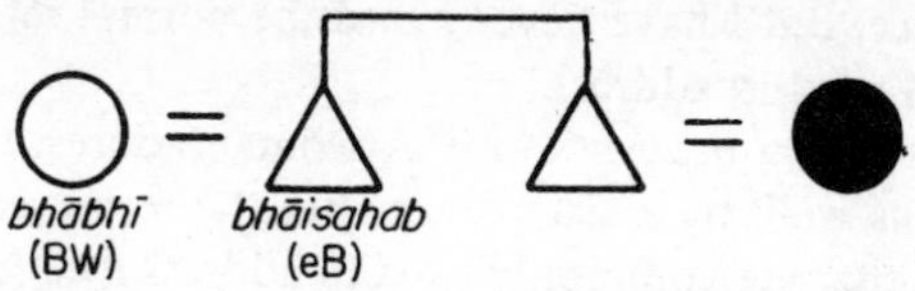

***Fig. 3.21.** Address form in an avoidance relationship. Ego uses her husband's term in addressing a kinsman whom she should traditionally avoid. She also adopts the husband's term for his brother's wife, instead of addressing her as a sister, in the traditional manner.*

addressed by a sibling term, and since senior in-laws are normally addressed by the term the husband himself uses, one solution to the problem presented by the abandonment of strict avoidance practices is to address the HeB by the genealogically appropriate term for eB, namely *bhāī-sahab*) (see Figure 3.21). Another approach, illustrated in Figure 3.22, is simply to append the respect suffix to the usual referential form: thus, *jeṭhjī* (HeB). While adding a respect suffix to the term of reference is the usual way of handling address to senior consanguineals, it is an awkward solution to the problem of addressing avoided relatives, as in-law terms are otherwise almost never uttered in a vocative context. Very often the entire issue is circumvented by using no direct form of address at all.

Since the HyB is junior in relationship to his brother's wife, his given name is normally appropriate for address. The relationship of HyB with eBW (*devar* with *bhābhī*) is one of stereotyped joking, in which intimacy and familiarity is permitted and even prescribed. However, if the *devar* is considerably older than his *bhābhī,* and if the senior generation is punctilious about the respect due old age, she may be instructed to address him by a kin term, either as *bhāī-sahab* or *devarjī,* or even to avoid him as she avoids the HeB and thus to use no term.

In address to the brother's wife, the relative age of the two men is again crucial: the HyB addresses his eBW as *bhābhī* or *bhābhījī,* while the HeB may use her given name or nickname or copy the usage of his parents and address her as *bahū* (SW) or by teknonymy. Traditionally, of course, he would have little occasion to use any direct form of address, and in a situation of rapid social change there is a great deal of variability to be ob-

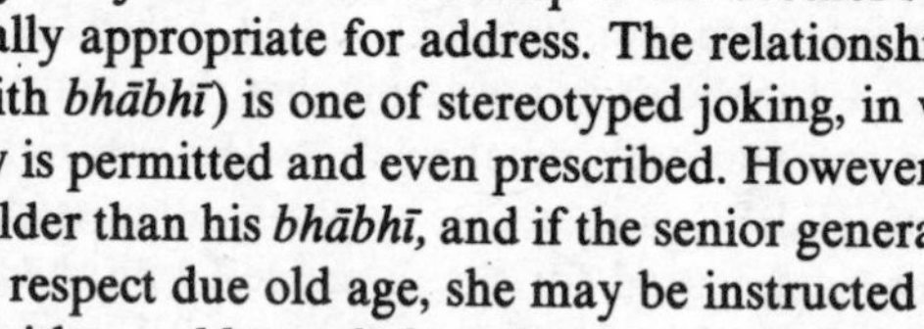

***Fig. 3.22.** Address form in an avoidance relationship. Ego uses an in-law term to address a kinsman whom she should traditionally avoid, while using a traditionally appropriate sister term of address for his wife.*

served in practice. But I have never heard the normal reference term for yBW (*bhābahū*) used in address.

Husband's sister and brother's wife. A woman addresses her HeZ, and often her HyZ as well, by a sister term. But the terms available are not limited to those that are commonly used to address true (*sagī*) or classificatory sisters. Instead, the terms *bahenjī* (literally respected sister) and *bībījī* (a rural term with a similar connotation) are heard most frequently. These terms are also used to address slightly older women who are at the periphery of the kinship network, affinal women for whom there is no distinctive genealogically specific term of address (WBW, *salhaj,* or ZHZ, *nanad*) and unrelated older female acquaintances, friends, and teachers. While relative age may be a factor in the address of husband's sisters, the kinship rank even of younger sisters of the husband is considered to be superior to that of an older brother's wife, and unless the HZ is very much younger than her BW, her parents may insist that she also be addressed by a kin term rather than by name.

Husband's brother's wife. In this relationship it is usual for the senior of the pair (the wife of the elder brother, regardless of the relative ages of the women themselves) to address the junior by name—or by whatever term their HM uses for her—while the junior addresses the senior with a kin term. The relationship of women married to a pair of brothers is conceived of as a quasisister relationship. The HBW is said to be like a sister or equal to a sister (*bahen jaisī, bahen ke samān, bahen barābar*), and this equation is followed through in the terms that they and their respective children use for one another's natal relatives (FBWB = MB, for example). The *jeṭhānī* (HeBW) is therefore typically addressed by one of the sister terms such as are used for the Z or HeZ (*jījī, bībījī, bahenjī*). If *daurānī* and *jeṭhānī* are close in age, or if the HyBW is older (this sometimes occurs when two brothers are themselves close in age or if the HeBW is a second wife), they may address one another reciprocally by given name. Occasionally the terms *jeṭhanījī* and *daurānījī* may be heard in address, but such usages are typically situational rather than customary forms of address within a family.

A modern trend in some families, accompanying the relaxation of avoidance taboos and the increasing use of the term *bhāī-sahab* for the HeB is to address the HeBW as *bhābhī* (BW), which is of course the term used for her by the speaker's husband (see Figure 3.21) as well as being the appropriate term to pair with *bhāī-sahab.* This usage appears to be spreading, despite the fact that several informants who reported or commented on it observed spontaneously that it is really quite inappropriate to blur in this way the distinction between two so different kinds of relatives as BW and HBW.

Father's brother and brother's child, father's brother's wife and husband's brother's child. The FB is distinguished terminologically in reference according to his age relative to that of one's father (FyB, *cācā,* and FeB, *tāū*). Address is normally also by these terms, often with the respect suffix —*jī*. Similarly, the FBW is addressed by the genealogically appropriate term according to the relative age of her husband (FyBW, *cācī,* FeBW, *tāī*). In large families where several brothers share a joint residence, some variation on this standard pattern may be observed in which children of a younger brother take on the usages of their older cousins in addressing the latter's parents. See, for example, Figure 3.18, in which Ego addresses his FeBW as *mammī* (M), retaining, however, the genealogically appropriate *tāūjī* for his FeB.

A recent trend with respect to FB and FBW, as well as to other collaterals of the first ascending generation, is the increasing popularity of the English-derived kin terms *ankal* (Uncle) and *āṇṭī* (Auntie). This is a similar development to that which one may observe in the use of English-derived terms for parents. However, it has broader implications for change in the system, because in this case more is involved than simply the replacement of a lexeme. Since English kin terms do not distinguish among the various first ascending generation collaterals as do the Hindi terms, the replacement of the latter with English forms blurs verbally the culturally important distinctions among different kinds of uncles and aunts. I do not have sufficient data to say to what extent the terms *ankal* and *āṇṭī* are in fact widely replacing the Hindi terms for all first ascending generation collaterals. My observations are that no systematic pattern has emerged and that there is a great deal of variability from one speaker to another and within the usage of a single speaker as he addresses various kinsmen of these categories, retaining the genealogically appropriate terms for some individuals while addressing others who may stand in a genealogically equivalent relationship with English-derived terms. The degree of modernness of the relative being addressed and of the speaker and his family seems to be a major factor in this variability. But there seems also to be some tendency for the newer terms to mean FB and FBW, while distinct Hindi terms are preserved for the parents' other siblings (see Figure 3.18).

Regularities in Family Address Usages

In order to interpret these data on address usages within the family, it is necessary first to examine them, and particularly the case examples, for discernable regularities and consistent patterns within the considerable variability exhibited. It is particularly important to look at this material from a diachronic as well as a static perspective and to look at address usages within each family as an integrated whole. For example, one ought ideally to observe the entire set of terms used by a given Ego for all Alters within his family as well as the set of terms used for a given Alter by each of those in the family who address him. In order to do such an investigation it would be necessary to have more complete data for a substantial number of families than I have been able to collect. Nevertheless, the information at hand is adequate for a beginning to be made in these various directions.

Viewing synchronically the overall configuration of address usages within the extended family for which I have information, the most striking feature is the widespread use of first ascending generation parental terms for lineals, and occasionally for collaterals, of the second ascending generation (see Figs. 3.8, 3.9, 3.11, 3.13, 3.15, 3.16, 3.17, 3.18, 3.20). Thus, one finds genealogical grandparents routinely addressed by terms that in a referential context, to nonintimates, would be used for the genealogical mother and father only. Furthermore, where an Ego so addresses his patrilateral or matrilateral grandparents, he invariably uses other than Hindi parental terms for his genealogical mother and father. Typically, in such cases the latter are addressed either by kin terms genealogically appropriate for junior uncles and aunts (see Figs. 3.10, 3.11, 3.18); kin terms for genealogical siblings or siblings' spouses (see Figs. 3.8, 3.9, 3.10, 3.11, 3.12, 3.13); other junior kin terms (such as *bahū,* SW, Fig. 3.14); other parental terms, especially those derived from English (see Figs. 3.13, 3.15, 3.16, 3.17, 3.18); or the given name. Ego almost never uses the same mother or father term to address two different members of his or her family. The only exception I have observed occurs in families in which there has been a polygynous marriage. For examples, in one household composed of a man, his two wives, and ten children, all the children address both women indescriminately as *mā̃,* distinguishing them only when necessary as "big mother" and "little mother," according to relative age. Although their father took a second wife because of the apparent barrenness of the first, both women subsequently bore a number of offspring, all of whom have lived since birth in a household with two mothers. It is more usual, however, to refer to and address the father's wife who is not one's biological mother as *mausī* or *masī;* this term is otherwise understood to denote the MZ. As in Figure 3.20, such a mode of address is usual when children of a deceased woman address their stepmother and frequent also in polygynous families where all children are the offspring of one wife.

The only other instance in my data that illustrates the use of a single parental term for two different individuals is one of leviratic widow inheritance resulting in a polygynous union (see Figure 3.9). This Raya Rajput household contains the wives and descendants of a pair of brothers, one of whom has been deceased for almost twenty years. The wives are sisters—each has married sons who themselves have offspring. As the diagram illustrates, Ego_2 addresses both paternal grandmothers as *mā̃,* while addressing her own mother as *bhābhī* (BW). In the former usages she follows the practice of her own mother and of the wife of her paternal uncle (FFBS), who also use the term *mā̃* for both of these women. Unfortunately, I do not have information on the mode of address used by the junior men of the family for these two women, but I would expect it to follow the pattern exemplified by Ego_1, who is their sister and cousin, respectively. It is relevant to a diachronic analysis of address patterns in this family to note that both daughters-in-law entered the household some years after their father-in-law had taken his dead brother's widow in marriage.

The pattern according to which one or both grandparents are addressed by a parental term while the genealogical parent is addressed by some other kin term or by name, is especially typical of lineally extended households, whether agnatic or uterine, or of families that have had such a household structure in the past. It is also observed in cases in which Ego's parents and grandparents, while maintaining separate hearths, still reside in close proximity. Figure 3.8 shows a very straightforward example of the typical patrilocal residence situation. Ego is a young Brahman girl who has been brought up since birth in a joint household with her paternal grandparents and several unmarried adolescent paternal uncles and aunts. She uses brother and brother's wife terms (*bhāī, bhābhī*) for her parents while addressing both grandparents by the parental terms *mā̃* and *pitājī*. Similar cases are very numerous in my data. However, it will be noted in the figures that the choice of terms for the parents in these households is quite varied.

Where residence is uxorilocal (as sometimes happens in the absence of male heirs), a similar pattern may be observed. Figure 3.16 shows a case of this type. Similarly, in Figure 3.11 we find the maternal grandmother addressed as *mā̃*, while the mother is called *bobbo* (Z). Ego lived for a number of years in early childhood in the village of his mother's family because his father's government job had caused him to be stationed nearby. Although maintaining their own independent nuclear household, he and his parents had lived in close proximity to his widowed MM, married MB, and the latter's children.

In contemporary urban families the more usual form of address for the parents in joint households is shown in Figure 3.15 (and also, with variations, in Figs. 3.13, 3.16, and 3.17). Here English-derived parental terms are used for M and F, while grandparents receive Hindi parental terms. Such a pattern may also be observed in uterine extended households, and it is beginning to spread into rural families as well. It will be interesting to see whether, as the present generation of young children becomes adult, these English-derived terms will in turn be used by their children to address their grandparents or whether the distinctions between *mammī* and *mā̃* and *pāppājī* and *pitājī* will come to correspond consistently to the distinctions M/FM and F/FF, as they do in many families today.[10]

Looking for differences in address usages between male and female siblings or younger and older members of a sibling set or set of cousins would make it possible to make some inferences about the possible influence of sex and of birth position on address practices. My data are unfortunately too scanty, particularly with regard to sex differences, to draw any firm conclusions on this matter. But some indication of the possible direction of variation by age is given in Figures 3.9, 3.13, 3.16, and 3.19, where the forms of address used by each member of a pair of elder and younger siblings are illustrated. In general, my data show that siblings, regardless of sex and birth order, tend to use identical terms of address for their shared parents and grandparents. In most cases, in fact, where I have shown a single Ego on a diagram, there are other siblings present in the household whose usages replicate those reported for the individual represented.[11] Furthermore, parallel cousins growing up in the same household also tend to use identical terms for their grandparents and in some cases also for their respective sets of parents. For example, in the household shown in Figure 3.18 the mother of one set of cousins is addressed by both sets as *mammī,* while the mother of the other set of cousins is called *cācī* (FyBW) by all of the children in the family.

However, there is some evidence that birth position may be associated in some households with the differential use of address terms by siblings. In two of my cases there is a difference in usage by an elder and younger sibling; in both it is the younger sibling who uses the parental term for their mother, while the elder addresses her as *bhābhī* (Fig. 3.9) or by her given name (Fig. 3.19). This phenomenon may be associated with fission of the household, or some other change in its composition between the births of the first and later siblings.

Another potentially revealing avenue of inquiry is that of change over time in the address forms used by a given Ego for members of his family. Schneider, for example, has pointed out that in American English such terms as *Mommy* and *Daddy* seem to be considered inappropriate by some mature speakers. While they are used by children, they tend to be replaced in adolescence by more formal terms; this tendency is especially marked in the case of address for the parent of the same sex as the speaker (1955:1198–1199). I suspect that a similar process may occur in Hindi, but I do not have sufficient evidence to confirm its presence.

It is also interesting to note, in the cases that have been presented, the widespread incidence of unpaired terms used in address to married couples. In other words, Tax's rule of uniform mates (1955:20)—which specifies as a general principle in the structure of kinship terminologies that "if a husband is called A and his wife is called B, then the wife of any A must be B"—is liberally disregarded in address within the family, although otherwise it is quite systematically adhered to, except when Ego's relationship to a particular married pair can be traced in more than one way. Note, for example, the following husband-wife terminological pairs: *cācā-bobbo*—FyB/Z (Figs. 3.10, 3.11), *pitājī-jījī*—F/Z (Fig. 3.12);

bābājī-bhābhī—FF/BW (Fig. 3.16); *bābājī-ammā*—FF/M (Fig. 3.17); *tāūjī-mammī*—FeB/M, *bāpūjī-cācī*—F/FyBW (Fig. 3.18). In most of these cases the nonuniformity of the terminological pair is such that the males are accorded genealogically appropriate terms while the females are addressed in some other way.

Interpreting Hindi Address Usages

It seems evident from the foregoing discussion that coresidence is commonly associated—though not invariably so—with the distinct pattern of address usage that I have been describing, and it is therefore logical to begin to seek within the domestic domain, at the level of household structure and the interpersonal dynamics of the Indian extended family, an understanding of its meaning and significance. A suggestion has been made, with reference to a very similar phenomenon in Japanese, that the terms used by any given Ego in address within his family reflect the positions of the various Alters within the group as a whole rather than their kinship position relative to the speaker (see Beardsley et al. 1959; Kitaoji 1977). That is, the terms of address used within the family are sociocentric rather than egocentric terms (see Service 1960) and form part of what Kitaoji has called a "positional" terminology of kinship (1971:1039–1042). Beardsley and his colleagues have elaborated upon this idea, suggesting that "the household rather than the individual person is the point of reference for use of kin terms. Thus, within the household one's personal relation to elder brother or elder son is less significant than his position as presumptive heir within the house; hence father and siblings alike tend to refer to him by the same term" (1959:245).

Carter has made a similar interpretation of his Marathi data on familial modes of address, which seem to follow patterns very similar to those which I have described for Hindi-speaking families. He suggests that the address terminology seems "to reflect the conceptual autonomy of the household as a distinct sphere of organization and the relations of seniority within it . . . Many aspects of address usage are a function not of kinship connection but of household membership" (1976:7; see also 1978:9–10). A similar approach underlies Drummond's discussion of an analogous pattern of intrafamily address and reference among Guyanese Creoles, in which the maternal grandmother is typically called Mother while the mother is addressed as Auntie. Drummond explains, "A young woman has her first child while still living with her parents . . . [and] the woman's child is thus incorporated into its mother's household where the child's grandmother stands in the . . . position [of] mother" (1978:36).

If we examine the accompanying diagrams, particularly those that illustrate the application of terms of address by a number of different Egos within the same family, it is clear that there is indeed a marked tendency for certain important roles in the household to be singled out by means of the application of one term by all or most members (see especially Figs. 3.9, 3.13, 3.14, 3.16, 3.19). A good example of this is seen in Figure 3.13, in which the oldest member of the family is called *mā̃* by all present and former members of the household and by their respective offspring. This woman is an eighty-year-old widow, the mother of several sons, who fostered her daughter's daughter from the time of her birth until her marriage. This is a particularly striking case because of the generation depth involved and because uterine as well as agnatic connections are present. But one could adduce many other examples to support the general observation that parental terms are commonly used for an individual or couple who holds the seniormost position in an extended family, in terms of age and generational level. Such persons tend to be addressed uniformly by all junior members of the household, regardless of their own generational standing; to that extent the use of parental terms may be said to reflect their status vis-à-vis the household as a whole. Further support for such an interpretation of these usages can be found in those cases in my data in which parental terms first begun to be used for an adult man or woman only after he or she had become a grandparent. Up to that time the form of address used by his or her offspring was a sibling or sibling-in-law term or even the given name. This reflected the addressee's junior or dependent status in the household in the earlier years, a parental term being awarded only when he or she eventually succeeded to a leadership position. In such cases, it should be pointed out, members of the household who have already established a customary mode of address for the individual concerned do not usually abandon that usage in recognition of a family head's new role; instead, the new parental term is adopted by those subsequently joining the household, in most cases by birth into it. A good illustration of this kind of situation may be seen in Figure 3.16. Here, the term of address used by Ego's M for her own M is *bhābhī* (BW), while Ego herself uses for this woman (her MM) the term *ammājī* (M), as do all her younger siblings and several cousins, the children of her MMBS, who live in a separate household but in the same building. The same principle can be seen to operate in other families of the more usual agnatic extended form.

On the other hand, a kin term used by more than one member of a family for a given Alter, a term that reflects that person's household status at an early stage, may eventually become a personal identity label and persist over time, being adopted by all newcomers to the household, until long after he or she has ceased to occupy the position to which it originally referred. Figure 3.16 also illustrates this process. Ego's FM is called *bhābhī* (BW) by her son, her daughter-in-law, and her grandchildren (daughters' as well as sons' children). While the term is one that may initially have served as a household status or positional term, reflecting the woman's place as a new bride when she first came to join her husband's household, it has become something else with the passage of time and the progress of the family developmental cycle. It does not at present reflect either this woman's position in her existing household or her relationship to any living member of that household. A similar persistence of a household status term through many decades of development of a household cycle is shown in Figure 3.14, where a mother is addressed by her son as *bahū* (*son's wife*). But if we examine our data on family address *in toto,* such persistence of a junior status term through several phases of the family cycle does not appear to be the usual pattern. It is probably most likely to occur in the case of persons of exceptionally strong personality. More usual is a situation in which the terms by which any individual is addressed vary with different speakers in the family at any one time and change over time with changes in personnel within the household throughout the developmental cycle, owing to demographic shifts with births, deaths, and marriages and other factors that alter the kinship composition of the household.

Thus, I would suggest that although the composition and structure of the household is indeed a significant factor influencing patterns of address usage within the family, the relationship between them is more complicated than has been proposed in the initial hypothesis. While the notion of household status as a determinant of address forms is a useful one, it is not adequate to account for the variety of actual usages to be observed within Hindi-speaking families.

Another approach to an understanding of Hindi address usages—one that is not inconsistent with the sociocentric terminology theory—may be sought in the usual ethnoexplanation of the phenomenon of the use of genealogically inappropriate terms for members of one's family. This is a feature of the way of speaking to relatives of which members of the culture are quite aware and that they explain as a consequence of patterns of child socialization. According to this line of reasoning, which one could label biographical or ontogenetic explanation of the origin and persistence of the practice, children who are brought up in an extended family household with other older children, either their cousins or their uncles and aunts, will simply imitate the modes of address they hear others using while they are still too young to grasp the concept of genealogical relationships or the proper connection between genealogy and kinship terms. As they mature they learn the correct referential system but out of habit continue to use the forms of address they acquired in infancy. So, for example, informants explain that "I heard my father's sister saying it, so I started to call my mother *bhābhī*," or, "Everyone else in the family called her *jījī*, so I did too."

This explanation rests upon the assumption that children learn their address usages simply by listening to what others say and do not receive any direct instruction or correction. Such an assumption is not entirely consistent with the observation that no confusion seems to occur in later life with regard to the referential uses of kin terminology while inappropriate address usages persist. Unfortunately, there is very little concrete evidence about the way that children learn to speak to and about their relatives, either in India nor in other parts of the world. Carter has recently carried out an investigation of levels of competence in the use of kinship terminology by children in Maharashtra. He finds that very young children do not have a systematic conception of the ways in which other persons are related to them and use kinship terms as titles for individuals known to them rather than as terms of relationship. But in his still unpublished report on this research he has not addressed the question of how these address titles are actually learned by the child or of the way in which particular forms of address are selected as appropriate for addressing specific individuals within the family and kindred (see Carter 1979). It is my own observation that there is in fact in India a good deal of explicit instruction of young children in this matter, concerning not only the appropriate way of addressing other persons but also the genealogical classification of kin and proper referential usage. The process of the acquisition of full competence—in the latter skills particularly—is of course long and gradual, but the fact that so much active teaching takes place belies the notion of purely imitative learning of address usages. There is even direct evidence from informants' statements that children do not simply learn to address the grandmother as *mā̃*—or the mother as a brother's wife or sister—by imitation. The following remarks, made by a young woman about an interchange I had overheard between her and an elderly woman whom I had never seen before illustrates this. It also illustrates the nature of the indigenous distinction—referred to above—between mode of relatedness and mode of address: "*mãi unko mā̃ kahtī hū̃.*" (I call her Mother.) "*vaise to mā̃ nahī̃ hai, nānī hai.*" (Actually, she is not my mother, she is my mother's mother.) "*mujhẽ nānījī kahnā cāhiye, par bacpan se hī apne ko mā̃ kahlātī rahī hai.*" (I should call her *Mother's Mother,* but ever since I was a small child she has had me call her *Mother.*)

A completely different approach to the problem raised in this essay is suggested by Bean's attempt to analyze the semantics of the word *ammā* (mother) in Kannada (1975, see also 1978). Bean formulates the problem as an essentially linguistic one, focusing on a particular lexeme and exploring its various meanings in Kannada discourse. She points out that the term *ammā* is used not only to refer to and address the genealogical mother but is also used in address for grandmothers, parallel aunts, and mothers-in-law, much as the similar lexeme is used in Hindi. *Ammā* is also used in a number of other senses, such as to politely refer to or address other women, to refer to or address goddesses, as a word for *pox,* and as an expletive indicating the need for succor. Her analysis of the meaning of *ammā* rests, in brief, upon a theory of polysemy according to which the word has a primary meaning (genealogical mother) and a number of other related meanings, indexical and referential, acquired through metaphoric and metonymic transfer. Using this approach to the data presented here, one might identify each of the terms habitually used in intrafamily address (*mā̃, bhābhī, bobbo, bhaiyyā,* and so on) and identify for each a primary meaning in the genealogical referent with metaphorical extensions to other kin. Carried to its logical conclusion this process would give us a set of terms for female relatives, for example, each of which has metaphorical extensions of meaning in the primary meaning of each of the other terms in the set. Aside from the circularity of such a result, this approach does not help us to understand such things as why the metaphorical extensions are realized in some situations and not in others or why certain terms are used most often when someone other than their primary referent is addressed. The questions with which we are dealing here go beyond the semantic level; Bean's approach is inadequate to our task because she is explicitly dealing with the meaning of kin terms rather than the meaning of kinship relationships.[12]

If we try now to focus on the relationships themselves in seeking to understand the significance of the observed ways in which family members address one another in north India, we are led to examine those relationships most commonly implicated in the use of genealogically inappropriate terms, namely the relationships of parent and child and of grandparent and grandchild. What are the cultural conceptions about the nature of parenthood, about the nature of the family, about the proper behavioral expression of kinship relatedness, and so on that can help us to understand the general pattern of addressing grandparents or other senior kinsmen with parental terms while parents are called by terms appropriate to more junior kin, in collateral rather than lineal categories?

I has often been observed of the Indian joint family that relations between parent and child, particularly between father and child and between husband and wife, are muted and undemonstrative in front of other persons—not only with outsiders but within the family circle itself. It has been pointed out that fathers are not supposed to show open affection to their own children in front of others. Though they may freely indulge the children of their brothers, they may not openly indulge their own, particularly when members of the senior generation are present. Open expressions of affection and concern between husband and wife are even more sharply circumscribed in the presence of other people. At the same time it is known and acknowledged by all members of the culture that parents in fact have deep and exlusive feelings of love toward the children they have borne and that the closeness of the bond of intimacy between husband and wife is unique and powerful. These feelings, which are considered to be wholly natural and universal, are not allowed open expression not because they are thought to be inappropriate as feelings but because their very intensity gives them a dangerous power to disrupt and divide the larger group within which husband, wife, and child are ideally embedded. The danger of disruption is most feared in the early years of a couple's marriage and when children are small; this is clearly reflected in the fact that cultural constraints on the expression of intimacy and concern are somwhat relaxed as a couple ages and their offspring grow to adulthood. In structural-functional terms one might say that the relegation of the expression of father love and conjugal love to the private sphere of interaction serves to delay and even prevent the emergence of fissiparous tendencies in the joint family, by enforcing a disemphasis on the emotional and affective separateness of the nuclear units within it.

Das, in a discussion of the Punjabi kinship system—closely akin to that of the Hindi-speaking area of northern India—presents a somewhat different formulation. She maintains that in the Punjabi view, "Human conduct is derived from a dialectic between [the] biological substratum and the socially constructed nomos" (1976:2). While biology is accepted as a given in kinship relationships, Punjabis feel that its demands should not be permitted public expression. This is not to say that sexuality is to be repressed or procreation hidden but rather that they are to be consistently kept backstage in the conduct of social life (1976:3–5).

The fact that these tendencies to what Das calls "backstaging" the natural ties that bind human beings in the family also affect very keenly the conduct between mother and child and between this pair and others in the extended family has been given much less attention in the literature. It is widely recognized that the achievement of motherhood is a goal of prime significance for a young Indian woman, not only in terms of the psychological benefits of having a child who is preeminently her own but also in terms of the social acceptance it gives her in a family that has heretofore regarded her somewhat as an interloper. Furthermore, the child gives her a base from which to begin to build toward a position of control over others. But it is not so often pointed out that there are strong constraints on the new mother's openly reveling in her accomplishment or seeming to wish to establish an exclusive and all-fulfilling relationship with the child. As Das has insightfully observed, "Not only may the daughter-in-law make no claims over her husband, but she should also *leave special ties with her children unstressed*" (1976:14, italics mine). Thus, "some women believe that the proper behavior for a daughter-in-law is to de-individualize her relationship with her child to the extent that any female member of the household can be entrusted with its care" (1976:15). A woman who is too possessive in her behavior with her child, who gives the impression to others in the family that she alone is capable of meeting her child's needs and discerning his discomfort, is readily criticized for her self-centered, and thus by definition antisocial stance.

These notions about the proper social conduct to be displayed by a mother to her child within the context of the wider family group are directly revealing of the cultural conceptions about the nature of motherhood that underlie them. Clearly, one element of this cultural construct revolves around ideas about the natural process of procreation and its implications for those who participate in it, as creator and product. The genetrix, the real mother (*sagī mā̃*), is felt to have a natural and indestructible affinity and love for the child of her own body (*apnī sharīr kā*). This special attachment and unwavering instinctual concern of the real mother for her offspring is believed to develop through the long, close association involved in pregnancy and nursing. There are many proverbs, folk tales, and common sayings that echo informants' statements about the unique status of the biological mother in the complex of conceptions that coalesce in the notion of motherhood. But in addition to this natural component are those social processes involved in the care and feeding and overall nurturing (*pālnā*) of a child in the years following its birth. While these are tasks that the biological mother is eminently suited to perform, she is not felt to be uniquely qualified to do so. Thus, the actual process of mothering, unlike the process of childbearing, may properly involve a variety of surrogates in addition to, or instead of, the real mother. This is even considered desirable. While it is of course a mother's natural desire to mother her own child, and to do so exclusively, such a desire is basically selfish, and it is not always in the wider family's interest—or in that of the child itself—to allow her to do so. In family life the tasks of mothering should be shared, as food and space and intimacy are shared, among all of its members according to their needs and inclinations.

A concept that is closely implicated in these ideas about motherhood, as it is also in north Indian ideas about sexuality and conjugal love, is that of *sharam,* a term that communicates notions of shyness, embarrassment, and shame. *Sharam* is a feeling associated, for a young married woman particularly, with the public acknowledgment of her motherhood. Such a woman is said to be affected by shyness (*sharam lagnā*) when in the presence of other people, especially before senior (*baṛe*) relatives. While this feeling affects her in her conjugal home, in the presence of in-laws and village neighbors, *sharam* is felt to arise especially strongly in a woman's natal home, in front of her own mother and father. The north Indian kinship system systematically segregates for a woman, symbolically as well as physically, those arenas in which she is a wife from those in which she is a daughter. In her natal home it is of course the latter identity that applies, and there the married state of a returning daughter is backstaged as effectively as possible. First, and most crucial, the daughter's husband is seldom present when she visits her parents. She is always fetched from his home by a male member of her natal family, and only when her in-laws wish to have her return does her husband or some other member of his family come to call for her again. When her husband does visit his in-laws the occasion is typically brief and formal. Husband and wife do not speak to one another and should not even acknowledge one another's presence by being together in the same room in the wife's natal home. Thus, a woman hides from her husband in her parents' house, and to have sexual relations there is considered improper and shocking in the extreme. Of course, the products of their intimacy—pursued in its appropriate place, in the husband's home—freely visit their mother's kin and are welcomed and coddled with openly expressed warmth. But to verbally allude to the mode and source of their genesis is nevertheless a cause of keen embarrassment to the young mother.

The sense of shame felt by a young mother in front of elders—whether in-laws or her own parents—is frequently alluded to by informants seeking to explain the typical pattern of addressing the mother and other members of the extended family. It is said that a woman is so shy about being called *mā̃* by her child in the presence of others that she teaches the child to call her something else and to use the mother term for some senior woman of the family, usually her mother-in-law. Such behavior is consonant with a culturally approved reluctance on the part of a young woman to seem to assert her own individuality and that of the new mother-child unit, against the family as a whole or to assume for herself a mother role in competition with the elder mother of the household. But this explanation cannot be taken literally as a replication of an actual process by which individuals strategically order a pattern of address usage. Empirically it is probably more common for the paternal grandmother herself to instruct the child to call her *mā̃* and to address his own mother by some other term. This is only one of a variety of ways in which senior women in a household may actively attempt to take over the mothering of a child, even trying to alienate its affections from its own mother. But whatever individual motivations and strategies may be pursued in a given instance, the cultural significance of Indian ideas about motherhood and mothering is clearly reflected in the widespread and generally accepted pattern of usages in which there is a distinct tendency to avoid the use of the genealogically appropriate mother term for the genetrix. It is somewhat ironic that when the mother term is preempted by the grandmother—either on her own initiative or at the instigation of the young mother herself—in order to reinforce her bond with her son's child and to reaffirm his belonging to the wider family group, the term adopted for addressing the natural mother usually comes to connote in turn the specialness and uniqueness of the mother-child relationship. This occurs whatever term is actually utilized for the mother, but a kin term that denotes a relative junior to the parent in generation or age is usually chosen, and appropriately so, as it is easily made to suggest an enhanced closeness and intimacy and a leveling of status asymmetry between the pair.

While I have ultimately focused most heavily on cultural perceptions of female parenthood—and justifiably so, since these patterns of use of kin terminology predominantly affect modes of address for female family members—I would suggest a parallel interpretation for the similar patterns of address for father and senior males, which have been described. The considerably reduced salience of the natural bond between father and son and the lesser symbolic power of the idea of fatherhood is, however, reflected in the fact that the genealogically appropriate term is more readily used for the male parent than it is for the mother. Furthermore, the connotations of intimacy which attach to the use of junior terms for the parents may be inconsistent with the heavy component of respect and/or deference which exists in the cultural definition of the father-child relationship.

Conclusion

There exists a widespread pattern of address usages within Hindi-speaking families in northern India that is characterized by a consistent tendency to employ genealogically inappropriate kinship terms for senior members of the extended family. Therefore, genealogical criteria cannot be said to account in any regular way for the choice of particular forms of address within the family: a knowledge of existing genealogical relationships among its members does not allow one to predict or explain address usages, nor is it possible by observing the manner in which family members address one another to deduce what their genealogical relationships may be. At least it is not possible for a casual observer unfamiliar with the internal cultural logic of these patterns of address.

The fact that the genealogical mother tends not to be addressed as such in Indian families and that she, and sometimes the father as well, tends to be assimilated terminologically to a younger relative or one of more junior generation and of collateral rather than lineal linkage is related preeminently to the cultural meaning of parenthood in that society. Factors relating this address pattern to the dynamics of family life in the joint household and to the symbolic separation of wifehood and daughterhood in the north Indian kinship system are also ultimately derivative of culturally shared notions about motherhood and fatherhood. Thus, habitual modes of address within the Indian family are, at the level of social conduct, a means of helping to assure that the presumably powerful natural ties among persons produced through the processes of procreation are kept in the background of ongoing joint family life.

The broader significance of this lengthy excursion into the meaning of a particular mode of intrafamily interaction in India lies in the demonstration that one can only properly understand the meaning of kin terms as they are actually spoken by understanding the meaning of the kinship relationships for which they are employed and by understanding the shared assumptions of members of the culture about the nature of these relationships and about the nature of kinship relatedness as such. There is abundant evidence in the literature, and the data presented here amply confirm, that while kinship terms may indeed have genealogical referents, their actual use in spontaneous communicative acts among members of a society does not always or only communicate something about genealogy (cf. Hunt 1969). Those who espouse a genealogical approach to the meaning of kin terms prefer to seek the solution to problems of this kind in the concept of extensions of meaning from that of the primary genealogical referent. But such an approach has not been helpful for understanding the kinds of family address patterns I have described here. Nor is an attempt simply to shift from an egocentric to a sociocentric perspective, while leaving fundamentally unchanged one's conceptions of the nature of meaning, wholly adequate to the task of analyzing data such as I have presented. A more enlightening approach necessitates turning from the meaning of the terms to the meaning of the relationships involved, in this case examining Indian cultural conceptions about parenthood and particularly about motherhood. By understanding something about what it means to be a mother within the context of the Indian joint family, one finally gains some understanding of the meaning of the way that kinship terms of address are customarily applied within this group.

4

The Ideology of the Householder among the Kashmiri Pandits[1]

T. N. Madan

> Because men of the three [other] orders are daily supported by the householder with [gifts of] sacred knowledge and food, therefore [the order of] householders is the most excellent order.
>
> *Manusmrti* III: 78

> Deliverance is not for me in renunciation. I feel the embrace of freedom in a thousand bonds of delight.
>
> *Gitānjalī* 73

IN THE COURSE of my field work among the Pandits of rural Kashmir, which has now stretched over many years,[2] I have been impressed by their preoccupation with personhood, that is, with their sociocultural identity. In order to delineate the Pandits' conception of what it means to be a Kashmiri Pandit, given the importance of kinship as an organizing principle of social organization among them, I have chosen to examine this question of personhood preeminently in the context of kinship. The domestic group is the domain where the phenomeological presence of the other is an abiding constant of everyday life. In fact, withdrawal from domestic life is not at all a highly prized goal among the Pandits.

Some Pandits among the many with whom I have talked about their culture and society have emphasized the central importance of going beyond personhood—man in society—and attending to the problem of selfhood expressed in the hoary question, "Who am I?" According to them, what sets off human beings (*insān, ādam, nara*)[3] from other living beings (*jīva-janatu*) is the former's intelligence (*buddhi*) and capacity for introspection (*vicār*)—in short, self-consciousness (*cit*). The religiophilosophical heritage of the Pandits is Kashmir Śaivism, which, unlike south Indian Śaivism, is monistic (see Chatterji 1917 and Dasgupta 1975). Though the common people in rural areas are only dimly aware of the doctrines of Śaivism, some of them do cite well-known aphorisms from the *Upaniṣad,* such as *tat tvam asi* (that thou art) and *aham śivam asmi* (I am Śiva), as the true answers to the question about selfhood. The Pandits who talk in such terms are, however, very few.

The majority of the Pandits I have talked with when confronted by me with the foregoing formulation averrred that such knowledge (*gyān, vidyā*) is beyond the comprehension of the common man and of not much avail to him, enmeshed as he is in "the veil of illusion" (*māyā-jāl*). They assert that the inward-looking emphasis on selfhood is not the common man's problem: his problem is the proper performance of social roles (*duniyā-dārī,* literally world maintenance) and the pursuit of *dharma* (moral conduct). In other words, it is the pressing if not paramount reality of everyday life, demanding constant attention and action, that is the primary concern of most human beings. Whether this is fortunate or unfortunate is another question.

In the context of such an involvement in everyday life, answering the question "Who am I?" remains important, as appropriate behavior between people is guided, animated, sustained, and controlled by such self-definition. The Pandit lives his daily life in and through meaningful social relations with other Pandits, who may or may not be his kin or affines, and with non-Pandits, notably Muslims. In order to decide how to relate to and conduct his intercourse with these others, he has to have a guide to action, and this is available to him in his understanding of what the entailments of being a Pandit are, or in his knowledge that there are such collective understandings.

I have elsewhere discussed some of these entailments and the manner in which they help the Pandits orient their relations with Kashmiri Muslims (Madan 1972:106–141) and with one another as wife-givers and wife-takers (Madan 1975:217–243). Here I am concerned with the more general problem of the cultural construction of the person among the Pandits. The work of David Schneider (1968, 1976) and Clifford Geertz (1973) has shown the heuristic value of the notion of person as a cultural construct as against the person on the ground, in the understanding of the interplay between culture and society. Thus, I am concerned here with what Alfred Schutz (1967) called "constructs of typicalities." These typicalities pertain to the purposes of life, to the procedures appropriate for their pursuit, and to the persons involved in them, acting together within a system of fundamental ideas and values, meanings, and symbols.

The kind of ideas I am interested in are those that the Pandits themselves employ to bring out the purposiveness and meaningfulness of their institutions: ideas that embody norms and values, stating what is axiomatic and not to be questioned, but enabling people to make choices in respect of both purposes and procedures where doing so is permissible. Social relations among the Pandits—as, of course, among any people, anywhere, anytime—are constructed by themselves. The ideas that animate them and sustain or alter social interaction between them, must be, therefore, understood. There is a need for caution, however, for, as Louis

Dumont (1970:36ff) has pointed out, ideas and values are not everything—they do not exhaust social reality, just as externally observable behavior does not do so. This is why both ideas and behavior, the total situation, must be taken into account.

The duality of ideas and behavior has to be retained, but they must not be mutually opposed. Rather, ideas have to be seen as the framework for the interpretation of behavior; and behavior, what actually happens, provides what Dumont (1977:27) calls "control," preventing the misunderstandings that an overweening emphasis on ideas alone might generate. My decision to confine attention to an explication of some selected Pandit ideas should not be, therefore, misconstrued to imply an argument against the importance of concrete behavior and its study. I have earlier attended to it at length (see Madan 1965). It is through it that ideas find expression.[4] I am not setting up a mutally exclusive dichotomy of culture and society but insisting that we recognize, following Max Weber, Alfred Schutz, Louis Dumont, and others, that social action is suffused with meaning, that intentionality is central to it. Purposes are not causes, however; nor do I want to explain anything. This is only an interpretive essay.

Now, people's ideas are intractable and difficult to get at and analyze. This, it seems to me, is the challenge of ethnography. The ethnographic text is not a faithful account of what has been seen and heard—as perhaps the videotape might be—but involves reconstruction and redescription of what has been seen and heard in the light of, first, the people's own concepts of everyday life and its larger purposes and, second, the ethnographers' theoretical presuppositions about the nature of social life and about the significance of people's ideas. This is true of the work of the native, formally trained anthropologist no less than of the anthropologist who studies a society other than his own. The present essay is based on the affirmation that the ideas of the people—enshrined in folklore, proclaimed in proverbs and sayings, talked about and discussed everyday, but often unexpressed—provide a significant point of departure for the anthropologist's work. The ideas are not there for him to pick up, as it were; he has to look for them and, indeed, ferret them out through intensive field work.

What is important is that one must seek a fusion between the view from within (ideas, meanings) and the view from without (behavior, rules), for anthropology is, as Dumont has rightly pointed out, understanding born of the tension of the encounter of the two perspectives (1966:23). "In this task," Dumont (1957:12) writes, "it is not sufficient to translate the indigenous words, for it frequently happens that the ideas which they express are related to each other by more fundamental ideas *even though they are unexpressed.* Fundamental ideas literally 'go without saying' and have no need to be distinct, that is tradition. Only their corollaries are explicit."[5]

It is obvious that to achieve the foregoing objective the ethnographer has to seek the companionship of informants in a joint endeavor of exploration for meaning in the minutiae of everyday life. He begins tentatively with questions of a specific nature about concrete behavior and builds on the informants' answers and goes on to further observation and bolder questions of an increasingly general nature. Informants are not always forthcoming with general formulations. As Weber himself pointed out, "Actual action goes on in a state of inarticulate half-consciousness or actual unconsciousness of its subjective meaning" (1947:111ff). The reasonable assumption that one makes in this regard is that it is inconceivable that a person does not have a view of life and its purpose, a *Weltanschauung,* even if he has not explicitly formulated it. The point really is that he can be expected to formulate it. The ethnographer, therefore, invites the informants to reflect on their everyday life, discuss their behavior, examine its purposes—not the specific intentions that prompt particular actions but general purposes—evaluate procedures, and assign meanings. One can do this retrospectively as Schutz (1976) suggests. In short, the ethnographer tries to make sense of social reality together with his informants. He tries to formulate explicitly what they know implicitly and vaguely, perhaps only confusedly. The answers ultimately are the informants', but the ethnographer structures them by the kind of questions he asks: the text is his. What the informants do, and what they say about what they do, are his data or facts. His task is to redescribe and translate these facts without loss of meaning, and finally to interpret what is given in the informants' beliefs and their ready and not-so-ready knowledge of their culture.[6] Belief, knowledge, and understanding are, of course, not one and the same thing.

Needless to emphasize, the ethnographer is not able to engage in and sustain such productive interaction with every informant. Fortunately there are intellectuals among informants, too, those who are curious about their own culture and think about it. There are others, however, who are not so interested or well informed about their way of life for the dialogue to continue fruitfully.[7] But everyone—man and woman, boy and girl, and even children—contribute to the ethnographer's knowledge and understanding. In the final synthesis that he endeavors to construct, the ethnographer assigns different types and degrees of significance to the various contributions, including his own. This, then, is the manner in which the data embodied in this paper were generated. I might add that none of my informants consulted any text in the course of conversation with me, nor have I drawn upon any such source in this essay.[8] What I am dealing with here is, therefore, the Pandit oral tradition.

Pandit Identity: Other Ascription and Self-Ascription

The Brahmans of Kashmir, generally known as the Kashmiri Pandits, refer to themselves and are referred to by other Kashmiri-speaking people as the Bhaṭṭa (singular and plural). The word *bhaṭṭa* is the Prakrit form of the Sanskrit *bhartr,* meaning doctor, "the designation of great scholars" (see Macdonell 1924). Very few Kashmiris, certainly not the non-Bhaṭṭa, however, attach any importance to the etymology of this term. As used by the Kashmiris to designate those among themselves who are not Muslims or Sikhs, the word is perhaps best translated as Hindu (or Hindus).

Now, too questions may be posed here. First, how does one know a person to be a Bhaṭṭa, or to revert to the more general usage a Pandit? And second, how do the Pandits themselves define their cultural identity and communicate it when the need arises to themselves and to others?

Visible Signs of Pandit Identity

There are many outward signs of recognition of a Pandit and of places and events associated with him. The traditional clothing of Pandit men, women, and children is different from that of their Muslim covillagers. Though a non-Kashmiri might not easily recognize these differences in the case of men and children, there can be no mistaking a married Pandit woman's traditional or contemporary sartorial style for that of anyone else (see plates in Madan 1965). The Kashmiris readily perceive these differences. Also many Pandits, particularly women, wear the very visible *tyok* on their forehead—a mark made with sandalwood or rosewood paste, saffron, or *sindūr* (vermilion), or combinations of these. When bare-headed a Pandit man or boy may be recognized by his tuft of head-top hair (*chog*), but this is now less commonly found than it was a couple of generations ago. An adult Pandit male who has stripped himself to the waist for bathing or some other purpose will always be recognized by the holy cotton threads (*yagñopavīṭa*), characteristic of the twice-born castes all over India, worn round the neck or round the neck and under the right arm.

Pandit houses look different from those of other Kashmiris both inside and outside (see Madan 1965:46–54 and plates). Their places of worship and cremation grounds are also distinctive, as are their religious, wedding, and funeral gatherings. The sight of flowers (particularly marigolds) and the sound of conch shells are characteristic of these events. Though they speak Kashmiri, like the others, the Pandits' speech is more laden with Sanskrit than that of the Muslims (see Kachru 1973). Personal and family names, with a few exceptions, are also different.[9] There is no particular kind of work that the Pandits alone do, but there are several chores that they never perform, such as making pots or shoes, forging agricultural implements, shaving other people and washing their clothes, and anyone seen engaged in such tasks can never be a Pandit. The contrast in all these respects is primarily between the Pandits and the Muslims. Its details are generally known and accepted among all Kashmiris:

agreement among the communities is built upon an explicit recognition of difference between them (see Madan 1972:138). For the Pandits, the Muslims are the others or outsiders, but not strangers (*vopar*).

Pandit Identity: Self-Ascription

By themselves the Pandits constitute not merely a single breed (*bīj, byol,* meaning seed) but, more significantly, one *zāt.* The notion of *zāt* is subtler than that of the community of kith and kin and of common customary behavior. In fact, the word is used in two senses. Generally, and rather loosely, it connotes the family name or the name of an occupational goup. It is also used to convey the particular idea that a people (*quom,* the anthropologists' ethnic group), whether the Pandits or any other, ultimately are what they are and do what they do because of their essential and inborn but alterable nature. Stones, plants, animals, human beings, gods all have their *zāt,* or essence. Among human beings it is considered to be a product of physical and moral elements: in fact, it may well be described and understood as the relation between the two. One's *zāt* may become refined through appropriate effort—what Marriott (1976) calls the process of maturation—or it may become corrupted through the neglect of moral conduct. *Zāt* connotes a complex, hierarchical relation in which the moral element encompasses the physical. As an informant once put it to me, "A Pandit is not the fruit of the pursuit of pleasure [*kāma*] but of moral duty [*dharma*]." The reference is to the paramount duty of the householder (*gṛhastha*) to beget children (*santān*), particularly sons (*nechiv, putra*) so that the lineage (*kula*) is continued and the manes (*pitṛ*) are assured offerings of water (*tresh, tarpan*) and food (*piṇḍa*) and their perdition is averted. In the process, the Pandit *quom* also survives.

A Pandit is thus born into the *quom;* there is no other way of acquiring this identity. One loses it by totally abandoning the Pandit way of life, as when one eats and lives with Muslims and marries a Muslim. Such actions result in a crucial alteration of one's *zāt.* A Pandit must, therefore, ever guard it. I asked a Pandit of Utrassu-Umanagri who had become a Muslim why he had done so. His answer was that it was some flaw in his *karma* (*karma khandit*) that blinded him and made him commit this sin. I do not mean to suggest that every Pandit converted to Islam has such regrets. The point rather is that one who is repentant thinks about it in terms of a moral lapse, a falling away from *dharma,* and, I might add, the consequent deterioration in one's *zāt.* Despite his regret, this man never even mentioned the hope of a restoration of his lost status.

The significant relation between moral and physical elements in the make-up of a person does not mean the denial of any importance at all to the physical dimension of personhood. On the contrary, it is dramatized at the beginning of all major rituals when the person performing the rite summons himself into existence, as it were, by pointing to, and naming and purifying different parts of his body, beginning with his feet and culminating in his head.

According to Pandit ethnobiology, conception cannot occur among biological beings (*jīva*) without sexual intercourse, though it may among supernatural beings. Sexual intercourse does not, however, guarantee that conception will occur. There may be something wrong with the body and the physiological processes of the wife or the husband. Barrenness is recognized as a physical incapacity. A childless wife may be advised by her friends to change her cover (*vurun*), that is sleep with a man other than her husband, but this, of course, would be a reprehensible breach of moral conduct. Barrenness among women and infertility among men may be produced by disease, sorcery, or the curse of people endowed with supernatural powers. But ultimately, whether a couple will or will not be blessed with children, the much sought-after sons in particular, is a question of fate (*prārabdha*), or *karma-lekhā* (the "written," that is, preordained, results of one's actions in the previous life). In the normal course of events, there is no escape from the consequences of one's actions; only divine grace (*anugraha*) can come to one's rescue, but this is hard to obtain (*durlabha*).

It is generally maintained that conception occurs when husband and wife reach orgasm simultaneously. Female orgasm is believed to result in the discharge of vital fluids into the womb, which also receives the male seed (*bīj*). Not only were my informants uncertain about the nature of the supposed female discharge, some of them also considered it to be of no consequence. The male seed is believed to contain in it all the requirements for the making of the complete human being: bones, flesh, blood, all internal and external organs, hair, nails, intellect, knowledge, ignorance, health, disease. It has the capacity to provide for the nurture of the fetus and subsequently of the newborn child. The mother's menstrual blood provides the soil or bed for the seed to grow in when it ceases to flow out and solidifies into the fleshy sack that envelops and nourishes the fetus. The mother is the feeder and preserver of the fetus. It is because of this fact that Hindus worship the black stone *śāligrāma,* the symbol of Visnu, the preserver, which resembles the womb in shape. The growth of the child's body, which is already in the seed, depends upon the mother and her physical and moral condition. The original planting of the seed in the womb sets in process the milk-producing capacity of the mother, who then suckles the child when it is born. In short, as one informant put it, the human seed is very much like the walnut, which contains in itself the full-grown fruit-bearing tree.

Despite the potency of the male seed, the father's role is seen as rather accidental and episodic compared to the mother's sustained and intimate involvement with the child during both the prenatal and the postnatal stages. A Kashmiri proverb proclaims this intimacy rather bluntly: *harāmuk yā halāluk panani dambik nav reth* (illegitimate or legitimate, the nine months of my womb); that is, though the physical bond between father and child may never be proven, there can be little doubt in the case of mother and child. Human life, the Pandits aver, consists in the obligation to repay debts (*ṛṇa*) incurred in the course of numerous lives: debts to gods, ancestors (including one's father), teachers, fellow human beings. There is one debt, however, which never gets repaid because it cannot be repaid: it is the debt one owes one's mother (*matṛ-ṛṇa*). There is no one—not to speak of one's father, not even gods—obedience to whom is enjoined more on human beings than to one's mother. The intimacy of the bond with one's mother is expressed in another proverb also: *Goda zāi ba ta maj ad zāv bab, doh painsha dab log ada budbab* (I and mother were born together, the father followed, the grandfather came still later). All one's kith and kin, including the father, may turn wicked, but never the mother; one may be evil oneself and ill-treat one's mother, but the bad mother (*kumātā*) is unknown.[10] The bond between mother and child is the moral bond of love par excellence—Fortes's axiom of amity—unsullied by the kinds of mundane consideration that enter into the father-son relationship. The Kashmiri woman is said to be a child worshipper (*baca-parast*). The reverence for human mothers is paralleled by the Pandits' reverence for mother goddesses, particularly their patron goddesses *Śārikā* and *Rāgnyā,* both addressed as *jagadambā,* universal mother, whom they accord a higher place in the divine hierarchy than their divine consorts. Mothers thus pervade both the human and the divine spheres.

Fathers also are obviously important: "The seed flows clearing the way for the flow of property" is how an informant summed up the significance of the father-son bond. When I suggested to him, and to other informants, that the way that the flow of seed clears is not only for the downward transmission of property but also the upward flow of food offerings, they agreed with me. But there is a problem in respect of the father-child relationship. The mother has milk, and she gives it all to her children. A woman may even die in childbirth, sacrificing her life for the sake of the child. The father has property and he shares it with his sons. The mother gives absolutely of what she has, but the father does not do so.

The father-child relationship is moral, even as the mother-child bond is, but it also has a material dimension: not only do sons share ancestral property with their father and inherit his share in it, daughters also expect a dowry and postnuptial prestations from their natal family. Inheritance by sons and gifts to daughters and their conjugal families are governed by law and custom, and these may often be manipulated by particular individuals to suit their own advantage. The Pandits often justify the actions of a son who fights his father over property, blaming the older man for such vices as covetousness or intolerance of others' points of view. They never condone the neglect by a son of the material needs of his mother, even if she is a stepmother. The contention of Edmund Leach (1968:9) that the constraints of economics are prior to the constraints of kinship morality does not hold good of the mother-child relationship among the Pandits; it applies to the father-son relationship, but only at the level of behavior and not in terms of ideology, in which filial piety is extolled as an imperative of *dharma*.

Property endures, as Leach (1968:11) has pointed out, but so do the moral bonds between parents and children. An adult Pandit's first action in the morning, after he has performed ablutions and before he eats any solid food—the pious will not even drink anything—is to offer water (*tresh, tarpan*) to his manes beginning with his own parents. Moreover, twice a year he performs the *śrāddha* ritual for his parents on their respective death anniversaries (according to the Hindu lunar calender) and on the appropriate days during the annual fortnight-long feeding of manes (*kāmbar pakṣa*). *Piṇḍa* (conically shaped lumps of cooked rice) are offered to them symbolically and thrown into flowing water or fed to birds after the ritual. Priests are fed the favorite dishes of the deceased parents.

Other ancestors also receive *piṇḍa:* five lineal male ascendants beginning with one's father's father, on the occasion of the father's *śrāddha,* and father's mother, father's father's mother, and so on up to FFFFFM on the occasion of the mother's *śrāddha.* Still other ancestors, notably mother's father, may also be offered *piṇḍa,* or—this is more likely—dry, uncooked rice, salt, and fruits (called *sīddha*) may be given to the family priest in the name of the dead person. Those whom one normally offers *piṇḍa* or *sīddha* and their descendants are one's *sapiṇḍa:* one is related to them through the ritual food offering,[11] and one must not take one's wife from among them, or give one's daughter or sister in marriage to them, within certain defined limits (see Madan 1965:105). It is obvious that the Pandits disapprove of the mixing together or confusion of categories and would no more derive their own successors (lineal descendants) from their ancestors (lineal ascendants) than they would give wives to those from whom they have taken them (see Madan 1965:105; 1975).

The nature of the parent-child relationship is thus given in *dharma,* which declares its moral basis and defines what should be its content. The Pandits are down-to-earth pragmatists and acknowledge that the dictates of *dharma* are often violated by people. Why should this be so? Why should considerations of economic gain emerge blatantly as prior to the dictates of morality in some cases? The Pandit answer is, *hawālyat;* that is the notion that you may receive from your children what you gave to them in the previous life. It is a matter of the give-and-take of the previous life (*purūjanamuk len-den*). In short it is *karma.* Fate (*prārabdha*) informs the parent-child relationship at every step: from the initial step of *kanyādāna* (the gift of a virgin by her father to her chosen husband), through the intermediate step of *garbhādāna* (the receiving of the seed by the wife from the husband), to the ultimate step of *piṇḍadāna* (the post-mortuary gift of food by a son to his parents and other ancestors). This threefold pattern of gifts given and received is the defining characteristic of the domain of kinship among the Pandits, forming the basis of a person's relations with (to borrow Schutz's terminology once again) his predecessors, consociates, and successors. More generally, it is the very basis of the Pandit way of life and of the definition of cultural identity. Birth and death are physiological events found among all living beings; it is the manner of his birth and death—what precedes, accompanies, and follows these events—that defines a Pandit and distinguishes him from the non-Pandit. Physiology, morality, ritual, custom, and law—all are elements in the definition of identity.

BHAṬṬIL: TRADITIONAL PURPOSES OF LIFE

The Pandits' conception of sociocultural identity is given explicit expression in their notion of *bhaṭṭil,* the Bhaṭṭa or Pandit way of life. Needless to emphasize, they consider *bhaṭṭil* the best—that is, the morally superior—way of life. It is constituted of a range of fundamental purposes of life (*abhiprāya*), largely centered in domestic life, and of appropriate procedures. These purposes and procedures have their basis in tradition. When children—the great questioners in every society—and even curious adults ask of those who might know why something should be done in a particular manner, or done at all, the answer that is usually given is: "It is *bhaṭṭil:* it is our way of life." If the questioner persists and demands a fuller answer, he is sought to be silenced by the utterance of the single exclamatory word *ada.* As an affirmatory exclamation *ada* would mean, "That is the way it is," implying, "That is the way it should be." Put negatively the connotation would be, "There is no reason," implying, "No reason need be given." *Ada* could also be interpreted as a counterquestion: "What else?" or, "Why should I tell you?"

The foregoing gloss, I must clarify, is my attempt to decode this powerful verbal symbol on the basis of careful attention to the contexts and manner of its use. My informants never explained the term to me but left me in no doubt about its significance. It stands for the attitude of unquestioning acceptance of the moral imperative. It is not employed in connection with the inevitability of natural or physiological processes, such as the change of seasons or death. There were many among them, the inevitable skeptics, who considered it the symbol of irrationality; as they sarcastically put it, "There is no higher *śāstra* [sacred text] among the Bhaṭṭa than the *ada-śāstra.*" It is obvious that we are here confronted with axiomatic truths that are the foundation of tradition everywhere.[12]

These truths have not ever been stated to me in any systematic form by my informants. Certain overarching notions have, nevertheless, emerged quite clearly in the course of my conversations with individual Pandits and through group discussion. A Pandit's most precious possession, I have been repeatedly told, is his self; and one's self is more than one's body (*śarīra*). The physical self or the body is really of little significance by itself. It is fragile, subject to deterioration, and readily perishable: it is *kṣṇa-bhangur,* that which may disintegrate at any moment. It is when body is joined to the inner self or soul (*antar ātmā*) that it becomes the vehicle of *dharma.* It is, therefore, a Pandit's first obligation to protect his *zāt* and, indeed, to try to enhance its merit so that the next life may be better than the present one. He who neglects this first among life's purposes turns out to be, in the words of an informant, who switched over to Hindi, *tīn janam kā bhūkā*—that is, one who remains (spiritually) starved through three lives, the previous, the present, and the future. One's present life's difficulties indicate the neglect of *dharma* in the previous one; one's present failures ensure the difficulties of the next one. How does one meet this primary obligation? Through steadfast adherence to *bhaṭṭil,* or *dharma,* in whatever one does and in the manner one does it.

The demands of nature, while the body lasts, are not to be denied but fulfilled in accordance with *bhaṭṭil.* When this is done, one acquires fame (*yash*) for righteous conduct in this world (*yahaloka*) and merit for the next (*paraloka*). The body is thus the meeting ground, as it were, between the past, the present, and the future or, to put it differently, the present is the link between the past and the future. How the present is filled is then, obviously, a matter of great import.

In the context of this concern with the present and with protection of one's *zāt,* it is important to note that the Pandits' whole way of life is pervaded by a sense of the pure and, consequently, by the fear of impurity. The source of this threat is seen to lie primarily in the manner in which a Pandit may be tempted to attend to the needs arising from his physical nature, from the fact of his being a *jīva.* Hence the obsessive emphasis on the questioning attitude, the exercise of doubt (*śankā*). The Pandit is a doubter because he is a believer. I have heard many Pandits say in good-humored self-depreciation that their undoing (in relation to the pursuit of pleasure, which is seen as the hallmark of the Muslim way of life) is doubt (*bhaṭṭa khyav śenki*). The Pandit is enjoined to exercise patience and restraint (*ced*), and to be ever prepared to resist the compulsion of bodily appetites until one is assured of their proper satisfaction as defined in *bhaṭṭil.* Thus it is *ced* that marks one out as a Pandit. This is an obligation and also the privilege of the human species (*manusya yoni*). Man is endowed with moral consciousness (*cit*), and he must cultivate it to resolve his doubts, or else he will lose it and become *jaḍa* (one lacking in the capacity for discrimination).

Their chequered history[13] has, however, taught the Pandits, that there are exceptional circumstances when the need for compromise arises and one is constrained to violate the dictates of *bhaṭṭil.* As is known (see Madan 1972), there are no Hindu service castes in rural Kashmir, and the Pandits are obliged to accept the help of Muslims—not only of butchers, cobblers, and cultivators but also of washermen, barbers, milkmen, and others. There is no solution to this problem, and the wisdom of folklore is invoked: *Yath na pūś tath na dūś* (Whereof one is helpless, thereof attaches no blame). The same is true of all unwitting breaches of proper conduct. Minor lapses, such as the unavoidability of physical contact with Muslims in certain situations, can be taken care of by the performance of routine corrective actions, such as washing one's hands. In more serious cases one could perform *prāyāscita* (ritual of atonement), though I have never witnessed one.

The questioning attitude (*śankā*), the exercise of restraint (*ced*), and the cultivation of the moral consciousness (*cit*), then, provide the framework within which a Pandit has to order his life. The pursuit of *dharma,* of *bhaṭṭil,* is not a call to an exercise in abstraction: it is in the everyday life of economic pursuits (*artha*) and bodily appetites (*kāma*) that *dharma* has to remain ascendant. It might be added here parenthetically that the Pandits themselves use these terms, though *dharma* is heard far more often in conversation than the other two words. In Dumont's terms, *dharma* must encompass *artha* and *kāma.*[14] This hierarchical balance can be achieved in the life of the householder (*gṛhastha*), which is the generally most highly valued identity of a human being in the Pandit scheme of life and values.

The Pandits' attitude to worldly concerns and rewards is one of joyful acceptance. They do not seek immediate release from them (*mokśa*) in the present life but try to accumulate merit for the future. Here and now they strive for health, wealth, and progeny, and pray for divine favor in the fulfilment of these wishes. When a man kneels with folded hands before a priest to have his forehead marked with red paste, the latter pronounces a blessing: "May you be long lived, may you be blessed with sons, may you be wealthy, may you be renowned, may you be wise, may you be greatly prosperous, may you be possessed with full faith in mercy and charity, may you be glorious, may you be one who lowers the pride of his enemies, may you be ingenious in trade, may you always be devoted to worshipping the feet of God, may you be doing good to all!"[15] Similarly, a married woman receives her blessing: "May you be blessed with money and sons, may you be devoted and faithful to your husband, may you always be dearly loved by your husband, may you be insightful, may you have correct understanding, may you live a hundred years!"[16]

The purposes of life are, then, well established in tradition. The emphasis is upon joy and plenitude within the framework of *dharma.* I have so far refrained from explicating the concept of *dharma,* apart from having suggested that it implies the obligation of moral conduct. The Pandits themselves refer to it broadly as the only way there is to lead one's life righteously. A righteous man is one whose thoughts and actions are pure: not only is his body pure but also his inner self. Hence the designation *dharmātmā,* pure in soul. More narrowly, *dharma* refers to a particular class of actions, namely those rituals and symbolic acts that fortify one's *zāt* and may indeed improve or mature it. The rituals are precisely known, being enshrined in texts. The symbolic acts are contingent and numerous: characteristic of them would be devotion to god and charity toward human beings. The pattern of such rituals and symbolic actions is differently described.

Bhaṭṭil: Traditional Procedures

The most comprehensive concept of action is that of *krama,* or ordered conduct. It consists of such general notions as customs and conventions (*rīti*), procedures (*vidhi*), and daily routine (*niyam* or *nityakarma*), and of specialized notions such as the technical acts (*kriyā*) that help one to awaken one's dormant power (*śakti*). A very important component of *krama* is the cycle of rituals (*saṁskāra*)—the so-called rites de passage—that must be performed in respect to each individual, in a prescribed sequence, beginning before birth and ending only after death. Thus there are the childhood rituals of purification (*kaha nethar,* performed on the eleventh day after birth), the first solid meal (*annaprāśana*), the first tonsure (*zarakāsai,* for boys only), piercing of earlobes (*cūdākarṇa,* nowadays for girls only), and the investiture of the boys with holy girdle (*mekhalā*) and the holy threat (*yagñyopavīta*).[17] Marriage (*nethar,* that which cannot be changed or undone) is the principal *saṁskāra* of adult life. The ultimate rite is that of cremation (*dahasaṁskāra*), which is followed by postmortuary rites. The general purpose of these rituals is to invest the person with the ritual status of a Brahman and to enlarge the repertoire of the roles that he or she may perform. It is what Marriott calls the maturing process. Marriage stands out as the most crucial ritual and social event in the life of every individual, enabling him or her to take on the highly valued role of a householder (*gṛhastha*).

Next to the *saṁskāra* it is the chores and rites of daily life properly performed, the *nityakarma,* that are the abiding concern of the Pandit and constitute his *bhaṭṭil.* These include the proper performance of ablutions (*śrocacār,* the purificatory process), the offering of water to the manes (*tarpan*), and prayers to gods and goddesses (*pūjāpāth*), the eating of proper food, the observance of anniversaries, the honest performance of one's work, and so on. As in the case of *saṁskāra,* the concern is with the protection and improvement of one's moral and physical well-being. The cycle of daily activities is seen in the context of transmigration: Does it add to the burden of the *karma* of previous lives or lighten it? The heavier the load of sins (*pāpa*), which alone would make the curses (*śāpa*) pronounced by others effective, the greater the chances of suffering as retribution. The Pandit view of life is a moralistic one, and whatever the immediate agency that brings about good fortune or misfortune, ultimately it is the inexorable law of *karma* that governs human life. One must not blame one's woes on god, for god does not discriminate and hand out joy to some and sorrow to others.

It is, therefore, imperative to follow the straight path of *dharma.* One can do nothing better about the present than mind the future, for it is the dialectic of the past *karma* and the present *krama* that determines one's fate. The content of one's *krama* is, therefore, of utmost importance. Partly predetermined, it also allows scope for choices made in the light of a cultivated moral consciousness (*cit*). Otherwise one remains tied to the wheel of *karma,* going round and round interminably, born again (*punarapi jananam*) to die again (*punarapi marnam*) to be conceived once again (*punarapi garbhanivāsam*). One attains release from one's sins only very gradually, through the performance of one's duties in full consciousness—*krama mukti*[18]—and in the attitude of submission to the divinity (*śaraṇa*), hopeful of grace (*anugraha*). Meanwhile, one should seek joy in the proper pursuit of the purposes of life. The words of a famous nineteenth-century poet, Parmananda, who belonged to the village of Mattan, about a dozen miles west of Uttrassu-Umanagri, have often been quoted (and sung) to me: *karma bhumikāi dizi dharmuk bal, santośa byāli bhavi ānanda phal* (Let the performance of *karma* be firmly grounded in *dharma,* sow the seed of contentment [*santośa*] and reap the harvest of joy [*ānanda*]).

ALTERNATIVES: BHAKTI

The inexorability of *karma* notwithstanding, the Pandits consider submission to divine protection as a value in itself. Filling one's self with the love of divinity (*lol barun,* love filling) is an act that is its own reward. Of course, if the divinity wills it, the devotee (*bhakta*) will be bestowed with the capacity for right thought and conduct and thus liberate him—that is, help him to liberate himself. (The expression used for liberation in the context is *moklāvun,* which would literally mean termination, the reference being to the termination of the cycle of birth, death, and rebirth.) Such is the nature of divine grace and blessing (*anugraha*). The Pandits say that the special characteristic of *kaliyuga* among the four eons of cosmic time is that a devotee does not have to engage in severe and long drawn-out austerities (*tapasyā*) to win divine favor. If the devotee's heart breaks from the pangs of separation from the divinity for just as long as a hailstone will stay on the tip of a bull's horn, divine grace will be assured. But such is the wickedness of human beings in the *kaliyuga* that only rarely is one so filled with divine love as to become a fit receptacle for divine favor, which is thus hard to obtain (*durlabha*). But one must not cease one's endeavor and prayer.

The longing for divine love and grace does not require one to abandon one's family and become a recluse. It simply so transforms and enlarges one's affections as to make them all partake of divine love. The devotee does not fall into the snare of rituals either, for love of god is an attitude of life. Rituals have their place in one's life, for they help to maintain *bhaṭṭil,* but rituals are only a means to the end. The devotee learns to be detached in the midst of involvement, concentrating on the one true attachment: that to the divinity. He knows himself to be alone (*keval*), though he has a family, and seeks union with the divinity (*kaivalya*). His attitude is one of utter humility and submission to god. In the course of my field work I have met a few people of whom others said that they were men of god and led pure lives though they were householders.

ALTERNATIVES: ŚAKTI AND SANNYĀSA

Kashmir has another celebrated tradition, that of pursuit of *śakti,* power through knowledge. According to popular belief the *veda* consists of a hundred thousand verses, of which eighty thousand deal with *karma* (ritual), sixteen thousand with *upāsaṇa* (devotion to the divinity), and the remaining four thousand with *bramhagyān* (knowledge of the godhead). This calculus is interesting in view of the light it throws on the relative emphasis on the three options available to a Pandit in the conduct of his life. Over the years I have met only one Pandit who described himself to me as a novitiate *śākta* (one in pursuit of *śakti*), but have been told of a few others, dead or alive, who were or are adepts. The *śākta* seeks, through *kriyā,* consisting of study, discussion, reflection, ritual, and *yoga,* the arousal of *śakti,* which resides in every human being but lies dormant, coiled like a somnolent snake (*kundalinī*). It can be aroused, however, and enable the seeker to realize his own divinity, his Śiva-hood. I have heard stories of the miraculous powers of the *śākta,* of how they can even control the processes of nature, such as seasons and earthquakes. I have also been told that the ordinary rules of *bhaṭṭil* do not bind a *śakta:* thus he may eat meat in places and on occasions when the ordinary Pandit dare not do so.

Now, my informant had been a householder, but his wife had died and his children were grown-up adults with families of their own. He maintained contact with them but claimed to feel no special attachments. He said that for the *śākta* there can be no personal family, but he may live in an exclusive household of his own, consisting of his family members. Preferably he may live with his preceptor (*guru*) and fellow seekers, and at a later stage have his own disciples (*śiśya*) minister to his needs. Thus, one of those may be adopted as a son so that funeral and postmortuary rites can be performed. The *śākta* is thus not exactly a man without a household, though he is different from ordinary householders.

I encountered no renouncers (*sannyāsī*), strictly defined, among the Pandits: such *sannyāsī* as one does encounter in Kashmir are non-Kashmiris. Some individuals, mostly men, may live away from home, but they do not go through formal initiation into any *sannyāsī* order. There is also no emphasis at all upon the termination of the *gṛhastāśrama* (the stage of the householder) in one's life. As one grows older, one is expected to become more and more god-centered, but no one is expected to live away from home. In this sense, renunciation is not merely postponed; its place in the life of the Pandit is denied. There are only two stages of life: that of the child who lives with his or her parents and that of the adult who has his or her children living with him or her. Both stages are stages in the life of the householder. The householder sustains the world.[19]

The attitude of the Pandits toward those who make claims of detachment, if not of renunciation, is generally one of skepticism. Individual men and women may command respect and even a following, but most of them are dismissed as charlatans. The general term of reference for such persons is *sād* (from the Sanskrit *sādhu*), and it is related to and rhymed with *bād,* or flatus (from the Persian word *ba'd* for air), in light-hearted banter. In a similar vein, an old saying warns the Pandit against the company of the renouncers, as they will make him give up his wife and never make him privy to their esoteric secrets.

In view of their almost total absence among them, why is it that the Pandits distrust and ridicule the self-styled renouncers? I do not think that the answer lies in the Pandits' having a higher standard by which to judge such claims; it lies rather in their commitment to the ideology of the householder. Apparently they are cynical about those who leave home because most such people have never had families of their own (either because they were unable to get married or because they became widowed before becoming fathers) or their relations with their kin have been unsatisfactory. At a deeper level one might detect a fear of the renouncer, for he poses a threat to the ideal of the householder. Unlike the former he not only seeks release from the web of kinship and other worldly ties but also denigrates those as a trap and an illusion. The renouncer is too powerful an adversary to be contemplated with equanimity. Individual renouncers are usually accorded respect in face-to-face encounters; they are fed and given alms. When talking about them, however, they are ridiculed and even reviled as their genuineness is generally doubted. The Pandits reduce the renouncer to a caricature of his ideal self. That the caricature is only too often an accurate enough portrait of the holy men one actually meets is another matter, and not totally irrelevant.

The pandit characterization of the four human types described above

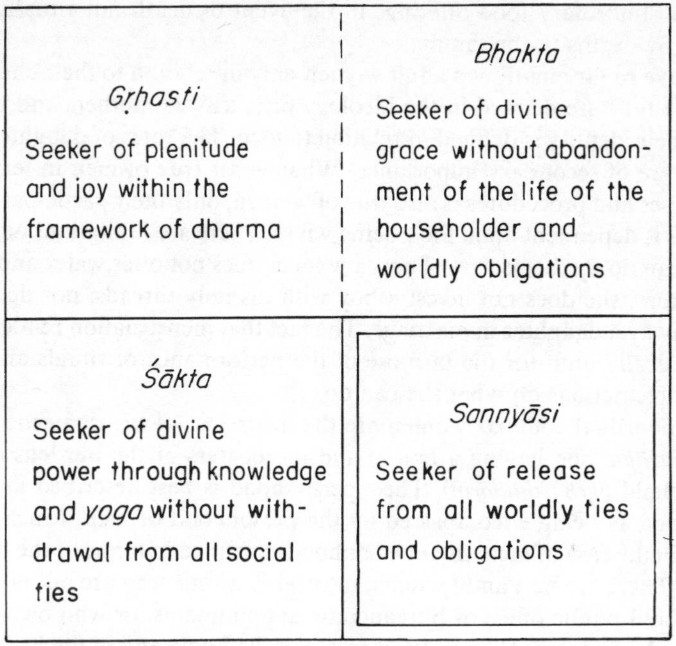
Gṛhasti
Seeker of plenitude and joy within the framework of dharma
Bhakta
Seeker of divine grace without abandonment of the life of the householder and worldly obligations
Śākta
Seeker of divine power through knowledge and *yoga* without withdrawal from all social ties
Sannyāsi
Seeker of release from all worldly ties and obligations

Fig. 4.1. *Pandit characterization of four human types.*

and their mutual relations, may be represented diagrammatically (see Figure 4.1). The householder and the renouncer are polar opposites; the devotee and the seeker of power through knowledge fill the intervening spaces. While the householder and the devotee are prominently present in the Pandits' consciousness, the other two types remain submerged, as it were, both as ideas and as empirical types. The broken line between the *gṛhastha* and the *bhakta* indicates the fluidity of the boundary between them: the roles may overlap. The *śākta* stands clearly demarcated from the *gṛhastha,* and so does (but much more emphatically, pointing to his virtual exclusion from the ideology of the Pandits), the *sannyāsī.*

The Place of Children and Women in the Ideology

In the context of *bhaṭṭil,* children take Pandit identity from birth, by the fact of birth. Their conduct is regulated under parental guidance till they are sufficiently grown up to become self-dependent. Many concessions are made, and lapses from proper conduct are condoned in respect of young children. But once a boy has been through his initiation (*mekhalā*) and a girl has been married, the full range of expectations and restraints of conduct that are a part of *bhaṭṭil* applies to them. Prior to these crucial events, boys and girls are yet without the status of ritual adults. This fact is dramatized in their being neither entitled to full funeral rites and postmortuary food offerings in the event of death nor ritually polluted by deaths in the family.

I have so far mentioned adult women only in relation to their children. In fact they are defined in the ideology primarily as mothers and wives, and their identity is defined in relation to men. The roles of daughter and sister are of secondary importance. Whatever is true of men in terms of purposes and procedures is also true of women; only their participation in rituals is dependent upon their being wives. There are limitations on what they can do by themselves. Thus, a woman does not offer water and food to manes; she does not invest a boy with his holy threads; nor does she give away a daughter in marriage. The fact that menstruation renders her periodically unfit for the purpose of the performance of rituals also imposes restrictions on what she can do.

In nonritual contexts women are the mistresses of the domestic scene (*gharavājin,* one having a home) and the bearers of the burdens of the household (*gṛhasthadārin*). Their personhood is best described and understood as being encompassed by the personhood of men. Much more than in the case of men, their personhood is defined in terms of the household. There are no Pandit women in rural Kashmir who are not married, who hold public office or bureaucratic appointments, or who own property independently of men. Women are of the home and in the home, the mothers and the wives.

Conclusion

I have tried to describe in this essay how the self-proclaimed abiding concern of the Pandits of rural Kashmir with their sociocultural identity turns out in effect to be a concern with the purposes of life and the appropriate procedures for their fulfilment. In other words, the Pandits define their personhood—that is, being a Pandit rather than a member of some other society—in terms of certain purposes and procedures. These are given in tradition and together constitute *bhaṭṭil,* or the Pandit way of life. *Bhaṭṭil* enables an individual to organize his life not only in relation to other Pandits but also non-Pandits and make sense of it.

Of the purposes of life the most crucial seems to be the concern with one's fate. One hopes eventually to obtain release from transmigration (*saṃsara*) by gradually accumulating merit through the performance of one's allotted tasks. These tasks, as the Pandits see them, are those of a householder. The home (*ghara*) is the place of one's abode, and family life (*gṛhastha*) is the normal and desired condition of life. As a householder, one legitimately may seek plenitude and joy, but only if these are informed by *dharma,* or the code of moral conduct. One seeks salvation through the affirmation of the obligations of family life and other wider worldly ties. The Pandit is a man in the world and not a renouncer. Willful submission to divine grace and a steadfast recognition of the bondage of transmigration teach one to look at domestic and otherworldly involvements in the proper perspective and not to run away from them. The life of a householder is a good and moral life so long as it is not divorced from *dharma*.

The emphasis on *dharma*, then, turns out to be a concern with procedures. Purposes are in a fundamental sense given, and the scope for the exercise of choice is severely restricted. In respect of procedures, however, there is a considerable scope for choicemaking. The choices that one makes determine one's future and are therefore of the very greatest significance.

An individual's sociocultural identity of himself as a Pandit is gained and sustained by being so categorized in the speech of others, Pandits and non-Pandits. Pandit-hood is invoked regularly in everyday life by oneself and by others as reminder and exhortation, as support and justification, or as disapproval and condemnation, respectively, of certain actions that one ought to perform, that one performs, or that one should not perform. One discloses oneself in one's actions. One is, therefore, expected to do all that, and nothing contrary to it, which one's name indicates: one is that as which one is addressed: a Bhaṭṭa. And the most characteristic Bhaṭṭa, ideologically and empirically, is a householder.

5

Hierarchy and the Concept of the Person in Western India[1]

Anthony T. Carter

So God created man in his own image, in the image of God
created he him; male and female created he them.

(Genesis 1:27)

When they divided the Man,
  into how many parts did they divide him?
What was his mouth, what were his arms,
  what were his thighs and his feet called?

The *brāhmaṇ* was his mouth,
  of his arms was made the warrior,
his thighs became the *vaisya,*
  of his feet the *sūdra* was born.

(from the "Hymn of the Primeval Man,"
Rg Veda X: 21, translated by
A. L. Basham 1963:243)

AS MAUSS HAS OBSERVED, the attributes and capacities that form the person and the signs by which persons may be known are created and imposed upon suitable objects by society. "La personalitié, l'âme, viennent avec le nom, de la société" (Mauss 1969:132; see also Dumont 1970:4–8 on the "sociological apperception," and Geertz 1966). The attributes, capacities, and signs of personhood may be imposed, of course, upon particular human actors, but they also may be imposed upon collectivities of human actors, as in the case of registered corporations or descent groups, or upon nonhuman entities, such as, among the Tallensi, the crocodiles that live in pools sacred to particular clans (Fortes 1973:285–286). In other cases personhood may be denied to particular human actors in whole or in part. Thus in the antebellum South slaves were denied personhood to the extent that they were regarded as chattel that might be owned by and subjected to the will of others but were granted personhood to the extent that they were held accountable for and might be tried and punished for their crimes (see Genovese 1972:25–49). Among the Tallensi, again, "no one can be certainly known to have been a full human person until he is shown, at the time of his death, to have been slain by his ancestors and therefore to deserve a proper funeral" (Fortes 1973:293). One who dies abnormally—by drowning, smallpox, or suicide—or who divination shows to have been killed by some agency other than the ancestors is said not to have achieved full or proper personhood and may be buried outside the community, away from the ancestral shrines, as if he had never been a person.

Conversely, it is by means of the attributes, capacities, and signs of culturally defined personhood that the particular human actor experiences himself as, and demonstrates to others that he is, the person he is supposed to be. "For it is surely only by appropriating to himself his socially given personhood that he can exercise the qualities, the rights, the duties and the capacities that are distinctive to it" (Fortes 1973:311). This aspect of personhood has been explored usefully in the Western context by such writers as Goffman (1959, 1961, 1963, 1967), Laing (1961), and Bateson (1971; see also Bateson et al. 1956), but an observation by the novelist Ralph Ellison is especially apposite. "Our names, being the gift of others, must be made our own. Once while listening to the play of a two-year-old who did not know she was under observation, I heard her saying over and over again, at first with questioning and then with sounds of growing satisfaction, 'I am Mimi Livisay? . . . *I* am Mimi Livisay. I *am* Mimi Livisay . . . I am *Mimi* Li-vi-say! I am Mimi . . .' " (Ellison 1966:151).

If personhood is imposed or made available by society, if it is a Durkheimian sociological fact and not a biological one, then we may usefully distinguish between particular actors and concepts of personhood. And more to the point, we may ask if different kinds of sociocultural systems regularly posit different kinds of personhood. This latter question is particularly interesting when explored in the context of a comparison between Indian and Euro-American sociocultural systems, for, as Dumont has shown in a series of seminal publications (1960, 1961, 1965a, 1965b, 1970, 1971, 1977), these two systems are in many important respects the mirror image of each other. In the Euro-American case the person is conceived of as an individual, ontologically prior to any collectivity and containing within himself all of the attributes of humanity. Conversely, in this "individualistic universe" society as a whole is regarded as *"in principle* two things at once: a *collection of individuals* and a *collective individual"* (Dumont 1971:33). In the contrasting Indian case the social whole, informed by the hierarchical opposition of pure and impure, is ontologically prior to any empirical actor. In this holistic universe particular human beings are regarded as possessing different and unequal attributes of humanity and are not associated with any normative principle.

Insightful as it is, however, this contrast between the Indian and Euro-American systems is incomplete. If in the Indian case we have a system that stresses a principle of holism and in the Euro-American case one that stresses a conception of the person, we still have to explore the conception of the whole in the individualistic universe as well as the conception of the person in the holistic universe. Dumont himself has suggested that individualism is confined largely to politicoeconomic institutions and that elements of holism remain elsewhere in the Euro-American system even if unstressed (1965a:55–61, 1965b:86). It remains to examine the nature of personhood in the Indian hierarchical or holistic universe.

McKim Marriott and his colleagues at the University of Chicago have begun to approach this problem with their conception of "dividuality." According to this view the particular human actor, or dividual, is a transmitter and manipulator of blood or blood purity and associated codes for conduct which together situate him as castemate and kinsman. But in South Asian as opposed to American culture, it is argued, code is inherent in and inseparable from substance and also is optative and subject to modification by action (Marriott and Inden 1976:7–9). Furthermore, dividuals are inescapably bound up in a system of transactions. "To exist, dividual persons [actors] absorb heterogeneous material influences. They must also give out from themselves particles of their own coded substances—essences, residues, or other active influences—that may then reproduce in others something of the nature of the persons [actors] in whom they originated" (Marriott 1976a:111). Finally, in this view transactions between dividual actors are at the same time transformations within such actors, while transformations of the actor are simultaneously transactions within the actor (Marriott 1976a:111–112; see also Marriott 1976b). As Barnett, writing from a somewhat different position, put it: "A person's [actor's] action must regulate the flow of material of higher and lower purity through his body (itself changing as a result of this flow) so that he can remain a KV. This suggests a KV view of substance fundamentally different from our own. Rather than substance being primary and separable from particular codes for conduct, the substance of KV blood purity *enjoins* a specific code for conduct. For KVs, there can be no relations of substance alone or of code alone" (1976:144–145).[2]

This line of investigation promises to be very interesting, but rather than being an analysis of the South Asian concept of the person it seems to me to be an account of a biological or psychobiological theory of empirical actors. A similar qualification applies to the analysis of "The Cultural Construct of the Person in Bengal and Tamilnadu" by Fruzzetti, Östör, and Barnett (1976; see also Barnett 1976, and Fruzzetti and Östör 1976). Concerned primarily with indigenous notions of conception and of the relations between natural substance and code for conduct, this analysis too is more nearly a psychobiological theory of actors than an analysis of personhood. Both of these accounts diverge in several ways from the view of personhood per se that is current in western Maharashtra. These theories do not differentiate among human beings nor between human beings and other living things, including animals and gods. As Marriott and Inden put it: "The organization of South Asian society is premised on the ancient and continuing cultural assumption that all living beings are differentiated into genera, or classes, each of which is thought to possess a defining coded substance. One of the commonest words for genus is most Indian languages, *jāti,* is derived from an Indo-European verbal root meaning 'genesis,' 'origin,' or 'birth.' It is applied to any species of living things, including gods and humans" (1978:983). The concept of personhood is much narrower than the category of living things, even if related to it, for in Maharashtra, at least, personhood is denied to all nonhuman living things and also to some human beings.

We should be forewarned, as well, that Dumont's own view of my problem might well be that it is no problem at all, that it is empty. His position seems to be that there can only be theories of actors in the Hindu context. Thus, while noting the exceptional position of the renouncer, Dumont argues that "for the traditional Hindu mind . . . the particular being acquires a reality only by epitomizing [through transmigration] in succession the sum of particularities found in the world; a chain of existences is the equivalent of a single, individual, existence in the West" (1965b:91). Or more generally, "from the point of view of the caste system *as a whole* (as opposed to one particular aspect, say the perpetuation of the groups), the smallest ontological unit (or normative agent) is that in which order (or hierarchy) is still present, i.e. a pair of higher and lower empirical agents, complementary to each other in a particular situation" (Dumont 1965b:91). Dumont's views on this question merit serious consideration, but at this point it may be noted only that there is at the very least a prima facie case for proceeding with an investigation of personhood in the Indian context. For just as I have been told that some human actors are not persons, so I have been told that others most certainly are.

Actor and Person in Maharashtra

In Marathi two overlapping sets of terms are used to speak of the person. When speaking of the person in the abstract one is likely to use *vyakti,* although *manus* might be used in more informal speech. The latter, however, also has the sense of human being or man, that is, a class of actors or agents who may or may not be persons. Though somewhat formal, *vyakti* is not an artificial word, used only for the benefit of the ethnographer by sophisticated persons with a great deal of education. In contexts unconnected with a discussion of personhood I have heard the term used in the following ways. A boarder, male or female, is *ekac vyakti* (one person) living alone in lodgings, while one's family of procreation as opposed to the wider extended family is one's *vyaktic kutumb* (personal family). In a discussion of genealogies and blood relationships one might hear, *"eka vyaktila don mulge ahet"* (Suppose there was a person with two sons) or in a discussion of village politics, *"vyakti titkya prakuti"* (There are as many dispositions as there are persons, or roughly, "Many men, many minds"). More to the point, one may say of a deceased infant, *"to khara vyakti nahoto"* (He was not really a person).

When asking about particular persons one is likely to choose from a series of terms, overlapping with the first, the elements of which show different degrees of respect and formality. Thus of a man one might ask, *"tya grhastha kon ahet?"* (Who is that householder? or, Who is that gentleman?) or, *"to manus kon ahe?"* (Who is that man?). Of a woman one might ask, depending upon respect, *"tya bai kon ahet?"* or, *"ti bai kon ahe?"* both having the sense, "Who is that woman?"

In order to qualify as a person (*vyakti*) one must be a living creature (*jiv*). The treatment accorded an image (*murti*) in worship resembles that accorded a person, both in its annual and in its daily routines, but an image remains a symbol or representation (*pratikay*), not a person, for an image is not a living creature. While an image is established (*esthapana karne*), a living creature is born (*janma dene*). But although to be born a living creature is a necessary condition for personhood, it is not a sufficient condition. Animals (*prani*), though born living creatures and linked to human beings by the cycle of death and birth (*karma*), never achieve personhood. Furthermore, some human beings (*manus*) fail to achieve, or having achieved, transcend or forfeit personhood.

These underlying criteria of personhood rest upon features of the Hindu cosmology, including the nature of living creatures, the nature of action, and the laws of *karma.* In the Hindu cosmology a living creature (*jiv*) is composed of a body (*sheri*) and a soul (*atma*). Most of the informants with whom I have discussed this matter go further and distinguish two aspects of the body: the *sthuladeha,* or gross, material body, and the *lingadeha,* or subtle, ethereal body. According to this view the subtle body is the seat or vehicle of the *atma* and an aspect of the particular or individual essence that survives through death from birth to birth. It is only the material body that is burnt at cremation.

All of the manifested or created matter in the universe, including the bodies of living creatures, is alike in sharing or being determined by a mixture of three *gun* (qualities or strands): *satvagun* (truth), *rajagun* (passion), and *tamagun* (darkness). The bodies of living creatures differ not in being based upon different qualities but rather in being based upon different balances among the same qualities. Thus, in human beings the *satva-* and *rajaguns* are dominant, while in animals the *raja-* and *tamaguns* and in plants *tamagun* are dominant (see also Davis 1976:10). As a result, of all the living things only human beings are capable of making moral judgments. As a Brahmin informant explained it to me, using an example that makes clear the range of matters included in the term *moral:* "The capacity for judgement (*vichar*) is a distinguishing attribute (*vi-*

shesh) of human understanding (*buddhi*). Animals (*janavar*) do not have the power to judge. If there is filth in the road an animal will not exercise judgement in going along. But a human being would be careful not to place its feet in such filth . . . The one whose intellect (*buddhi*) does not include the power of discrimination (*vivek*), that one is termed an animal (*prani*). The one whose intellect does include the power of discrimination, that one is termed a man."[3] The various forms of manifested matter also are united by the doctrine of *karma.* A single soul, in successive births and according to the fruits of its actions, may be reborn as or embodied in any or all of them.

The Hindu notions of the body and the soul differ from Euro-American notions in more than the positing of a subtle body (*lingadeha*) which persists after death from birth to birth. In addition, important functions, especially mental functions, are differently distributed over the two major components of the living creature in the two traditions. To the *lingadeha,* not the *atma,* are ascribed agency, intelligence, consciousness, and sentience: "Hence the innate intelligence of the newborn animal to seek the breast and to cling to its parents" (Molesworth and Candy 1857:719).

A human being, like other living creatures, obtains its body (*deha*) as a result of an act of conception by its parents, followed by subsequent sex acts and by nursing, from which the child receives various forms of parental blood: semen, uterine blood, and breast milk. In order for the union of parental blood to be accomplished or to endure, however, and for a viable fetus to be formed, there must be present, as a result of its own *karma,* an *atma* with its *lingadeha.*[4] The blood that one receives from one's father in the form of semen contributes to one's bones and to the "hard" parts of one's body generally and links one to a series of male agnates, deceased, living, and not yet born. From one's mother's blood in the form of uterine blood and breast milk one receives the "soft" parts of one's body and the active part of one's being and is linked to a network of nonagnatic, matrilateral relatives. Very importantly, blood may be altered by a variety of actions, especially the sacrament (*saṅskar*) of marriage. Thus in some contexts it is said that upon marriage a woman ceases to be a blood relative (*raktaca natevaik*) of her brother and father and becomes a blood relative of her husband.[5]

Although different Hindu texts approach the problem in different ways, they agree in assuming that action and the consequences of action are an inherent property of matter rather than dependent upon a vivifying soul. As the *Bhagavad Gita* puts it at one point,

> O great-armed one, these five
> Factors learn from Me,
> Which are declared in the reason-method doctrine
> For the effective performance of all actions.

The (material) basis, the agent, too,
  And the instruments of various sorts,
And the various motions of several kinds,
  And just Fate as the fifth of them.

With body, speech, or mind, whatever
  Action a man undertakes,
Whether it be lawful or the reverse,
  These are its five factors.

This being so, as agent herein
  Whoso however the self alone
Regards, because his intelligence is imperfect,
  He does not see (truly), the fool.

Whose state (of mind) is not egoized,
  Whose intelligence is not stained,
He, even tho he slays these folk,
  Does not slay, and is not bound (by his actions).
(XVIII:13–17; Edgerton 1972:84)

In his commentary on this passage Jnanadev, the famous thirteenth-century poet-saint of Maharashtra, identifies the second factor in this analysis, the agent, with the soul and observes,

> The second cause of action is to be known as the doer, the reflection of consciousness,
>
> When the water from the sky falls upon the earth it forms pools and reflected in them the sky seems to have the shape of a pool.
>
> In a deep sleep a king forgets his kingship and dreams that he is a beggar.
>
> So also consciousness, forgetting its own true nature, identifies itself with the body and takes on that form.
>
> In this sense the universal consciousness is called the individual self; and this self promises to remain attached to the body in every respect.
>
> It is matter that performs actions, but owing to delusion the individual self claims the credit for them; for this reason he is called the doer.
>
> (*Jnaneshvari* XVIII:319–324; Pradhan and Lambert 1969:252–253)

Thus action is inevitable and unavoidable or as the *Gita* puts it again,

For no one even for a moment
  Remains at all without performing actions;

For he is made to perform action willy-nilly,
Every one is, by the Strands that spring from material nature.
(III:5; Edgerton 1972:18)

And the soul becomes implicated in action, reaping its inevitable fruits in the form of *karma,* only by its attitude to action, not by any agency of its own. The one who is deluded by the mental faculties of the body and whose soul, imagining that it acts, becomes attached to the fruits of action, whether good or evil, is bound to the endless cycle of rebirth.

But who takes delight in the self alone,
The man who finds contentment in the self,
And satisfaction only in the self,
For him there is found (in effect) no action to perform.
(*Bhagavad Gita* III:17; Edgerton 1972:19)

Or again,

Who this My doctrine constantly
Follow, such men,
Full of faith and not murmuring,
They too are freed from (the effect of) actions.
(*Bhagavad Gita* III:31; Edgerton 1972:21)

A surprising number of lay persons, in remote villages as well as centers such as Poona or Alandi, are aware of these classical texts, but it is more usual to hear the problem of action and its consequences discussed in terms of *ichchha,* or wishes. Thus, a fetus is believed to develop a heart about the fourth month and to start desiring things. This causes a pregnant woman to have cravings (*dohale*), and birthmarks and congenital defects may result from neglect of these longings. Inherent in the subtle body (*lingadeha*) as well as the gross body (*sthuladeha*), these wishes persist after death, and it is for this reason that deceased ancestors (*pitar*) are given offerings at annual memorial services (*shraddha* and *mahal*). The soul, unfortunately, becomes attached to these wishes in the great majority of cases, and it is for this reason that the quality of one's wishes at death has such an important effect upon the subsequent rebirth. Those whose wishes are evil or simply unfulfilled may become demonic beings such as *bhuts* and *pretas.*

What begins to stand out in all of this is that the particular soul is immortal, proceeding from birth to birth in accord with its accumulated *karma.* The state of an embodied soul's *karma* may be assessed by an astrologer. The soul's horoscope is cast only once with each human embodiment not long after birth and in terms of the date and hour of birth, but it may be read more than once. The initial position of the planets indicates the *karma* with which the embodied soul was born, while subsequent readings may indicate changes in *karma* during the course of a lifetime. In Sri Lanka similar developments may be assessed by palmistry (Kemper 1979), but I do not know if this can be done in Maharashtra.

An unsophisticated view of the doctrine of the reincarnation of the soul according to *karma* is contained in a folk tale *(hakikat)* that was told me in explanation of the women's fast on Rushpanchmi.

> There once was a married woman who neglected to sit outside the house during her monthly menstrual period. As a result of this sin (*pap*) the woman was reborn as a dog (*kutrichya janmala geli,* literally "went to a dog's birth"), and her husband was reborn as a bullock. Their son performed their annual memorial service (*mahal ghatla*). He prepared a great deal of sweet rice (*khir*) to feed his guests at this function, but unknown to him a snake vomited its poisonous saliva into the food. The dog, formerly the mother, saw what happened and, realizing that the people would die if they ate the poisoned food, ate it herself. Seeing the dog eating the food and ignorant of the reason, the son's wife beat the animal and drove it away. That night the dog was moaning in the bullock's pen, and then the two of them acquired speech. The bullock explained to the dog that they had come to these births as a result of her own sin. Now women fast on Rushpanchmi so that if by mistake a little of their own menstrual discharge falls in the house, they will not obtain such births themselves.

I have gone into all this at some length, while avoiding as much as possible dogmatic simplifications of metaphysical subtleties, in order that I may be in a position to make a crucial point, namely that the notion of personhood is quite distinct from that of the self or soul. In the *pravachanas,* or religious addresses, which are popular all over Maharashtra, the speaker not infrequently advises his listeners, as Krishna advised Arjuna in the *Bhagavad Gita,* to ask themselves, "Who am I?" (*mi kon ahe*). An appropriate answer to this question is *mi parmeshvar svarup ahe* (I am a manifestation of god). One's essential self resides not in one's personhood but in one's unique or individual soul or ego, one's *atma.* But if one's soul is a major aspect of one's personhood, it is not the whole of it. Though a soul possesses continuity from birth to birth, its successive embodiments may qualify as persons only if they are human beings and are not the same person even then. Nor do disembodied souls—and such do exist in a variety of forms—ever qualify as persons. This distinction between personhood and soul, clearly reflected in the language, cannot be emphasized too much, for to miss it may lead to comparisons of quite disparate phenomena, perhaps missing the Indian concept of the person altogether in the process. It is inappropriate, then, to compare the Euro-American notion of personhood, individualism, either with the Indian notion of the soul or ego (see Biardeau 1965) or with the Indian renouncer (see Dumont 1965b), for the former is only a component of personhood while the latter, as wel shall see, has left his personhood behind.

Rites of Passage and the Distribution of Personhood

Not surprisingly, informants who are asked straight out, "What does *person* mean?" (*vyakti mhanje kay*) generally are unable to give the inquiring anthropologist much help. There exists, nevertheless, a series of customary procedures that may be regarded as diagnostics of personhood in a manner paralleling divination and funerals among the Tallensi. These are the *sańskar,* or sacraments, which complete, alter, improve, or mark the termination of personhood. The primary meaning of the term has to do with these rites de passage (Gennep 1960), but it also refers to the operations involved in preparing cooked food (Molesworth and Candy 1857:836). Just as the aim of cooking is to render edible foodstuffs into cultural products, "so that it is both auspicious (*shubha*) and pure for the people who handle it and for those who consume it" (Khare 1976:44), so the aim of sacraments is to confer upon human beings the cultural qualities of personhood.

In Western Maharashtra there are said to be sixteen *sańskar.* No one in my experience either regularly performs or imagines that anyone else regularly performs the full series of sixteen rites. The *sańskar* that are performed are not carried out in the manner prescribed by the *shastras,* nor are they referred to by their Sanskrit names, Marathi terms being used instead. Nevertheless, a wide range of informants is aware of the full sequence and of its implications, particularly of the manner in which the sequence is applied to different categories of human actors. It is by attending to this aspect of the classical series of sixteen *sańskar* that we may obtain an initial understanding of the Maharashtrian conception of personhood.

The list of *sańskar* in Molesworth and Candy's Marathi dictionary (1857:836) closely corresponds to those produced, often with gaps, hesitation, and/or the help of ritual handbooks, by several of my informants (see also Pandey 1949; Chatterjee 1965; Kane 1941:188–549 and 1953:179–333):

1. *garbhadhana,* a rite performed at or before conception to help ensure that male offspring are produced
2. *puńsavana,* to help ensure the vitality of the fetus
3. *anavlibhana* and
4. *vishnubil,* additional rites during pregnancy
5. *simatonnayana,* to ensure easy delivery
6. *jatkarma,* rite performed at parturition, including preparation of a horoscope

7. *namakarma,* the naming ceremony performed twelve days after birth or later
8. *nishkramana* and
9. *suryavalokana,* the first outings of the child when it is presented to the moon and then to the sun
10. *annaprashana,* a rite to mark when the child is first fed rice, at about eight months or when the child has cut its first teeth
11. *caul,* the child's first hair cutting, at the end of its first year
12. *upanayana,* investiture with the sacred head (*yajnopavita*), fastening of the girdle (*munja*), and initiation into the status of *brahmacarin* (student) in the fifth, eighth, or sixteenth year, depending on *varna*
13. *mahanamya,* instruction in the Vedas
14. *samavarttan,* loosening the girdle (*munja*) and initiation into the status of *snataka*
15. *vivaha,* marriage and initiation into the status of *grhastha* (householder)
16. *svargarohana* or *antyeshti,* funeral obsequies.

It will be noticed that this list of *saṅskar* differs from that in Inden and Nicholas's account of Bengali kinship (1977:35–66). The differences are of two kinds. The Maharashtrian series contains major ceremonies that are not included in the Bengali series, most notably *antyeshti.* In addition the Maharashtrian series differs from the Bengali in treating *garbhadhana* as a rite directed at the fetus rather than at its mother or parents and hence in beginning the series with *garbhadhana* rather than *vivaha* (marriage).

The incidence of *saṅskar* may serve as a diagnostic of personhood in a variety of ways. Most broadly, eligibility for *saṅskar* is different for men and for women and also for the four *varna:* Brahmin, Kshatriya, Vaishya, and Shudra. Shudras, as is well known, are ineligible for Vedic instruction and the *saṅskar* concerned with instruction—*upanayana, mahanamya,* and *samavarttan*—are not performed for them. They are not twice-born (*dvija*), for they are not reborn through initiation. The full series of *saṅskar* may be performed directly only for men of the first three, twice-born *varnas.* Initiation (*upanayana*) and the other *saṅskar* concerned with Vedic instruction, as also *caul,* the first hair cutting, are not performed for twice-born women, at least not directly. Kane (1941:293–296) and my informants agree that the all-important *upanayana* is not performed directly for women, but although I can find no textual support for it, there is a suggestion that it is performed indirectly for women as part of marriage. Thus, in Maharashtra a groom with pretensions to twice-born status puts on, during the marriage ceremonies and on behalf of his wife, a second sacred thread (see also Stevenson 1920:32, and Kane 1941:413).

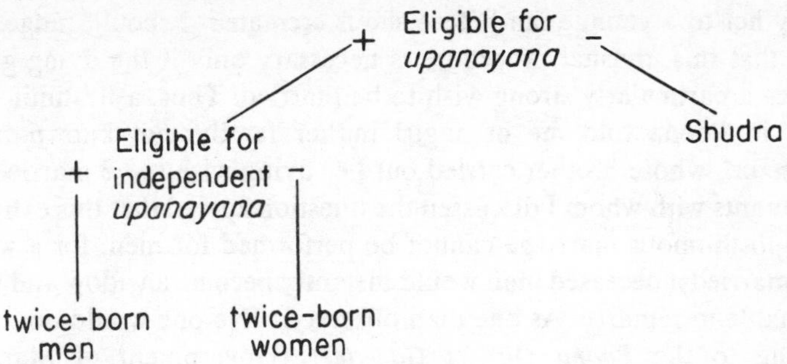

Fig. 5.1. Classes of persons discriminated on the basis of eligibility for upanayana.

These discriminations among *varna* and between males and females are summarized in Figure 5.1.

In addition the performance of *sanskar* in a variety of anomalous circumstances permits one to distinguish between what might be called incipient and full personhood on the one hand and between full personhood and forfeited or transcended personhood on the other. In brief, the achievement of full personhood and its proper termination are marked by funeral obsequies centering upon cremation.

To begin with, in practice as well as in theory very small children are buried (*jamini madhe purne*), while older persons are cremated (*titi var jhalne*). The most commonly given point for the switch from burial to cremation is the appearance of the first teeth. A child who dies within its first year, however, is likely to be unnamed, as there is a tendency to delay *namakarma* or *barsa,* as the naming *sanskar* is called in Marathi, for children who are unwell. Death pollution (*sutak*) is not observed by relatives of a small child, and it is regarded as not really a person (*vyakti*). Rather it is a *mul,* or child, not in the sense of the offspring of a parent but in that of nonadult (see Molesworth and Candy 1857:660). A human being does not really become a person, some informants explain, until after he or she is married.[6]

The procedures that may be followed in the case of human beings who survive the first several years of life but die before they are married are different for men and women. In general it is felt that such a human being is incomplete or unfinished. He or she is likely to have unfulfilled wishes (*ichchha*) that will prevent the soul from obtaining release (*moksha*) from the vicinity of the cremation ground and hence render it unable to obtain a suitable rebirth. There is fairly widespread awareness of these procedures, and some say that they have been employed in their family, but I have no direct knowledge of their use.

In the case of a girl who dies unmarried, it is said to be possible to marry her to a young man before she is cremated. I should judge, however, that this unusual procedure is necessary only if the dying girl expresses a particularly strong wish to be married. Thus, a Brahmin informant in Poona told me of a girl in her family, not known by my informant, whose brother carried out her dying wish to be married. The informants with whom I discussed the question agreed that this extraordinary posthumous marriage cannot be performed for men, for a woman who married a deceased man would instantly become a widow and would be unable to remarry. As one man observed, "No one would do it." According to the *Poona District Gazetteer* (Government of Marashtra 1961:117), however, if a male dies while still a *brahmacari, samavarttan* may be performed upon the corpse followed by *arkavivaha,* marriage to a twig of the milkweed plant (*rui*), and full funeral obsequies at the cremation ground.

In any case my informants were agreed on the necessity of completing the full series of educational *sańskar, upanayana* through *samavarttan,* as a prerequisite for full funeral obsequies with cremation (*antyeshti*). If a man dies while still in the status of *snataka,* that is, after the performance of *samavarttan* but before *vivaha,* then his cremation may be performed without further ado. If, however, he dies while still, or even not yet, a *brahmacarin* it is thought appropriate to perform *samavarttan* posthumously before cremation. For this purpose a small stone is obtained and the unperformed *sańskar* up to and including *samavarttan* are performed upon that. The stone is called *ashma* and is the same as that used in the latter stages of the funeral rites, ten days after cremation, when offerings are made to the deceased. It represents, or is a sign of (*kun*), the deceased's *atma.*

All of this applies to ordinary people. People who are out of the ordinary in various ways are treated, in principle at least, differently. Some kinds of deviant actions are said to be punished by forfeiture of personhood, temporary or permanent, although it must be added that much of my evidence here is historical and concerns practices that would not be allowed in the present day. Those guilty of very severe offenses might be sentenced to death in a way that denies that they ever were persons. In pre-British times the murderers of Narayanrao Peshwa (1755–1773) as well as some intercaste adulterers were put to death by being trampled by elephants (Telang 1961:150–151). What seems to be significant about this form of punishment is that it precluded the performance of the usual funeral obsequies. The deceased was doomed to perpetual torment as a malevolent ghost, and his relatives were forbidden to observe death pollution (*sutak*). Other offenders, while not being killed, may have their personhood stripped from them. Steele (1868:32) reports that a woman who is guilty of adultery with a man of lower caste, of the attempted murder of her husband, or of procuring an abortion may be divorced and outcasted (the same word, *ghatasphot,* applies to both aspects of the punishment). The woman is banished, and her funeral rites are performed by burning an effigy made of *darabh* grass. Death pollution is observed for the banished woman.

There are others who are out of the ordinary in a positive way who also are not given the usual funeral obsequies. These latter actors have not forfeited personhood, but somehow have shown themselves to have transcended it, to be more than ordinary persons. All of these actors are renouncers; some, but not all, are *sannyasins.* A man, but not a woman, may become a *sannyasin* by performing his own funeral obsequies. After this he ceases to be a person in the ordinary sense. His relatives do not observe death pollution for him, nor does he observe death pollution for them. Most significantly he may accept cooked food from a wide variety of others, including persons whose caste is lower than that of his own origin. When he dies, his remains are buried rather than cremated.[7]

In and around Alandi, a pilgrimage center ten miles north of Poona on the right bank of the Indryani, have lived a number of renouncers. The most famous was the thirteenth-century poet-saint Jnanadev. The son of Vitthalpant, a Brahmin who was outcasted for returning, on the instructions of his preceptor, to the life of a householder (*grhastha*) after being initiated as a *sannyasin,* Jnanadev is revered all over Maharashtra as the author of the *Jnaneshvari,* a Marathi commentary on the *Bhagavad Gita,* and as a founder of the Varkari Sampradaya, the fellowship of saints devoted to the worship of Vithoba through *bhakti* (love).[8] Jnanadev and at least one other well-known Alandi renouncer, the nineteenth-century *sannyasin* Narasinha Sarasvati, ended their lives in an extraordinary manner by taking living (*jivant* or *sañjivan*) *samadhi* (release). Now illegal, this apparently consists of having oneself shut up in a vault. What is believed to happen then is not perfectly clear, but it is clear that such people receive no further funeral obsequies, none at all if they were not *sannyasins.* Some people believe that Jnanadev's material body remains quite unchanged, still in a meditating posture, in the vault in which he took leave of it. Among their devotees, the taking of living *samadhi* by renouncers is accepted as convincing proof that the actor concerned was more than a person. They are regarded as persons and as *avatars* (incarnations) of god at the same time. Thus Jnaneshvar is said to be an *avatar* of Vishnu, while Swami Narasinha Sarasvati is said to be an *avatar* of Datta. The *samadhi* of each is now the site of a large temple in Alandi.

Some fifteen miles northwest of Alandi, Dehu, lived another of the poet-saints of Maharashtra, Tukaram (1598–1650). A renouncer in the tradition of the Varkari Sampradaya, but no *sannyasin,* Tukaram was a Kunbi shopkeeper with two unsympathetic wives. He is said to have been carried to the paradise of Vishnu, with his body, in a miraculous *viman* (airplane). Thus Tukaram received no funeral rites, nor is he anywhere memorialized by a *samadhi* (monument). Although not himself an *avatar,* he is believed to have achieved *moksha* (release) through his spiritual devotions and to be residing permanently in heaven.

In Maharashtra, then, personhood is not inherent in the constitution of particular human actors, nor is it equivalent to any partial aspect of their nature as actors, for example, their unique or individual souls. Rather, personhood is something that may be achieved by qualified human actors and conferred upon them by the performance of *sanskars.* Members of the twice-born *varnas* are qualified to achieve a fuller or more complete personhood than Shudras, while men may become fully persons than women, but actors of either sex and of all *varnas* are incomplete persons as long as they are unmarried (see Inden and Nicholas 1977:45–46). To achieve full personhood one must be married and, in the case of a man, a *grhastha* (householder), or in the case of a woman, a *suvasni* or *grhini* (female householder). Moreover, personhood is terminated, even for actors who are still biologically alive, by the performance of funeral obsequies.

Personhood and *Sansar*

Further insight into the nature of conferred personhood in Maharashtra may be obtained by attending to the content of *sanskars* as well as their distribution. The sequence of *sanskar* that is actually performed in Maharashtra differs from the sequence prescribed in classical texts in a number of respects. The Marathi names of several of the ceremonies are different from the Sanskrit names. Some of the classical *sanskar* are omitted altogether, while others, particularly the three educational *sanskar* may be combined in a single performance so that the full contemporary sequence, although variable, is always shorter than the classical sequence. The contents of the parallel contemporary and textual rights also differ quite considerably.

Here I will concentrate on those rites that mark the achievement and the termination of full personhood, but first I should make a few observations concerning the lesser preceding rites. Rites at birth in Maharashtra are minimal. Few parents obtain horoscopes for their children, and those who do so require an informal consultation with a qualified Brahmin priest rather than a formal ceremony for the purpose. The major rites for an unborn or young child include *dohala,* when the cravings of the mother, originating in the wishes (*ichchha*) of the fetus, are indulged; *barsa,* the naming ceremony; and *javal,* the first hair cutting for boys. In these ceremonies the pregnancy of the mother and the legitimacy of the child is acknowledged and certain aspects of the child's personal identity are discovered or conferred. Thus, at *dohala* the mother is asked to choose blindfolded between two kinds of sweets. If the wishes of the fetus impel her to choose *barphi* it is discovered that the fetus is male, while if she chooses *peda* it is known that the fetus is female. Again, the child's *karma* may be discovered by preparing its horoscope. At *barsa* the child is named and its ears are pierced in a manner that shows that it is a Hindu. Every child in Maharashtra has three names: a given name, its father's given name as a middle name, and a surname. The surname of an upper-caste person, especially a Maratha or Brahmin, is a patronymic, while that of a lower-class person may be either a patronymic or a caste name. The true or cradle (*palna*) given name is chosen in astrological accordance with the time and date of the child's birth but is seldom used, as every child also acquires one or more nicknames (*topan nav*). Most people choose a nickname as well as a true name at *barsa,* and it is by this name that the child is called by its seniors. Very often the community at large chooses another nickname for a child as it grows older. In most circumstances it is disrespectful to call to or address a person by his real name, so that nicknames are used in normal social intercourse. There are, however, occasions on which the use of real names is prescribed. A woman changes her name upon marriage and a man changes his name if he becomes a *sannyasin.*

Although marriages (*lagna*) and thread ceremonies (*upanayana*) differ in many elements, they are alike in that they both may be divided into a series of preliminary rites plus core rites commencing with the singing of sacred verses (*mangalastaka*). Below are listed the preliminary rites with which the marriage ceremony (*lagna*) begins. For convenience of exposition I describe these rites as they are performed by members of the two lineages (*bhaubund*) of the Kadam clan of Marathas resident in Girvi, a large village some sixty-five miles south of Poona in Satura District. While others perform these rites over a period of days or weeks and divide them between the bride's village and the groom's, the Kadams perform nearly all in the bride's village in a single day.

1. *supari phodne.* Representatives of the families of the bride and the groom crush and share a betel nut (*supari*) to show that marriage has been agreed upon. The marriage is usually celebrated a few weeks later.
2. *akshat dene.* Early on the day of the wedding a senior man from among the bride's near agnates accompanied by the village priest delivers rice (*akshat*) consecrated with red powder and verbal formulas to the village deities and to the bride's fellow villagers as a sign of invitation. Written invitations are sent to more distant relatives and friends.
3. *sakhar pudha.* Accompanied by five *suvasni,* married women who have never been widowed, the groom visits the bride in the *lagna ghar,* her father's house. There she is given ornaments such as anklets and a sari. The bride's lap is filled (*oti bharne*) with a coconut and other foodstuffs.

4. *telavni.* Another purificatory rite performed by five *suvasni,* this time for the groom at the *janvas ghar,* the house allocated to the groom's party.
5. *haldi kunku.* A paste made of ground turmeric and water is applied to the head, shoulders, and knees of the bride and also of the groom. The bride's party apply *haldi kunku* to the groom, and the groom's party annoint the bride. Again married women take the lead.
6. The clan deities and totems (*kula devat* and *devak*) are worshipped.
7. *simolangan.* The groom ceremoniously enters the bride's village, riding on a horse if possible and accompanied by fireworks. He first visits the Maruti temple, for Maruti is a *brahmacharya,* or celibate, and lives outside the village. Recrossing the village boundary the groom's party is greeted by an elder of the bride's lineage. The groom also must give a present to the representative of the village service castes in recognition of their contribution to the raising of the bride.
8. *tila.* The groom is presented with a turban, a shoulder cloth (*uparne*), a gold ring, and possibly a new suit of clothes. His forehead is marked with an auspicious sign (*tila*). Dowry also may be announced at this time and a portion actually paid to the groom's father.

The parallel preliminary rites in thread ceremonies are as follows.

1. *ghana.* A purificatory rite that is performed by *suvasni.*
2. The worship of deities, beginning with the auspicious Ganpati and ending with Agni.
3. *upanayana.* The initiate is made to see his reflection in water, and water is sprinkled on his head. The boy's father cuts a few strands of hair from each side of his head and then the rest of the boy's head is shaved by the Barber (*Nhavi*), save for a tuft or topknot at the back. My informants gloss *upanayana* as "opening new eyes."
4. The initiate shares a final meal with his mother, eating from the same plate.

The effect of these preliminary rites is twofold. They confirm in the presence of witnesses that the subjects of the marriage *saṅskar* have the necessary qualifications. If the bride or groom is blind, deaf, or otherwise handicapped, the proceedings may be abruptly terminated.[9] Similarly, the agnatic affiliations of the couple are displayed and it is made manifest that their clan totems and deities are, as they should be, different. The situation of the bride as family, lineage, and village member is acknowledged with suitable gifts to all those who have been concerned with her upbringing. At the same time the preliminary rites, by bathing and the application of auspicious or pure substances, raise the subjects of the *saṅskar* into the pure state required for the performance of the core rites. In the case of marriage the groom and bride are regarded as deities, *navradev* and *navradevi,* and are appropriately dressed with garlands and crowns.

The core portion of both marriage and initiation opens with the singing of sacred verses (*mangalastaka*) at an astrologically chosen auspicious moment. In thread ceremonies the initiate stands facing his father or a substitute such as the father's brother, the initiate on the west and his father on the east. The initiate and his father are separated by an *antrapat,* a white cloth decorated with a red *svastika.* Behind the initiate stands his mother's brother holding a knife with a lemon stuck on it to protect against evil spirits. First the officiating priest and then the assembled guests sing *mangalastakas* and throw consecrated rice (*akshat*). In marriages the bride and groom face each other, the bride on the west and the groom on the east, and each is guarded by his or her mother's brother. As in thread ceremonies, benedictory verses are sung, and consecrated rice is thrown by the assembled guests led by the officiating priest. In both ceremonies the *antrapat* is removed when as many guests as wish to have sung and the principal parties to the *sańskar,* the initiate and his father in thread ceremonies and the bride and groom in marriages, are regarded as prepared to complete the core rites. *Mangalastaka* is concluded by the presentation of publicly announced gifts of cash to the sponsor of the ceremony, the father of an initiate or of a bride or groom, from the guests who have participated in and witnessed the ceremony.

In thread ceremonies *mangalastaka* is followed by the investiture of the initiate with his sacred thread (*pavita*). The initiate's father or his substitute then teaches him the *gayatri mantra,* whispering it into his ear while covered with a cloth, gives him the equipment required by a *brahmacarin,* or student, including a girdle of *munj* grass, and instructs him in the duties of a *brahmacarin,* especially chastity. The initiate then mimes the life of a *brahmacarin,* begging uncooked food from his mother.

The core rites following *mangalastaka* in marriage are listed below.

1. *kanyadan* (gift of a virgin). Switching places, the bride now on the east and the groom on the west, the couple seat themselves on either side of a large brass tray. The priest wraps around the couple a string (*kankan*), unwinding it from a brass pot full of turmeric water that is passed clockwise with the help, usually, of a crowd of excited little girls. While the couple is thus encircled, the bride places her cupped hands over those of the groom, both reaching out over the tray. Holding a few coins, the mother's brother (*mama*) of the bride places his hands above those of the bride. The priest pours water into the hands of the bride's mother's brother and the coins and water are allowed to fall through all three sets of hands into the tray. The same

actions are repeated, this time with the mother's brother of the groom taking the place of the bride's mother's brother. In some cases the feet of the groom are washed by the bride's *mama,* while the feet of the bride are washed by the groom's *mama.* Finally, the encircling string is taken up by the priest, who breaks it into two pieces. The bride ties one piece of the string, together with a small piece of sprouting (*le-kurvali*) turmeric root representative of their offspring, on the right wrist of the groom and he ties a similar *kankan* on the left wrist of the bride. The couple is now, as one informant put it, "bound together forever."

Following *kanyadan* the couple move on to a sacrificial altar (*bahule*), where a further series of rites is performed. The couple sit side by side facing east with the groom on the bride's right. The sequence of these rites is highly variable. Among non-Brahmins steps two through five do not require the offices of a priest.

2. The bride and groom "take" one another's names. The groom utters the name that the bride receives from her mother-in-law upon marriage, consisting of a new given name, her husband's given name as a middle name, and her husband's surname. If a married woman dies and her husband remarries, his second wife takes the married name of his first wife. Younger guests regard this as uproariously funny and subject the embarrassed bride to considerable teasing.
3. *gath marne* (to make a knot). The clothes of the bride and groom are tied together. *Gath* refers to an early fetus as well as a knot and so is regarded as suggesting the children the couple will have.
4. *saptapati* (seven steps). The groom leads his bride over seven heaps of rice uttering injunctions concerning the quality of their married life.
5. The couple are served cooked food and, again amidst much teasing, are urged to feed each other.
6. *hom.* Supervised by a priest the couple construct a small fire and worship it with ghee and other offerings.
7. The groom is invested by the priest with a second sacred thread (*janve*), and the bride receives her marriage necklace (*mangalsutra*), a black thread strung with gold.

The remaining rites are performed away from the *bahule.*

8. *sade.* The couple together with, in most cases, the bride's father and the groom's father worship a bamboo basket containing oil lamps made out of dough. The bride's father performs *namaste* (worship) to the groom's father. The groom's father gives a sari (known as *sade*) to the bride and a turban (*poshakh*) to her father. In addition, a number of other gifts of clothes (also *poshakh*) are made among persons who are cross- and/or affinal relatives (*soyre*), to and from the parties of

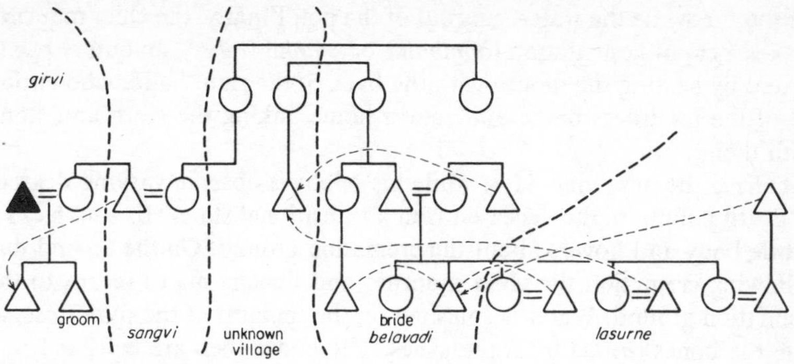

Fig. 5.2. Gifts of poshakh *at* sade.

the bride and groom as well as within each party. One informant explained these worshipful prestations as "oaths binding the two families together." The gifts given at *sade* at a Maratha wedding in Girvi are shown in Figure 5.2.

9. *varat.* The bride and groom are taken in procession to the Maruti temple and then on to the groom's quarters (*janvas ghar*). While in procession they are entertained by groups of male dancers. Later the bride returns to her own home.
10. *solava.* A ceremonial bath and feast marking the first arrival of the bride at the groom's house, usually sixteen days after the wedding.[10]

Funerals are known in Marathi as *uttarkarya, shevatca vidhi* (last rite), *agni saṅskar,* and so on. More clearly than marriages, funeral obsequies involve distinct rites of separation, transition, and incorporation (see Gennep 1960). The rites of separation begin on or before death, when the body of the dead or dying person is placed upon the ground with the head to the south. After death the body is washed and wrapped in a white cloth. Within a few hours, when the materials for the pyre (*chita*) have been assembled and the chief mourner, preferably a man's eldest son or a woman's husband, is present, the body is carried in solemn procession to the cremation ground. Four male agnates carry the bier, and a fifth leads the procession carrying an earthen pot containing a little rice and a few coins. At the edge of the village the procession halts, and this pot is broken against the ground.[11] Arriving at the cremation ground the deceased's lineage mates construct the pyre, while the chief mourner bathes in a nearby field well and the Barber (*Nhavi*) shaves his head and beard. Placing on his right shoulder a white cloth (*ashma*) and another clay pot (also *ashma*), this time containing water, the chief mourner circumambulates the fire three times in a clockwise direction. The pot is then punctured with a stone (*ashma* again), and the chief mourner continues to circle the fire while the water runs out of the pot. Finally, the chief mourner makes a cry of lamentation (*bombalne* or *shanka vadne*), an outcry punctuated by beating the mouth with the back of the right hand, whereupon all of the mourners bathe and return home, taking the cloth and stone with them.

During the next nine days, while his relatives observe varying degrees of death pollution, the deceased is in a transitional state. His soul lacks a subtle body and hovers about the cremation ground. On the second day following cremation the chief mourner and lineage mates return to the cremation ground. Water is splashed on the remains of the pyre to separate the bones (*asthi*) from the ashes. The bones then are collected in a clay pot and the ashes are gathered together in a small triangular shrine (*samadhi*), which is worshipped with flowers, red powder, and the performance of *namaste.* Within the next few days the chief mourner disposes of the bones at a sacred bathing place on a nearby river.

Mourning is brought to a close on the tenth day with the performance of *dehava* or *daspind,* a rite of incorporation attended by cross- and/or affinal relatives of the deceased (*soyre*) as well as by his lineage mates (*bhaubund*). *Soyre* who attended *daspind* for a Maratha who died in Girvi are shown in Figure 5.3. The proceedings open with all of the participants returning to the cremation ground, where they construct another shrine with the ashes of the deceased. The shrine may be elaborately decorated, but its principal ingredient is the stone that was used to puncture the pot of water with which the chief mourner circumambulated the funeral pyre and which now represents the deceased's soul. Offerings of balls of rice (*pinda*) and water are made to the deceased's soul, which has been lingering around the cremation ground as a *pret* or ghost. The desired effect of these offerings is to give release (*moksha*) to the soul and permit it to join the ancestors (*pitar*). Some say the offerings accomplish this by providing the soul with a subtle body as a vehicle. The acceptability of the offerings is shown by their being taken by a crow. All of the participants sit a little distance away to await the arrival of a crow, and if one does not come soon they may call them or repeat the offerings. The day's proceedings end with a feast and the gift of a turban to the chief mourner from an affinal and/or cross-relative (*soyre*), which together mark the end of formal mourning and of death pollution.

As I have suggested, human beings enter into full personhood by the performance of marriage or, for a man, perhaps by initiation (*munj*) alone. In any case, the two now often are combined in a single ritual performance. One leaves personhood by the performance of funeral rites. Significantly, neither the uninitiated boy, the unmarried girl, nor the *sannyasin* is thought to have *dharma* (religion, duty, or code).[12] The deaths of none of these occasion full pollution, if any, for their relatives nor do *sannyasins,* at least, observe death pollution for others.[13]

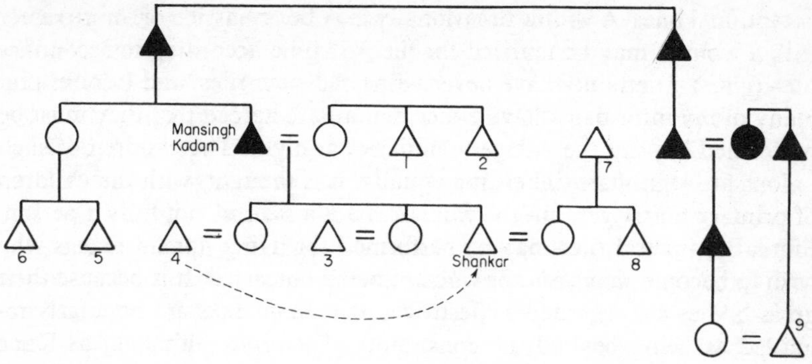

Fig. 5.3. Participation of soyre *in* solava. *Shankar Kadam was chief mourner for his father, Mansingh. His guests are numbered 1 through 9. The gift of a turban to Shankar from 4 marked the end of mourning and of death pollution.*

The marriage *sanskar* alters the condition of the groom and that of the bride. He becomes a *grhastha* and she a *suvasni;* both are fully persons. The transformations are brought about by the use of verbal formulae (such as *mangalastaka*) as well as by material substances (tumeric, knots) and have bodily effects, especially as regards the bride. She is now regarded as a *raktaca natevaik* (blood relative) of her husband and his agnates and as a *lagnaca natevaik* (wedding relative) or *soyre* of her father and his agnates. The rites also look forward to the couple's bodily unity as parents of children. While they both live, the couple together may make burnt offerings (*hom*). Separately and jointly the couple is bound up in an ongoing series of prestations involving agnates (gifts of *aher*), cross- and/or affinal relatives (gifts of *poshakh*), and persons of other castes, all of whom have contributed materially to their being and who witness and acquiesce in the achievement of personhood.

Just as in marriage personhood is conferred on a fully qualified human actor, that is one who is possessed of material substance from his or her parents and also from other castes, of a *karma*-bearing soul, and, where it is appropriate, invested with *dharma,* so in funerals actors are divested of personhood and the components of their being are dispersed. The gross body is destroyed and the soul, equipped by the deceased person's nearest agnates with a subtle body, is transformed into an ancestor. For three generations it will be invited to annual ancestral feasts, but ultimately it will be reborn according to its *karma,* perhaps as an offspring of one of the deceased's own descendants. Again, those who contribute to one's being and who witness the achievement of personhood, *soyre* as well as *bhauki* (here agnates) also witness the transformation to ancestorhood.

The central point here, that these *sanskar* confer and terminate personhood, is further borne out by comparing the usual procedures with exceptional ones. A widow occasionally may be remarried or, more rarely still, a woman may be married for the first time according to secondary rites (*gath*). I certainly have never witnessed such rites, and I doubt that many of my informants have either, but all are agreed that they must be performed beyond the village boundaries at night. The children of such unions are legitimate, inheriting equally, it is thought, with the children of primary marriages, but the woman is not a *suvasni,* not fully a person. Similarly, funeral rites may be performed for living human beings who wish to become *sannyasins* or who are being outcasted. It is because their gross bodies are regarded as destroyed that *sannyasins* are popularly regarded as being beyond the constraints of *dharma,* although, as Kane notes, not all authorities concur in this. Thus, according to Kane, Apastamba "combats these ideas by saying that such sentiments were opposed to the sastras laying down rules about ascetics, that by realizing the Self, he cannot be free from the effects of what he does or the consequences of having a body" (Kane 1941:940).[14] In abandoning his personhood and destroying his body the *sannyasin* also abandons his name, taking a new one given him by the preceptor who initiates him.

Another way to put it is to say that one who has achieved personhood is fully situated in the world of *saṅsar,* understood not merely as flux and illusion but as the world of caste and kinship in all its ramifications. My peasant informants were not given to dwelling on these matters. They were clear, nevertheless, that to be caught up in *saṅsar* or *prapanch,* as married persons are, is to be linked with, obligated to, and dependent upon others, especially one's spouse but also one's family and relatives and the society generally in which one tries to pursue the ends of personal existence: *dharma, artha,* and *kama.* Moreover, to be situated in *saṅsar* involves one in moral choices (*vichar*). And try as one may these will be difficult and painful (*dukha*).

Conclusion

In Maharashtra personhood as a cultural concept is distinct from the psychobiological actor. Rather, it is a species of office which qualified actors may hold. This would appear to be true of most sociocultural systems, but it perhaps may be objected that the concern with personhood evidenced in Maharashtra is a result of the emphasis there upon *bhakti,* the path of devotion, with an attendent moderating of the principle of hierarchy and holism.

Maharashtrians, however, are not alone in their concern with *bhakti.* In an all-Indian context the Hindi writings of Kabir and Tulsi Das, central to the Vaishnavite *bhakti* tradition of north India, are undoubtedly better known than those of the poet-saints of Maharashtra (see Allchin 1964), as is Surdas (see Pandey and Zide 1966). Indeed, several generations of Maratha Kabirbuvas, hereditary followers of Kabir, have lived in Alandi next to the Jnanadev Mandir, participating in the annual Varkari pilgrimage to Pandharpur and preaching all over the state, Maharashtrian devotional singers revere the Hindi songs of Mirabai as highly as those of their own region. Dimock (1966) has described devotional Vaishnavism in Bengal, and Marriott (1966) has traced aspects of its spread into the region around Mathura. And of course Singer (1966) and Venkateswaran (1966) have given us excellent analyses of devotional worship in Tamilnadu.

More broadly, although the *bhakti* tradition stresses personal devotion, its concern is not with personhood as an office. Rather, the stress is upon the relationship between a loving god and one's particular *atma*. Through love the embodied soul may win god's grace and so achieve *moksha*. Far from being unique to Maharashtra or even to *bhakti* traditions generally, this notion of self or ego principle seems to be a central aspect of Hinduism, one that is the complement of hierarchy and holism. Thus Biardeau (1965) suggests that in the Upanishads the *ahamkara* or ego principle is at once a cosmic principle in speculative thought and a stage of Yogic religious quests.

It is not surprising, then, that the various ethnographic phenomena that I have detailed are not unique to Maharashtra. As far as I know there is no other account of Indian material that explicitly stresses personhood as office. Nevertheless, as I have tried to suggest through references and footnotes, the implications of personhood for the distribution of *dharma* and pollution over categories of actors as well as for *sańskar* are both widespread and based on solid precedents in the *dharma shastras*.

We reasonably may ask, then, how the Maharashtrian conception of personhood as a species of office is related to holism and the Indian hierarchical opposition of purity and impurity. It appears not to be the case, *pace* Dumont (1965b), that personhood is an office that may be held by particular souls in a succession of births or by ranked pairs of actors, for example a married couple. The first solution mistakenly equates the self (*atma*) with personhood, whereas the self is in fact associated with different persons in each successive birth and, as the case of *sannyasins* shows, is stripped of personhood when it is separated from the body. Against the second solution one may argue that while marriage completes two persons (see Inden and Nicholas 1977:45–46) or confers personhood upon two actors, it does not create a single office held by two actors. Thus, in theory at least, a man may be completed by marriage to a milkweed plant and may himself participate in the completion of several women.

The most obvious consequence of hierarchy is that there are ranked varieties of personhood. The personhood that may be achieved by Shudras is lower than that which may be achieved by members of twice-born *varnas*, while that which may be achieved by twice-born men is higher than that available to twice-born women. And if Heesterman (1971:46) is correct that in the Indian context renunciatory values provide a necessary, transcendent point of reference with which to validate the worldly values of hierarchy, then it also is appropriate that personhood is an office that may be resigned by *sannyasins* and other renouncers.

At the same time the holistic aspect of hierarchy is reflected not in the absence of a concept of personhood but in its contrasts with Euro-Amerian individualism. Although the person, in a manner of speaking, is a responsible officeholder who may be expected to maintain his own *dharma* (*svadharma*), he is not an autonomous individual. His *svadharma* is not (*pace* Inden 1976:44, and Marriott and Inden 1976:7–8) the *dharma* of a particular South Asian dividual actor, let alone that of a Euro-American individual. Rather, it is that appropriate to his *varna* (Dasgupta 1932:502). To quote the *Bhagavad Gita* once more

> Better one's own duty (even) imperfect,
> Than another's duty well performed.
> Action pertaining to his own estate [varna]
> Performing, he incurs no guilt.
>
> (XVIII:47; Edgerton 1972:88)

Just as holistic social science involves a "sociological apperception" (Dumont 1970:4–8), so Indian holism conceives of persons as embedded in and dependent upon *saṅsar*, the hierarchical, holistic world of caste and kinship.

6

From Kanyā to Mātā: Aspects of the Cultural Language of Kinship in Northern India

R. S. Khare

FOR THE SAKE of making an analytic advance in Indian kinship studies it may now be increasingly relevant to approach the kinship system as a language of certain fundamental cultural constructions and their meaningful transformations.[1] We may begin to look for that language used by the people themselves that orders social experience as well as cultural purpose, one in terms of the other. In this pursuit an inviting view of kinship is one that handles it "as a cultural system; that is as a system of symbols" and meanings (Schneider 1968:1, and further elaborated in 1972, 1976). Here kinship is found to be in its concrete and abstract aspects a comprehensive language of the cultural system as a whole, where dimensions of social action and cultural meaning, context and norm, action and idea, are handled according to the perspective generated by the cultural system at hand. The logic of relations is found to be guided by a scheme of culturally relevant ideas and meanings.

However, to study a cultural system in this way is also to come upon that fundamental problem (see Dumont 1966:17–32; compare Khare 1975a:20–58) that the two approaches, one from within the system and the other from without, bring with them in the Indian context. I prefer to take the system-from-within approach, thus making a comparative stance more demanding in exactness than ordinarily so but, I hope, neither obscure nor less revealing (cf. Needham 1974:60, 70; also Tambiah 1973:191–229, for a relevant exercise). My stance is implicitly comparative, handling the specific features of a cultural system in a manner that opens it to comparison.

Though generally directed toward a study of that language of cultural significance on which kinship patterns itself in northern India, the aims and scope of this essay are specified and limited. Empirically, I hope to exemplify how a culturally crucial vocabulary is systematically approached by the twice-born Hindu as a source of those cultural directives and meanings that guide his kinship relations. The material for such a discussion is provided by a small region of northern India where my field data come from; my observations on practice-related contextual meanings will hold true only for that region. Conceptually, however, the systemic and structural connections suggested are much wider; here my sights are on the cultural genres of kinship relations, and an all-Indian (that is, the twice-born Indian) model is under consideration. This makes further methodological stipulations necessary for this essay.

I do not wish to describe kinship behavior under any set of specific ethnographic contexts—especially since kinship behavior is meaningful for the people themselves—but rather those cultural units and their interrelationships that set up a basic paradigm of social direction and meaning for the people under study. These units are the conceptual constructs of the people themselves, and they may be examined for the cultural directives they contain and the manner in which they are arranged by the people as a part of that language that guides them in their social relationships. Since the system under discussion—the twice-born Hindu system—has several levels, clusters, and competing sources (textual, regional, and contextual) of directives, values, and meanings, it is necessary to study a segment of this diversity that enables us to connect the textual ideal and the normative to the contemporary directive and its interpretations by my informants. Thus, I have discussed the conceptual constructs provided by texts in terms of those constructs that my informants in the field talk about. These are cognitive, structural connections, not limited to specific situations or cases. These connections also point towards the syntax of that underlying cultural language that guides my informants in the act of being properly related toward each other.

I have accorded much fuller explanatory roles and implications to those internal cultural constructs and social action complexes (*dāna, ṛṇa*) that Dumont (1957a, 1957b, 1966), with some reluctance, admitted into an analysis of Indian kinship. My attempt may suggest that it is necessary to recognize kinship not simply as being the logic of one's social rights and obligations but, more deeply, as an integral part of an entire cultural language and conception. There is a world of explicit and implicit systems of meanings and senses behind that logic of kinship relations. To study kinship this way is to study it more completely and probably more accurately (cf. Khare 1975:245–261).

My empirical data for this study come, once again (see Khare 1975), from the Lucknow-Rai Bareli region of Uttar Pradesh, collected in the Rai Bareli region during 1972 and in the city of Lucknow during short visits in the summers of 1974 and 1976. On questions of what one could call systemic significance, including textual information, my informants in 1976 were either traditional literati or those highly educated intellectuals who were inclined to inspect the normative kinship order by juxtaposing it with their images and experiences of what is now going on. On contextual significance my guides were middle-aged and/or old men and women, that is, those who had repeatedly handled the full fare of births, marriages, and deaths of those near as well as distant. Additionally, from within these groups of informants also emerged a smaller third group that helped me trace the continuities and discontinuities of the two simultaneously operating systems of cultural guidance. My rural informants from the Rai Bareli region, it could be noted, also fell within these three categories, and they provided a convergent, though generally less systematized, body of information, but one often containing better-recalled examples and experiences.[2]

Cultural Constructs and Practice

Though what people do and what they think about are not always directly or simply related, and though all they speak of is not found in practice, there are almost always some sufficiently deep connections between guiding cultural constructs and practice among the twice-born of the Lucknow-Rai Bareli region, allowing us to discuss their kinship practices against the backdrop of a primary set of guiding cultural categories and constructs.[3] An understanding of these principles is necessary in order to explain some of the northern system's comparable as well as unique features. Actually, I found a consideration of these aspects to be inescapable in my case, and the field demanded such a discussion once broad features of practice and some immediate (or contextual) rules were known accurately enough. The northern system has been sufficiently studied to offer such information in a reliable manner (see, for example, Dumont 1966, 1975; Vatuk 1969, 1971, 1972, 1975; Madan 1975; and Khare 1970, 1972, 1975).

However, in order to facilitate the presentation of data and the pursuit of specific analytical aims in regard to primary cultural constructions, I must present at the outset a group of distinctions that emerged from my data and that helped me in seeking interconnections between languages of performance and meaning for a kinship system. From the field data that I had collected in the Lucknow-Rai Bareli region since 1972, it became evident that externally observable social behavior guides one to consider those questions of meaning that are either only partly visible or implied in behavior. Calling someone *bhāi* and *bahén* in numerous different contexts is an example. The fact that people unambiguously assign a specific meaning to these usages in each context and yet they carry an overall meaning gives us the evidence that an observable segment of behavior implies not only social action but an idea of overlapping sets of meanings. Thus, there are contextual rules that help distinguish between

Z, FZD, and MZHBD, while all are called *bahén* and all may fall within the category of nonmarriageable (cf. Manu II:133, for such a recognition). Contextual rules are normally subsumed under an established collective norm. All members of the society, therefore, readily agree to share and uphold this norm, even as they recognize the contextual rules within this norm on the one hand and its assumed but not always known connections with Hindu law—to *Dharmaśāstras* as well as modern legal codes—and textual ideas on the other.

These norms, which are emphasized in our anthropological discussions of a kinship system, are gateways to further cultural constructs. Given the increasing generalization in Hindu ideals, they are not as independently complete as they at first seem. Thus, *bahén* as a kinship category that sets up a systemic structure for north Indian marriage must connect with an entire range of cultural distinctions that apply to women in general.

Beginning with a completely nonkinship, popular usage of *bahén* (Z) as a form of address for any woman, except one's wife, who is approximately of one's own age and ending with those few women closest to one's own blood in the same generation, using the term becomes a way—a cultural viewpoint—of relating toward women at large. Thus, as the Kanya-Kubja Brahmans say, "In this world all women are my mothers or sisters, except the one who could be (or actually will be) my wife." But they also emphasize that this is a norm concerning what ought to be and not what actually is. There is many a slip between the two in reality, and hence actual social behavior demands a different observation. Actually those very Kanya-Kubja Brahmans who speak about this norm also say, "There are only counted true *bahéns* and the rest are *bahén*-like; one looks at one's *bahén* as *bahén* and the rest of the women as women, not *bahén,* as it should be." The reality almost inverts the view the norm proposes. Put another way, the term *bahén* represents a way of looking at those women who cannot become one's wife and those who, being distant or strangers, are merely women of the same age.

However, once the category of *bahén* is considered beyond the kinship context in the Hindu system, it quickly merges with basic cultural constructions of woman (*nārī, strī*). A *bahén* is always a woman, carrying all those womanly properties that Hindu thought awards to woman; however, a woman is not always a *bahén.* Accordingly, law-giving texts most often discuss the woman, a generic cultural category, and sister only contextually (on sister, see Manu II:50, V:151, and IX:118; cf. entries in the index on woman, Bühler 1886:611–612). If woman is thus what we would call a primary cultural construction in *dharmasāṣtra* literature, where it represents the most inclusive significance, then there are a series of derived key constructions that give, directly or indirectly, content and direction to what we distinguish as present norms for *bahén.* For example, consider the *nārī* (primary construct) as *kanyā, suhāgin, jananī,* and *vid-*

hawā; and also as *mātā, bahén,* and *putrī* (derived key constructs). While the latter constructs must fundamentally take after the former one, they are of course further derived and specialized according to social contexts and purpose.

Thus, the distinctions that help us connect observed behavior with several successively deeper cultural meanings involve first, that social action that is only partly observable; second, those rules that presage the presence of a norm on the one hand and a concrete situation on the other (where *dharma* context is provided by either of the two); third, collective norms, which the people under study readily admit as guiding their social actions and experiences and which at the same time readily connect with some ideological formulations of the culture; fourth, derived-key constructs (which I place as being parallel to Schneider's "galaxy"),[4] which help us see interconnections between norms and primary constructs; and fifth, primary constructs themselves which provide basic cultural premises, postulates, propositions, and principles (cf. Schneider 1976:203, who assigns these and other such properties to culture). The last category is most directly concerned with cosmological and cosmogonic questions concerning the nature of the universe and the man's place in it. My emphasis is on derived key constructs and through them on regional norms on the one hand and primary (systemic) constructs on the other.

There is another equally important qualification about Hindu cultural constructions. Since they come from various trains of thought and from different times, only the chosen context of our conceptual discussion will help us develop a clearly delimited set of meanings. However, this context will come primarily out of, and fall between, constructions themselves. For example, a norm that classifies most of one's same generation members as *bhāi* and *bahén* must become a context for derived key constructs and the constructs a context for the primary ones. However, the reverse process is rather more appropriate to the Hindu system. In this emphasis the primary cultural construct is also conceived to be the primal context par excellence. Ideally, for the Hindu all that is problematic and anomalous in practice (*lokācāra*) and in intermediate normative constructions (as in *Dayābhaga* and *Mitākaṣāra* systems of Hindu traditional law) must be resolved within this primal (*sṛuti* and *smṛti*) context.

Dharma: A Pervasive Order

Now we can turn toward the internal conceptions, categories, and relational alignments involved in the language of cultural significance produced by Hindu kinship categories as cultural constructs. One fundamental feature is approached when kinship is seen as an integral part of the Hindu conception and categories of *dharma* (that which is firm; compare *dhṛ* of Sanskrit with *firmus* and *fretus* of Latin). A common Hindu's language of cultural significance is most often a language of *dharma* and *adharma.* (The depth and power of this system of meanings becomes evident once its usage is found extant in the field—from the illiterate to the most authoritative text or informant. For a revealing range of lexical entries, see Apte 1965:522–523).

All kinship norms and constructs are in principle designed to inculcate *dharma* and contain *adharma.* If there is a contextual *dharma* that does not always correspond with the systemic (whether *smṛti* and/or *sṛuti* or *sadācāra* enjoined) *dharma,* there are procedures available for making a decision or establishing priorities (see Lingat 1973:3–17 for a summary of some traditional provisions). In contemporary practice, familial or lineage customs constitute what Lingat (1973:14) calls "good custom" or *sadācāra* and *siṣṭācāra* and are powerful guides of people's social actions. Yet they are not without erosion, ambiguity, and conflict over time, and hence require adaptive procedures. Nor is the contemporary Hindu without an authority to mend them, which often rests with the most knowledgeable and the old.

When my informants were unable to connect their contextual *dharma* with the age-old *dharma,* it was either because they thought they were ignorant but that someone more informed would know, or because they felt the Kali age has deformed and erased, though not irretrievably, the connections that should be evident, or because their *lokācāra* (customs and practices) is now irreversibly corrupted by man's folly. Some others thought that their practices are in outright response to extraneous (secular social) forces, bearing little or no resemblance to the systemic thought the classical Hindu represented. The first three reasons, which dominated in the groups I studied, assume the overriding importance of *dharma.* People often said so: "Though it is Kali age and ignorance on this matter abounds, the serious seeker can always uncover such connections, for they are not absent or severed but only masked."[5] At this point in an interview would be mentioned one or several knowledgeable men—*prudentes*—whom one could consult to know further. The latter are significant not as much for their consistency of thought or close argumentation as for the underlying constant effort to weave the images, categories and relations of *dharma* through and through into what is socially seen, known, and expected as proper.

My interviews concerned the distinctions between *kanyā* (virgin), *saubhāgyavati* (married, unwidowed woman), and *mātā* (birth-giving or adopting or fostering woman). Of course this set of categories is complemented by one of *putra* (son), *patī* (husband), *pitā* (father), and *pitra* (*manes*), and the two sets together may provide a necessary kinship vocabulary from within. As these cultural categories are distinguished from one another and then arranged in varied sequences, they bring forward a language of cultural significance, a language of the *dharma* order, at both contextual and systemic levels. The scope of this attempt will not allow a treatment of the second set. However, methodological points illustrated for the first set remain valid for both.

Three Key Constructs of Dharma

The *kanyā,* an unsullied symbol of total *dāna,* is a derived key construct for any unmarried (most often virgin) girl among the Kanya-Kubja Brahmans, Thakurs, and Kayasthas of the Lucknow-Rai Bareli region, except those few who are aware of finer textual distinctions.[6] Calling a pregnant unmarried girl a *kanyā* is as culturally anomalous as a *vidhawā* becoming pregnant. This is because *kanyā* is a key construct for the Hindu that involves the idea of *dāna:* a *kanyādāna,* ultimately a proper marriage yielding a proper birth. A *kanyā,* therefore, inevitably brings the question of marriage to the mind of a Hindu. As some of my Kanya-Kubja Brahman informants pointed out, *kanyādāna* is one of the *mahādānas* (cf. Kane 1941:869), and to be able to perform it one's sisters and daughters must remain virgin until married. Conversely, *kanyā* as a construct entails the *dharma* of virginity while her parents must provide protection and appropriate *dāna.*

For an orthodox Hindu even today *kanyā* fundamentally represents these two cardinal properties of *dharma.* It is as much a *dharma* of womankind to yield culturally proper women as it is of mankind to retain or improve upon this *dharma.* The point is important since it shows integral conception of the system whereby each upholds the construction of the other rather than each being responsible for itself alone. Manu, looking at the *kanyā* from within the man's world, finds her (one's daughter) "as the highest object of tenderness" (IV:185). Neither should one quarrel with unmarried women of one's family. For they represent one of the most vulnerable—*dharma* harming—spots within the social system.

With these general remarks on the *kanyā,* let us see how this category translates itself along the five conceptual distinctions we proposed earlier. In order to focus the discussion, it is useful to consider some of the central cultural deferentia (*lakṣaya*) such as age, virginity, menstruation, and marriage. Statements repeatedly produced by my informants offer not only examples of the spoken language but clues to the language of cultural significance.

As Table 6.1 demonstrates, in text and context *kanyā* represents a heterogeneous range of meanings, but it still has a shared cultural direction and sense. The primary feature is defined by that cultural idea of virginity that may terminate only after a proper marriage. (Cultural and biological components of virginity are not coterminous or coextensive within this system.) Age and menstruation are secondary classifiers, as the texts clearly record from early times, as features of preference and ideals but are only loose guides for practice. A technical textual definition of *kanyā* is not popularly known, and the term is used rather flexibly, though not in

TABLE 6.1. CULTURAL CONSTRUCTION AND CLASSIFICATION OF *KANYĀ*.

CULTURAL CLASSIFIERS	INFORMANT'S STATEMENTS	ANALYTICAL REMARKS AND NOTES
1. Virginity	*Cāheiñ jo bhi zamānā ho, kanya to vahi hai jiskā kaumārya nā bhanga huā ho.* (Whatever the age, kanya is one who has not lost her virginity.)	States a collective norm and its relation, a key (*dhārmika*) construct in the *smritis.* For example, see Manu VIII: 367; Apte 1965:333.
2. Virginity and age	*Kanyā to vahī kahalāyé gī jo kumāri ho, jiskā kaumārya na bhanga huā ho; kanyā kèval umar sè nahiñ hotī.* (Kanya is called one whose virginity has not been violated; she is not [defined] by age.)	States a limited disjunction in text and context insofar as a *kanyā* is said to be only that girl who is ten years old (see Kane 1941:444). The contemporary usage favors *kanyā* being an unmarried virgin girl or even woman (see Apte 1965:333, his first and fourth meanings).
3. Virginity and quasi-(socially passable) virginity	*Aja kal to kabhì kabhi larkiyan galata kadam uta lètiñ hain, phir bhi kanyā kahalātī hain aur unka vivaha bhi ho jata hai.* (These days once in a while girls take the wrong step [i.e. lose their virginity] yet they are called a *kanyā* and are even married as a *kanyā.*)	States a disjunction between the cultural norm and the passable social practice, showing that the latter vitiates the construct.
4. Age, menstruation, and marriage for the virgin	*Sach meiñ to kanya rajasvalà hoté hi kanyadan ka dharma yāda dilātī hai.* (In fact, a *kanyā* reminds [us] of her marriage as soon as she begins to menstruate [but now we most often fail in this duty].)	States a limited disjunction between textual and contextual rules about marriage and age (and menstruation); primacy of marriage for *kanyā* remains undisputed, but not whether it should be before or after her menstruation. However, texts (e.g. Kane 1941:438–446; Manu IX:88) provide several not always con-

TABLE 6.1. *Continued*

CULTURAL CLASSIFIERS	INFORMANT'S STATEMENTS	ANALYTICAL REMARKS AND NOTES
		sistent guidelines in this area, probably a product of the times in which they were written. Thus, the disjunction, as some of my informants in fact argued, is not a true contradiction of the key construct (i.e. *kanyādāna*) for which *kanyā* stands. Notice also how today the onset of menstruation is clearly a cultural marker but without any special name given to it (see the *nāgnika* category in the text; see Kane 1941:440–441).
5. Contemporary constructs of the virgin	*Kanyā kanyā hi nahin nārī matra ki murtī hai: wahī hamārī jananī hai. Yahi ādi saktī aur prakrati ka pratīka hai: yadi māyā hai to bhī aprampāra hī hai.* (A *kanyā* is not merely a *kanyā,* but she foreshadows womankind: she is [thus] our Mother. She also represents primal *shakti* and *prakriti.* If she is an illusion she is still unfathomable.)	States normative and primary cultural constructs one after the other to let the discussion of the *kanyā* rest on most basic ideals. This is a typical instance of how the contemporary informant lifts various ideological constructs and weaves them together to convey his ideal. Obviously, therefore, the *dharmaśāstra* literature alone will not suffice for textual parallels. However, see Kane 1941:574–581, particularly 597–581, for a spirited defense of woman. Compare also Prabhu 1963:263–268 on discussion in the *purānas;* see also 274–276.

violation of the dictionary meaning (cf. Apte 1965:333). A *kanyā* can be an unmarried virgin girl or even an unmarried virgin woman. (*Spinster* in English is not its accurate equivalent, since unmarried state and age, not virginity, are the primary criteria of classification.)

Under the Hindu system, therefore, virginity is found to be the most definitive single feature of the *kanyā.* However, it is equally important that the *dharma*-based conception of this *kaumārya* (virginity) be understood; it conjoins, rather than excluding one at the expense of the other, the *ḍṛṣta* (seen) and *aḍṛṣta* (not seen) classifiers of virginity. Whether its referents are thus physical and biological or not, it is always a formulation of *dharma* within the Hindu system. So approached, a *kanyā's* virginity is basically understood as a state of *dharma* rather than merely a physical condition of continued sexual continence. A voluntary as opposed to involuntary loss of virginity, for example, introduces a significant *dharma* classifier, whereby the latter will tend to be received more kindly than the former. A mythological example of illustrious Hindu *kanyās,* all of whom are blemished in one way or another (see Prabhu 1963:263–264), is provided by the following verse, given here by two versions, recited by my twice-born informants during their daily worship. It means, in essence, daily recital of the names of Ahalya, Draupadi, Sita, Tara, and Mandodari, the five *kanyās,* destroys one's mortal sins.

Ahilyā Draupadī Tārā Kuntī Mandodarī tathā
Pañcha-kanyam smaré nittyam mahāpātaka nāśanam

(recorded in the field)

Ahalyā Draupadī Sīta Tārā Mandodārī tathā
Pañcha-kanyam smarén nityam mahāpātakanāśánam

(quoted in Prabhu 1963:263)

Prabhu points out how these *kanyās* actually remained unblemished despite the blemishing circumstances each had gone through because of "the purity of their motives and of their ideals" (1963:264). However, in the first version, substitution of Sitā with Kuntī complicates in part such an explanation, as Kuntī received god-lovers voluntarily as well as involuntarily. My informants, however, explained the case with reference to the contextual (*lokācāra*) versus the larger (*adhyātmika*) *dharma,* whereby the latter always wins, rectifying the circumstantial irregularities. To them these *kanyās* were divine, hence capable (*samartha*) to transcend the contradiction. Impregnated by a god, one remains a virgin even after giving birth (cf. Leach 1976:69–70).

These statements on a key cultural construct demonstrate how people derive a range of meanings, ideal and practical, from such formulations as listed in Table 6.1. It is usually done by variously classifying, declassifying, and reclassifying the key cultural construct. For example, consider the construct of *kanyā,* first as classified by virginity and age (prepuberty), and second as reclassified by quasivirginity (see items 3 and 4 in Table 6.1.) and marriageable age (postpuberty). Over time, the Hindu system could be shown to have performed such exercises on the key construct of *kanyā* from the Vedic times (when postmenstrual *kanyā* existed) to that at present (when, once again, there is increasing preference shown to this sort of *kanyā* over one who had to get married before menstruation).

Suhāgin: Total Wifehood

The importance of this derived key construct cannot be overemphasized if the Hindu kinship system is to be understood from the point of view of the woman. This construct has a crucial place in identifying and understanding the female principle itself within the cosmological system.

As an ethnographic term *suhāgin* is a popular corruption of *saubhāgyavatī,*[7] a word the literate use to denote a woman in the blessed state of wifehood. As Apte correctly explains, a *saubhāgyavatī* is "a married woman whose husband is alive, a married unwidowed woman" (1965:1001). Such a formulation remains valid for situations of a long-absent husband, an emigrated, even an unfaithful or remarried husband. A living husband is thus the most important single condition that keeps the woman a *suhāgin.* (We shall use this corrupted form in our discussion, as it is most commonly used in the region of my study.) Thus, for example, a married woman who first receives the news that her *pardesi pati* (a husband residing away from home) is dead and then the news that he is still alive must undergo a priest-conducted reinstatement of *suhāga,* but no remarriage.

A more hypothetical situation is provided by the idea of *satī,* in which, as several of my informants observed, a wife "unites with her [dead] husband without becoming a widow, for a *satī* defies widowhood by sacrificing herself at her husband's funeral pyre. However, if such ideas vary in the field, a glorification of the *satī* still exists, especially in the context that it is the Kali age and not a better appreciation of British morality that has made this cultural ideal unattainable. Textually, however, the concept of *satī* is not culturally as simple as many of my informants supposed or as common sociological discussions make it out to be. The most popular of these conceptions is concerned with what Kane (1941:627) calls the rite of *sahamaraṇa* or *anavārohaṇa,* the burning of a widow on the death of her husband, voluntarily or involuntarily. (For other distinctions as in *anumaraṇa* and *mahāsati,* see Kane 1941:624–636.) Still, it is striking that Kane (1941:636), not unlike many Kanya-Kubja Brahman informants, argues in favor of correctly appreciating the cultural significance of this, now socially dead, custom.

Ideally the *suhāgin* attains her best in being what my informants called *satī sāvitri,*[8] an image of absolute fidelity and coexistence in relation to her husband. However, most informants expressed a commonly shared ideal: "A *suhāgin* always wants to die a *suhāgin,* in the lap of her [living] husband." In fact, those women who die *suhāgin* are popularly recalled as being, or being as good as, a *satī.* Clearly, all such statements about *satī* extol *suhāga* (wifehood) and decry pitiable widowhood. If a proper *kanyā*-hood culminates in *suhāga* by way of such cardinal marital rites as *kanyādāna, paṇigrihana,* and *saptapadī, suhāga* culminates by yielding a lifelong *suhāgin,* and, as some informants critically added, a potential *sādhvī* (a virtuous woman) and *mātā* (mother). The marital rites underscore the point that what *kanyādāna* starts is concluded only by *saptapadī,* creating a *suhāgin.* There is no other intermediate status available to *kanyā.* (For a textual description of these marital rites, see Kane 1941:527–538, 869; also Manu VIII:227).

Hindu wifehood, like virginity, is a *dhārmika* construct. In practice it only implies rather than always insures commensurate action. Thus, a woman who may enjoy *suhāgin* status even when, as my informants put it, "she is known to have lapsed into less than virtuous conduct," needs to be corrected to return to her *dharma.* As in the case of virginity, wifehood is also a state of personal as well as collective *dharma;* being well placed in the context of such norms means being properly related to oneself and the society at large. A social recognition of the violation of these *dhārmika* norms produces conditions of serious social disapprobation, but in practice probably more for *kanyā* than *suhāgin,* since the former cannot easily mask a lapse, and her marriage becomes very difficult, if not impossible.

The *dhārmika* construction of these two statuses is further conveyed when virginity and wifehood are seen as ritual states, though in practice wifehood may seem to be more so than virginity. A *suhāgin* is irrevocably a full wife just as soon as the seven-step rite of marriage is completed (here several texts and the contemporary practice are identical), for if her husband were to die moments after his ceremony, she will be a complete widow, even though her marriage was not physically consummated. However, texts offer complicated provisions for handling a widow under the categories of *vidhwā* and *punarbhū* (widows up for remarriage). (See Kane 1941:538–593; 608–619). But even so, and current ideas support this, a marriage based on lifelong fidelity is considered to be the highest *dharma* of man and wife (Manu IX:101).

A state of being directly dependent on another person's life and his life alone, wifehood is, as women informants pointed out, a fragile relationship: "It rests in the hands of God, where one's *karma* and God's *kripā* [blessings] play the most important part." If women find *suhāga* a fruit of good past *karma,* its termination is accepted with utter helplessness, with only one's past *karma,* once again, to blame. If a *suhāgin* is very young and she becomes a widow, she is called *bāla-vidhwā,* a condition of maximum social and supernatural punishment. Even though in age she is like a *kanyā,* she is in social fact and in conception a complete widow, beyond wifehood and motherhood. (There is no such word as *kanyā vidhwā* in Hindi, since the *kanyā* construct ceases to exist after *kanyādāna.*)

A *suhāgin* must protect her wifehood in two ways: first, by ritually preserving and prolonging the life of her husband, and second, by remaining faithful (*pativṛta*) to her husband and in turn expecting but not assuming that her husband will be faithful (*éka patnīvṛta*) to her. This definition of *suhāgin* is both normative and normal for the twice-born Hindu in northern India, though it should also be recognized that a *suhāgin* retains all of the ritual symbols and activities of wifehood even when she or her husband has been unfaithful or when her husband has deserted her to marry another woman, as is allowed to him under the customary norms. This practice is not structurally or culturally inconsistent with the normative definition of *suhāgin,* especially since this status comes to a woman but once in her lifetime, and only her husband's death rather than any other contextual blemishes can snatch it from her. The same reasons make widowhood a condition of such total deprivation for a woman—a glaring loss of her feminity, sexuality, and social status.

In the language of some of my rural informants, a *suhāgin* is like "an appropriately offered, and rightly received field [*khéta*] that is ready for sowing." Here the ideas of legitimate transfer of a woman to her husband, like a piece of land, and of his undisputed rights "to sow and to produce" were quite dominant. This is the man's view, of course, included in which is the implication that a *suhāgin* normally assures sexuality, pregnancy, and motherhood. But in practice, since the latter may not inevitably come to a *suhāgin,* we may note that her *suhāga* does not depend on such realizations. The auspiciousness and positive social status accruing to her as a *suhāgin* remain secure even if she cannot flower and fructify (*phūlanā* and *phalanā*).

Though *suhāgin* is not a term of address, and it does not specify patrilocal or virilocal residence, it is used with such terms as *bahū* or *bétī.* Older women greet and bless younger ones by wishing them *saubhāgya* (*saubhāgyavatī rahō̄* is the usual phrase). *Suhāgin bahū* and *bétī* are clearly distinguished from widowed *bāhūs* and unmarried or widowed *bétīs.* In comparison to the concept of *kanyā, suhāgin* can absorb more blemishes without falling apart. It is thus important that we know what *suhāgin* as a construct of crucial cultural significance within kinship means under different conditions. As Schneider so succinctly points out in this connection, "What is necessary to know is which of the many meanings applies when, and which of the many meanings does not apply or is not relevant under what circumstances; and finally, how different meanings of the word relate to each other" (1968:4).

An internally consistent cultural formulation of *suhāgin* is that she represents a vital dimension of *sṛajana dharma,* the duty to procreate. She symbolizes coexistence, harmony, amity, and mutual inclusion between the cosmogonic—male and female—sexual principles. Though undoubtedly her existence anticipates and negotiates motherhood and progeny, and the culture must value her for this reason, she is given a definite significance of her own. To be and to remain in the blessed state of conjugation is as much sought by human beings as by gods and goddesses (for the stories of paradoxical Shiva, see O'Flaherty 1973). From the *suhāgin's* point of view, progeny is one natural consequence of her existence; however, she does not exist for it but exclusively for her husband. Giving birth to one's dead husband's child is a case in point, in which a woman is impregnated as a *suhāgin* but is obliged to give birth as a widow.

For my rural male informants *suhāgin* represents either a prepared or sowed field, hence always a source of expected and arriving happiness. For the women she brings the best from both this and the other world; she symbolizes *khāné-khélané, pahanané-oḍhané ké din* (the period of enjoyment and personal care) and a stage for easily earning religious merit. The *suhāgin* as a key construct must, therefore, generally underscore two sets of logical relations: one of transition toward motherhood and the other of coexisting (preferably for life) with one's husband. Relationships of coexistence and transition are so arranged in this construct as not to be contradictory but mutually overlapping, enriching, and fulfilling.

Mātā: Image of the Earth[9]

Another key cultural construct of the Hindu kinship system, *mātā,* is by no means a simple representation of *dhātra dharma.* Its popular as well as textual usages are so diverse and so figurative that it would be hazardous to try to point out its single most specific common denominator. God, for example, quickly becomes a mother and a father at the same time, as in the verse *tvaméva mātasca pitā tvaméva.* However, returning to common social usages, *mātā* is usually a potential or actual mother. Mother, motherlike (*mattravata*) and motherliness (*mattratva*) are general categories of reference and description that are included in this social usage of the term. Thus, married but childless women and old unmarried women may be either addressed or referred to as *mātā-ji.* The usage is justified by seeing these women as potential or metaphorical mothers; they may be seen as a mother or motherlike, and in turn these women may also be motherly without actually being mothers. (In northern India usages of *bhāi* and *bahén* also follow a comparable metaphorical pattern, though their cultural depth may not be the same.)

Though one is tempted to associate *mātā* with older women, it is not a trouble-free formulation, particularly since the *dévī* cult and its popular emphasis on seeing in *kanyā* a reflection of the mother goddess superimposes the idea of mother on young women. (Compare this view of woman with that cited earlier in which women of one's own age become sisters and those much younger become daughters.) Moreover, if *suhāgin* represents a legitimate *kshétra* (field), *mātā* stands for a legitimate *kshétra* with legitimate *bīja* (seed) in it. Alternatively, *mātā* is fruition of the *dharma* inculcated by *kanyā* and *suhāgin.* For our purposes, *mātā* is a construct that fundamentally brings together the Indian cultural notions *bīja* and *kshétra* and inevitably poses conjunctions between the *sagī* and the *sautélī* mother, an example for illustrating the *dharma* of motherhood.

In popular as well as textual usages (see Prabhu 1963:252, summarizing a discussion of the mother's position in Mahabharata), the mother is accorded an impeachable primacy by informants because "she rears us in her womb for nine months, a work which only she gladly performs despite great physical pain and inconvenience; her position must therefore remain unchallenged." Most popularly it is believed that the mother should be honored because "she bore us" (*usné hamkō janama diyā hai*). Texts express the same by making the mother the sole cause (*hétuḥ*) of the conjugation of *bīja* with *kshétra* (seed with soil), awarding actual existence to the coveted *putra* (son)–*patī* (husband)–*pitā (father)-pitra* chain. Manu (II:145, 225–237) extols the mother for similar reasons: she is characterized as the earth, as "presiding over the earth" (Manu IV:183), a figurative expression concordant with her being a *kshétra.* Kane (1941:580–581) summarizes mother's superior status in the *dharmaśāstra* texts, including how a son may favor her over his father because she "bore him." While seeing mother as representing *kshétra* and as nurturing *bīja* in *kshétra,* we must again recognize that these are constructions of *dharani dharma* (duty of bearing), which link up with wide-ranging sets of metaphorical analogues of the Hindu cosmology.

One chain became apparent to me after I put together informants' and textual statements on the *bīja* and *kshétra* interrelationships (cf. also Prabhu 1963): *bīja:kshétra :: karma:daiva :: vāyu:agni :: téla:dīpaka :: chakra:ratha :: bhojana:udarama.* (Approximately glossed as: seed:field :: action (effort):destiny :: air:fire :: oil:lamp :: wheel:chariot :: food:stomach.) The central point of the expanding analogic chain, which is by no means exhaustive, is to show how the Hindu system, even under popular formulations, handles systemic interconnections by widely juxtaposing the sphere of effort (*karma, purushakāra*) to fate or destiny (*daiva*), making it a thread that connects *bīja* to *kshétra* as forcefully as *bhojana* is connected to *udarama.* The *bīja* represents the necessary *karma,* and *kshétra* is the field where the fate or destiny of this *bīja* becomes known.

Progeny, like a fruit, is held to be a result of the conjugation (*samyoga*) of both, where one displays dependence on the other. Beyond it, divine will prevails. However, while granting the above, my informants moved on to raise the primacy of *bīja* over *kshétra* for what the former encodes and the latter cannot. According to Hindu creation and cosmology, I was told, the cosmic egg (*hiranyagarbha*), not the *kshétra,* holds prominence; the former ideologically survives without the latter. "A *kshétra* nurtures all *bījas* indiscriminately, hence only the latter can carry all the necessary distinctions for the *dharma* to be distinguished from *adharma*" (Compare Khare 1970).

In settling the primacy of *bīja* over *kshétra* my informants produced another analogue from the Bhagavad Gita, where *bīja* is the knower of the field (*kshétrajna*) while *kshétra* is the field, the physical body itself. The former is interpreted as the unchanging, superior cultural principle within the system. (For the exact idea, see Zaehner 1969:332–350, 352). This analogue is extended to human procreation and its social evaluations, so that like the Purusha a man "plants the seed" (cf. Gita 14:3) for his progeny giving him his own social characteristics.

Thus, at present *mātā* as a cultural construct brings forward a wide range of symbolic interconnections for the *bīja-kshétra* analogy whereby views are shifted from the social to the cosmological to the way one analogy connects with another one. Thus, the ideological superiority of *bīja* is juxtaposed with the logical and practical prominence *kshétra* occupies for human procreation, bringing about among the contemporary northern Hindus (as also in the *dharmaśāstra* texts) a secure superiority of *bīja* (*pitā*) for preserving their social classification. Contributing to this security is a complementary—and only as systemically logical and necessary—idea of honor, respect, and protection of *kshétra* (*mātā*). In the mother's case, as Manu (II:225–237) clearly points out, and as it is attested by the contemporary Hindu, there is a definite effort to accord a sentimental priority (homage of heart) to the conception of the mother (an aspect only logically extended and intensified in the *shaktī,* or goddess, conception and worship). The mother continues to enjoy a strong support from the son's *dharma* toward her; this support is strong, as the son's *dharma* toward her is made to be uniquely direct and unflinching.

Within the system *mātā* also symbolizes that entire cultural idea of the process of transformation by which the seed decodes itself. The nine-month period spent in one's mother's womb is therefore a very powerful (and equally verbalized) reason for being in her eternal debt. In one's *jananī* do the *bīja* and *kshétra* effectively conjoin and the *prākritika* (natural), *laukika* (worldly), and *pāralaukika* (otherworldly) *dharma* simultaneously take over, according to the popular conception. The first forms the body of the child, while the second not only classifies its social placement but brings forward all that love and emotional attachment (*mamtā* and *moha*) that *mātā* fundamentally signifies. From her point of view, it is the latter that takes precedence over social and spiritual relationships. One usual way to say it is that her *dharma* is to be a figure of love: "One does not find a *ku-mātā*" (bad or unmotherly mother). A literate informant played on words: "A *mātā* is born the moment a *suhāgin* knows that she is pregnant, and she thereafter prepares to receive her child as a full mother."

If *mātā* as a construct implies a discussion of *bīja* and *kshétra* and the transformations the two undergo as they conjoin, it also entails a discussion of the *dharma*-ordered conception of sexual principles and their differentiations. However, we can mention this issue only in passing.[10]

It is further helpful to distinguish between *sagī* and *sautélī* mothers and the principles of *dharma* underlying them. A *sagī* mother is of course one's *jananī,* the woman who has actually given birth to the person in question. She normally represents the total conjugation between that *bīja* and *kshétra* that gives body to the child under *dharma;* and she does so by being a proper wife (a *kshétrin*). The child is thus neither a widow's progeny nor a *kanyāgarbha* nor *kanyāputra* nor *kanīna*—the terms Sanskritic texts employ to designate the son of an unmarried daughter.) As remarked before, she is the birth giver (*jananī* or *janmadātrī* or *janītrī* or, as popularly put, *janma dénéwālī mātā*) as well as a fully socially recognized mother.

However, further cultural (*dharma* generated) distinctions appear when the situations of *sautélī* (or father's wife who did not give birth to the person in question) or other nonbirth-giving (including figurative) mothers (also called *mātā*) are simultaneously considered. A foster mother (popularly called *dhāya,* or in texts she is *dhātri* or *upamātā*) is distinguished from the *sautélī* and both from any other related or unrelated woman who, though not charged to be a foster mother, can become motherlike under situations of *mā kī mamtā* (motherly attachment).

Informants readily offer mythological examples to explain the nature of these *dharma*-ordered (and not simply biologically-based) distinctions. Kaikéi is a celebrated example of *sautéli mātā* for Rama and Yashoda of a *dhāya* or *upamātā* for Krishna. Kaushilya, in contrast, is an example of perfect *jananī-mātā,* since her attitude toward her *sagé* and *sautélē* sons is not governed only by the criterion of giving birth. Yashoda is also given prominence for similar reasons. Her charge is to be a good *dhāya,* but she comes out just like (for some even better than) a birth-giving mother; she is a *jananī*-like *mātā,* a point culturally greatly elaborated. In Krishna's case, his birth-giving mother (Devaki) is overshadowed and equalled by Yashoda by following the *dharma* of being an actual mother even if she did not give birth to Krishna. In the popular conception, *māmtā* of motherhood is present in every woman, and she can truly express it even if she is not a mother.

These illustrations are another way to focus on the two basic components of motherhood: the act of giving birth (*apné péta se janama dénā*) and rearing a child (*pālanā posanā aur baṛā karanā*). It is as much the *mātra dharma* of a pregnant woman too nourish and deliver the life in her womb as it is to rear the child afterwards. However, which of the two dimensions should acquire a greater cultural value is not easily settled. In fact, depending on the context, either one (consider Devaki and Yashoda) can be proved to be more important. If giving birth is considered essential and necessary to make one a complete *mā,* then there is also the argument, expressed by one informant, that "one does not become a mother simply by bearing a child in one's womb, for this is what the animals also do. One must also have the *pālana dharma* and *mamatā* (attachment) of a *mā* toward one's child "to make him a *mānava* (human being)." Normally, if it is admitted that a birth-giving woman naturally (*svabhāvataḥ*) develops an attachment toward her child, it is also argued that mother's true love (*mā kā sacchā pyār*) is not limited to the birth-giving mother (*saccī mā*) alone. Intense *mamātā* (attachment) of a foster mother like Yashoda is repeatedly described as the *dharma*-ordered ambience of true motherhood.

As a key construct, however, *mātā* is a progeny-emphasizing category that must successfully handle the *dhātrī* (bearing) and *pālana-poshana* (nurturing and upbringing) *dharma.* For the man within the system *mātā* is crucial because she helps obtain continuity of line. For the woman she symbolizes fruition and culmination of the woman's role within the system by displaying qualities of holding, bearing, preserving, sustaining, protecting, and loving her progeny. However, if as a *suhāgin* she loves her husband and as *mātā* her progeny, the balance tilts, according to men and texts, in favor of the latter. For a *suhāgin mātā* herself, as a Kanya-Kubja woman remarked, it is always a feat of "striking balance between husband and children, for both together are the source of my happiness and satisfaction."

The discussion of three key constructs of northern Indian kinship allows us to observe some of those features that the Hindu cultural system seems to emphasize. In terms of both ideology and context, each of the three constructs shows multiple connections with successively wider classes of meaning, where each embodies at least one culturally crucial principle of meaning organization (for example, virginity for *kanyā,* living husband for *suhāgin,* and progeny for *mātā*), and where each forges through this principle bound (*sāgī bahén* and *sagī mā*) and unbound (*bahén* and *mātā* under general usage) meanings. However, the bound meanings tend to link with the unbound ones in so many ways that the distinction remains purely analytical, and one's attention quickly moves to figurative procedures by which concordant systems of meaning (such as the *bīja-kshétra* chain for *mātā* and *suhāga-satī* connection for *suhāgin*) are elaborately produced against the unendingly resilient canvas of *dharma* and *karma.* Actually, it is feasible in the field today to compose a list of critical concordance for the scores of distinguishable usages of such a word complex as *mā-mātā-mātā-jī,* showing how, and for what cultural reasons, consistencies or variations in meaning appear in usage and whether the boundaries of such meanings are collapsible.

As for some figurative procedures, ranges of syntactic similitude and overlap (such as *sautéli mā* as *mā* and any woman as *bahén*), balance (as in being mother and wife at the same time), antithesis and contrast (as in *kanyā* and *suhāgin,* and *suhāgin* and *mātā*), and figurative (metaphorical and metonymic) comparisons and extensions (*suhāgin* being auspicious, *mā* being a figure of *māmata* and *tyāga,* or sacrifice) all may be seen to produce the described clusters of meanings. However, since these procedures work in terms of an inclusive notion of *dharma* and *karma* in the common man's mind, they yield, directly or indirectly, a concordant, holistic system of expression and meaning.

Two Cultural Transformations

From kaṇyā to suhāgin, a dāna-order transformation. Though this will not be the place to outline even essential features in the Hindu conception of *dāna* that apply in our example, we will consider those that draw attention to *dāna* as a primary cultural process that transforms a cultural category like *kanyā* into *suhāgin.* To study *dāna* in this context is to study the transformation itself. Under the Hindu system *dāna* represents a *dhārmika* act in its most pervasive sense (cf. Manu III:77, 78, 80). Its cultural conception is extremely rich. It begins with the cosmic order itself (where the Purusha himself may engage in *tapas, yajna,* and *dāna* to bring the creation about; cf. Kane 1941:837), and it still remains one of the most widely accepted components of the Hindu's daily ethic. A Kanya-Kubja Brahman priest characterized it as a "complete sacrifice where *tapas, homa,* and *yāga* simultaneously culminate and fructify" (cf. Kane 1941:841–842).

In our example, *kanyādāna,* which is the precondition for a ritually successful *pāṇigrihaṇa* (holding of hands by the couple) and a completed Brahma *vivaha* (see Prabhu 1963:173–175), is responsible for transforming a *kanyā* into a *suhāgin.* It is one of the ten *mahādānas* (the supreme gifts) one undertakes in life (Kane 1941:869), and it is at present as powerful a metonym for *kanyā* as for *dāna.* It thus readily comes to parents today as soon as a marriageable *kanyā* (one's own or another's) is mentioned by name or is implied in a domestic conversation (cf. Manu IX:4). Social pressures for *kanyādāna* remain unremitting on a girl's parents and brothers, displaying in social reality the enormous powers the *dāna* is accorded as a process for affinal transformation.

The indigenous conception of *dāna,* as useful for our purposes, could be classified between what we shall call formal, informal, and figurative *dāna.* (*Śulka* should be clearly distinguished from these.) The first, as Kane (1941:842–843) points out, requires the appearance of a vedic *mantra,* and it explicitly or implicitly carries "the idea that [the donor] will derive from that act some unseen spiritual result (*adṛṣta* or *puṇya*)." (The word *pratigraha* is applied to this type of *dāna.*) The second type is illustrated by giving *dāna* to a beggar on the street, where no *mantra* intervenes and the purpose met is generalized. The third type is exemplified by *vidyādāna* (such as a gift of education as by a teacher or by those who financially support educators, educational institutions, and pupils). An additional type is *dharmadāna* (that which is given to a worthy person solely because it is the donor's duty). A *kanyādāna* is almost always of the first type, though when a benefactor helps perform or performs *kanyādāna* for an orphan girl it falls into the last category.

Furthermore, *dāna* is seen to have six dimensions (*añgas*) in the texts, which, if not in similar words, are essentially still distinguished by the contemporary Kanya-Kubja Brahman and other twice-born caste groups I have studied. They are: giver (*dātā*), receiver (*pātra, pratigrahīta*), charitable attitude or faith (*sraddhā*), the proper thing donated (*déyam*), proper time (*kāla*), and proper place (*désha*) (summarized from Kane 1941:843). A *kanyādāna* invariably requires a careful consideration of all six dimensions; it is a culturally complete statement on *dāna* for a contemporary upper-caste member.

The notion of *dāna,* quite importantly, carries the emphasis on *sraddhā* (charitable attitude or pleased attitude of mind) (cf. Manu IV:226–227). Actually, the idea of superior (*uttama*), middling (*madhyama*), and low (*adhamam*) *dāna,* depending on whether the giver goes to the receiver to give or the receiver goes to the giver to receive or the receiver begs the giver to give, is central (Kane 1941:111–114). A *kanyādāna* on such a scale now occurs at the giver's place where the receiver comes to receive (seemingly a middling *dāna*). However, we must also recall that all marriage negotiations in the north start with the proposal from the giver, who goes to the receiver to give (a superior *dāna,* but compare also Kane 1941:532). My informants argued that it is this first step, where the receiver is given the *māna* (honor or respect) at his place, that sets the tone for the entire succeeding stages of *dāna.* A *kanyādāna* with *māna* of the receiver by the giver elevates the cultural quality of the whole *samaskāra.* (Such a formulation is logically consistent with that *dāna* model whereby Brahman is generally a receiver in the worldly order.)

The Hindu concept of *dāna,* as is ethnographically verifiable, normally underscores a logic of addition, multiplication, and division.[11] As givers give and receivers receive, both cause addition or multiplication in seen (*dṛṣta, laukika*) and unseen (*adṛṣta, alaukika*) dimensions. *Dātā* (givers of *dāna*) add or multiply their (the unseen) *puṇya* as they give away the (seen) cows, foods, virgins, clothes, money, and so on; receivers, being properly authorized to receive and by proper use of what is given to them, add or multiply their (unseen) *puṇya*. (Remember that the unseen merits sooner or later help secure the seen objects under the Hindu belief.) Subtraction logic, whereby *dāna* brings about a permanent loss, is anomalous within the system.

In this context *kanyādāna* illustrates a cultural principle and logic of conversion. It is for initiating a total, irreversible conversion of the idea and identity of a person under *dāna* (*déyam*); its conjugation with such vital ceremonies as *paṇigrihaṇa* (holding of hands), *homa* (fire sacrifice), and *saptapadī* (taking seven steps together) represents an entire cultural process of conversion. (For textual evaluation of *kanyādāna* and other central ceremonies, see Kane 1941:529, 531; also 532–538 for a list of ceremonies.) On taking the seventh step this transformation is held to be complete (see Manu VIII:227; for an ethnographic description see Khare 1976a:214), and wifehood (*saubhāgya*) is fully attained. A *kanyā* is so irrevocably converted into a *suhāgin* that if her husband were to die during the next hour under the marriage canopy, she would be a full widow (*vidhwā*), while her husband, if she died, would be a full *vihur* (widower), except that he could eventually remarry. The conception of consummation (if the idea were applicable in the same sense as in the West) is ritualized, and it is ritually achieved once a *kanyā* becomes *suhāgin.*

This transformation occurs through a series of ritual procedures, often by employing arrangements of cultural mediators, modifiers, markers, and reclassifiers that come from that cultural language that *kanyā, suhāgin,* and *mātā* represent as interrelated cultural constructs. Briefly, such conversions are brought about by ritual converters, usually those which the Hindu normatively employs in *samaskāras,* particularly since the latter concern themselves with symbols and signs of changing body and being and express a fitness either by removal of taint or by generation of fresh qualities (see Kane 1941:190–193). Table 6.2 illustrates a few such converters that appear under the marriage canopy; however, the list is merely suggestive, not exhaustive.

The cultural procedure for a *kanyā's* transformation into a *suhāgin* is marked by supernatural initiators, converters, and markers on the one hand and a firm resolution to give and to receive irrevocably among the human participants on the other. *Mantras,* publicly audible and reciprocal, form the resolution (*saṃkalpa*) to accomplish the total transformation for the *kanyā* (cf. Prabhu 1963:163–172). (The supernatural initiation of this transformation is underscored by the textual idea that the bride comes to her human bridegroom by way of her three prior divine husbands: Soma, Gandharva, and Agni (see Prabhu 1963; Kane 1941).

For the contemporary Hindu the idea of *dāna, māna,* and *saṃkalpa* epitomize the nature and consequence of *kanyādāna* and of the cultural

TABLE 6.2. INTERRELATIONSHIPS AMONG THE RITUAL CONVERTERS DURING MARRIAGE.

MAJOR CULTURAL TRANSFORMERS	MAJOR RITUAL COMPLEX	MAJOR SETS OF LOGICAL FUNCTIONS
Gauri-Ganesha	*Homa* (fire sacrifice)	Opening marker, mediator, modifier
Fire-*Prajāpatī*	Gauri-Ganesha *pūjana*	Initiator, facilitator
Mother goddesses	*Matṛkāpujana*	Invocators of the female principle (*shaktī* and *kula dévī*)
Vishnu-Tulsi	Vishnu-Tulsi *pujana* and circumambulation	Divine certifiers
Saṃkalpa (resolutions) of *dāna*	*Mantras* and rituals of successive resolution for *dāna.*	Verbal markers of the successive stages of transformation
Upahāra-dakshinā	Ceremonies of *upahāra-dakshinā* (combinations of *dāna* and *sulka* ethics)	Markers of transition and its completion
Dhruva (Pole Star)	*Dhruva darshana* ceremony	Stabilizer of the transformed
Departing gods and goddesses	*Devavisarjana* ceremony	Send-off marking successful completion of the transformation.

depth of transformation that it invariably involves for the near and dear ones of the bride. As informants as well as texts readily recognize, *samkalpa* (resolution) helps start, accomplish, and maintain the *dharma* of *kanyādāna.* Without *saṃkalpa* and *sraddhā* (proper bent of mind, faith, in the *samaskāra*), the *kanyādāna,* my informants repeatedly argued, is "meaningless, just as any other crucial practice"—*sadācāra*—"would be under those circumstances."

Suhāgin to mātā: a sapiṇda-order transformation. Here the introductory caveat is the same as in the first example. I cannot sketch even the essential features of this fundamental conception in the Hindu kinship system. Some relevant points for us, however, are the following. It is about coexistence and distribution of shared particles[12] among one's relatives related through one's parents. It normally builds upon only a successful *dāna*-order transformation, and it represents that principle and logic of coexistential[13] *dharma* that circles of ascendents and descendents (*pitra, pitā,* and *putra*) have toward each other within the system.

This transformation represents two central concerns: first, how the segment of biological facts of sexuality, pregnancy, and motherhood are handled within the system as a *suhāgin* becomes a *mātā* (along that *dharma* axis of conversion represented by *vadhu* and *var, patnī* and *patī, jananī* and *janaka,* and *mātā* and *pitā*) and how it symbolizes the coming together of *kshétra* and *bīja dharma* and the creation of another locus (progeny) for the *sapiṇda* and *srāddha* complex to extend itself. The latter complex leads us toward that system of meanings that dominates the Hindu conception of consanguinity (for the unusual cultural depth and significance of these key constructs, *sapinda* and *srāddha,* see Kane 1941:334–551.

The *srāddha* complex also makes a general point about the procedure to handle the natural: one always attempts to exhaustively impregnate the latter with *dharma* as one tries to ritually anticipate, control, and interpret the cause, process, and effect of the natural, and in doing so this approach sets up its own dominant systems of meanings and their boundaries. We find that *kshétra* and *bīja, sapiṇda* and *srāddha,* form a basic cultural cluster for the indentity of one's body and being, which a *suhāgin* materializes by becoming a successful *mātā* (that is, by giving birth to a normal, healthy child at full term and by rearing it to physical maturity). The popular conception of shared *rakta* or *khūn* (blood), now being discussed by anthropologists, is housed in, and acquires its meanings from, this key cultural cluster. My only indirect reference to *rakta,* which has a culturally secondary (auxillary rather than primary or key) position for us, is to be explained in the above frame of reference.

This prepares us to take up the popular cultural (*dharma*-based) conception of biological facts that a mother implies or represents. Our examples aim to illustrate the *dharma*-based conception and control of the biological. *Kshétra* and *bīja* have a double meaning for my informants: they refer to a natural fact (whenever *kshétra* and *bīja* are allowed to come together, they remain capable of yielding a pregnancy, whether legitimate or not) and to a *dharma*-ordered classification of that fact. A brother and a sister represent *bīja* and *kshétra* (and a potential for the same natural consequence between them if they are allowed to come together) that are by one *dharma* shared and by the other not meant to mix. Put another way, whether *sapiṇda* or not, *nara* and *nari* fundamentally represent *bīja* (seeds of *srajana* and *utapatti*) and *kshétra* (a system for *dhāraṇa* of that *bīja,* and a woman is in fact called *dhātri*). The metaphor of *ghrita* (*ghī*) and *agni* (fire) is often employed to convey their natural attraction: "One indiscriminately seeks the other unless carefully discriminated along the *dharma* and *adharma,"* observed one of my informants. If the *kshétra* approaches the *bīja,* as I was told, under the regular order, it is still the *bīja* that carries and manifests all relational and positional distinctions.

As a related point, my informants discussed at length the biological in terms of the properties and conditions of the body (*sāririka dharma*). Coming together of husband and wife for *sahagamana* (sexual intercourse) is also placed and evaluated within this cultural scheme. One of my educated informants, for example, sought to symbolize this relationship by "63" (those who face each other) while a *bhāi* and *bahén* dyad was merely "36" (those who have their backs turned toward each other). Another informant likened a proper conjugal relationship to the proposition whereby 1 (*pati*) facing 1 (*patnī*) yields 11, rather than 1 + 1 = 2—a quality of consanguineal relationships. Meanings ranging from psychosexual to metaphysical are extracted from such popularly shared cultural formulations. They are proposed to convey a basic cultural point: only a controlled and proper expression of sexual urge (even if it is a part of *sāririka dharma*) can accomplish the preferred transformational value (of *vriddhi*) that the above examples propose.[14]

Thus also as a *suhāgin* becomes a *mātā* she not only fulfills the hope of *vriddhi* (an increase or multiplication) but brings along a *kula deepaka* (literally a lineage's lamp, a powerful metaphor for a progeny that, with supposedly added honor and merit, carries forward the ancestral line), is a carrier of *vīrya* (semen) on the one hand and a performer of *srāddha* (ancestral rites) on the other. Actually, a *suhāgin* fully fructifies (*phūlti phaltī hai*) her husband's status "only when she provides a *putra* to perform *srāddha* and a *kanyā* for *kanyādāna,* as one informant said.

The *suhāgin-mātā* transformation is also represented in the field as an ethnographer records the fact that the *pati-patnī* relationship is, in meaning and world view, irretrievably transformed as soon as a child is born to them. A *suhāgin* pregnant for the first time may therefore represent that stage in which fully formed affinity is found, giving rise to its antithesis: still forming consanguinity. However, as soon as the child is born, this transformation is complete, and it inescapably enters and transforms the *pati-patnī* relationship. As my informants pointed out, "It alters one's whole view of social existence, even the view of one's body, age, attitudes about conjugal love, and standards of speech and behavior." One formulation was that the parents begin to see themselves and their relationships through the child; they are to each other mainly or only that which a child's presence, now or in future, would make them to be. Their bond of *rakta* (notice this usage of *blood* for *sapiṇda* and its cultural construction) with the child selectively masks, attenuates, and finally even dominates a view of their own relationship.[15] What we call teknonymy is in several informants' eyes evidence of this conquest by the child: one's wife becomes one's son's or daughter's mother, and vice versa.

The first-time pregnant *suhāgin* and the first-time mother (*jananī/mātā*) represent the two most crucial thresholds of cultural transformation available within the household (*grihya*). The first culminates the *dharma* of *kanyādāna* and *paṇigrihaṇa,* and the second interlinks *mātā, pitā, pitra,* and *baccé* (*bhāi/bahén*) orders of relationships and meanings.

If the first-time pregnant *suhāgin* represents a condition of total inclusion; the construct translates for the Hindu as "husband being inside his wife to be a child" (see Khare 1975:254 for Manu's enunciation of this point). Conceptually, a pregnant mother subsumes both husband and child in her body until she is transformed into a *jananī,* when regular parent-child social distinctions take over. It is an arrangement that probably the *bīja-kshétra* complex alone can bring along.

The *suhāgin-mātā* transformation is found to be culturally indispensable because it critically controls the *pitra-putra-dharma* so crucial for the Hindu social system. Internally, however, the view is inverted: *putras* (sons) exist because *pitras* (ancestors) exist. Texts make this point through a blessing: "May the *pitrs* who throng around the bride to see her grant her happiness endowed with progeny" (Kane 1953:346). My informants bless a bride, *"dūdhoñ nahāo pūtoñ phalo"* (May you bathe—or be so prosperous as to bathe—in milk and bear fruit by having sons).

Here *pitra* and *putra* connect with each other by sharing *piṇda.* Put in other words, *pitra* can link with *putra* only in the womb of a bride. Consistent with the male-dominant view, *pitra* must help beget *putra.* Kane (1953:346–347) in this context notes a well-known mantra, "Oh *pitṛs!* deposit (in this wife) an embryo [*garbham*], a child that (will wear later) a garland of lotuses so that he may become a grown-up male, [which is] repeated when the wife of the performer of the *srāddha* eats the middle one out of the three *piṇdas."*

Thus, when one marries, there are two interpretations of the event within the system. One is the male-dominated view that places the *pitra-putra* axis at the center of the stage, making the *suhāgin-mātā* transformation subservient to this axis. Here *pitras* cause a married woman to have *putra,* and it is this that texts and my informants, consistent with their patrilineal (*bīja*-based) cultural ideology, express and emphasize. Sons, therefore, by definition stand in debt (*ṛṇa*) of *pitṛa,* and they must repay that debt by performing *srāddha,* which, it is important to note, is a combination of two primary ritual complexes (see Kane 1953:482): *yajna* (sacrifice) and *dāna* (gift). In popular language this *karzā* (debt) is one of the most important ones one must repay in one's own life, and one expects one's sons to do the same after one is gone. In a culturally fundamental sense, if the *kanyā-suhāgin* transformation is dominated by the *dāna* (gift) *dharma,* the *suhāgin-mātā* transformation underscores *ṛṇa* (debt) *dharma.* Both transformations are there to support the *pitra-putra* coexistence, their consubstantiality, as one could say. Looked at from the woman's side, however, *pitras* exist because *putras* are there, and the latter must come from a *suhāgin's* womb. To become a *mātā* is therefore truly to create the factual basis for the *pitra-putra* axis—the relatives and relationships on which the Hindu *bīja* ideology survives. Instead of *dāna* and *ṛṇa* principles, the emphasis in the woman's world is on dharma *vṛtas* (vows) of *suhāga* (wifehood), *pativṛta* (fidelity), and successful motherhood. Following the first two means, as the law givers (Manu IX:12; V:151, 154) repeatedly emphasize, supporting the *bīja* (and social status) ideology of the system as a whole.

Conclusions

The discussion of the three cultural constructs and their two cultural transformations illustrates an initial but necessary step toward considering a kinship system as a cultural system. The Indian cultural system is particularly well suited for such an exercise, since it emphasizes a methodological holism that allows segments to be fundamentally conceived and defined in terms of the system as a whole. The language of direction, purpose, and meaning that the north Indian kinship system follows flows from the returns to the cultural system as a whole.

In order to demonstrate this feature I have followed certain methodological controls. An interconnected series of key cultural constructs works as connective tissues between the textual idea, the contemporary conceptions of the shared ideal and the normative, and the customarily variable systems of meanings. I do not seek to place an emphasis on texts or contexts, or texts and contexts under some mysterious balance, but on the ways they connect with each other, consciously or unconsciously, in the minds of the people studied here. I have found that the Indian kinship categories as cultural categories display a wide-ranging system of directives that guides their ranges of preferred, possible, and precluded meanings; that when people behave as relatives they do so for certain culturally valued reasons; and that what is called kinship is also, simultaneously and fully, the stuff of which the Hindu system itself is made. I found my informants connecting themselves with the ideal, either textual or popularly shared, but the quality of connections they made varied. They would interpret, invent, mythologize, and argue to construe, but all under a strong conviction that the texts and their practices, as one said, "cannot be very far off from each other, for they are always meant to be parallel if not always identical or converging." This cognitive datum on the twice-born is by itself crucial, despite the scholarly evidence (Lingat 1973; Kane 1941) that clearly cautions us against assuming such an interrelationship between texts, norms, and practices in Indian society.

What does this research imply for an anthropological attempt? The answer must come in terms of the methodological premise of the inquiry at hand. If an inquiry sets out to prove that specific customs follow specific textual ideals (or origins), or if it goes about cataloguing concordance between the textual recommendations, specific regional norms, and concrete social practices, we know the exercise would soon be doomed. If, however, our eyes are on the features of that fundamentally shared rela-

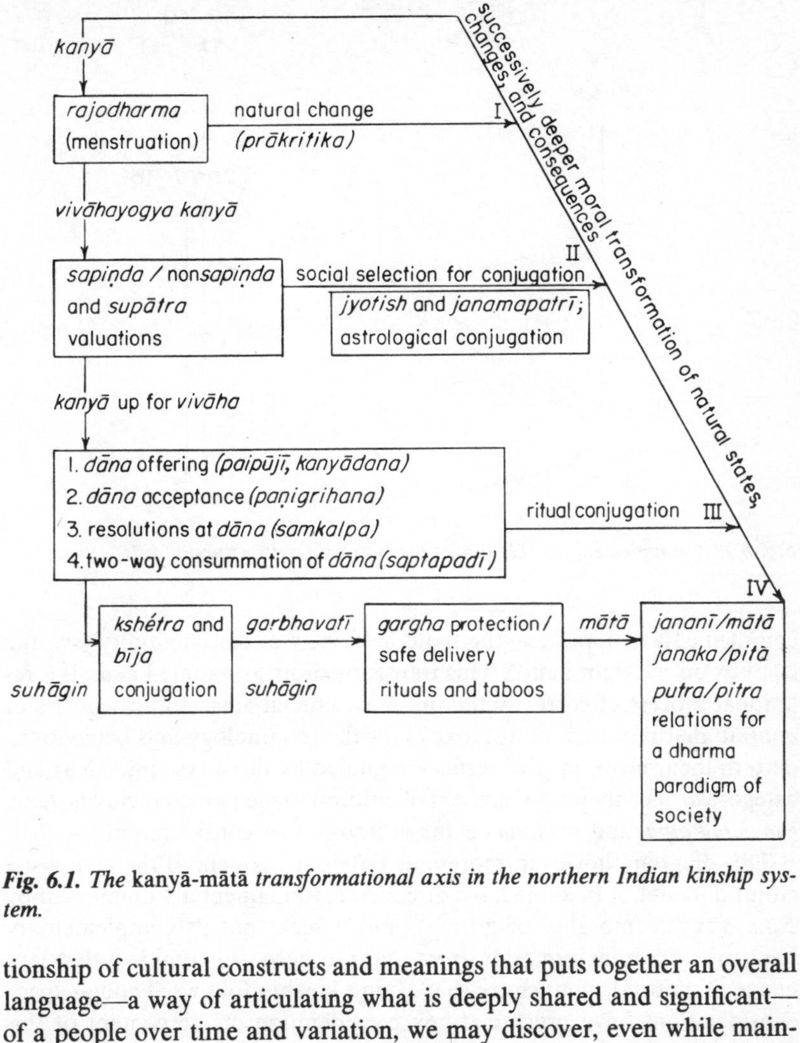

Fig. 6.1. The* kanyā-mātā *transformational axis in the northern Indian kinship system.

tionship of cultural constructs and meanings that puts together an overall language—a way of articulating what is deeply shared and significant—of a people over time and variation, we may discover, even while maintaining respect for the Indologist's diligent caution, sufficiently recurring cultural perspective regarding the ways in which people make sense of and set priorities on what they think, say, and do. An anthropological attempt like this one works at the level of the structure of cultural language itself.

There are two cognitive-conceptual models that help us coordinate major alignments that the *kanyā, suhāgin,* and *mātā* bring forth for the northern kinship system. Figure 6.1 summarizes an essential chain of cultural transformers (see boxes in the diagram) that help convert a *kanyā* into a *mātā.* In other words, it also presents a woman-centered view of Hindu affinity in northern India, leading us up to the emergence of its

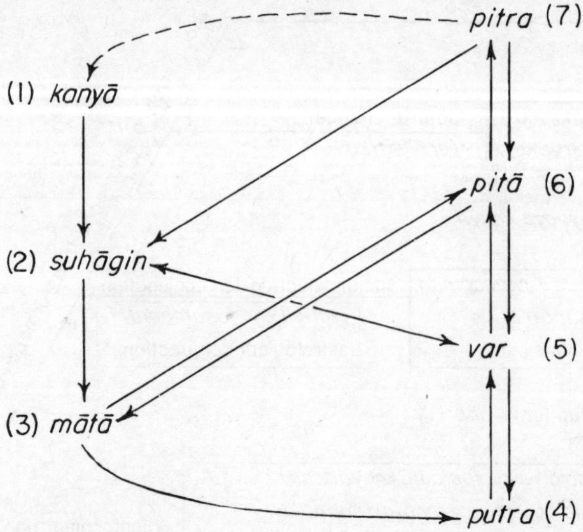

Fig. 6.2. A complementary relation of the putra-pitra *transitional axis.*

complementary opposite—the male-held view of consanguinity (see the last box on the right hand). This transformation, as handled here, is a relational process of correctly linking those crucial ideas and categories of *dharma* that represent cultural keys for the terminology and behavior to pattern themselves on. Kin terms are guided by these systemic ideas and categories, once their total context of cultural usage (which includes *dāna, ṛṇa, saṃkalpa,* and *srāddha*) is taken into proper consideration.

This diagram, however, represents only one segment of the composite cultural model. It is, as we have discovered, fundamentally dominated by *dāna dharma* (morality of gifting), and it seeks out its complementary segment—the transformation from *putra* to *pitra*—to complete that language of cultural significance that Hindu kinship follows. Though space considerations have precluded any consideration of the content of this complementary transformation, which is dominated by the ideas of *pitra ṛṇa* (debt towards one's ancestors),[16] the conceptual model seen in Figure 6.2 brings the two transformations together within the system. A systemically proper appreciation of the second diagram emerges when the first three categories and their interrelationships are considered to lie behind the other four, for the three woman-related categories will then be in line with the dominant patrilineal ideology of the system, showing a proper infrastructural alignment of the female principle in relation to the male. In other words, here we have stretched the model sideways so that the *kanyā-mātā* axis that normally lies underneath the *putra-pitra* one is placed on its side for a better comparison.

There are also five interrelated features we have demonstrated or variously implied in the above discussion.

1. This kinship system is found to run along certain key constructs of cultural significance; they guide the system of meaning that the majority of contemporary twice-born Hindus seek by their practice.
2. These constructs interrelate with each other under a transformational grammar, displaying how they are linked to key concepts of *dharma* and *karma* that weave through contexts and norms but are not context bound; they are culturally deep and stable but neither static nor possessed of axiomatized, invariant relations.
3. A chain of key cultural constructs like *kanyā, suhāgin,* and *mātā* not only exemplifies the above but also leads us toward uncovering the fundamental significance of such crucial nondualistic complexes of meaning-cum-action (idea into action and vice versa) as *ṛṇa* (debt), *dāna* (gift), *saṃkalpa* (resolution), *srāddha* (rites in faith). These link the language of meaning to the language of performance in a culturally correct manner.
4. As these cultural constructs and complexes undergo a series of transformations, they illustrate a syntax and a way of conceiving interrelationships between meaningful units that the twice-born Hindu follows in making sense of what he does regarding kinship and marriage, offering culturally good reasons.
5. Interrelationships available between the contextual and the general, the practical and the ideal, and kinship and nonkinship repeatedly show how this system is predisposed to treat a segment in terms of the whole: the language of kinship is unmistakably the language of the cultural system as a whole.

7

Widowhood among "Untouchable" Chuhras

Pauline Kolenda

> One etymology of *devara* is *dvitīya vara,* meaning "second husband" or "groom." This appears to reflect the fact that in some ancient *śāstras* or code-books a husband's brother might be appointed to beget a son upon his brother's widow (Bühler 1969:57–65). Inasmuch as this practice is not approved by contemporary Bengalis, they prefer to derive the term from *deva,* "god."
>
> Inden and Nicholas 1977:124

> The Jat father is made to say, in the rhyming proverbs of the countryside—"come my daughter and be married; if this husband dies there are plenty more." Ibbetson 1903:76
>
> Cited by Lewis 1958:4

WIDOWHOOD REPRESENTS the last and lowest stage in life for the Hindu woman. She starts in girlhood before pubescence as pure, a *devi,* a goddess, so pure that among the "untouchable" Chuhras,[1] who are not served by Brahmans, she receives the ritual gifts that a higher casteman would give to a Brahman; and pure, she is given in marriage. In menstruation and childbirth, by contrast, she is impure, and her touch and nearness must be avoided, for her pollution is communicable. As a *sūhāgin,* a woman whose first husband lives, she is welcomed as auspicious, especially if she is also a mother of sons. However, as a widow she is inauspicious, a reminder of death, and should be absent from all blessed occasions such as birth ceremonies and weddings.

For lower castes such as the untouchable Chuhras, there are ranked statuses within widowhood. Through them the Hindu widow can be understood as a cultural unit. Certain basic symbols underpin social norms (Schneider 1972:38), here for the symbolic activity of widow-mating, an indigenous category that means something distinctively different from remarriage. If we use a layer model, we may picture the indigenous basic symbols as being beneath or underlying the articulated norms or rules for behavior. Both the basic symbols and the norms relate to decision making and to action based on those decisions (see Table 7.1).

TABLE 7.1. LAYER MODEL OF AN ACTOR'S MENTAL RESOURCES IN DECIDING AND ACTING.

Action
↑
Decision
↑
Norms
↑
Basic Symbols

Indigenous conceptions operate at the level of "culture-as-constituted," or "certain regularities which are generally agreed relations between sign and meaning in this community" (Schneider 1980:131), and also at the level of "culture-in-action or culture-as-lived" (Schneider 1980:126, taken from Sahlins 1979). Linking the two levels are the norms, which are consistent with, indeed express, the basic symbols and evaluations but which are also directives for action. People—here the Chuhra widows and those who take responsibility for them—make decisions with the norms in mind. They, of course, may accept or reject those norms.

The questions to be addressed are these: What does an examination of widowhood within a small symbolic system and within a petty sphere of action tell us about the untouchable Chuhra widow as a cultural unit? What does it tell us about the more general Hindu cultural unit of widow? What does it tell us about the Chuhra kinship system, about the north Indian kinship system, and about the relationship between high-caste and low-caste cultures?

Caste Differences in North Indian Kinship

There are four aspects to the issue of caste differences in north Indian kinship practices: first, the treatment of caste differences in kinship by cultural analysts, specifically Dumont and those inspired by Dumont and by Schneider (1968); second, a presentation of a paradigm for comparing high-caste and low-caste cultures; third, a comparison of high- and low-caste cultures in Khalapur, the village studied; and fourth, the comparison as treated in Hindu law.

Cultural Analysts on Caste Differences in Kinship

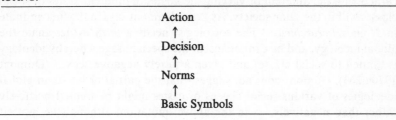

The cultural analysts who have scrutinized Indian kinship, those advocating the analysis of culture or ideology as distinct from the analysis of social structure, have been alike in treating what Dumont has termed "a basic ideology," "the global ideology," "the ideology of a society" (Dumont 1970a:263–264), as though it were uniform throughout the various social groups and segments in the society, as though there were a social unanimity, a unanimous ideology. They have not been very much concerned with the different or varying ideologies of different castes or social classes within the same society. As Louis Dumont says in the first endnote in *Homo Hierarchicus:* "The sociologist needs a term to designate the global ideology, and he cannot accept the special usage whereby ideology is limited to social classes and given a purely negative sense" (Dumont 1970a:263). Dumont does not suggest that the partial or less-than-global ideologies of various social classes or castes might be treated positively rather than negatively, as in the above quotation, although he himself treats a partial ideology in his analyses of north and south Indian regional kinship systems.

In a discussion of the kinship practices of the lower castes as compared to the higher castes in northeastern Uttar Pradesh, Dumont says: "On the whole, it is not easy to summarize the picture of marriage rules and intermarriage among the lower castes. One way out of the difficulty which I here reject, would be to fancy that there were different systems in vogue in different social levels. I believe, on the contrary, that there is in the matter of kinship a regional pattern which each group exemplifies in its particular way" (Dumont 1966:109). Thus, Dumont asserts his belief in a regional pattern of kinship.

That cultural analysts like Talcott Parsons (Parsons 1951) and Dumont himself (Dumont 1970a) were especially interested in comparing the ideologies of different societies does not invalidate their general uninterest in ideological variation among the social segments, categories, classes, and castes within the particular society under study. This consensus in methodology, the delineation of a single global ideology for a society as a goal for cultural analysis, can be traced from Parsons (1951) to Dumont's work on caste and kinship (1966, 1970a) to Schneider's *American Kinship: a Cultural Analysis* (1968). Schneider himself did not avoid the problem of class differences in American kinship (Schneider and Smith 1973), and other anthropologists (Yanagisako 1978a, 1978b; Drummond 1978; Chock 1974; Schneider 1980:121–122) took up the matter. However, it has not been faced in the Indian context.

It is Schneider's book on *American Kinship* (1968) that has served as the paradigm for the cultural analyses of regional kinship systems in India (Inden 1976; Inden and Nicholas 1977; Fruzzetti and Östör 1976; Barnett 1976; Fruzzetti, Östör, and Barnett 1976). It is not that these, as scholars of a unanimous ideology, are unaware of the question of variation among castes, social classes, or other social categories. Some of the works of the cultural analysts have been limited to high-ranking castes (Inden 1976; Barnett 1976). The two more general treatments of Bengali kinship, the one by Inden and Nicholas (1977), the other by Fruzzetti and Östör (1976), both admit that there are "problems of variation and change," that there may be differences between "urban and rural Bengalis," and "educated and uneducated persons" (Inden and Nicholas 1977:xii), "between high and low caste kinship, male and female kinship" (Fruzzetti and Östör 1976:102), but both opt to postpone examination of such variations, the former being more "convinced that a single coherent pattern of symbols . . . underlies most of the specific variant forms" (Inden and Nicholas 1977:xii) than the latter. Inden and Nicholas assume, furthermore, that there is much similarity in kinship practices in north India generally. They say:

> Our preliminary comparisions with other anthropological accounts of kinship in India have shown that categories of kinship in North India, if not also in the South, are structured in much the same way as the Bengali categories. That this is so is also confirmed by data derived from texual accounts of Indian kinship. Much of what we say about kinship in Bengali Hindu culture is derived from ancient and medieval Sanskrit texts; Bengali Hindus share these with Hindus throughout South Asia, implying the existence of an all-Indian "culture of kinship." (Inden and Nicholas 1977: xiii)

Dumont also, in his strenuous efforts (1966, 1975) to find that north Indian kinship expresses affinity even as south Indian kinship does (Dumont 1957b), was striving for a single Indian kinship ideology.

The cultural analysts thus strive to establish regional or all-India kinship systems. This is consistent with Schneider's emphasis in *American Kinship: A Cultural Account* upon the value of finding "one central symbol," "a firm, fixed core which provides the defining feature for every kind of person" in defining a relative (Schneider 1968:113). This, indeed, is the challenge of making a cultural account, to find the account that everyone in a cultural group accepts as correct (Nicholas and Inden 1977: xvii). Differing with Schneider, Yanagisako finds that in defining relatives there is a cultural order of Japanese-American kinship that is different from the cultural order of American kinship (Yanagisako 1978b:23–24).

We may ask: Is there a cultural order of untouchable Chuhra or low-caste kinship and a cultural order of Rajput or high-caste kinship? Since, at this point, we only know that we are concerned with widowhood, and we do not know what cultural units we will need to compare high-caste and low-caste cultures, we can only seek general guidance for making comparisons. There are, of course, Schneider's suggestions for comparison, first, of rates at which practices occur. We can answer in advance for widow mating and widow sale. There is none of either, at least publicly, among the high-caste population of Khalapur, while there are frequent instances of both among the untouchable Chuhras. Schneider further suggests that one may look at alternate and variant norms and forms and at differing outcomes of strategy decisions that individuals make

(Schneider 1968:16–18). He concludes, "Whether one can usually distinguish different kinship systems within the United States, or whether there is a single system depends on how the problem of variance is posed and how it is solved" (Schneider 1968:18). All of Schneider's remarks have to do with defining a relative. Here, that is not what is problematic. We are looking at practices—widow mating and widow sale—that occur with frequency among the untouchable Chuhras of Khalapur and almost never occur among the highest castes—the Rajputs, Brahmans, and Baniyas. Do we see this difference as part of different kinship systems, or is this a matter of an alternate set of norms and symbols within what is essentially one marriage system? The answer depends upon the other cultural units with which the alternate definitions of the widow as a cultural unit coexists to form a kinship system. Are these definitions largely the same in the highest and lowest caste except for the alternates of widow mating and widow sale, or are these also different?

Comparing High- and Low-Caste Cultures

In making such a comparison, we should also consider the process by which similarities or differences between high-caste and low-caste culture come about. As an aid for analysis, let me present a paradigm (see Table 7.2) that summarizes the various processes identified in recent social anthropological literature. We can specify which of these processes occurred between Chuhras and high-castes of Khalapur. The paradigm does not exhaust all possibilities, and there is logical overlap between categories—for example, any kind of incomplete emulation of high-caste culture would seem to result in a mixed culture.

The paradigm serves, nonetheless, to summarize a number of different processes that have recently been discussed. Elite emulation (Lynch 1969:218) has been a dominant theme in discussions of intercaste relations for some decades, whether in the form of Sanskritization (Srinivas 1966), Rajputanization (Sinha 1962:71–75), Vellālaization (Gough 1960:57), or the following of a kingly or priest model (Barnett 1970; Beck 1972:76–77). The social structure of a number of low castes residing together may be, in fact, a minicaste structure. Moffatt has provided an example of "accomplished emulation" (see the concept in the first box of Table 7.2) for a set of untouchable castes in a locality in Chingleput District, Tamilnadu; they recreate among themselves the entire set of institutions and ranked relations from which they have been excluded by the higher castes (Moffatt 1979:217).

Dumont has treated lower-caste kinship practices, comparing them with those of the Sarjupari Brahmans in Gorakhpur District in eastern Uttar Pradesh (Dumont 1966:108–110). His model might be considered to be what I call impoverished emulation (see Table 7.2, box 1). He talks

TABLE 7.2. PROCESSES OF LOW-CASTE EMULATION OF A HIGH-CASTE MODEL.

	HIGH-CASTE MODEL IS RELEVANT	HIGH-CASTE MODEL IS NOT RELEVANT
High-caste and low-caste cultures are similar	1. Emulation a. accomplished emulation b. impoverished emulation c. lagging emulation d. relaxed emulation	4. Reverse emulation a. universalization
High-caste and low-caste cultures are different	2. Contrast a. Involuntary contrast b. advocated opposition c. reformist opposition	5. Emulation of other models such as Westernization, Islamicization, Christianization, Persianization 6. Cultural pluralism
Low-caste culture is mixed	3. Mixed culture	7. Syncretism of Hindu-Muslim cultures 8. Partial modernization

about the wife-givers and wife-receivers as two sets of affines among the Sarjupari Brahmans: he sees the relationship between the two affinal sides as essentially hypergamous, the wife-givers having to maintain a perpetual gift giving as part of a permanent relationship of subordination to the wife-receivers. Influenced by his earlier study of repeated or perpetual alliances (Dumont 1957b) between minimal matri- or patrilineages in South India, he also has sought for repeated or perpetual alliance in north India; hence his focus on the repetition of intermarriage, by which he means repeated marriages between a pair of villages.

> In the matter of marriage rules, informants are most often clearly conscious of the hypergamic ideal, but they also recognize that the practice in their own group and in their immediate surroundings is different, and some of them state clearly that only the rich can afford to follow the higher customs. Among a caste of Banias, three devices are in vogue for making marriage less costly. The first is exchange, *badlā,* the second consists in abandoning to the bridegroom's family the honour of celebrating the marriage ceremony. This represents for the bride's father a severe loss of face, but it is characteristic of these small traders, economically-minded as they are . . . The third device consists in marrying not an unmarried girl but a woman who has already been married; it is called *sagāī* and appears only exceptionally and among the most destitute as the first marriage of a man . . . It is

> thus impossible to figure the pattern of intermarriage among the lower castes as an alternative to hypergamy; it stands under the shadow, so to speak, of the hypergamous pattern. What we are accustomed to calling rules in South Indian marriage is here replaced in part by the half unattainable ideal of higher and more well-to-do castes . . . To a great extent their practice is in their own eyes a makeshift, a manner of putting up with the actual conditions in their setting; it is not governed by fixed principles or rules. (Dumont 1966:108–110)

Dumont seems to be suggesting that the lower-caste customs are customs by default; that is, the lower castes resort to these practices because they cannot afford to follow the practices of the admired high-castes—specifically, for Dumont, the hypergamous relationship between wife-givers and wife-receivers. Dumont sees hypergamy as setting the regional kinship pattern, even though the lower castes can adhere to the pattern "only partially or weakly" (Dumont 1966:109). Inden and Nicholas also mention that the poor do "saṃskāras in very abbreviated form," another example of impoverished emulation (Inden and Nicholas 1977:36).

The term *lagging emulation* (see Table 7.2, box 1) was coined by Ernestine Friedl (1964): "The emulation in question is the process whereby social groups of lower prestige, upon the acquisition of new wealth or other forms of opportunity, imitate and often successfully acquire what they conceive to be the behavior of those with greater prestige; the emulation 'lags' in that the behavior imitated is that which reached its acme as a prestige symbol for the higher social group at an earlier period in its history, and is now obsolescent" (Friedl 1964:569). Bernard Cohn gave an example of lagging emulation in his comparison of untouchable Chamars with high-caste Thākurs in the eastern Uttar Pradesh village of Madhopur (Cohn 1955): "The Thākur model for the family appears to be influenced by the urban, Western family, while the Camār mode is based on the family of the Thākurs fifty years ago" (Cohn 1955:67–68). This phenomenon is undoubtedly widespread in India, as higher-castes Westernize and lower-castes move up socially.

Relaxed emulation (see Table 7.2, box 1) refers to emulating what is convenient to emulate along with ignoring what is inconvenient to emulate. The Chuhras of Khalapur were attracted by many aspects of high-caste Rajput style of life, but most did not want to give up eating pork to have a more Rajput style, nor did the Chuhra men show any interest in giving up widow mating or widow sale.

Involuntary contrast or structural opposition (see Table 7.2, box 2) is illustrated by one of the few systematic comparisons between high-castes and low-castes with respect to kinship: Kathleen Gough's comparison of Brahmans with "the lower non-Brahman tenant castes of cowherds, peasants, artisans, washermen, and barbers, and of the 'exterior' castes of

Pallans and Parayans" (Gough 1956:844) of Kumbapettai, a village in Tanjore District, Tamilnadu, south India. Gough admits to certain similarities in the kinship systems of Brahmans and lower castes: both are patrilineal and patrilocal and both use Dravidian (bifurcate merging) kinship terminology; both prefer cross-cousin or sister's daugter marriages, although few close-relative marriages actually occur. In contrasting Brahmans and the lower castes, Gough emphasizes particularly the assymmetrical relations among Brahmans—the father as superordinate to the son, the elder brother to the younger brother, the husband to the wife, the mother-in-law to the daughter-in-law, the sister's husband to the wife's brother, the father's sister's son to the mother's brother's son. These contrast with the egalitarian relationships among the lower castes, brothers being peers rather than ranked one over the other; the adult son as an independent wage earner being equal with his father; the wife as a wage-earner being close to equal to her husband; brother and sister being equals. Of particular interest to this paper on the levirate is Gough's contrast between the relations between brothers. Among the lower castes social equivalence and unity with their brothers is more strongly emphasized than among Brahmans (Gough 1956:843). Among the lower castes there is also the practice of what she calls the "optional levirate" (Gough 1956:846), and brothers substitute for each other in other contexts. She speaks of the "social equivalence and organized solidarity" of brothers and adult married men among the lower castes (Gough 1956:840).

Consistent with the optional levirate among the lower castes is a man's assumption of affinal relations with his brother's affinal kin as well as with his own. This does not occur among the Brahmans. Furthermore, relations between brothers-in-law (wife's brother and sister's husband) are egalitarian among lower-caste men. These egalitarian males express more open aggression toward each other, as opposed to the aloofness and distance between ranked males among the Brahmans (Gough 1956:847).

Unlike Brahman women, lower-caste women "are not assimilated to their husbands, but in marriage remain equal and 'opposite' to them"; "a low caste woman does not become terminologically assimilated to her husband" (Gough 1956:845). The Brahman woman, on the other hand, is assimilated to her husband; she is one flesh with him (Gough 1956:842). Women in the lower castes are not considered to be dangerous to their men's spiritual lives either, as among Brahmans; the latter believe that sexual activity is a deterrent to spirituality (Gough 1956:841). Lower-caste women retain greater rights in their natal families than do Brahman wives (Gough 1956:846). While *satī* (a widow's committing suicide when her husband dies, usually by throwing herself on the husband's funeral pyre) and permanent widowhood are practiced among the Brahmans, lower-caste women are allowed divorce and remarriage and, presumably, are not encouraged to become *satīs* (Gough 1956:842–843).

Gough explains the differences between the Brahmans and the lower castes as being due to two factors. The first is the contrast between the Brahmans as landholders and the lower castes as wage earners. The equality between adult son and father and between husband and wife result from their separate and more or less equal status as wage earners. Thus, the difference is caused by differences in relationship to production; it is not a matter of impoverished emulation. The second factor is the lower castes' lesser concern with Sanskritic religious beliefs and practices, such as a concern for Vedic writings and rituals, mystical meditation, and freedom from rebirth. Presumably, it is this lesser Sanskritization that accounts for lower-caste women's not being spiritual hazards for their husbands. Possibly it is the requirement that a man must have a wife in order to perform Vedic rites with him that is connected with the wife's assimilation to her husband among the Brahmans. It would appear to be the economic rather than the religious factor, however, that account for a lower-caste woman's more equal rights in both her marital and natal homes and her equality with her brother. Among the higher castes, the control of land inherited by men may foster degradation of women in order to exclude them from a share in inheritance.

The impoverished emulation described by both Dumont and Gough emphasizes the importance of economic roles. Each writer is, of course, concerned with different features of the kinship culture—Gough with the quality of family relationships, Dumont with the giving and receiving of wives. Gough finds much more consistency in the lower-caste practices than does Dumont, who finds little consistency in the rules for bride-giving among the lower castes, except for their impoverished emulation of higher-caste hypergamy. His conclusion about north Indian kinship can serve as an example of a mixed system, one combining Sanskritic kinship vocabulary with "the type of affinal prestations which is part and parcel of the 'Dravidian' kinship system" (Dumont 1966:102). "The complexity of the scheme, its relatively unsystematic or astructural type, would then be the fruit of a compromise between a Sanskritic verbal heritage and a 'Dravidian' practice" (Dumont 1966:102). Similarly, Dumont found a mixed culture among the Nayar. He explained the Nayar *tali*-tying rite, after which a woman was free to take a series of lovers, as indicative of a cultural compromise made by a matrilineal people to "perpetuate themselves" in a "patrilineal milieu" "by subordinating their productive marriage to the regional pattern of the principle-primary patrilineally productive marriage" (Dumont 1964:85).

To return to Table 7.2, box 2, to the prcesses called advocated opposition and reformist opposition, examples here would include political movements such as the DMK in south India, which, in its earlier forms, was very much against north Indian high-caste religion and religionists—Brahmans. Reformist opposition might be illustrated by the Arya

Samaj, strong in northwestern Uttar Pradesh, where Khalapur is located, a religious reform movement that also was anti-Brahman, or the Lingayats in south India, similarly anti-Brahman and reformist. Turning from the intercaste cultural processes in which a high-caste model is relevant to those in which a high-caste model is irrelevant, I have listed as an example of high-caste and low-caste cultures as similar the process of reverse emulation (Table 7.2, box 4). An example is universalization, which Marriott speaks of, whereby elements of folk tradition, including low-caste tradition, are taken up by Brahmans and refined and made part of the Sanskritic high culture and adapted into a universal culture (Marriott 1955:197–199). Krishna, as a local folk hero of the Mathurā region, is an obvious example. We may ask whether there has been similar universalization of lower-caste kinship practices.

As to emulation of other models (Table 7.2, boxes 5 and 6), as in Westernization, Islamicization, and Christianization, undoubtedly much research could be done on the influences of these as well as other models upon Hindu kinship. T. N. Madan points out that the term *rishta,* as in *rishtadar,* and *ashnav,* both meaning affinal kin, are Persian words. He comments:

> The absence of words derived from Sanskrit for the categories under reference is rather intriguing, particularly because the vocabulary of kinship among the Pandits is very largely so derived. In fact, there is no other major notion in the field of kinship for which a term of Sanskritic derivation is not available. Could one argue that under the influence of Islam affinity has acquired a greater salience than it earlier had—that formerly marriage ties were subsumed under kinship ties and were therefore of much less significance than now, and the principle of descent was dominant? (Madan 1975:222)

Here Madan is suggesting a compromise system of kinship combining Sanskritic consanguinity and Persian affinity; as we have seen, Dumont saw a compromise between Sanskrit terminology and Dravidian affinity. The issue of the origin of north Indian affinity is an interesting one. The influences of Persian culture or of Islam on north Indian kinship practices have yet to be thoroughly studied.

A representative of the cultural pluralism view (Table 7.2, boxes 5 and 6) is Irawati Karve (1961) who holds, "It is the caste which is mainly responsible for the variety in behavioral patterns found in India" (Karve 1961:10). For Karve, *jatis* are like tribes: both *jatis* and tribes are endogamous, have a territorial spread, and are self-governing. Both tribes and *jatis* come together to exchange services and products. She sees the interaction between *jatis* as "peripheral and tangential" (Karve 1961:55): they interact "without actual mingling" (Karve 1961:109). *Jatis* are "semi-autonomous cells" (Karve 1961:57). She holds that this type of society of juxtaposed ethnic or tribal groups arose when different peoples came together, without any single people being strong enough to impose its political or cultural dominance. Such a pluralistic society persisted because it accommodated new elements and offered security through a long period of political instability and foreign domination. Caste is "a loose structure which could take in new units and rearrange old units" (Karve 1961:108). She contrasts this patchwork society with Christian Europe, with its "fundamental uniformity" (Karve 1961:109). In India, the state was culturally unimportant, she asserts, and a church never emerged. In contrast to Dumont, she does not see either king or Brahman as integrating the caste system, either locally or in India generally (Dumont 1970a; 1970b). Such integrating principles as hierarchy, pollution, and *karma,* ideas spread by holy men and wandering dramatists, sat lightly over the coalesced tribes (Karve 1961:116). The apical status of Brahmans was always contended (Karve 1961:114). The three *varnas* continually competed with one another. Caste society was "an ever changing pattern of alliances and rivalries" (Karve 1961:114). Karve is not impressed by processes of elite emulation. Those of lower caste who imitate a higher caste in dress or speech are most often ridiculed, demeaned rather than praised (Karve 1961:119), she observes. Those castes which through conquest had declared themselves to be Kshatriyas might imitate those of higher rank after attaining higher rank themselves, not before (Karve 1961:121).

Her disproof of any all-India pattern of kinship inheres in this passage: "The variety in family organization is equally great. Polyandry and polygyny are both found. There are groups which are matrilineal, others which are patrilineal. The taboo on consanguine marriages changes from region to region and from caste to caste . . . The modes of inheritance and succession are also different" (Karve 1961:5). Karve, in an original mode, sees the source of cultural diversity among *jatis* in the diversity of origins and histories of the various *jatis* within the same region. She does not see Sanskritization as either attractive to lower castes or important, nor does she admit to the cultural dominance of any elite; she does not admit even that there are model elites.

We will not tarry over the last two intercultural processes, syncretism and partial modernization (see Table 7.2, boxes 7 and 8). This paradigm helps guide us in the comparison of high-caste and low-caste cultures. It suggests certain key questions to ask in the comparison of lower-caste with higher-caste kinship practices. These are:

1. Is the lower-caste group aware of an elite model of kinship culture?
2. Are they attracted to emulate this elite model?
3. Are the differences between lower-caste practices and higher-caste practices due to differences in economic roles and resources?

4. Are the differences between lower-caste practices and higher-caste practices due to differences in history and origins?
5. Are other models besides that of the higher caste relevant?
6. Can the kinship practices of lower castes and higher castes be seen to be expressions of the same symbolic system?

Low- and High-Caste Cultures in Khalapur

Khalapur is a large village in western Uttar Pradesh in southern Saharanpur District. It is composed very largely of a single huge clan of Rajputs (Hitchcock 1956, 1960; Minturn and Hitchcock 1966). In the mid-1950s, when I did field work there as part of a team of Cornell University researchers, the Rajputs composed over 42 percent of the population of five thousand people.[2] The Rajputs were the dominant caste, owning and controlling almost all the land. Ritually, they ranked below the Brahmans, but the Brahmans were few and poor. The Rajputs used the untouchable Chamars—the second largest segment of the population, about 10 percent of the total—as field hands. The other half of the population was distributed among almost thirty other caste groups, almost all of which were Hindu (about 10 percent of the population were Muslim). There were Brahmans, Vaishya (Baniyas) shopkeepers, Goldsmiths, Carpenters, Barbers, Launderers, Potters, Shoemakers, and so on. At the bottom of the caste hierarchy were the Scavengers, called either the Chuhras or Bhangis; they were about 5 percent of the population and numbered about 250 people living in two colonies on different sides of the village. The colony of Chuhras among whom I worked were composed of under one hundred people.

The *jajmāni* system was a thriving institution, and each reasonably prosperous Rajput, Brahman, Baniya, and Goldsmith family had a complement of servants—a Water-carrier, a Barber, a Launderer, a Scavenger, a Carpenter, and a Potter. Among the Scavengers, teams of women, usually mother-in-law and daughter-in-law or two brothers' wives or mother and daughter—more rarely husband and wife or mother and son—served a dozen or more *jajmān* families, cleaning their cattle yards, making dung cakes for fuel, and cleaning any womens' latrines. From each *jajmān* family they received thirty pounds of grain semiannually after each harvest, clothing twice a year, and daily food at midday, feast food on festival days, and something from kitchen and fields regularly, whatever might be available.

While some of the other castes that provided *jajmāni* services were gradually becoming unemployed owing to technological improvements (courtyard pumps displaced Water-carriers, manufactured metal dishes were displacing the pottery made by Potters), the Chuhras continued to be indispensable. Most of the scavenging work was done by the women, the Chuhris. The elderly headman worked as scavenger-sweeper at the high school; another young man worked for the American project in the same capacity. All of the adult men had worked in cities of the region at various times, where they were employed on sanitation crews or in commercial or private establishments as sweepers and scavengers. A few were absent in the cities while we were working there. Within the village the men did some agricultural work, limited almost entirely to cutting grain at harvest time; they raised and sold pigs; some looked after cows or water buffaloes, either their own or those of some higher-caste owners. A few worked occasionally on house construction. A group of the younger men had a brass band that was on hire for weddings. Some men were occasional drummers for various higher-caste ceremonials like birth and wedding rites.

A part-time avocation of a number of the Chuhra men—there was usually one in every patrifraternal joint family—was serving some minor gods as a devotee (*bhagat*). The god, in return for offerings of food and drink, acceded to being a tutelary spirit, helping the *bhagat* to communicate with harmful spirits of the dead, which caused illnesses and female misfortunes like barrenness and miscarriages. There were *bhagats* in some of the other low castes of Khalapur. Occasionally higher-caste women patronized these lower-caste *bhagats* to effect needed cures. To a minor extent, this was a source of income for Chuhra men.

Both Chuhras and Rajputs, as well as all of the other castes of Khalapur, were patrilineal in organization and patrilocal in residence rule. Virtually all Rajput males could trace descent from a common male ancestor whose sons seem to have settled in the village in the first half of the sixteenth century (Hitchcock 1956:64, 66). The Rajputs were strict in their enforcement of the rule of patrilocality, probably owing to the pressure of population on land resources, strong disincentive to share land with affinal male kin or with outsiders. The Rajput wives all came from other villages, since Rajputs, like all other *jatis* in Khalapur, rigorously adhered to rules of village and patrilineage exogamy.

The Rajput ideal, which the Chuhras and other castes also tried to achieve, was the maximization of marriage ties with as many different caste chapters in as many different villages as possible. All also tried to practice directional hypergamy, giving daughters to one set of villages, said to be in a westerly direction, and taking brides from another set of villages, said to be in an easterly direction. Exchange marriages, either between families or between villages were proscribed. A rule of three- or four-*gotra* exogamy was followed by the Chuhras and other castes. *Gotras* were patrisibs: one inherited *gotra* membership from the father, and members of *gotras* were *gotra* brothers, *gotra* sisters, *gotra* uncles, and so on, to each other. A person was not permitted to marry into his or her own *gotra* nor into that of the mother, the father's mother, or the mother's mother. A woman did not change her *gotra* membership to that of her husband upon marriage. The *gotra* rule, in effect, prohibited marriage with first cousins of either parallel or cross variety.[3] Directional hypergamy and the prohibition on marriage with cousins seems to be characteristic of north Indian kinship generally, as Dumont has pointed out (Dumont 1966), and is generally followed by the Chuhras, as well.

The female segment of the populations of all castes of Khalapur fluctuated in number and composition, because wives, with their children, often went for long or short visits to their natal home and village, and married daughters with their children, came to Khalapur. The two visits within a family were often coordinated; as a wife left, a married daughter came. Among the Chuhras, the male segment also fluctuated, as men stayed out of the village to work or to visit with relatives elsewhere. The Chuhras also had much more flux in their core population, because the rule of patrilocality was much less rigidly adhered to. The family of a married daughter might settle with her parents and brothers, or a wife's brother and his family (or in one instance a wife's sister and her family) might settle with the married sister. At one point in 1955 the Chuhras of the western colony of Khalapur, among whom I worked, numbered about ninety persons. The core of the group was a patrilineage (of thirty-six persons) tracing descent from a common ancestor, husband of a daughter of the eastern colony of Chuhras who had returned to settle in Khalapur six or eight generations ago. An additional thirty-six persons were related to this core, either through daughters of the patriline who had returned after marriage with their children, and sometimes with their husband to live in their parental village, or through wives' brothers who had settled with their married sister in her husband's village. This patrilineage plus its accretion of maritally related families formed one cognatic descent group or faction. Another descent group composed of the remaining eighteen persons was made up of an elder and the families of his two married sons plus that of his wife's married sister's family who had recently migrated to Khalapur from another village.

A key difference between Rajputs and Chuhras, then, is that there is much deviance from the rule of patrilocal residence among the Chuhras but virtually none among the Rajputs, and there is much flux in the population as families change residence. The occasional uxorilocal rather than the more usual virilocal residence means that there are among the Chuhras a number of *ghar jamais,* men living in their wives' natal houses. *Ghar jamais* are looked down upon. They do not have inherited rights to *jajmāni* clients nor to participation in the *kunbā* (descent group) council. A *ghar jamai's* male descendants may, of course, remain in their mother's village and found a new patriline.

Among the Chuhras, the largest solidary group is the *basti,* or residential colony. It is composed of all the Chuhras living in the western quarter of Khalapur. The colony is a single monocaste neighborhood. They do not feel any unity with the Chuhras of the eastern quarter, although some wives have kinship ties with members of that quarter, and of course the ancestress of the main patriline in the western quarter was a married daughter of the eastern quarter. There have been a number of disputes between the two colonies; possibly at one time they had a more solidary feeling.

Within the *basti* the next largest unit is the *kunbā.* This is a patrilineal descent group of male descendants from a grandfather or a common male ancestor or more remote generation, plus wives and unmarried daughters. A line must have had at least three generations before being considered to be a *kunbā.* The families of four *ghar jamais* thus have no *kunbā;* they number twenty-three people. Affinal relatives through either wives or through married daughters are not members of a *kunbā.* There are four *kunbās* among the Chuhras of the western colony: Ram's, composed of thirty people; Lakshman's, composed of six people; Gokal's, composed of eleven people; and Munshi's, composed of ten people. The first three represent a core patrilineage (Ram's) plus two patrilines descended from men who were originally resident by virtue of one being a wife's brother and the other a daughter's husband to Ram's lineage. Except for the elderly Chuhri, Sumi, who was married first into Munshi's *kunbā* and then into Ram's, there were neither agnatic nor cognatic relations between the first three *kunbās* and Munshi's. The three related *kunbās* formed a faction; Munshi's formed the other faction. The first three referred to their faction as the *bagar* (residential compound). Munshi had his own *bagar.* Each *kunbā* had its own tutelary godlings and ancestors for worship. Each *kunbā* had its own *chaudhuri* (headman). The entire *kunbā* suffered birth pollution and death pollution if a member was born or died. And the *kunbā* had a reputation, a name (*nam*), had its honor (*ijjat*) to preserve. If a wife of the *kunbā* had an illicit affair with a lover, "the whole *kunbā* was angry" and she "gave the *kunbā* a bad name," one Chuhri explained.

Members of the *kunbā* who were not one's close lineal or collateral kin were referred to by an appropriate kinship term prefixed by *kunbā.* So one's brother (*bhai*) born of the same parents as oneself was a *saga bhai.* The sons of one's father's *bhais*—his elder brother is one's *taū,* his younger brother is one's *chacha*—were *chacha-taū-bhais.* Other members of the *kunbā* who were neither *saga bhai* or *chacha-taū bhais* were *kunbā bhais.* Similarly, one distinguishes between a *khās* (one's own) *tau* or *khās chacha* or *khās baba* and a *kunbā tau, kunbā chacha, kunbā baba.* All the members of a *kunbā* were called *kunbewale* (people of the *kunbā*); so one might say *kunbāwala bhai.*

The Rajputs were more likely to use the word *ḳhāndān* for the patrilineal group. Some Chuhras said that *kunbā* and *ḳhāndān* were synonymous. One of the high school boys among the Chuhras said that a *ḳhāndān* would be men descended not just from a *baba* (father's father) but from a *parbaba* (father's father's father). The idea seemed to be that the *kunbā* was a patriline of shallow generational depth, while a *ḳhāndān* would have deeper generational depth. This distinction in terminology, indeed, reflects a difference between the two caste communities. While Chuhra patrilines went back at most six or eight generations, members of Rajput patrilines (*ḳhāndāns*) claimed to go back sixteen, even twenty generations.

There were two kinds of residential houses in Khalapur, one entirely for men, the other very largely for women and their small children. The latter is usually referred to as the *bagar.* It is a series of rooms built in lines forming a rectangle around an open-air space. Depending upon its size, this inner space may be a courtyard in which many activities take place, or it may be merely a wide passage or thoroughfare. The courtyard would be found in the large women's houses of prosperous landed Rajput *ḳhāndāns.* The thoroughfare was found in the Chuhra *bagars.* The entranceway to a room in the *bagar* was usually partially walled, and in this walled entranceway, in an inside corner, would be one or more floor-level, horseshoe-shaped, dried mud burners; it was here that most cooking for the *ghar* (household) was done. All of the people who ate from a *chulha* (hearth) were a *ghar.* The sixteen *ghars* among the Chuhras were the smallest kinship units. Of the sixteen, six were nuclear families, five were supplemented nuclear, one was a supplemented collateral joint family, one was a lineal-collateral joint-family, one was a supplemented subnuclear family, one was subnuclear, and one was a single-person household (Kolenda 1968:362). The women sharing the room or rooms of a *ghar* were related by birth or by marriage; they slept in the room with their small children. The men slept on the *chaupāṛā,* the sitting platform, raised three or four feet above the street; it had a long room at its rear where men and boys of the *kunbā* or *kunbās* sharing a *chaupāṛā* slept. The men sat on the platform during waking hours to smoke, talk, and care for small children; there, occasionally they also performed ceremonies.

The family cycle tended to be similar for both Rajputs and Chuhras and for the other castes of Khalapur as well. Elderly parents lived with married son or sons, the daughters-in-law doing most of the household work, the elderly mother-in-law looking after the small children (the elderly father-in-law often looked after a grandchild while he sat on the *chaupāṛā*). Adult married brothers usually divided into separate *chulha* groups as their children increased in number. By the time both of the elderly parents were dead, virtually all sets of brothers separated into separate *ghars.* Their wives and children would continue to live in adjoining *ghars,* or in ones very close to each other. It was the *kunbā* that functioned as a large extended family, since its members took a very personal interest in the affairs of one another. It was the *kunbā* elders who arranged marriages for the children of its constituent *ghars* or who should arrange such marriages.

The Chuhra *basti* was located on the furthest northwestern edge of Khalapur village. The double *bagar* of the three related *kunbās* was not fully walled in; it opened at one end onto a pond which separated it by a few hundred feet from the huge *bagar* and *chaupāṛā* of a very prosperous Rajput *ḳhāndān*. The *chaupāṛā* of the Chuhra men of the three *kunbās* faced the *ghars* of some of their women. The women in the houses facing the *chaupāṛā* could easily observe the men's activities on the sitting platform, and the men, in turn, could easily observe the women's activities. While women were forbidden to step onto the *chaupāṛā,* women could easily hear the men's discussions going on there, and bold women did not hesitate to call out remarks on what they heard.

High-caste Rajputs men and women were much more separated from one another than were the Chuhras. Among the Rajputs, the *bagars* were completely walled off from the village streets, and while the men's *chaupāṛā* might adjoin the *bagar* or be very close to it, the thick mud walls of the *bagar* thoroughly insulated the women's activities from the men's. The men could, of course, easily monitor their women's movements out of the *bagar.* Since they were strictly restricted, kept in *parda,* little should take place. High-caste women visited other *bagars* by crossing from one to another over the flat rooftops where *bagars* adjoined one another. The men could also easily monitor those going into the *bagar* from the street.

Since all the Chuhris went out to do their scavenging and sweeping work daily, they also were watched by their men sitting on the Chuhra *chaupāṛā.* It was the Chuhris' services, as well as the services of other *jajmāni* household servants, that made it possible for high-caste women to be secluded. The women passing through the Chuhra *basti* streets on their way to and from work could easily chat with the younger men of the community; they, like the higher-caste women, were prohibited from speaking to men older than their husbands and, indeed, they were to keep their face hidden in the ends of their head scarves (*oṛnās*) if such older men were close by. This covering of the face was called *ghungaṭ.* But they could talk with children and men younger than their husbands.

The Chuhris had ready access to high-caste culture, since they frequented high-caste homes daily to clean latrines; they also saw high-caste men in their cattle yards when they went there to collect the animal dung and make dung cakes, used for fuel, and they were on friendly bases with many of the families for whom they worked. Part of the high-caste culture that the Chuhris could easily observe were the details of the various Hindu calendrical rites and life-cycle rites celebrated in their *jajmāns'* homes. And indeed the Chuhris emulated these in an impoverished way. One element of impoverishment, of course, was the lack of a Brahman priest for household *havans* and *pujas.*[4] Among the Chuhras, an elderly Chuhra man performed these rites. Part of the *jajmāni* rights for a Chuhri was receiving some of the rich foods that high-caste women always prepared on each of the thirty-odd Hindu festivals celebrated annually in the village. The Chuhra religious life was, hence, Sanskritized by this emulation. They supplemented these festival celebrations with worship of their own deities and with the curing rites by their own *bhagats.*

Among the Chuhras, as among other castes in Khalapur, marriages were arranged, bride and groom not seeing each other until the day of the wedding. Both were usually under the age of sixteen, and sometimes brides were tiny girls of six or eight. Grooms usually were at least fourteen, although there were some instances of child grooms. Expenses in marriages were especially heavy for the bride's people, since the groom came from an outside village with a party of male guests who had to be fed for three or four days. The bride had to be provided with ample jewels, ornaments, and *saris,* and she had to take with her to the groom's family's home in his village clothing, toys, and sweets for her husband's people as well as permanent housekeeping equipment such as vessels and linens, a sleeping cot, and so on. Sizable amounts of money were not given at that time by a bride's people for a groom, a groom price, nor was bride price given either, at least not openly; this is not to say that bride price might not have been customary in the past. Rajputs and some other of the higher-caste families gave groom price,[5] and their trousseaus and other gifts were, of course, more lavish than among Chuhras, but even an untouchable Chuhra or Chamar bride departed from Khalapur adequately equipped.

Elopement, love marriages, and premarital sexual activity were strongly disapproved, both for men and women, to be sanctioned by ostracism from the caste community, or worse. A high-caste girl becoming pregnant premaritally was said to deserve to be killed by her father. In fact, such cases either ended in a rapid arrangement of her marriage, or, rarely, in suicide. Chuhra women would be married off or even sold under such circumstances.

There were two parts to a wedding. The first part, called the *shādī,* involved the *pheras,* or rounds made by the wedding couple, her *sari* tied to his head scarf, circling a sacred fire. The Chuhras generally referred to marriage as the *pheras.* It was the *pheras* that bound a woman to her husband; by this ceremony, she became irrevocably his wife. The *shādī* often took place before the bride had reached puberty. Preceding the *shādī* were rituals including the *roknā* (the formal agreement between the fathers to have the children marry), the *sagāī* (the engagement ceremony), and *lagan* (sending the confirmation of the date for the wedding), all described in Vatuk for Meerut (Vatuk 1975:160–161). The second part of the wedding, the *gaunā,* usually took place a few years later, after the bride had reached puberty. Again the groom, with a party of male relatives, neighbors, and friends came, and after feasting and ceremony, took the bride to his village and household, to his mother, brothers' wives, and unmarried sisters. Usually the marriage was consummated at this time, although the bride only took up residence with her husband gradually. During the first years of marriage she was in her parental home as much as or more than in her husband's, or more correctly her father-in-law's place (her *sasurāl*).

The same kind of asymmetry in the relations between the relatives of the bride, the bride-givers, and the relatives of the groom, the bride-takers, was found in both high and low castes in Khalapur, as found by Vatuk (1975) for the Meerut high-caste townspeople and for the eastern Uttar Pradesh rural people studied by Dumont (1966:95). The Chuhras all entered into perpetual gift giving in this asymmetrical relationship very much as Vatuk described (1969:174).

In both high caste and low caste, the young married woman spent as much time in her parental home and village as in her father-in-law's home and village. And in neither group could her mother, her sisters, or her brothers' wives visit her in her marital home. She must be invited to her natal home and be escorted there by father or brother, and upon her return to her father-in-law's home and village, she must bring gifts for her husband and his close kin. Both the high and the low castes idealized the joint family. Both allowed joking relationships between *bhābhī* (elder brother's wife) and *der* (husband's younger brother) and between *sālī* (wife's sister) and *bahanoi* (sister's husband). In both high caste and low caste there was a strong tie of affection held to be appropriate between brother and sister and between *sālā* (wife's brother) and *bahanoi* (sister's husband). Both groups required that a woman avoid her father-in-law and husband's elder brothers, never speak to them, and be veiled (*ghunghaṭ*) in their presence. This rule was extended to all men older than her husband in her husband's home, caste chapter, and village. A woman was transformed to the identity of her husband's wife during the *pheras* at the wedding, and she never lost her assimilation to the identity of the *pheras* husband.

Neither high caste nor low caste favored polyandry. There were no cases of polyandry in Khalapur. Polygyny also was disvalued, although an occasional case of it occurred. I never heard Khalapur people discuss polyandry; they seemed to be unaware of its existency in the not so far distant Punjab and northern districts of Uttar Pradesh. The view on polygyny was that cowives quarrel and fight all the time. The worst epithet by which one could address or refer to a woman was as a *sauk rānḍ,* a woman who was both a cowife and a widow. Raheja (1981) explains this epithet by saying that a woman whose husband takes a second wife is like a widow, a woman with no sexual partner. Of course with widow mating, a woman could be both a widow (of her *pheras* husband) and a cowife to the wife of her second mate. Raheja, who worked in a rural locality in Meerut District, may have found such an interpretation of the term, because it fits castes that allow polygyny but prohibit widow remarriage. The Chuhras, of course, allow both.

All Chuhra women went to their first husband in *pheras.* A minority remained *sūhāgins*—women married to their first husband—throughout their lives. However, life expectancy among these untouchables was short, and anyone, man or woman, who had reached the age of forty or fifty had very likely gone on to a second or even a third spouse. In contrast to the Rajputs and twice-born high-castes, among whom widow remarriage was prohibited (Minturn and Hitchcock 1966:28; Vatuk 1969:108), the untouchable Scavengers of Khalapur practiced widow remarriage. Indeed, widow remarriage is one of the defiling practices that constitute the impurity of the lower castes. The Chuhras were not alone in practicing widow remarriage or the levirate in Khalapur; all Shudra and untouchable castes allowed it.

By traditional high-caste standards, a woman should have only a single sexual partner during her lifetime, and he should be her husband given in sacred ceremony with community sanction, gifts, and dowry. A woman, and along with her her family, is made impure by her relations with any subsequent sexual partner she might have. An adulterous wife or widow should be cast out, even executed. In Khalapur a Rajput widow, void of jewels, remained in her dead husband's household, raising her children, serving others, assured of maintenance for life from her husband's property, but forbidden to marry again (Minturn and Hitchcock 1966:28–29). Chuhri widows were similarly reasonably secure economically because it was women who did the *jajmāni* work. A lone woman such as a widow could support herself and her children. After a husband's death her standard of living might not change much, provided she and her daughter, son, or daughter-in-law could continue working for the *jajmāni* clients. She had a right to live in her mother-in-law's house for life. However, Chuhras practiced widow mating and even widow sale, so that her economic security did not make the Chuhri close to equal to men; the men could pressure her into taking another mate; they could even sell her, so that she would be lost, separated from all her kin.

Of special interest is the key difference of widow mating. It does not occur among the Rajputs, nor of course does widow sale occur among the Rajputs. It is the Chuhra men's practice of selling women that clearly makes Chuhris subordinate to the men. They are economically independent. A woman has a right to live in her mother-in-law's house for life, and she has a right to *jajmāni* clients who belong to her mother-in-law, so she is economically reasonably secure and self-sufficient, but it is the Chuhra men's capability of selling a woman that makes her clearly inferior to men and dependent upon men.

The summary in Table 7.3 shows that Rajputs and Chuhras share the same kinship system to a very large extent. It is hard to say whether Chuhras, once in a hoary past, learned the kinship system of the Rajputs; if so, it represents an example of accomplished emulation. The differences between the two systems are largely matters of conformity to shared norms. Lack of land means that the Chuhras have been more mobile, less anchored to a locality than Rajputs have been. Hence, the genealogical depths of their patrilineages, their *kunbās,* are not as great as the genealogical depths of the Rajput patrilineages, their *ḳhāndāns.* There is also more flux in the composition of a *basti* community, with more *ghar jamais* and resident affinal male relatives present. If Chuhras are emulating Rajput patrilineality, we might label this impoverished emulation.

Because of their poverty, the Chuhris work outside the home and thus get to know the ways of their higher-caste *jajmāns* and also get to know *ders* (husband's younger brothers), as well as other women and children of the village; Rajputanis are secluded within their *bagars* and are less mobile. We might, therefore, consider the *parda* etiquette of the Chuhris to be attenuated, another example of impoverished emulation. The main contrast between the two groups is with respect to marriage and widow mating. The Rajputs give bridegroom price (sometimes mislabled as *dowry*); the Chuhras do not. The Rajputs prohibit widows from taking a second mate; the Chuhras allow widow mating.

If we compare the Chuhras and Rajputs of Khalapur with the lower-castes and Brahmans of Kumbapettai, Tanjore, described by Gough, we may note that the Chuhras and Rajputs seemed to share a common kinship culture, more so than did the two extreme caste groups in Kumbapettai. There did not seem to be such egalitarian relations among Chuhra men and women and between Chuhra fathers and sons or between brothers as there was among the lower castes in Tanjore. The Chuhras may have been more Sanskritized in terms of ritual celebrations than were the lower-caste of Kumbapettai, and Chuhri wives seemed to be assimilated to their husbands more completely than the low-caste wives in Kumbapettai. The greater Rajputanization of the Chuhras than Brahmanization of the Kumbapettai low-castes is perhaps due to an accessibility of Rajput culture to the Chuhris and an exclusion of lower-caste people from contact with high culture by the Tanjore Brahmans.

WIDOW MATING IN HINDU LAW AND ITS DISTRIBUTION

What about the difference in widow mating between the Rajputs and higher-castes versus the lower-castes of Khalapur? Is this an example of cultural contrast? Is widow mating non-Sanskritic? Is it prohibited in the

TABLE 7.3. CULTURAL UNITY AND NORMS IN KINSHIP: CHUHRAS AND RAJPUTS COMPARED.

ALIKE	DIFFERENT
Kinship Ideology	
1. *Kunbā* (Chuhras), *ḳhāndān* (Rajputs): local patricians	*Kunbā* is of less genealogical depth than the *ḳhāndān*
2. *Bagar* (women's quarters), *chaupāṛā* (men's quarters) as residential buildings	
3. *Ghar:* room or rooms in *bagar* occupied by a woman or related women and small sons; those who eat from *chulha* (hearth) or *ghar* form the smallest kinship unit	
4. Family cycle with break-up between adult married brothers with children	
5. *Kunbā* (or *ḳhāndān*) or *ghar* celebrate various life-cycle and calendrical rites	
6. Elderly males of *kunbā* or *ḳhāndān* govern clan by arranging marriages, adjudicating disputes, and so on	
7. Western Hindi kinship terminology	
8. Affection between brother and sister emphasized	
Marriage Ideology	
1. Maximize marriage ties with as many families and villages as possible	
2. Directional hypergamy	
3. Proscribe elopement, premarital sexual activity for both males and females, self-arranged marriages, exchange marriages, and polyandry	
4. Disvalue polygyny	
5. Proscribe marriage with cousins called by terminology *bhāi* (brother) and *bahan* (sister)	
6. Bride and groom are teenaged strangers	
7. Expenses of wedding greater for bride's side than groom's	Rajputs pay bridegroom price, Chuhras do not

TABLE 7.3. *Continued*

ALIKE	DIFFERENT
8. Two sets of wedding ceremonies: the *shādī* and the *gaunā*	
9. Bride is transferred to her husband's *ghar* family in the wedding and becomes irrevocably her husband's wife	
Women's Affinal Relations	
1. Wives live at *sasurāl* (village and house of husband's father): patrilocal residence	Some deviance from sasurāl norm among Chuhras, with daughters' husbands (*ghar jamais*) or wives' brothers (*sālās*) or sisters' husbands (*bahanois*) residing with wife's father or brother or with sister's father-in-law
2. Women keep *ghungaṭ* and do not speak to men older than the husband at the *sasurāl*	
3. Wives may joke and be friendly with men younger than husband at *sasurāl*	Chuhris have more chance to interact with *ders* (husband's younger brothers) than do Rajputanis
4. Asymmetrical gift giving from women's kin to husbands' kin	
5. Widow belongs to husband's patrifraternal contingent	Chuhri widow may mate with her husband's unmarried brother. The dead husband's patrifraternal contingent may transfer or sell the widow. The Chuhri widow has the right to live in her mother-in-law's house and to serve her mother-in-law's *jajmāns* The Rajput widow lives in her dead husband's *ghar* and lives off the proceeds of her husband's land. Rajputs idealized the *satī,* worshiping a *satī* shrine as the first ceremony in every marriage; no recent *satīs* have been committed, however
6. A wife as a *salhaj* may joke with her *nandoi* (husband's sister's husband)	
7. She is respectful to women in her *sās's* (mother-in-law's) generation at her *sasurāl*	

TABLE 7.3. *Continued*

ALIKE	DIFFERENT
Men's Affinal Relations	
1. Joking and friendly relations between a man and his *sālā* (wife's brother), a man and his *bahanoi* (sister's husband), and his *sālī* (wife's sister)	
2. Respectful toward *sasur* (father-in-law) and men of his generation; avoidance of *sās* (mother-in-law) and women of her generation	

Hindu classical religious texts? Although it is often assumed that the prohibition on widow mating and upon the levirate is Sanskritic and Brahmanical (Mandelbaum 1959:259; Blunt 1969:71, O'Malley 1932:92) and that widow remarriage is, therefore, non-Sanskritic and non-Brahmanical, study of old Hindu texts, both religious and secular, indicates that this assumption is not quite correct. Four different positions on the lot of the widow were taken in ancient Hindu law. The first position was that a widow could be married again, usually to her husband's full brother, but if not to him then to a nonuterine brother or to a more distant *sapinda* (of the same mourning group), *sagotra* (of the same patrisib), or *sapravara* (of the same worhship group) brother of the dead husband. This position is taken in Kautilya's codification of fourth century (B.C.) custom, the *Arthaśāstra:*

> In the case of husbands who have long gone abroad . . . who have become ascetics, or who have been dead, their wives, having no issue, shall wait for them for the period of seven menses; but if they have given birth to children, they shall wait for a year. Then [each of these women] may marry the brother of their husband. If there are a number of brothers to her last husband, she shall marry such a one of them as is next in age to her former husband, or as is virtuous and is capable of protecting her, or one who is the youngest and unmarried. If there are no brothers to her lost husband, she may marry one who belongs to the same gotra as her husband's or a relative, i.e., of the same family. But if there are many such persons as can be selected in marriage, she shall choose one who is a nearer relation of her lost husband (Shama Sastry 1967:183).

Similarly, in the epic the *Rāmayāna:* "We are told that when Rāma hotly pursued a demon in the forest for his skin, this demon raised a loud cry for help. Sitā, hearing this, thought that Rāma was in danger, and asked Lakshmana to hasten quickly to his brother's help. Lakshmana hesitated and Sitā wildly cried out, 'You wish to see Rāma dead so that you may get me [for your bride]' " (Kapadia 1947:98). Not only in the *Arthaśāstra* and in the *Rāmayāna* are there clear references to widow remarriage as an acceptable institution but also in a number of the ancient law books. In those of Baudhyana, Vasistha, and Yajnavalkya there is discussion of a *samaskāra* (a ritual transformation occurring during the life cycle) for a second marriage called the *paunar bhava samaskāra* (Kane 1941:II, 612).

So the first position taken by old religious texts with respect to widows is the remarriage of a widow, preferably to her husband's full brother. A second position was the custom of *niyoga.* Cited in the religious law books of Gautama (600–300 B.C.), Narada (A.D. 100–400), Baudhayana (800–400 B.C.), and Manu (200 B.C.–A.D. 200), *niyoga* was a service provided by a dead man's brother when the latter had left no surviving son. The brother was to have sexual intercourse with the widow until she had conceived one (or sometimes more) sons. The sons were heirs to the dead man. Besides the brother, a priest or Brahman was also sometimes allowed to be the *niyoga* seed provider (Kapadia 1947:94); some law books allowed more distant cognatic brothers (men whose relationship was traced through the mother) to perform the *niyoga. Niyoga* is similar to the levirate in the Old Testament. Some anthropologists (Radcliffe-Brown 1950; Bohannan 1966:119–120) believe that the term *levirate* in anthropological analysis should be limited to these ancient practices in which a man raises up seed for his dead brother, procreating children who count as the dead brother's. Murdock, however, defines the levirate less rigidly as a "cultural rule prescribing that a widow marry by preference the brother of her deceased husband, thus often becoming his secondary spouse as he is hers" (Murdock 1949:29; 1959:25). Rather than extend the levirate term, Radcliffe-Brown distinguished the "true levirate" from "widow inheritance," "in which a brother takes over the position of the husband and father to the widow and her children" (Radcliffe-Brown 1950:64). I prefer to use the term *widow mating* because unless the man has left an unmarried brother, there is rather careful decision taken in assigning a widow to her next mate, so it cannot be seen as inheritance among the Chuhras. A man does not inherit a widow as he might inherit a clientele of *jajmāns.* Secondly, the Hindu view, one shared by Chuhras, is that any subsequent mating is not a marriage, legal and accepted though that mating may be. It should be understood, however, that the dead husband's brother who mates with the Chuhra widow becomes her husband, the children procreated are his, and he has a right to the widow-wife's domestic and sexual services. It is, in other words, a full conjugal relationship.

The ancient Sanskritic pedigree of either the *niyoga* or full marriage-levirate is indicated by passages in the most ancient Hindu religious work, the *Ṛg Veda:* "What sacrificer invites you [Aśvins] in his house as a widow invites a brother-in-law [*devara*] to her bed or as a young damsel her lover" (*Ṛg Veda* X 40.2, cited by Kane 1941:II, 606, by Kapadia 1947:99–100, and by Chattopadhyay 1922:37). Instances of either *niyoga* or widow remarriage with her dead husband's brother (it is not always clear which) also appear in the *Mahābhārata,* the other great Hindu epic (Kapadia 1947:93, 96, 98). Kane suggests that the kin term *devara* may be a form of *dvitīyo varaḥ,* or second husband (Kane 1941:II, 615). Kapadia, however, thinks it is derived from *div* (to play) and refers to the joking relationship between a woman and her husband's younger brother (Kapadia 1947:101).

A third position in the Hindu scriptures is one prohibiting either remarriage or *niyoga* for a widow, celibacy being lauded. The most popular of the Hindu religious law books, that by Manu, is inconsistent, having some passages seeming to sanction *niyoga* and others seeming to forbid any form of widow remarriage. So verse 59 states, "On failure of issue [by her husband] a woman who has been authorized, may obtain [in the] proper [manner prescribed], the desired offspring by [cohabitation with] a brother-in-law or [with some other] *sapiṇḍa* [of the husband]." But verse 64 reads, "By twice-born men a widow must not be appointed to [cohabit with] any other [than her husband]; for they who appoint [her] to another [man] will violate the eternal law." And verse 162 reads, "No where is a second husband declared for virtuous women" (Manu IX:59–70, 162).

Reference is made in Manu to the rule of a king Vena, under whom there was inter-*varna* marriage, disruptive to the natural order of the class system, hence evil. Since his time, Manu says, "the learned of the twice-born," the higher *varnas,* have seen *niyoga* as "fit for cattle" (Manu IX:65–67). Other law givers suggest *niyoga* cannot be sanctioned in the present evil era, the Kaliyuga. The lawbook clearly suggests that it may be a custom appropriate for Shudras, the low-caste *varna,* but not for the twice-born *varnas,* the high-caste *varnas.* Kane points out that the most recent, the latest law books, do not mention widow remarriage or *niyoga* at all (Kane 1946:II, 615). Commenting on times since the laws books, Kane says: "Among the brāhmaṇas and castes similar to them and holding or endeavouring to hold a high place in the hierarchy of castes, widow remarriage has been forbidden for centuries . . . among Sudras and other lower castes widow remarriage has been allowed by custom, though it is held to be somewhat inferior to marriage of a maiden" (Kane 1941:II,615). We may conclude, then, that the levirate and *niyoga* were ancient customs by which a widow re-"married," but that by the early Christian period these practices were no longer favored by the upper castes; they were acceptable for the lower castes, however.

A fourth and most severe position to be taken with respect to widows in ancient Sanskritic literature is a demand for *satī.* While a passage in the *Ṛg Veda* may be taken to be a *satī,* and some instances occur in the epics, the custom seems to have been rare, and the early law books do not emphasize it. There is one law giver, Aṅgiras, however, who wrote, "For all women there is no other duty except falling into the funeral pyre, when the husband dies" (Kane 1941:II,633). Law books by Apastamba and the *Suddhitattva* prescribe penances and rituals for women preparing themselves for *satī* (Kane 1941:II,633). Kane is of the opinion that *satī* arose in Brahmanical India a few centuries before Christ, that the practice was originally primarily for royal wives to perform, that by the medieval period (A.D. 800–1500) it began to occur increasingly and also to be prescribed (Kane 1946:II,635). About the medieval period, Basham says, "During this period even child virgin widows were not allowed to remarry, and sati was encouraged as were customs degrading the widow through tonsure, requiring her to sleep on the ground and carry through a life of drudgery in the dead husband's family" (Basham 1954:186). These, then, were the four possible treatments of widows in the ancient literature: full remarriage, usually with a husband's brother; *niyoga;* prohibition on remarriage with celibacy; and *satī.* There are ample examples of widow remarriage in that literature. By the medieval period, however (beginning around A.D. 800), high-castes were advised not to allow widow remarriage or the *niyoga,* and in fact, to some extent, suicide for the widow was advocated. Even in the medieval period, however, secondary marriage for widows was allowed for the castes belonging to the lowest Shudra *varna.* A common Sanskritizing move has been for a caste striving for higher rank to try to enforce a prohibition on widow remarriage and the levirate within the *jati* (Karve 1953:295; O'Malley 1932:93).

Widow remarriage is actually widely practised in India. Mohinder Singh reported that almost all depressed castes in northern India allow widow remarriage (Singh 1947:169). William Crooke reported for an earlier period, saying that in northern India, "The higher castes do not permit it, while it is common among those of lower rank" (Crooke 1907:209). Mandelbaum says that the 1891 census of India suggested that 60 percent of the population of Madras allowed and practiced widow remarriage (Mandelbaum 1957:257). A number of recent village studies report widow remarriage among the middle- and lower-ranking castes: Dube for a village in Telangana (Dube 1955:122), Mayer for a village in Malwa (1960:234–235), Carstairs for one in Madhya Pradesh (1957:136), Dumont for the Pramalai Kallar of western Madurai District (1957:180), Alan Beals for a Mysore village (1962:31), Lewis for a Jat village near Delhi (1958:190–191), Vatuk for a Raya village near Delhi (1980:289). There are also many reports of widow remarriage among so-called tribal peoples: Hutton for the Rengma of Assam (1961:63), Hivale for the

Pardhan (cited by Mandelbaum 1957:255), Naik for the Bhils (1956:128), Karve for the Bhils, Baigas, Gonds, Korkus, and Savaras (1953:539).

The levirate is not as widespread as widow remarriage. Karve speaks of "Marathi-speakers between the Tapti and the middle course of the Godavari and upper reaches of the Krishna who do not allow marriage of a widow with the younger brother of the husband" (1953:539–540). Chattopadhyay is of the opinion that levirate is largely absent among those speaking Tamil, Telugu, Malayalam, Kanarese, and Marathi, except in areas bordering on the north where other groups practicing levirate might be contiguous (1922:41). Karve is also of the opinion that levirate is largely absent in the south (1965:224). Gough (1956) did find "optional levirate" among lower castes in Tanjore, Tamilnadu, however.

There are also areas where the levirate is absent and widow remarriage is prohibited among middle and lower castes. Abbé Dubois seemed to have been in such an area in Tamilnadu (1906:24), and the practice seems to be very rare in Kanyakumari District of Tamilnadu, where I have done field work myself. Obviously, the reliable mapping of levirate and widow remarriage has yet to be done. There have been some good but brief descriptions of the levirate among untouchables (Briggs on Chamars, 1920:39–41; Stevenson on Dheds, 1930:67). That the levirate was a favorite of early anthropologists—Westermarck, Bachofen, Lowie, and McLennan, all of whom emphasized the fact that it is very widespread throughout the world—is well known.

To return to the six questions posed earlier, we may answer the first two (is the lower-caste group aware of and attracted to the elite model) by saying the Chuhras and the Rajputs seem to share a common kinship system to a very large extent. Whether the Chuhras self-consciously emulate the high-castes is hard to say; probably they did in the distant past. In answer to the third question, on the role of economics, differences between Chuhra practices and Rajput practices are indeed related to economic differences. With respect to question four (are the differences between lower-caste practices and higher-caste practices due to differences in history and origins), the differences between Rajputs and Chuhras on widow mating seem to relate not so much to differences in their history and origin as to different models for twice-born *varnas* as opposed to models for Shudras given in the Hindu law books. While by medieval times the law books prohibited widow mating for the twice-born, it was still acceptable for Shudras. So we should add to the paradigm in Table 7.2 a category under "high-caste model is irrelevant" and in the box "high-caste and low-caste cultures are different" a rubric of "following a Shudra model." This would answer the fifth question (are other models besides that of the higher caste relevant). Yes, a Shudra dispensation allowing widow remarriage for Shudras, granted by Hindu religious law, is consistent with Chuhra custom.

An examination of the treatment of widow mating in the ancient holy books suggests a different cultual relationship between high and low castes—not one of the low castes emulating high castes or emulating some other model but rather one of the higher castes, those affiliated with the twice-born *varnas,* changing and refining their culture during the medieval period. There were a number of other cultural refinements introduced for the twice-born during this period, of course, including much stricter caste endogamy. What were the factors that brought about the medieval refinement of high-class culture? I cannot answer, but our attempt to understand the relationship between high- and low-caste cultures has raised the question. The low castes, then, were left to follow practices that all classes followed in ancient times. Their practices are not so much non-Sanskritic or anticlassical as archaic. This gives the status of widow mating a much firmer position in north Indian kinship. It would appear to be an ancient north Indian practice which higher castes have given up, rather than being a tribal custom that has not yet been Sanskritized. Given both the antiquity of widow mating and its wide geographical distribution, we can argue that it can be considered to be an alternate norm within a north Indian kinship system, and that it does make sense to look at the practice in one low-caste population as a beginning to understanding its relevance to a north Indian kinship system. We may answer the sixth question (can the kinship practices of lower castes and higher castes be seen to be expressions of the same symbolic system) with a yes. Both seem to be consistent with Hindu religious law.

The Culture as Constituted for Chuhra Widows

One of Louis Dumont's brilliant insights was his recognition of the fact that the principle of hierarchy pervades the domain of marriage as well as the domain of caste in Hindu ideology ("Marriages are strictly hierarchized," Dumont 1970a:123). Among other ways in which he showed this was his emphasis upon the uniqueness of the first marriage for a woman. He wrote, "A woman must be married, and can be married in the strict sense and with full ritual only once" (Dumont 1964:82). Later he wrote: "The true marriage, a woman's first marriage—*primary* marriage—is universally unique (but not indissoluble). The difference is between castes who forbid and castes who allow the woman, if her first marriage is ended by widowhood or divorce, to contract a kind of inferior marriage, which we shall call a *secondary* marriage. In direct opposition to the absence of the woman's secondary marriage, the custom of levirate or it would be better to say quasi-levirate is widespread" (Dumont 1970:111).

A number of earlier observers (O'Malley 1932:92; Blunt 1969:72) had made note of the same ranking of primary over secondary marriages. Of particular interest is the fact that the secondary marriage has a distinctively different name from the first marriage. Mohinder Singh lists some of these names as *dharawa, sagāī, karāwa, sangha* (Singh 1947:167). Also of interest is the fact of the very much abbreviated rituals celebrating the new union. Crooke, writing early in the century, said: "Widow marriage . . . is not attended by the rites which sanctify a regular marriage, but is done secretly at night, and the only formality is the feast which signifies that it is approved by the brethren" (Crooke 1907:209). O'Malley wrote: "The marriage of widows is permitted by many low castes, but the parties frequently have to obtain the sanction of the caste council, which gives its consent only after it has considered the propriety or advisability of the marriage. When the marriage takes place, the ceremony is conducted with maimed rites: there may even be nothing more than the presentation to the bride of some clothes and ornaments including bangles" (O'Malley 1932:93).

In my own field work among Jats and Minas of Jaipur, Rajasthan, the ceremony was called *churi painthna,* the putting on of bangles, in which the dead husband's brother puts bangles on the widow's arm. Mohinder Singh describes a different ceremony: "The ceremony is extremely simple. It may be merely the rubbing of *sindur* (vermilion) on the parting of a woman's hair, or the recitation of a *katha* and the knotting together of the clothes of the pair . . . But there is invariably a feast for the caste brethren" (Singh 1947:167). Mrs. Sinclair Stevenson, writing about the Dheds, an untouchable caste of Gujarat, dramatically reports on their practice of the junior levirate. "The young widow's parents-in-law call some witnesses, and then carry the girl, even if screaming and protesting, within the house; there they seat her on the bed-covering beside her deceased husband's brother, and in the face of her struggles tie the corner of his scarf and her shawl-like overdress together. This done, the pair are married, and the girl's own parents cannot take her away and remarry her to the man of her choice without a divorce, for which they will have to find the money" (Stevenson 1930:67). In the ceremonies described by both Singh and Stevenson, the key element is also a key element in the classical Hindu wedding—the knotting of the garments of the couple. The couple is tied together. The legitimacy of all of these secondary weddings is affirmed by the permission of a caste council or by witnesses from the couple's caste community.

The Chuhras of Khalapur also distinguish between primary and secondary marriage by distinctively different terms. The woman's first marriage is one confirmed by *pheras,* wedding rounds. This refers to the classical Hindu custom by which the ritual act that transforms the couple into a married pair is their circling of the sacred fire. The bride is led by the groom, the bride's head covering tied to the groom's turban or scarf. The widow remarriage is called *karāwa* or *baiṭhna denā* (given to stay with or sit with).

The Chuhras shared the belief that a widow, whether remarried or not, is of lower status than an unmarried girl or a woman married to her first husband. Once a widow, always a widow. She could never lose that inferior status with a new mating. An older woman who had children was not considered so unfortunate as a younger widow. Nevertheless, only the ceremonial marriage to the first husband was a real marriage. All subsequent unions, even if they were aproved by the caste community, were not equal in status to first marriage. Secondary marriages were not celebrated with elaborate ceremonials among the Chuhras, nor was a bride given much in the way of a trousseau. There might be a feast for part of the community to celebrate the new union, and the woman's natal kin might offer some gifts to her affinal kin.

The Chuhras' characterization of the first marriage by the word *pheras* is firmly in the classical Hindu tradition. A number of lawgivers affirm that it is by the wedding rounds, the *pheras,* that a marriage is made irrevocable (Kane 1941:II,539). Before the *pheras* it is still possible for one or the other of the couple to withdraw from the arranged marriage; it is not yet accomplished; but "even the *Kāmasūtra* quotes the unanimous opinion of the *acāryas* that the marriages celebrated before the fire as a witness cannot be revoked" (Kane 1941:II,540). That the tying of the *sari* or head covering to the groom's scarf or turban is also classically given is also noted by Kane: "The digests like Grhastharatnakāra of Candesvara say (p. 54) that in the case of sūdras the marriage will be complete when the sūdra girl holds the fringe of the garment of the bridegroom" (Kane 1941:II,540). As we have seen, some of the customs of lower-caste peoples are not non-Sanskritic. They are prescribed in classical literature, but prescribed for Shudras, the servant castes. In the word *pheras* we have the Chuhras' basic symbol for marriage. The couple has gone through a transforming ritual, the wedding rounds, and it is that ritual act that makes them married.

Let us turn to a consideration of the norms for widow remarriage among the Chuhras. These norms or rules I induced from Chuhras' own statements, from their accounts of widow mating. There are twenty rules—eight concerned with the status of a widow, five concerned with the levirate, four concerned with widow sale, and three concerned with love-marriage. These are, first, the rules concerning the status of the widow:

1. A woman, once married, belongs to the patrifraternal contingent of her husband's paternal family. That is, she belongs to her husband, to her husband's father, and to her husband's brothers. She has come to this patrifraternal contingent in *pheras.*
2. An adult of reproductive age should have a mate, so a widow of reproductive age should be given in *karāwa* to another man.

3. A widow should not be given in *karāwa* except by her dead husband's patrifraternal contingent group.
4. It is wrong for any man of this patrifraternal contingent to sell a woman who has come to them in *pheras.*
5. It is wrong for anyone else to sell a widow while she belongs to the patrifraternal core group, but if this occurs, this group has the right to the money received from her.
6. A widow should not settle in her father's village and take a new mate there. She may take a new mate in her first husband's village, or she may go to a new mate's village to live. A widow can reside in her father's village only as an unremated widow.
7. A widow who has grown children when her first husband dies may decide to remain unmated and celibate and so declare this decision to the community.

Rules concerning the levirate are:

8. A widow should be given in *karāwa* to her dead husband's unmarried brother, whether he is younger or older than her first husband.
9. A widow is not required to be given in *karāwa* to her dead husband's married brother. The widow must consent to marrying him, and the married brother and his wife must consent to his taking his brother's widow to mate.
10. A woman may be given in *karāwa* to her dead husband's *chacha-tau ke bhāi* (patrilateral parallel cousin), called in this Hawaiian-type cousin terminology *bhāi* (brother), but her consent must be taken as well as the consent of her father or brother. A similar requirement holds with respect to her dead husband's *maman-phupha ka bhāi* (matrilateral cross-cousin) taking her in her remarriage; in that instance also, the woman and her father or brother should consent first.
11. If a widow is given in *karāwa* to a *maman-phupha ka bhāi* or to a *bhāi* who is even more distant who takes her to live in a village other than the one in which she was living with her first husband, he must pay for her.
12. If a widow is given in *karāwa* to a man other than her husband's full unmarried brother, her consent and that of her father or brother (the head of her natal family) should be taken. The man's consent also must be taken. Even when she is given in *karāwa* to her husband's unmarried full brother, the formality of taking consents is gone through, even though this is a prescriptive secondary mating. She must be given in *karāwa* to the husband's unmarried full brother.

Rules concerning widow sale are:

13. Virgins and virtuous women married to their first living husbands should not be sold.

14. Married women or widows who commit adultery or engage in illicit affairs may be sold.
15. It is wrong for the men of the first husband's family, the patrifraternal contingent of his natal family, to sell a woman, because she is a bride who came to them in *pheras,* but her husband's cousin-brothers, either *chacha-tau ke bhāis* or *maman-phupha ka bhāis,* may sell the widow once she has mated with one of them. (See also rules 4, 5, and 11 involving widow sale.)
16. A bought wife may be resold.

Rules concerning love matings are:

17. Elders or heads of families should arrange matings. A couple should not establish a sexual relationship on their own initiative.
18. A couple carrying on an illicit sexual affair should be punished by the caste community by being fined and beaten if they promise to desist or outcasted if they insist upon continuing the relationship.
19. A woman cannot marry a man who is an affinal kinsman of her dead husband or one who is his consanguineal kinsman in either an ascendant or descendant generation to the husband—some man who cannot be classed as the dead husband's brother.

Let us recapitulate who are the brothers involved in a widow's remating. She should sit with her husband's unmarried full brother (*sagā bhāi*) whether he is older or younger than the dead husband; and although her father's or brother's agreement is requested, it is prescribed that she should sit with the husband's unmarried brother. If there is only a married brother available, then both the widow's consent and that of the married brother and of his wife must be taken. However, no full brother (*sagā bhāi*) of the dead husband has the right to sell the widow, because she has come to the patrifraternal contingent of her husband's family in *pheras.* If there is no unmarried brother of the dead husband, and she does not sit with the married brother of her husband, she may be asked to sit with her husband's *chacha-tau* brother, or, more rarely, a *maman-phupha* brother (her husband's mother's brother's son). If she does mate with a dead husband's *chacha-tau* brother and that man lives in her dead husband's locality, he pays nothing for her but does have the right to sell her. If a brother, such as the dead husband's *maman-phupha ka bhāi* takes her, and takes her from her husband's place to his residence in another village, then he must pay the husband's brother for her. He, of course, then has the right to sell her if he decides to do so.

What do these norms tell us about brothers in north Indian kinship? In his analysis of north Indian kinship terminology, Louis Dumont says that the *bhāi* term is the "richest, the most 'collectivizing' in the system" and is "the central category (together with 'sister', etc.)" (Dumont 1966:99). Dumont raises the question of the meaning of *bhāi,* as to whether its wide use should be seen as an extension from the "proper brother born of the same father and mother" to a "man approximately equal in age to Ego in his village and beyond," or whether it is a word which "has in essence a very wide connotation." He concludes that

> my "brother" is a man of my generation with whom I have one ascendant in common, his ascendant being, in the nearest case, the father or the mother (or both), and in the furthest case, a remote ancestor. Thus, . . . the category of "brother" is not defined logically, but empirically: the relationship ceases only at the point at which attention is no longer given it, where "memory" ceases. On the other hand, nothing prevents its being extended indefinitely and its including all the members of an endogamous group or of the sub-caste (within certain age limits), as there is a vague notion of their being of the same blood. All men might even be included, insofar as they are all sons of Adam, or Manu. The transition is thus easy to the extra-kinship uses encountered in address. (Dumont 1966:100)

Vatuk suggests that the *bhāi* relationship is "theoretically capable of infinite extension by means of certain covert equivalence rules" (Vatuk 1975:175), and Turner has demonstrated the rules of transformation by which kin are transformed into brothers, pointing out, "The equivalence of same-sex siblings is a fundamental principle of this kinship system" (Turner 1975:276). The importance of the principle of equivalence of or solidarity of brothers is shown in the requirement that a widow stay with her dead husband's unmarried brother.

There has long been recognition in anthropology of the correlation, the functional integration, of the levirate with patrilineality. Radcliffe-Brown uses the levirate as a prime example of his principle of equivalence of brothers (Radcliffe-Brown 1950:64). Consistent with this is the usual characterization of north Indian kinship as patrilineal and patrilocal. In recent writings on north Indian kinship, on the other hand, notice has been taken of the native concept of distance in kin relations. So Madan says that the Kashmiri Pandits speak of relatives who are *nazdik* (close) and those who are *durik* (distant) (1975:225). In Bengal, Fruzzetti and Östör tell us, the terms are *nikat* and *dur* (1976:91, 103, 119–102). It is a matter of courtesy, however, to address a distant brother by the term for the closer relative (Khare 1975:256). So, according to Dumont (1966:101) one says *bhāi* (brother) rather than *mausiyaut bhāi* (cousin-brother, mother's sister's son). And although the term *bhāi* is widely extended, there are qualifying terms that may be used in reference to make the relationship clear. Madan (1975:223, 225) speaks of *kaka-baba bhāi* (father's brother's son) and Khare of *sage bhāi* (brothers of the same parents), *sautele bhāi* (step-brothers), and *caceri bhāi* (father's younger brother's son, cousin-brother) among the Kanya Kubja Brahmans of central Uttar Pradesh (Khare 1975:253–256). Similarly, as we have seen, the Chuhras of Khalapur speak of *chacha-tau ke bhāi, maman-phupha bhāi,* and *sage bhāi.* The gradient of distance in this extension of *brother* is thus recognized in native thought rather exactly.

Since there is a gradient of distance in American kinship thought—we also speak of close and distant relatives (Schneider 1968:62–66)—the Hindu concept may seem to be perfectly natural. However, Schneider's challenge that the "genealogical grid" may be a conceptual framework of the anthropologist's own invention (1972:51) raises a question about closeness and distance in Hindu thought. Think about the problem in this way. Inden (1972), Nicholas and Inden (1977), David (1973), and Barnett (1976) have all spoken of the transformation of the Hindu bride into the same substance as her husband. She becomes one body with her husband through the ritual act of the wedding. If so, then the substance of cousin-brothers should be the same, since their fathers are of the same substance, and although their mothers are different persons, the two mothers have presumably been transformed into this same substance. All four parents, then, are of the same substance, and the children taking their substance from these substantially homogeneous parents would be of the same substance.

Now, quite frankly, the Chuhras of Khalapur never talk this way. As we have seen, they talk about wives coming to a family in *pheras*—a wife belongs to a father-sons set, the male side of a family of orientation. Easy to observe are their living arrangements. The father-sons set eat from the same kitchen, food cooked by the mother and sisters. After marriage, brothers and their wives might well eat with the parents until the death of the parents. After both parents are dead, brothers and wives and children do not share a joint kitchen, do not have a common grain store. Clearly, the economic units of *chacha-tau ke bhāis* and *sage bhāis* are different. Distance based on distance of households correlates well with distancing in terminology and custom. So the *saga bhāi* is likely to be in the same hearth group; the *chacha-tau ke bhāi* is likely to be in the hearth group next door; the *maman-phupha ka bhāi* is likely to be in the mother's parents' village some miles away. *Kunbā bhāi* or *biradari bhāi* (brother because of the same *jati*) may be in the neighborhood or may be more distant. The distance is distance of residences on the ground. This view of distance relies on a principle of those agnates who have shared a *chulha* as being closer, those who share a *chulha* with someone who used to share a *chulha* with members of one's own *chulha* group being next closer, and so on. The distancing between these types of brothers is expressed in economic terms with respect to widows. A *saga bhāi* of the dead husband cannot sell the widow; a *chacha-tau ke bhāi* can sell her, and a *maman-phupha ka bhāi* or any other *bhāi* must pay for her, but he has the balancing right to sell her. Distance, then, in Chuhra life can be understood in terms of residential distance; one does not need to attribute to the

Chuhras some form of genealogical thought whereby different descendants of the same ancestors have different genes because their fathers have married different wives. If the Chuhras have some genealogical conceptions, they did not tell me about them.

Both Khare and Vatuk have mentioned that there is a fading out of recognition of kin as they become more and more distant, that this makes it possible for relatives to become over the generation strangers, and that marriages between strangers is the preferred pattern, so the fading out returns relatives to strangerhood (Vatuk 1969:111–112; Khare 1975:252–258).

R. G. Abrahams (1973) has recently criticized the idea that the older and younger brothers related by the levirate are equivalent, one being perfectly substitutable for the other. He takes as his inspiration Meyer Fortes's statement, "Siblingship does not cancel the uniqueness of the individual" (Fortes 1949a:243). Abrahams says: "The point is that if the 'equivalence of siblings' is a general principle at work in human kinship systems, so too is the 'individuality of siblings,' and it is perhaps worth emphasizing that such individuality—as we have learned to understand through Fortes, and more classically through Durkheim—is as much a social and a cultural fact as is its opposite 'equivalence' " (Abrahams 1973:167). So in the Chuhras' preference for the dead husband's brother there is equivalence of brothers, but there are also distinctions between brothers. There are certain qualifying definitional and practical wedges. So the dead husband's *saga bhāi* (full brother) is not the dead husband, as indicated by the fact that the wife becomes a widow after her husband's death; she is no longer in her primary marriage; she sits with the husband's brother in a secondary marriage. She has come to the father-sons set of her husband's family in *pheras,* so none of them can sell her, but she is wife to the husband's brother only in a secondary mating, not a primary mating. The wedge between dead husband and his *chacha-tau ke bhāi* comes in the latter's right to sell her, and the wedge with other brothers is through any one of them's having to recompense the dead husband's father-sons contingent in order to take the widow away. It is these qualifying economic wedges that distance the brothers from the dead husband. There is a solidarity, an equivalence of brothers, but also a distancing expressed through different economic obligations with respect to buying and selling the widow.

To return to the idea of hierarchy, we may note that the hierarchy of preference in widow remarriage is a kind of verticalization of this lateral gradient of distance between the dead husband's brothers. The hierarchy of marriage types among the Chuhras, then, are these:

1. Marriage by *pheras*
2. Sitting with husband's *saga bhāi*

3. Sitting with husband's *chacha-tau ke bhāi*
4. Being sold to a man who is a brother to the husband, such as a *maman-phupha ka bhāi*
5. Being sold to a stranger

These norms concerning the widow remating tell us something about the differences between brothers in north Indian thought as well as about the equivalence of brothers. What is particularly surprising, however, is the revelation of a basic kin unit in north Indian thought: the father-sons unit. A woman comes in *pheras* to the male contingent of her husband's family, to the father-sons set. Indeed, *sage bhāi* are likely to contribute to the same household income, but *chacha-tau ke bhāi* contribute to different household's incomes. At the time of one of the *sage bhāis'* marriage, the other *saga bhāi* contributes to the expenses, but at the time of a *chacha-tau ke bhāi's* marriage, the other *chacha-tau ke bhāi* only lends money or goods needed. This is another practice indicating the basic social unit of father-sons. This analysis suggests that the family is basically the father-sons unit plus sisters, wives, and mother. By the time the father dies, the sons have separated, each to establish his own father-sons unit.

That a patrilineal-fraternal joint family is assumed in north Indian thought is indicated by other practices. Among the Chuhras, the work teams are usually mother-in-law and daughter-in-law, sometimes mother and daughter, or two brothers' wives. A husband's brother's wife may nurse her husband's brother's wife's baby. There is inheritance from mother-in-law to elder daughter-in-law of a family necklace composed of silver rupees. One silver rupee should be added to the necklace for each son born to the family. These work and inheritance practices suggest the social unit of mother-in-law and daughter-in-law, a female contingent of the father-sons family unit.

Recent analyses of north Indian kinship, initiated by Dumont (1966), have taken a focused structural approach. The objective has been to find the ways in which north Indian kinship terminology expresses marriage through a classification of bride-givers and bride-takers. Dumont found that Dravidian (south Indian) kinship terminology expresses marriage; more specifically, that the kinship terms, which divide into parallel and cross relatives, form quasimarriage classes of consanguineal and affinal relatives. Dumont concluded that north Indian kinship terminology did not express such affinal classes. There are not classes of a "truly structural system" that "would classify the whole universe of kinship through the application of a number of principles of opposition" (Dumont 1966:96). The division between wife-givers and wife-takers in nothern Indian he found not in the kinship terminology but in the elaborate system of gift giving that goes on in northern India between those who give a daughter and those who take her in marriage (Dumont 1966:98). The north Indian kinship terminology Dumont found expressed not affinity but a broad extension of siblingship. The term for brother (*bhāi*) and for sister (*bahan*) are very widely applied (Dumont 1966:98). Thus, north Indian kinship terminology introduces a third principle besides the two principles of affinity and consanguinity: siblingship. Subsequent discussion of north Indian kinship (Vatuk 1969; Turner 1975; Fruzzetti and Östör 1976), taking a lead from Dumont's 1966 article, has been concerned with the question of whether there are classes of kinship in north Indian terminology and what the logic is by which siblingship is extended.

As we saw in the analysis of rules for widow remarriage, there is a class of husband's brother in the Chuhras' thinking. The widow must marry a man in the class of husband's brother, and this class includes real brothers, cousin-brothers, and brothers of the same patrilineage; it excludes his affinal kin—*sālās* (a brother's wife's brothers) as well as men of higher or lower generation to her husband. So for widow remarriage the Chuhras assume a class of brothers, but these brothers do differ from one another along a gradient of spatial distance, and distance correlates with the vulnerability of the widow to being sold.

As Fruzzetti and Östör (1976) and Barnett (1976) have demonstrated, it is quite possible to look at north Indian kinship in some other terms. Dumont has said, "The importance of affinity is marked in North Indian terminology only by the great number of terms for affinal relatives" (1966:114). A naïve student might, in fact, say that the difference between south Indian kinship terminology and north Indian is that there are no affinal terms in south Indian terminology, not, at least, if you play by Dumont's rules for what counts as a kinship term (Dumont 1966:97), while north Indian terminology has three sets of affinal terms: her terms, his terms, and their terms. Affinal terms used by both male and female speakers are:

dādasarā	HFF/WFF
dādas	HFM/WFM
nānasarā	HMF/WMF
nānas	HMM/WMM
sasur	HF/WF
sās	WM/WM
chacharā	HFyB/WFyB
chachari	HFyBW/WFyBW
tayasarā	HFeB/WFeB
tāyas	HFeBW/WFeBW
maulasarā	HMB/WMB
maulas	HMBW/WMBW
phūpasarā	HFZH/WFZH
phūphas	HFZ/WFZ

mausasarā	HMZH/WMZH
mausas	HMZ/WMZ
bhābhi, bhāwaj	BW
jijā, bahenoī	ZH
samdhi	SWF/DHF
samdhin	SWM/DHM

Affinal terms used by male speakers only are:

sālā	WB
salhaj	WBW
sālī	WZ
sārhū	WZH

Affinal terms used by female speakers only are:

devar, der	HyB
jeth	HeB
daurānī	HyBW
jethānī	HeBW
nanad	HZ
nandoī	HZH

The principle of hierarchy pervades the joint family also, men having rank over women, older having rank over younger. Some pairs of kinship terms express relative age, and presumably relative degrees of authority within the joint family. One must state whether the father's brother is older or younger than the father, choosing the term *tau* for father's older brother and *chacha* for father's younger brother; a husband's father's older brother is a *tayasarā,* and a husband's father's younger brother is a *chacharā.* Their wives are similarly distinguished. A woman, likewise, must distinguish her *jeth* (husband's elder brother) from her *der* or *devar* (husband's younger brother), and the *jethānī* (husband's elder brother's wife) from the *daurānī* (husband's younger brother's wife). A woman must keep her face covered (*ghunghat*) from all men older than her husband in her husband's household, neighborhood, caste quarter, and village; she must also keep *ghunghat* from very elderly affinal female relatives like the *dādas* (husband's father's mother) and *tāyas* (husband's father's elder brother's wife). The affinal kin toward whom a woman must show avoidance and greatest respect are thus clearly marked.

On the other hand, a woman has a joking relationship and friendship is allowed with her husband's younger brother, her *der.* Her husband has a matching joking relationship with his *sālī,* his wife's sister, and a woman may joke with her husband's younger sister's husband, or *nandoī* (Vatuk 1969:109). These two latter relationships, however, are rarely implemented, since in neither case are the relatives likely to reside together, owing to the rule of patrilocal residence. The *bhāwaj* (brother's wife) and the *der* (husband's younger brother) do usually live in the same *kunbā, bagar,* and often *ghar* (household). The unmarried *der* is, of course, also the preferred second mate for the *bhāwaj* if her husband dies.

The women's affinal terms are quite consistent with joint family living in a patrifraternal joint family. Rudra Datt Singh has shown from his own village in eastern Uttar Pradesh that the joint family etiquette also supports the more distant relationships within a joint-family at the expense of relations between members of the component nuclear families. Thus, a child is cared for by his father's mother rather than by his own mother; a man shows affection openly to his brother's children, not to his own children; husband and wife do not speak to each other in the presence of elders, and so on (Singh 1962:75–152, 236–244). The terminology, the family etiquette, as well as the rule of widow mating in giving preference to the husband's brother as a second mate all seem to rest upon an assumption of the existence of the patrifraternal joint family, that is, one built on a structure of a father and his sons. The man's affinal terms are suffused with a connotation of sexuality. The attitude is that these are the wife's kin who have given her to be abused by means of sexual intercourse. These terms are favorite epithets. Just as an American might call someone a son-of-a-bitch, so a north Indian villager calls another man a *sālā* (wife's brother) or calls a woman *sālī* (wife's sister) or *sās* (mother-in-law). The most serious insult for a woman, however, is to call her a *sauk-rānḍ,* a widow-cowife, a term that suggests a widow mating that creates a polygynous household, at least in a widow-remarrying milieu. Sexual embarrassment, shame (*sharam*), determines the use of terms within the nuclear family. Children do not call their mother *man* (mother), because this would call up images of the mother in the act of procreation, nor does one call one's father *bap* (father). Rather one calls him *chacha* (father's younger brother), and one calls one's mother *'bahu'* (son's wife).

The key point about the affinal terminology, of course, is that it fits very well with the practice of widow mating with the dead husband's younger brother. Vatuk has recently pointed out the fact that such a joking relationship as that between *bhāwaj* (brother's wife) and *der* or *devar* (husband's younger brother) is often interpreted by anthropologists as anticipatory of subsequent marriage. However, among the higher-caste subjects of her study, such marriages did not occur, since widow remarriage was prohibited among them (Vatuk 1969:108). Remembering that such marriages are very ancient and were accepted and approved up to the medieval period for high-caste as well as for low-caste, and remembering that the leviratic type of secondary marriage is very widespread in northern India among the lower castes, we may indeed confirm that this kinship relationship and terminology is consistent with and possibly could be said to express the widow's mating with a husband's younger brother.

Culture as Lived In

Let us turn now to the data showing the way in which Chuhra widows actually have been reassigned to subsequent mates, the way in which the norms actually work out in real life. Sumi was a grandmother of perhaps fifty-five or sixty when I knew her. She had been married four times. She first married the boy Phulwā in *pheras.* Before the *gaunā* Phulwā died, so she actually had her *gaunā* with Phulwā's little brother Jhankā, a child much younger than Sumi. As often happens in such leviratic child-groom marriages, the full-grown bride had an affair with another man. In this case it was with her *tayasarā* (husband's father's brother) Shyam, a man with whom she should have had an avoidance relationship since he was, a Chuhri informant said, "a kind of father-in-law to her." Since the community would disapprove of such an affair, the couple ran away. They lived in various cities, working as scavengers. Sumi had two sons by Shyam. They were last in Hyderabad, where there was another family of Khalapur Chuhras, unrelated to Sumi or to Shyam. After the wife of this family died, and after Shyam died, Sumi married the widower, Jammal, as a fourth husband. By him Sumi had two more sons. The elders of the Sweepers pronounced the last two marriages of Sumi as *māra kām* (bad work). Yet when Jammal and Sumi and their sons returned to the village, ten years before I knew them, the community accepted them. Of course, by this time the wronged *devar* (husband's younger brother) was long dead, and Sumi was now married to a man who was not in a fatherly generation category of men forbidden to her, as Shyam had been.

There are three principles reflected in the criticisms of Sumi's marital career. First, a woman should remarry only into a category of men of her dead husband's own generation. That is, a woman should have an avoidance relationship with all men older than her husband in her husband's patrilineage and locality. Similarly, she should not marry a man of lower generation, a man to whom she would be a mother. Second, marriages should be arranged. There is a hierarchy of marriage arrangers, the highest rank ("good work") going to marriages arranged by the elders of the *kunbā,* secondary rank ("doubtful work") going to those arranged by a bride's father or brother, and lowest rank ("bad work") to a woman and man arranging a marriage by themselves. Called love-marriages, such self-arranged marriages are widely condemned in Indian society. Such individual actions go against the collectivity orientation of Indian culture. Among the Sweepers of Khalapur, self-arranged marriages were "bad work." Arrangement of marriage by elders of the *kunbā* was good work. Arrangement of marriage by a father or a brother was in between. If a marriage that had not been arranged by a father in consultation with elders went wrong, little sympathy was given, evoking the general response: "He went ahead without consulting anyone. What can he expect?" Third, the Sweepers practice a prescriptive levirate. A widow must be given to sit with (*baṭhnā denā*) her dead husband's unmarried brother. This often is a small boy, as was the case for Sumi. There is little or no ceremony involved. The disposition of the widow is determined during her husband's funeral by the elders of her husband's *basti* (local colony). The widow's father or brother usually attends the *Terahvin* held the last day of the mourning period when rites are performed, and he is consulted about the widow's new husband. If there is an unmarried brother of the husband, this consent is merely pro forma. The dead husband's father or brother is given a rupee coin and a turban to indicate consent. The widow will sit with the husband's unmarried brother. Neither the widow nor the brother has any say in the matter.

This brother, as we have seen, cannot sell the widow-wife, because, it is said, she has come to his family in *pheras.* The widow does not have to sit with a married brother of her dead husband. Her consent, as well as that of the man's wife must be taken. Rarely do the two women agree to the widow's sitting with the married brother. If the two women were to agree, then the widow's father or brother would also be consulted. Among the fifteen cases of widows whose husbands had left a full brother, there was only one instance of a widow agreeing to a polygynous marriage. Everyone recognizes that cowives inevitably quarrel, so generally there is little pressure on the widow by the community to sit with a married brother of the husband. The man himself may desire the widow as a second wife, of course.

As a matter of information, for twenty-four widows whose histories I recorded, at least fifteen husbands had left full brothers (see Table 7.4). In only five instances am I sure that no full brother (*sagā bhāi*) survived the dead husband. Among the fifteen men with full brothers, eight or ten left unmarried brothers. The probability, then, of a husband's leaving a full unmarried brother for a widow to marry was somewhere between two-to-one and one-to-one odds (between .50 and 1.00).

As Table 7.5 shows, there were three instances in which a dead husband left an unmarried brother who was sexually mature. In all three instances in which widows married mature unmarried brothers, they stayed married to them. However, for those five widows who had to sit with brothers who were small children, four went on to have affairs with some other man. Of these, two were caught and sold, and two ran away with their lovers and were not caught.

When an unmarried brother is not available and the widow rejects a polygynous marriage with a married brother, or there is no married brother, there are two options. A widow can declare herself a permanent widow; she says at the funeral that she will not marry again. If she is be-

TABLE 7.4. WAS WIDOW'S DEAD HUSBAND SURVIVED BY A BROTHER?

KIND OF BROTHER	NUMBER OF CASES[a]
Full brother survived	15
Unmarried full brother	7
Married full brother	5
Both married and unmarried full brothers	1
At least one brother, but unknown whether married or unmarried	2
No full brother survived	5
Unknown whether a brother survived	4

a. Out of 24 Chuhra widows.

yond child-bearing years, or if she is younger but has a number of children, her decision to remain a celibate unremarried widow may well be accepted by the elders. If she is of child-bearing age and has few children or none, she is likely to be pressured by the elders into accepting some other brother of her husband.

The logical candidate of the *chacha-tau ke bhāi* (a father's brother's son). All parties would be consulted—the men in question, the widow, her father or brother. This is a serious decision, especially for the widow, because her husband's *chacha-tau ke bhāi* can sell her. Once she sits with him, she is no longer protected by the *pheras;* she can be sold. Mating with the *chacha-tau ke bhāi* is transforming for the widow in the way that remarriage with her husband's *sagā bhāi* is not. His position is a mixed one. If he lives in the dead husband's locality, he does not pay for the widow, but he can sell her. Although she can refuse to marry him, if a widow becomes pregnant by the *chacha-tau* brother of her dead husband, even without her public consent (through his taking advantage of her sexually), the baby is considered to be acceptable by the community. He thus is seen to be quite appropriate as her second husband, and by the pregnancy becomes so, but she is changed into a saleable woman by submitting to his sexual overtures. In the twenty-four cases of widows that I collected, none had sat with a *chacha-tau ke bhāi* of the dead husband, although I knew of three instances in which widows—or in one case the widow's stepfather—pointedly refused such men. In all three instances, there was considerable reason to believe that the *chacha-tau ke bhāi* was motivated to sell the widow to a stranger because of long-standing quarrels—either over debts shared with the dead husband or over the disposition of the widow herself.

As Table 7.5 shows, women whose husbands leave either no brother or only a married brother often return to their natal villages. These are

TABLE 7.5. POST-MARITAL CAREERS OF VARIOUS UNTOUCHABLE CHUHRA WIDOWS.[a]

1. Widow whose husband leaves mature unmarried brother (3 cases) →	marries mature unmarried brother (3 cases) →		
2. Widow whose husband leaves an unmarried brother who is a child (5 cases) →	marries child groom (5 cases) →	affair (4 cases) →	caught (2 cases) → sold (2 cases)
			not caught (2 cases) →
		no affair (1 case) →	
3. Widow whose husband leaves either no brother or only a married brother (16 cases) →	marries brother for polygynous marriage (one case) →		
	sold by in-laws (one case)		
	returns to natal village (5 cases) →	sold by in-laws (5 cases)	
	declared selves widows (9 cases) →	innovated solution (8 cases)	
		remained permanent widow (1 case)	

a. Based on 24 cases.

young, usually childless widows. The women then have affairs with men in their natal village. Once the widow has had sexual relations with a man other than the *pheras* husband or with his brother in a leviratic secondary marriage, she is considered to be saleable. To legitimize an affair, the lover must pay a sum of money to her dead husband's family. If he cannot, she must run away with him or else be caught and sold elsewhere. The widow who is sold under such circumstances is stigmatized. The prohibition upon the dead husband's family against their selling a woman who has come to them in *pheras* is cancelled once the woman has taken another sexual partner. The *pheras* husband's brother or father is entitled to the money for which she is sold. If she has an affair in her home village, she may well be sold by her own brother or father. Then the *pheras* husband's people are likely to have difficulty getting the money from the woman's father or brother. There may then ensue a long quarrel and case before the *panchāyat* (caste council).

Since it is generally assumed that a wife who has been sold has committed adultery, the status of a bought wife is considerably lower than that of a *pheras* married wife or of a leviratic wife. In circumstances in which a dead husband's *chacha-tau* brother would appear to want to sell a widow who had not committed adultery, an innovative solution seems to arise. The community willingly colludes in whatever deception or fiction might be involved. In one instance a stepfather, himself a leviratic husband, whose young stepdaughter's husband left no full brother and who did not want her to marry the *chacha-tau ke bhāi* proposed, arranged an entirely new marriage for her, complete with *pheras.* His Rajput *jajmāns* and village officials abetted him, warning him only that he should not take money for the daughter. In this instance, the girl had not yet had her *gauna* and was thus most probably still virginal. The stepfather passed her off to the new affinal kin as a never-married virgin. This was quite contrary to established custom. In another instance a woman accepted her dead husband's *maman phupha bhāi* (mother's brother's son) as a husband. He had a childless wife in his own village. Such an outsider would not have been allowed to sell the widow-wife. Meanwhile, since she was remarried, she was protected from being sold by her husband's stepbrothers, who might have been tempted to sell her if she had continued to remain celibate.

Dumont's statement that there are legitimate subordinate types of marriages certainly holds for the Chuhras. Both the sitting-with leviratic marriages and marriage-by-sale are acceptable marriages. The couple so joined is accepted by the community as married and as having a right to live among them. The mating that is unacceptable is the self-arranged affair between lovers. This can be made acceptable by the lover paying the dead husband's family for the widow. This is possible only if the lover is of the Sweeper caste and in the husband's own generation (hence a kind

TABLE 7.6. HIERARCHY OF ACCEPTABLE AND UNACCEPTABLE UNIONS.

STATUS	ACCEPTABLE MARRIAGES	UNACCEPTABLE UNIONS
High	*Pheras*	Sweeper of husband's generation and in marriageable *kunbā* and *gotra*
Middle	Sitting with dead husband's brother Sitting with dead husband's *chachā-tau* brother	Sweeper of a different generation from husband and/or forbidden by *kunbā* or *gotra*
Low	Widow sale to a brother of the husband	Intercaste union
Lowest	Widow sale to a stranger	—

of brother to the dead husband), not in the widow's father's patrilineage nor in a set of prohibited patrilineal sibs (*gotras*)—those of the widow's and the man's father's, mother's, father's mother's, and usually mother's mother's *gotras.* So an intercaste affair or an intrapatrilineage affair can never be made legitimate, that is, acceptable to the community. The community refuses to allow such couples to live among them, equivalent to an outcasting or ex-communication. Unless the couple leaves the *basti,* the erring widow will be sold to some other Chuhra man. Thus, one can formulate a hierarchy of acceptable marriages and unacceptable unions varying in status (see Table 7.6).

How do we assess the prescriptive levirate rule of the Chuhras? Quite frankly, the data suggest the problem that students always raise when the anthropology instructor tells them about the levirate: What if the dead husband has no brother or no unmarried brother? As Table 7.5 shows, out of twenty-four widows, only five ended up permanently married to a husband's brother: three to a mature unmarried brother of the dead husband, one to a child groom who was a husband's brother, and one to a mature married brother, the widow thus becoming a *sauk-raṇḍ,* a widow-cowife to the married brother's first wife. Mating with a child groom appears to be quite unsatisfying to most women, who then go on to having affairs with some other man.

Our usual answer to students is that if a real husband's brother is not available, then she would remarry a classificatory husband's brother. But in fact that is not what happened among the Chuhras, who would appear to have prescribed levirate. And with good reason. The failure of any of the women to mate with a *chacha-tau* brother of the husband shows clearly how much widows dislike the idea of being saleable, for the *chacha-tau ke bhāi* can sell the widow. If there were space, case histories could be presented to substantiate this observation. Despite the desire to avoid being sold, however, one-third of the widows did in fact end up being sold, and sold to strangers. They were sold either because they had had affairs and were caught and sold or for some other reason. They were sold by either their husband's brothers or father or some more distant brother of the dead husband, or possibly they were sold by their own natal kin, a brother or other kinsman. Women also avoid entering full houses—ones already occupied by a man with a wife; they do not want to be *sauk-rāṇḍs,* widows who are cowives. Only one woman out of the twenty-four ended up in such a situation, and her husband had left no other kin at all. So, one of our first conclusions is that the prescriptive levirate rule does not work very well, so far as settling a woman into a satisfactory marital relationship goes.

Another point that might be made about these data is that except for the assignment to the husband's unmarried brother, the widow's own consent must be taken if the husband's *kunbā* elders want her to sit with someone else. She is granted, as a person, the right of consent, even though any money from her sale must go to her dead husband's patrifraternal contingent. So the widow as a person has the right to have her consent taken before she is made to sit with a new mate other than her husband's unmarried brother. The widow (if she is of child-bearing age) as a person is not granted the right to remain celibate, even though nine out of the twenty-four widows did originally, upon the death of their husbands, declare that they would remain widows. For eight of the nine, the widow and her relatives found some other solution that was not a sale. The ideal of the celibate widow seems to be attractive to Chuhris, and women generally admired a woman who wished to remain unremarried and celibate—in other words, women admired the high-caste ideal. Male Chuhras, however, put much pressure on a widow to give her consent to sitting with some man in the category of brother to her dead husband. As one widow's brother said to her, "Ours is a working caste; among us, a woman should have a man." This seems to be another way of saying, as do several of the Hindu law books, that among Shudras widows may mate again. "We are a working caste" is equivalent to "We are Shudras." There is also the fact that Chuhris do earn daily bread as well as grain and other food and goods from their *jajmāni* service; this gives an economically stable base to a family's income; hence, men benefit from having a wife, widow or no.

There is, furthermore, the prejudice against a widower taking a virgin as a bride.[6] It is generally agreed among the Chuhras that a widower must buy a wife, and some of the widows who were sold, in our corpus of cases, were sold to widowers, usually with children to be raised. Thus, the market for the sale of widows is largely the host of widowers who need mates for household work and care of children. Among the Rajputs, whether a widower can marry a virginal bride depends upon his wealth. A wealthy widower can command a virgin who would probably come to him with very little, if any, groom price, so she is likely to come from a poor Rajput family. Poor Rajput widowers are also rumored to have to buy their virginal brides. All of this suggests that there is a native category of widower and that the widower is an undesirable first husband. Widows are not under pressure to marry a widower with children, any more than they are under much pressure to join the household of the dead husband's married brother. Oddly enough, a child groom is not considered to be similarly inappropriate.

Conclusion

In this paper, I have asked: Is there a cultural order of untouchable Chuhra or low-caste kinship and a cultural order of Rajput or high-caste kinship? The answer seems to be: they share a common regional kinship system characterized by a strong patrilineal bias and the importance of the extensive category of "brother"; the woman is assimilated to her husband in marriage and belongs to his patrifraternal joint family. But the Chuhras, and probably other low castes that permit and/or prescribe widow remating, must be seen as having a variant kinship system. This variant is not non-Sanskritic; it is rather the persistence among the lower castes of practices that seem once to have been shared by all *varnas.* During the medieval period, Hindu lawbooks began to advocate the preferability of celibacy and even suicide for the widow, and some explicitly stated that celibacy for the widow was appropriate for twice-born communities while widow mating was appropriate for servants, the *varna* of Shudras.

The existence of a Sanskritic model for Shudras has not been recognized in the literature on the Indian caste system. This discovery of a special set of rules for the lower castes with reference to widowhood may stimulate study seeking other aspects of a Sanskritic Shudra model. The joking between *devar* (husband's younger brother) and *bhābhī*, a prescribed pattern widely followed in northern India, would appear to be a survival of the ancient widow-mating custom that was shared by all but is now adhered to only by low-caste people.

There are other differences between Chuhra and Rajput kinship practices. The Rajputs give a bridegroom price (often called a dowry); the Chuhras do not. The combination of a widow remating and no bridegroom price versus widow celibacy with bridegroom price in the two opposing social segments suggests that bridegrooms are in short supply in high castes while it is wives who are in short supply in the lower castes. This would be quite consistent with hypergamy, and, of course, Dumont has labeled north India as a hypergamous milieu. Exactly how such variants in the north Indian kinship syustem relate to hypergamy is also yet to be thoroughly studied; the hypergamy of bride-givers being inferior to bride-takers is shared by both Rajputs and Chuhras. Is there some other kind of hypergamy that we must discover in order to see the varient kinship systems as integrated into a single intercaste kinship system? Must we look more thoroughly for patterns of intercaste mating in north India to solve the issue?

The changes in medieval Hindu religious law concerning marriage are usually considered by scholars to be a process of refinement in the recommended customs, and these include much stricter *varna* endogamy. Stricter endogamy would, of course, not be consistent with a hypothesis that higher-caste men must be taking lower-caste mates, thus making it possible for high-caste widows to remain celibate or to commit suicide. Since the Rajputs were well known to be a community that practiced female infanticide as well, we may be puzzled by a set of customs that seem to say that bridegrooms are very valuable when, in fact, it is Rajput women who must be in short supply, that yet says that Rajputs should marry only Rajputs. Possibly, it is other twice-borns who are or were strictly endogamous. These are all questions for further research.

With respect to widow-mating among Chuhras, it has been seen that bride sale is very much part and parcel of the levirate among them, that a gradient of distance between brothers correlates with the widow's becoming saleable. This suggests that the closeness and distance dimension regularly found in north Indian kinship usage does have various corollary connotations and meanings for action. There are many aspects of their widow mating that need to be understood more: child bridegrooms, the process of selecting the "classificatory brother" to be the second mate, and the woman's own strategy in her plight as widow. As Schneider has pointed out, differences in kinship among different social classes and social categories may be a matter not just of rates, alternates, and variants but also of "strategy decisions which individuals make" (Schneider 1968:16–18).

Conclusion

Ákos Östör
Lina Fruzzetti
Steve Barnett

ALTHOUGH THE CONFERENCE did not reach unambiguous, firm conclusions, it did raise very important questions, some of which are relatively old, some relatively new.[1] They concern problems of terminology, primary and extended meanings, indigenous and a priori analytic categories, substance and hierarchy, central or key symbols, usage and practice in relation to concepts, and structural, cultural, and ethnosociological (monistic) approaches. The discussions, therefore, contributed not only to the study of kinship but to anthropology by casting light on these problems and revealing the contradictions and inconsistencies of previous approaches. It now appears that the terminological data are arbitrarily restricted and the legitimacy of the interpretations of their meaning are constrained by structural correlates to the classical terms of decent, affinity, filiation, and the like.

The convergence we perceived among our differently situated participants, of the more recent and dramatic theoretical departures in kinship studies, was also supported by the conference. Yet, despite the novelty of the approaches and new data, the central issues of the conference were those of anthropology in general: How do we analyze and/or understand relationships among people? What are the boundaries of domains? What constitutes meaning in social relations? What are the categories and symbols through which domains are constituted and understood? Whose symbols and meanings (how, where, and when) are we studying? How is anthropological knowledge constituted? How do we understand caste, kinship, and marriage in India? What constitutes these relations, what sets of data are we to include, and how do we interpret them? What are the contexts of kinship? How are we to resolve the problems of kinship theory in India? How do we arrive at new interpretations, and how do we evaluate them? Are traditional approaches to kinship inadequate? What semantic fields, practices, terminologies, and usages do we have to consider, analyze, interpret, understand, include, or exclude? Are there kin types, and how do we determine what these are? Are there primary and extended meanings in terminologies? How do considerations of the person, conception and birth, and other indigenous constructs and theories contribute to understanding and to resolving the problems of traditional social anthropology? In other words, what is or should be an epistemology for anthropology?

A related set of questions concerned symbolic or cultural approaches: What are these approaches in relation to more traditional social anthropology? What do they contribute that other anthropologies don't? How are they related to the basic questions of kinship, marriage, and caste in India? These questions also raise others about the problems of Indian sociology and social anthropology to date: What are the terminologies we analyze? How are kin terms to be interpreted? What are terms of address, and how are they to be dealt with? Similarly, questions were asked of rival cultural approaches: Are there "central" symbols in culture? What are these central symbols? What are monistic and dualistic approaches? What are moral constructs, and how do they interpret kinship? How can we make comparisons at all? How do we avoid cultural solipsism?

Put this way, we were asking quite a lot of ourselves. But these questions grew naturally out of the present state of caste and kinship studies in India. The range of these studies covers the spectrum of a splintered universe of contemporary anthropological schools—ethnosemantics, structuralism, symbolic interactionism, structural-functionalism, symbolic, mathematical, and psychological anthropology. Therefore, in challenging this diversity rather than embracing any one approach, we necessarily raise the most wide-ranging and basic issues and find it necessary to retrace our steps along a complex epistemological path. These were some of the questions asked of the papers in the course of the conference. Discussions of the person served as a useful way of introducing new considerations for a sociology of India and provided a renewed attempt at the comparison of regional variants of kinship, marriage, and caste in India.

Three years ago we thought of such a volume with the aim of making progress towards an all-Indian perception of kinship, caste, and marriage. Now, after the discussion and revision of these essays, we see the problems in a somewhat different light. Although we did not come up with an all-encompassing, all-India theory of kinship and caste, we were able to do something more immediately interesting: we discussed regional variants in relation to each other and in relation to India as a whole. With the extensive and successful revision of the conference papers, we have studies of similar problems in different regions of South Asia: Kashmir, Maharastra, Uttar Pradesh, Tamilnadu, and Bengal.

For better or worse, no new school, no new orthodoxy emerges from these pages. An overriding factor unifies these divergent essays, and that is the authors' dissatisfaction with previous kinship studies and their conscious attempt to reformulate questions, to discard inadequate though venerable theories and approaches, to reach toward new domains for analysis unrestricted by conventional boundaries. Thus, Vatuk writes on the household domain, Carter and Madan on the ideology of the person, Khare on moral constructs, Kolenda on the concept of woman among the lowest caste groups in India, and Fruzzetti and Östör on seemingly anomalous relationships and ritual domains.

The results also differ in their greater or lesser inclination to assimilate a new approach to more traditional concerns. There are yet other, more significant divergences. One bone of contention is the status of terminological studies. Dumont, Tambiah, and Yalman stressed, throughout the discussions, that the analysis of kinship terminologies, consanguinity and affinity, jural rights and obligations, inheritance and dowry should not be ignored, and that these older concerns should be assimilated to the newer ones brought up in the papers. On the other hand, the rest of the group expressed dissatisfaction with previous approaches and insisted on the legitimacy of cultural, symbolic, semantic, and other new departures. However, this did not yield an agreement about what the direction and contribution of these approaches should be.

Fruzzetti, Östör, and Barnett's *Contributions* papers built on Dumont's accounts but went beyond the kinship terminology to a cultural study of kinship, caste, and marriage in Bengal and Tamilnadu and to a comparison of alliance in south and north India. In discussion Dumont argued that the structural study of Bengali terminology (Fruzzetti and Östör 1976a) should be pressed further, especially in breaking down compound terms and in defining the fundamental terminological categories. The cultural study (Fruzzetti and Östör 1976b) is valid though incomplete because terms of consanguinity and affinity should not be discarded and because alliance should be constructed out of the latter rather than the former.[2]

Fruzzetti and Östör felt that a mere terminological study could not resolve the puzzles raised in the anthropological literature, and that the addition of marriage and death rituals and other Bengali constructs and practices to a kinship universe was called for in order to advance beyond our current forms of understanding. They drew attention to the great difficulties and inconclusive results of Dumont's most recent terminological study of north Indian kinship (1975) and emphasized the striking difference between Dumont's economic-political-religious studies of India, in which social domains are analyzed through indigenous ideologies, and his kinship studies, in which Dumont takes the domain to be defined through a priori relations of consanguinity and affinity. This inconsistency is not only a feature of Dumont's work; it comes up again in Tambiah's and Yalman's. If, indeed, kinship terminology can be explored fruitfully, despite all of our cautionary analyses, and if terminological analyses contrast with indigenous, cultural, or symbolic accounts, then Dumont has to face the problem of how we can possibly have terminological categories in kinship and indigenous ones in economy and religion.

Calling for some sort of universal formulation of consanguinity/affinity or kin/marriage as a general account of kinship is all very well, yet this cannot be the aim and end result of our endeavor. On the contrary it powerfully introduces the coming task: to formulate the particular cultural case and the construction of indigenous domains. Since there is no assurance that a general theory of kinship can be arrived at, or is even worth pursuing, the task is reflected into the comparative sociology of constituting cultural domains in and through the dialectical encounter of universal and particular, in this case kinship, marriage, and caste and Indian constructions of person, marriage and alliance, line, hierarchy, segmentation, and the like. To emphasise one or another side of this interplay as an exclusive absolute is surely to vitiate the whole project. Put this way the eventual alternatives are positivist (pseudo)science and cultural solipsism, an outcome that is both unacceptable and unnecessary. Since anthropological formulations are necessarily incomplete, our understanding can be progressively deepened through the practice of refining the attainment of universal and particular linkages. General disciplinary notions of kinship and marriage are useful in approaching South Asian cases, which in turn reflect on our notion of universals. But the crux of the matter is the comparative, relational linking of these and the understanding yielded by such practice. Needless to say it behooves anthropologists to pay more attention to what they are doing when engaging in this kind of practice. As we have tried to explore these questions in other publications and in other contexts, we were consistently led to the same fundamental epistemological issues for social science.

Nicholas had further objections to the Fruzzetti and Östör studies, calling the lessons of the terminological critique (1976a) unresolved, since all terms will deliver whatever is asked of them. For this reason Nicholas expressed a preference to work through the central symbols of Bengali culture, resulting in the discovery of the eight prior and fundamental categories of kinship (Inden and Nicholas 1977, see Appendix). There is a structure in Bengali kinship, and it can be perceived through the shared body relations of kinspeople. Fruzzetti and Östör doubted that culture can be concretized to this extent, if there were any such central symbols, if any terms could be understood this way, and if substantive notions of the body can sufficiently differentiate hierarchical relations among people. The distinctions Bengalis hold among a range of relationships can be generated neither through this nor through terminological approaches.

Hence, in their paper Fruzzetti and Östör proceeded to domains beyond strict kinship, terminology, and substantive body and blood in an attempt to solve a puzzle in their data.

In the consideration of Barnett's paper the discussion turned to the question of bounded groups in South India. Kolenda and Tambiah raised the problem of the position occupied by *kulams* (lines) within the *vakaiyaras* (kindred). Furthermore, they found difficulties with the notion of kindred in Barnett's essay. Tambiah argued that Yalman's *pavula* (kindred) were open ended with boundaries renegotiated while the *vakaiyara* were closed. Kolenda wondered about comparable data from elsewhere in south India: she herself found exogamous groups in the Kanyakumari District of Tamilnadu. Going further, Dumont queried the argument that *vakaiyaras* were central to alliance, calling these groups an extreme form of hierarchy and not a condition of the latter. In reply, Barnett noted that his point was not to suggest a single ordering of *kulams* and *vakaiyaras;* rather KVs represent one possible configuration in the south Indian conceptual framework of hierarchy and ecompassed equivalence. And even among KVs there is not a monolithic interpretation for these terms. To assume such a unitary approach would recreate prior modes of analysis that missed the flexibility of use and definition of these terms in concrete situations. Barnett tried to show that this diversity of interpretation could be seen within an understanding of hierarchy and ecompassed equivalence that did not initially separate caste and kinship.

Barnett felt that Dumont's point raised crucial epistemological questions. One might approach south Indian culture as an exercise in regression, in the construction of a flow-chart system, where A is logically prior to and entails B, which in turn is logically prior to and entails C, and so on. Then it is possible to say that *vakaiyaras* are, say, G in such a flow-chart system, and that if we really want to understand what is central to alliance, we must start with A. It is important to keep in mind that such a strategy requires that we provide and stick to an initial definition of alliance that is formal to the extent that it is abstracted from a range of types of actual instances. Therefore, the regression may conceal a tautology implicit in all formal definitions: what we claim to discover as A may in fact have simply been built into the abstract definition of alliance itself.

Alternatively, one could say that where a form of alliance coexists with *vakaiyaras* on the ground, and where people cannot think of one without the other, in that case the reciprocal meanings of alliance and *vakaiyara* must be sought together, not in the putatively logically prior aspect of either. In this approach we do not start with an abstract definition of any element of the analysis as if that element can be factored out whole from the totality in which it is embedded. Alliance will not be the same without *vakaiyara,* although of course we might imagine a different notion of alliance without a strong notion of *vakaiyara.* Once we understand alliance and *vakaiyara* together, we can then ask what underlies the form of their interrelation, but this is very different from asking what underlies alliance alone as an abstraction, what underlies *vakaiyara* alone as an abstraction, and then combining these two abstractions. Barnett felt he was explicating a KV sense of the coherence of caste and kinship, a coherence that includes but goes beyond alliance and *vakaiyara.* Although KVs are greatly concerned with purity, their "extreme form of hierarchy," to quote Dumont, is not the mechanical grafting of *vakaiyara* onto an already intact alliance but rather the dialectical nature of their relation. Finally, Barnett suggested that recent ethnographic work in Tamilnadu was showing *vakaiyara*-like structures in castes not overly concerned with purity (especially in Moffatt 1979).

The problem of terminology was raised in a different way by the papers of Carter, Khare, and Vatuk. Carter argued for a distinction between primary and extended, or secondary, meanings of polysemic, polyvalent terms. Several discussants noted that there is a difficulty here with the identification and definition of primary meanings. Such attempts become either a substantive search for contents or an a priori derivation of meaning. Schneider contrasted semantics and pragmatics, noting that in the former meaning adheres to the value of particular lexemes in grammatical form, as a syntactical element. Yet most meanings are not semantic; rather they are defined by the context. Any element is not a meaning. A primary meaning, therefore, suffers from inadequate interpretation. Related meanings emerge through the variety of contexts and rules of usage in adherence to a culture.

Khare, and to a lesser extent Carter, imply not only that there are internal and/or primary meanings to terms but that these can be directly apprehended or discerned (note Khare's "proper relatedness" and moral constructs) and that they can be known and collected in the field. Nicholas goes even further with his conviction that internal meaning is directly elicitable, given the prior item of belief that culture, much like a concrete edifice, consists of particles to which indigenous terms are attached somehow (see Inden and Nicholas 1977; Marriott and Inden 1976; Marriott 1976). Thus central symbols are reduced to representing one particular and basic thing.

Regrettably, Nicholas decided not to include his thought-provoking paper in this volume. Nevertheless, much of the discussion turned on the more general approach to kinship developed by Inden and Nicholas (1977), of which the paper became an instance. In the latter Nicholas set out to link the apparent absence of incest at the cultural level in India to the exogamous/endogamous requirements of *jāti.* In extending the *ek-deha* (one body) argument to account for an anomalous case, Nicholas noted that the body as central symbol is shared by father and married daughter (through *piṇḍa* being regarded as shared ancestral body). This relation is severed in a change of *gotra* at marriage, when the daughter comes to share her husband's *gotra* (clan) and body (*piṇḍa* in this case). A complex system of sharing and exchanges would then account for other classes of relationships as well.

Our critical remarks are of necessity restricted to Nicholas's published work. We value and commend the cultural and symbolic project and share many problems and concerns. We also recognize the contribution of the Chicago ethnosociological school (Marriott 1976a and b; Marriott and Inden 1976; Inden and Nicholas 1977). Yet, we note our own critique of this approach (Barnett, Fruzzetti, Östör 1976, 1977). As one of us has written in a review of *Kinship in Bengali Culture,* the approach

> conceives of culture or "substances" defined by Bengalis across space and time, . . . deals with contents, not relationships, and assumes that cultural items can be defined as unitary containers, which are then to be aggregated into the edifice of "Bengali culture" (which in turn becomes the final arbiter of "meaning"). The argument is problematic. It raises a number of questions about who thinks what and about whom in the constitution of Bengali kinship.
>
> . . . The book leaves open some residual ambiguities concerning the position of women as wives and as daughters of *baṅgśa* ("lines"), the notion of male line, and the position of women as carriers of male lines. Through their one central symbol of "body" as container, the authors have adopted a definition of "blood" as mere substance and have as a result substantivized "line" and "male blood." (Fruzzetti 1979)

In the general discussion of central symbols Barnett wondered how we proceed from blood or body to what we want to understand. Not a question of terms, this, but rather of how does body/blood become central? In addition Maybury-Lewis argued very cogently that incest categories do not appear in indigenous ideologies since the problems they refer to are subsumed under other cultural assumptions. Our task, therefore, is to study relationships through native ideologies. He pointed out, however, that this program presents great problems, many of which are illustrated in the varying degrees of difficulty experienced by all participants in transforming indigenous categories into analytical ones for comparison and understanding.

The papers of Nicholas, Carter, and Barnett brought up the question of substance and code in kinship relations. Several saw a convergence between Barnett's and Nicholas's work in this regard. Carter argued that since code is inherent in substance, a code for conduct has to be acted out. Thus, the substantive person in Maharastra is completed in action through the *saṇskars* (Hindu sacraments). Such a notion of the person can be constructed from Marathi verbal usages and from the tasks assigned to the *saṇskar* life-cycle rituals, also based on verbal usages. In a different vein Nicholas argued for the substantiality of the body as central feature of Bengali kinship. Different particles constitute the body and hence define different kinds of kin. The most general problem with this position is the difficulty of separating the varied and layered meanings in different relationships of a category, since everything is ultimately and substantively accumulable into concrete culture. How are we to understand distinctions wrought by marriage, male links, female links, blood, line, purity, hierarchy, and relationship relations? Like Carter, Nicholas allows for central or primary meanings on no justifiable grounds. Hence, Dumont called attention to *piṇḍa* as a term of offering (meaning, among other things, the funerary ball of cooked rice) rather than shared body, the latter being the crucially central meaning in Nicholas's scheme. In the same manner Madan distinguished between the qualities of *mā* (mother) and *bāp* (father) as dual and irreducable in constructing relationships. Nicholas is thus led to dispose of what he calls the "nonexistent incest taboo" by assimilating wives to sisters and, coincidentally, husbands to brothers. Primary and central meanings close the door to symbolic constitution of social reality.

Carter and Nicholas converge to some extent in looking at *jāti* as substance transmitted to persons by birth. Substance, whether innate in a code (Carter) or particles of body (Nicholas), replaces an indigenous cultural understanding. Code and substance are transmitted through generations marrying within the same group. But what of differentiation within the sameness and oneness of *jāti,* between one person and another, one group and another? How is hierarchy constituted in these cases? Is it merely imparted, without warrant, to the contents of an a priori substance, which is then transmitted?

Regarding the apparent similarity between his, Carter's, and Nicholas's views, Barnett distinguished his use of Schneider's analytic terms, biogenetic substance, and code for conduct. He felt these terms could be partially taken over in the south Indian context not because they are a universal ground for a theory of the person across all cultures but because they bear precisely upon the interface of holism and individualism and so are relevant to a comparative effort that involves a Western anthropologist and Indian culture. Thus, he does not reduce substance and code to biology or to monism or to some simple generative mechanism (innateness or particles). In fact, the use of substance and code in these very different analytical approaches has led to a number of premature attempts to suggest that these approaches all derive from a single school.

In responding to the cultural construction of the person posed in different ways by Fruzzetti and Östör, Barnett, Carter, and Madan, Tambiah among others argued against the notion of the person, not recognizing such constructs in their own data. It was also pointed out by Dumont, especially in view of Carter's paper, that if there are different categories of the person, then the unitary concept itself is dissolved, and we have to pursue further subdivisions and relationships in a more conventional way. It appears that Carter, in objecting to Fruzzetti, Östör, and Barnett's stopping short of such an overall construction of the person, recognized the difficulty but chose to go further, to substantivize a general concept in much the same way that anthropologists have previously substantivized the genealogical notion of kinship. For Fruzzetti, Östör, and Barnett the construction of the person is useful in introducing new categories, new data, and new domains for analysis and understanding and not in supplanting the genealogical kinship approach by a substantive person approach. Madan, on the other hand, also tried to avoid the latter pitfall by discussing the concept of the acting subject—the person and way of the Kashmiri Pandits. Madan stays firmly within the local ideology regarding the actor in social relations. The logical extension of his approach would be a further analysis of the terms thus constructed in relation to other kinship, marriage, and caste categories and domains. Nevertheless, in a broader sense, Carter's and the editors' studies are convergent in their careful attention to indigenous constructs and their attempt to extend the traditionally narrowed kinship universe.

In his provocative paper Khare offered a view that claims access to an internal position by elaborating a set of moral constructs that shape action. This analytical strategy of interpreting Indian culture provided the stimulus for brisk discussions about the ways these moral constructs are constituted in relationships and are to be recognized in particular situations and in terms of their relevance to rethinking kin domains and categories.

Vatuk's was one of the earlier studies that take terms of address seriously instead of ignoring or dismissing them. Since then Bean (1978) appeared, and a whole session on terms of address was held at the 1980 meetings of the American Anthropological Association. Yet the discussion did not go beyond Vatuk's paper and did not resolve the problems raised here. Vatuk's discussion also raised the intriguing possibility of approaching the household domain, previously encountered through production and exchange, from the vantage point of terminology and address converging with studies of kinds of economy. Vatuk suggested that usages of address and approach extend terminological boundaries and show how persons in the household constitute relationships in category and conduct. In the discussion Schneider raised the crucial distinction between terms and tactics, noting that while the latter contribute useful data in showing a manipulation of terms, the domain, household or other, still has to be constituted culturally and structurally.

Madan's full ethnographic narrative considered a new set of data. While it stopped short of offering a theory, it did go beyond conventional discussions of kinship. Dumont noted the subtle relation between *dharma* and *karma,* while *krama* contributed the actor's subjective point of view. He also praised the link thus forged between Indology and sociology. Madan noted the all-India aspects of the Bhaṭṭa ideology: the concepts of mother and goddess do not form a maternal, in opposition to a paternal, distinction.

Kolenda's paper called attention to the opposition of Brahman and untouchable as a cultural reality in India. Even though the Chuhra community is not preoccupied with purity, untouchables have to be understood in relation to Brahmanic notions. Remarriage for women is a rite of passage, though a degrading one. Thus, concepts of widowhood are constructed out of people's definition of events and out of the ways in which people are related to each other through these events. As a consequence the idea of women as persons is also affected and is expressed through cultural values and categories. Kolenda's recognition of the variations in the local construction of women should be related to previous studies of purity, marriage and hierarchy (especially Yalman's and Tambiah's), and to ongoing investigations of the person.

Finally, several papers (especially Nicholas's, Carter's, and Khare's) brought up the question of texts and textual studies in sociological discussion. The use of textual materials in the analysis of *saṅskars* (Carter), of body concepts (Nicholas), and of moral constructs (Khare) raise the issue of meaning and for whom: Where do the terms come from? What difference is made by time and locality? Can terms be juxtaposed from different contexts of time? Most significantly, whose system do they help construct? In view of Nicholas's discussion Dumont queried whether *dharma dhatu,* a compound term originating from different ideologies, can legitimately be collapsed in a single etymology without regard to how it may have changed in meaning through time and locality. In the least the categories have to be constructed in and through social relationships, not direct derivation from texts.

Although we stated that we stand for no new orthodoxy, we may note the direction in which the results of this volume may be leading us. Here we shall speak for ourselves rather than for the conference group as a whole. On the most minimal level we expect that greater attention will be paid to the constitution of the person in the studies of kinship, caste, and marriage in South Asia. This is already evident in quite a number of pre- and postdoctoral research projects being pursued at several of our leading universities. Some of this effort may be sharply different from our own (see the work at Chicago already referred to); nevertheless it shares the same basic concerns. Theoretical stances may differ, the new controversies now taking shape will, we hope, benefit the whole of anthropology.

In a more ambitious vein we expect these new approaches to reconstruct the domain of kinship, caste, and marriage in India, regionally and subcontinentally, and to reformulate the links between kinship and other domains, culturally constituted. We view this continuing broad endeavor as demystifying kinship, too long a privileged section of the anthropological project. Too long have we labored under the sometimes hidden, sometimes all too clear assumption that systems of kinship and marriage are somehow more exact, measurable, elegant, and representational than other domains in society, deserving of anthropology's claim to scientific status, albeit of a nineteenth-century positivist kind. The aim, however, is not deconstruction; rather it is the extension of the current ferment to the accomplishment of alternatives. In our own work the study of kinship is to take its place alongside religion, politics, and economics in the dialectical encounter of advanced industrial and other societies, comparative science and indigenous ideologies, cultural domains, and local practices. Continued refinement of universal formulations will thus be pursued not separately but in close, mutually reflexive relation to indigenous constructions. Only in this manner can we hope to sustain the anthropological project so succinctly formulated by Mauss (Dumont 1978).

Specifically, this volume takes its place as the third in a series concerned with a common theme (Harvard Studies in Cultural Anthropology). The first (Maybury-Lewis, ed. 1979) situated itself in Brazil, the second (Fox, ed. 1980) in Indonesia. With the contribution of India the stage is set for a reaffirmation of the comparative project, on a far more sophisticated level than before, in the holistic anthropological endeavor.

In more global terms the comparative cultural-symbolic-structural approach we advocate has wide-ranging implications for the practice of anthropology.[3] Within contemporary social science, and especially cultural anthropology, the study of meaning as culture or ideology creates an immediate and profound impasse posed as the problem of self-reflexivity: Do the forms through which one understands another culture reflect aspects of the analyst's culture? Put another way: Can we develop methods for analyzing culture that are founded on rational (verifiable operational) procedures—procedures that by definition are not simply products of a historical epoch but that can stand independent of history as epistemological first principles? Such rational attempts to comprehend systems of meaning vastly different from the analyst's own often include claims that the analyst can get inside the informant's head—that the analyst can reproduce as a kind of cognitive map the meanings of symbols as given to the informant, or that the analyst has an overall typological classification that can include as an element of the typology any indigenous culture, the indigenous culture becoming "an instance of . . ."

Against this kind of rationality we advance our alternative approach that would make a virtue of the limitation placed on us as members of particular societies anchored in particular places and times, subject to particular ideologies, yet practicing a comparative science. As we already wrote in another context, here we reaffirm Dumont's formulation of the anthropological project. We can understand something of ourselves by seeing ourselves in terms of other cultures; and we can understand something of others in terms of ourselves. Since social science is analytical, and analysis implies critical distance rather than simple acceptance, and since there is no generally accepted standard of rational inquiry—ultimately, one cannot argue for verification and operationalism—Dumont suggests that we can begin to loosen ourselves from our own ideology by comparing it with one basically distinct from it, and then not losing the point of the comparison by dissolving that distinctness in our own constructions. Stated this way, the point perhaps seems an anthropological shibboleth; however, while most anthropologists pay lip service to it, few make it central. Most anthropologists use other cultures merely as a kind of foil for extending the domain of the rationalizing process (Barnett, Fruzzetti, Östör 1976).

The title of our volume is faithful to the tenor of the papers and discussions. Some of us were more concerned with the person as such, others with ideology in relation to conduct and/or the ideology of the person, yet others with conduct in relation to ideology. Some of us tried to press the accepted boundaries of domains farther than others. Some regarded the person, or at least South Asian versions of it, as a legitimate focus; others used different constructions of persons to get at old problems of caste, kinship, and marriage. Despite our disagreements we showed an overriding necessity and desire to reach beyond the conventional wisdom of kinship studies and to include new kinds of data for analysis and understanding in the wake of the shattered, separate domains of kinship and caste. Since we stand for no new orthodoxy, the approaches given here may lead to new work in many different directions. Some may reach toward cross-cultural psychiatric studies in pursuit of the person, others toward a reassessment of women and purity in hierarchy, yet others toward broader cultural studies in relation to the age-old problems of comparative sociology. The way is open for new constructions of epistemology for anthropology. As Tambiah summed up the impact of the discussions, for all of us intense and demanding beyond previous conference experience: in the least a whole new domain has been opened up for analysis, and at the very most a new interpretation has been sketched out. In either case the departures await further informed critical discussion, further field research, and further evaluations.

Notes
References
Index

Notes

Concepts of Person: Fifteen Years Later*

* The Harvard Conference which led to the book was held in December 1976. The original volume, published by Harvard University Press, appeared in 1982.

1. The positions we allude to here have been summarized in the original Introduction and Conclusion to this volume (see especially pp. 2–6, 222–26). See also our articles on 'Bad Blood in Bengal' and 'The Cultural Construction of the Person in Bengal and Tamilnadu', Chapters 2 and 1, especially pp. 8–12, 24–30, 31–38.

2. These articles were published before *Concepts of Person* appeared but they discuss our essays on kinship in the winter 1976 issue of *Contributions to Indian Sociology*. These articles in turn formed the basis of the discussions at the 1976 Harvard Conference which resulted in the present volume.

3. Vatuk went on to study, very successfully, a much enlarged field of marriage exchanges and terms of address (see Vatuk 1975 and this volume).

4. Here we are thinking specifically of marriage exchanges and ritual.

5. The situation can change through time: note the *kulin* lines of Bengal. Even the most extreme *kulin* case can tolerate divergence since not the whole endogamous group is involved in a marriage cycle of ranked groups. The very idea of *kulinism*, with the same groom likely to contract several marriages (even dozens or hundreds) belies a ladderlike scheme of groups recruiting and passing women up and down the ranks of the line.

6. We refer, of course, to a comparison of particular cultural constructs, not external sociological constructs such as status groups and the like with which *Concepts of Person* did not attempt to deal.

Notes

Introduction

1. For lists of the seminal works by those who came to the Harvard discussions, see References. Among the items not given in these bibliographies are Yalman 1962, 1967; Tambiah 1965, 1973; Vatuk 1972; Kolenda 1969, 1976, 1978; Maybury-Lewis 1965, 1979.

2. The arguments on pp. 3–4 and 5–6 are adapted from the editors' 1976 essays (Fruzzetti, Östör 1976a:63–64, 66, 67, 1976b:97–98; Barnett 1976:155; Barnett, Fruzzetti, Östör 1976:629) and are reproduced here by permission of the publishers, *Journal of Asian Studies* and *Contributions to Indian Sociology*.

1. The Cultural Construction of the Person in Bengal and Tamilnadu

1. Reprinted by permission from *Contributions to Indian Sociology* 10, no. 1 (1976).

2. For a different approach to south India in a different context, see Yalman 1967.

3. While we do not elaborate a theory of comparision here, the reader can see that we are not looking at surface aggregation and similarities or differences of content; instead, comparison proceeds at the level of structure.

4. See Fruzzetti and Östör 1976b:101–102 for limitations on the use of *Bengali* in this context. A more elaborate discussion of relationships among persons can be found in "Seed and Earth."

5. Acceptability for outcasting differs for Bengal and Tamilnadu and raises questions about caste that we plan to discuss in a separate essay.

6. We recognize the ambiguity inherent in speaking of caste in kinship in north India and kinship in caste in south India. Our approach to both regions, Bengal and Tamilnadu, attempts to reduce the ambiguity by refusing to adopt a priori, universalist constructions of kinship and caste based on genealogy in the former case and stratification plus transaction in the latter.

7. Dumont's achievement in *Hierarchy and Marriage Alliance* was the recognition of the fallacy involved in discussing cross-cousin marriage. Situating his study in caste hierarchy, Dumont arrived at a theory of alliance based on the equivalence of brothers-in-law. In north India, however, Dumont found a practice not dissimilar but without the alliance rule.

8. Dumont's profound contribution to our discipline is his theory of hierarchy. His insistence that caste hierarchy does not stop at the boundary of kinship is particularly significant for our argument.

9. We must not forget that the smallest unit, *baṇgśa,* is also the unit within which no marriage can take place, given *gotra* and blood exclusion. Alliance, then, is a way through which larger units of equivalence can be established. Within *jāti* equivalence only shared blood and *gotra* stand in the way of new alliances, yet not all lines are related by marriage, and there are smaller, often local units of equivalence established by marriages.

10. The Sinhalese *pavula* is an example of a nonclosed kindred. We must be aware of this ethnographic possibility for south India as well. The degree of closure may be variable and open for research for different castes in different regions (see Yalman 1962).

11. It is of course in the logic of the system that all lines are encompassed by *jāti* equivalence, while sets of allied lines are differentiated within the *jāti.* These sets, however, are not concrete groups; rather they are constructs formed by principles. This circumstance differentiates our case from hypergamy, since the lines of *jāti* are not ordered for unidirectional marriage. Alliance should be understood as a set of principles through which two persons of two lines are deemed worthy of marriage in the light of previous marriages throughout the sets of allied lines on both sides.

2. Bad Blood in Bengal

1. Lévi-Strauss (1973:140).

2. The first three essays appeared in *Contributions to Indian Sociology* as Fruzzetti and Östör 1976a and b, and Fruzzetti, Östör, and Barnett 1976.

3. See "Seed and Earth" (Fruzzetti and Östör 1976b) for elaboration on *baṇgśa, gotra, āttiya,* and classes of *āttiya.*

4. The in-marrying woman's change of *gotra* and her continuing relations with her father and brother prompt a further problem for adherents of transubstantiation: What, then, differentiates a sister from a wife?

5. For an elaboration of marriage exchanges see Fruzzetti 1982.

6. See Kapadia (1947:92) for the adoption *mantra.* See also Fruzzetti (1982) for the elaboration of the marriage rituals and the adoption of males for the continuation of the line.

7. Here we disagree fundamentally with the one-dimensional interpretation put forward by Inden and Nicholas (1977).

8. *Bhāśur* (HeB) is a compounded word, *bhātr śvaśur,* meaning a brother who is also a father-in-law. One's HeB name is never uttered. He maintains a distance from his yBW, while she covers her head in his presence and avoids conversation with him. It is said that even if the yBW is drowning, her *bhāśur* cannot rescue her, since to do so he would have to touch her.

3. Forms of Address in the North Indian Family

1. This is a revised version of the paper originally prepared for the conference on kinship and caste in India. I would like to thank all of the participants in that conference for their stimulating discussion of the paper and for many constructive criticisms. The finished version has also benefited from discussions in a seminar in the Department of Anthropology at the University of Washington in Seattle and at a symposium on language in South Asian social life, held at the annual meeting of the American Anthropological Association in 1979, where I presented some of this material. In addition, I am grateful to Veena Das, Lawrence Fisher, and Gloria Raheja, each of whom gave an earlier version of the manuscript a careful reading. I am also indebted to Ved Prankash Vatuk, who recorded some of the original data on which this paper is based. Responsibility for any errors of fact or interpretation are, of course, entirely my own.

2. I should acknowledge here the influence on my thinking of R. S. Khare's work on kinship in north India. In an earlier, unpublished version of his 1975 publication, his insistence on the value and feasibility of the contextual observation of actual kin term usages brought home to me the significance of things that I realized I had been seeing throughout my field work but had tended to suppress in my writings on the subject in the interests of systematization.

3. By using the phrase "genealogically inappropriate," I do not mean to imply that such usages are in any way improper or incorrect, either from the point of view of the speakers, or from my perspective as an analyst of the system. Furthermore, I do not thereby intend to make any judgment as to the relative merits of the genealogical approach to the study of kinship terminology as against any other approach. I simply use this as a convenient catchphrase to indicate that the kin term used in address is not the one that one would predict had the form of address been selected purely on the basis of the known genealogical relationship between Ego and Alter.

4. In the cited paper I did not question the accepted dictum that one can separate out a domain of fictive kinship from that of real kinship, in which former domain the use of kin terms in referential and vocative contexts is a consequence of the metaphorical extension of the genealogical model to nonrelatives. Today I would probably handle this issue somewhat differently, but inasmuch as I am here dealing almost exclusively with intrafamilial kinship, where the presence and knowledge of genealogical links among the members is unequivocal and culturally significant, a discussion of the matter would take me too far afield.

5. The distribution and use of the respect suffix *-jī* is itself a subject of considerable potential interest and merits sociolinguistic investigation, varying as it does by individual speaker, locale (rural-urban and regional), social class, and probably other dimensions as well. The suffix is bound in the kin terms *mātājī* and *pitājī* (in other words, /*mātā*/ and /*pitā*/ do not normally occur as such in reference and address among family members), but with most other kin terms, and with personal names, its use is optional, though contextually determined. Urban speakers tend to utilize it more liberally than do ruralites, as do those with higher levels of formal education, and in general it is employed more extensively in address than in reference. While it most commonly functions as a deference marker, its occurrence may indicate the formality of a situation or mock defer-

ence or emphasis—for example, when the person being addressed does not respond immediately to a summons.

6. The letters within parentheses indicate the genealogical specification of the cited kin term as it would be employed in a referential context or when an informant was asked to define the term. In the phraseology I am using in this paper, it is the genealogically appropriate referent of the term.

7. Numbers in brackets refer to the figures in which the usages cited are illustrated from actual case data.

8. The whole question of naming patterns in north India, and the impact upon them of Westernization and social change, is one that would reward further investigation. As far as I am aware, it is a matter on which very little has been written to date.

9. The conventional explanation for the abusive connotation of in-law terms is that, when used to address someone who is not in fact related genealogically as an in-law, the implication is conveyed that the speaker has had, or intends to have, illicit sexual congress with one of the hearer's female consanguineal relatives. Thus, to address someone as *sālā* (B) implies a sexual liaison with his sister; to address him as *susarā* (WF) implies such a relationship between his daughter and the speaker, and so on. The in-law terms to which this explanation applies assume, of course, a male speaker. But parent-in-law terms, unlike other in-law terms, are identical for male and female speakers and are avoided in address by both. Other in-law terms used only by women, such as *devar* (HyB) or *nanad* (HZ), are not considered obscene, although they are also rarely employed in address. While this rationale for the abusive connotation of certain in-law terms accords with the indigenous view and is probably satisfactory analytically at the surface level, it raises questions worthy of further study, whose answers could shed considerable light on the cultural significance of affinity and female sexuality in north Indian society.

10. One might debate the issue of whether the terms *mammī* and *pāppā* should be considered together with the parental terms of Hindi derivation or whether they should be placed, as I have done here, with the genealogically inappropriate terms for mother and father. While these English-derived terms are on the one hand clearly appropriate genealogically in the context of the English or American kinship systems, they are, in a Hindi-speaking cultural setting, functionally analogous to genealogically inappropriate terms—*jījī* (Z), *cācā* (FyB), and so on, in the way that they replace the Hindi parental terms in address for genealogical parents.

11. Note that the diagrams do not necessarily include all members of the particular families whose address usages are being illustrated. Only those persons have been included for whom there is the relevant information and about whom such information is pertinent to the discussion at hand. In most cases, if there is more than one sibling in the family all of whom use the same term for a designated relative, only one Ego appears on the corresponding diagram for the sake of convenience.

12. Another quite different interpretation of the kind of phenomenon being discussed here is provided by Beck, with reference to what she calls "slippage," or "the ease with which usages slip across generational lines" in the use of kin terms in Tamil (1972:227). As examples she cites the habit of referring to and ad-

dressing the (geneaological) father by the term for elder brother or father's father and points out, as I have done here, that one cannot determine by observing the ongoing use of kin terms in the family what the actual genealogical relationships are among its members. In the light of my data for Hindi and Carter's for Marathi, it is interesting to note that Beck observed in Tamilnadu "no similar 'slippage' associated with the terms for mother and sister" (1972:227). Beck's interpretation of this pattern associates the "widespread disregard for generational distinctions within the nuclear family" with a general lack of generational emphasis in the terminology as a whole (1972:227). However appropriate such an explanation may be for such a pattern in a kinship terminology of Dravidian type, I have not found it relevant to the Hindi terminology.

4. The Ideology of the Householder among the Kashmiri Pandits

1. An earlier draft of this essay was presented at the seminar on new approaches to the study of Indian society held under the auspices of the Department of Anthropology, Harvard University, in December 1976. I owe warm thanks to Ákos Östör and Lina Fruzzetti for the invitation and for their hospitality. The discussion that followed the presentation of my paper, particularly the comments by Louis Dumont and Nur Yalman, have been of invaluable help in its preparation for publication. I would also like to thank the Wenner-Gren Foundation for Anthropological Research, Inc., and its director of research, Lita Osmundsen, for making it possible for me to visit the United States for the seminar. Later, I read the paper to the research colloquium of the Department of Sociology, Delhi University. I am grateful to Professor J. P. S. Uberoi for the suggestion that I do so and for his criticism of the essay. Among other members of the colloquium whose searching questions have enabled me, I hope, to improve the paper, I would like to make particular mention of Dr. Veena Das.

2. My first and longest spell of field work was carried out in 1957–1958, mostly in the village of Utrassu-Umanagri in the south of the Kashmir Valley. I have since then paid several visits to this village; the last of these took place in 1975. My discussions with Pandits of other villages, whom I had occasion to meet in their own village, in Utrassu-Umanagri or elsewhere, has convinced me that there is a uniformity in the patterns of Pandit culture in the rural areas, and this emboldens me to speak of the Pandits of rural Kashmir generally. In fact, I have reason to believe that what I write here is largely applicable to Pandits anywhere in Kashmir. Though the Pandits are divided into two subcastes, priests and non-priests, and differences of socioeconomic status also are found among them (see Madan 1965), these differences are not relevant in the context of the problem dealt with in this paper.

3. Most Kashmiri words are either of Sanskrit or of Persian derivation, but the difference of pronunciation between the original and the derivative words is often considerable. Thus, Kashmiris hardly ever use aspirated consonant sounds. For the sake of comparability of the linguistic material, I have used the original Sanskrit words whenever I could identify these. A glossary at the end of the paper lists all the native words used and the correspondence between their Sanskrit and Kashmiri forms.

4. Cf. "Behaviour must be attended to, and with some exactness, because it is

through the flow of behaviour—or, more precisely, social action—that cultural forms find articulation" (Geertz 1973:17).

5. Also cf. "To be sure, the more standardized the prevailing action pattern is, the more anonymous it is, the greater is the subjective chance of conformity and, therewith, of the success of intersubjective behaviour" (Schutz 1967:33).

6. The need for interpretation arises when we are confronted with data about the experience of a person or persons that is apparently meaningful to him but the meaningfulness of which is obscure even to the actor himself. Interpretation, therefore, involves the process of clarifying the obscure through bringing out implicit linkages and the significance of these linkages between the components of information readily available to the researcher from different data sources.

7. Schutz (1967:61) referred to this phenomenon as the "social distribution of knowledge": "Each individual knowing merely a sector of the world and common knowledge of the same sector varying individually as to its degree of distinctness, clarity, acquaintanceship, or mere belief." In this connection I might add that my informants in the village of Utrassu-Umanagri accept without demur the fact that some of them know more than the others about certain matters. One does not question what one does not know, but other fellow villagers do on even such basic matters as religious belief, ritual performances, kinship ties, and so on. I have written elsewhere about the general lack of interest in genealogical materials (see Madan 1975b:141–146). Rather uncomfortable about such a state of affairs, I expressed my anxiety to my informants on several occasions till one of the most intelligent Pandits of the village resolved my doubts in a rather simple manner. He asked me if I believed in the methods of science and whether I used electrical gadgets. When I answered him in the affirmative, he asked if I could repair a broken-down radio. I had to admit that I could not. Triumphant, he concluded: "If your ignorance and consequent dependence upon a radio repairman does not shake your belief in science, why do you expect us to know everything that we believe in?"

8. Though there were literate members in all the Pandit households of Utrassu-Umanagri during 1957–1958, not many of them possessed any books other than almanacs and the schoolbooks of the children. The most commonly found religious text was the *Bhagavadgītā,* in about half the homes. Some households owned astrological books, the epics *Mahābhārata* and *Rāmāyaṇa,* and prayerbooks such as the *Bhavanīsahsranāma,* containing the thousand names of the mother goddess.

9. It is interesting to note that a common family name among Kashmiri Muslims is Bhat (Bhaṭṭa), just as it is among the Pandits. It has obviously survived conversion of Hindus to Islam.

10. Stepmothers are, however, different. They are generally said to be cruel to the children of their husband's deceased wife, particularly when they have children of their own. I even heard stories about the attempts of some women to poison their stepchildren. Adoptive mothers are unpredictable. If a child has been foisted upon an issueless woman by her husband's relatives she may not feel very attached to it, but mothers do often treat their adopted children with the same love and care as natural mothers do. Between the pangs of bearing (*zenadod*) and the toils of rearing (*racchnandod*), the Pandits aver, it is hard to arbitrate, but in the ultimate analysis, the Pandits say, "blood simmers in one's veins."

11. Legal texts translate the word *sapiṇḍa* to mean those connected by particles

of one body (see, for example, Mayne 1950:146); in doing so they follow Vijnāñeśwara's twelfth-century text known as the *Mitākṣara.* It would seem that this usage is also commonly employed by Hindus in Bengal in defining the category of one's own people who are seen related to oneself as *eka-śarīra* or *sapiṇḍa,* that is by the same body (Inden and Nicholas 1977:3). The literal meanings of the word *piṇḍa,* it must be noted, include not only body but also balls of cooked rice offered to manes.

12. Cf. the quotation from Dumont on page 101 above and from Schutz in note 5.

13. Since the coming of Islam in the twelfth century Kashmiri Hindus have had to live on their wits and on compromises. It is remarkable that they should have survived at all. For an account of the vicissitudes through which they have passed, see Kilam (1955). It is, however, a poorly researched and badly written book. Also see Bamzai (1962).

14. "There are three 'human ends,' *dharma, artha,* and *kāma,* duty, profit, and pleasure. All three are [necessary and] lawful, but they are so graded in a hierarchy that an inferior ideal may be pursued only as far as a superior one does not intervene: *dharma,* conformity to the world order, is more important than *artha,* power and wealth, which in turn is above *kāma,* immediate enjoyment" (Dumont 1960:41).

15. Blessing for men: *Om ayuṣmān bhava putravāṇ bhava śrimān yaśasavi bhava praynyāvān bhava bhu✕ ri bhūti karuṇa dānaika nistho bhava tejasavi bhava vairi darpa dalana vyāpār dakśo bhav śrī śambhorbhava pāda pūjanaratah sarvopakārī bhava!*

16. Blessing for women: *Om dhanaputravatī sādhvī sattam bhratr vallabhā manognyāgnyān sahita tistha tvam śharadahśhatam!* Both invocations are in Sanskrit.

17. What is called the *upanayana* ceremony elsewhere in north India is called *mekhalā,* or *yagñyopāvīta,* among the Pandits, and very great importance is attached to it both as a ritual and as a social event. It takes place usually in the seventh or ninth year of a boy's life. In all, twenty-four rites are performed on the occasion, beginning with *bījvapānam,* for ensuring the fertility of the parents of the boy, which may not have been performed as it should have been in the father's twenty-fifth and the mother's sixteenth year. All other rites, which should have been but may or may not have been performed, are also performed, culminating in the investiture of the girdle (*mekhalā*) and the holy thread (*yagñyopāvīta*).

18. "The knowledge of the Absolute, *parā vidyā,* which secures immediate liberation (*sadyo-mukti*) is possible only for those who are able to withdraw their thoughts from worldly objects and concentrate on the ultimate fact of the universe. The knowledge of *Iśvara* [the Supreme as God], *aparā vidyā,* puts one on the pathway that leads to deliverance eventually (*krama-mukti*). The worshipping soul gradually acquires the higher wisdom which results in the consciousness of the identity with the Supreme" (Radhakrishnan 1953:579).

19. There is a category of exceptional people who should be mentioned here. They act like madmen and madwomen but one learns to recognize them as people "touched by god" (to quote an informant). They develop clairvoyance and give indications of the will of the divinity. They have the power to bless and

curse. They do not acknowledge family ties and obligations nor indeed the rules of *bhaṭṭil,* including the rules of purity and pollution. Such people are more feared than revered by the Pandits.

5. Hierarchy and the Concept of the Person in Western India

1. This paper is based upon data gathered during two periods of field work in Maharashtra. From October 1965 through September 1967 I resided first in Deccan College, Poona, and then in Girvi, a large village (pop. 3841) some seventy miles southwest of Poona in Satara District. From March through August 1976 I resided, this time with my wife and our two daughters, in Alandi, the site of Jnanadev's *samadhi* and a major pilgrimage center, some ten miles north of Poona. The first trip was supported by a graduate fellowship and research grant from the NIMH and the second by a grant from the NSF (SOC74-19108). Further material on the site of my first field work on the region generally may be found in Carter (1971, 1974a, 1974b and 1975).

A first draft of this paper was presented at the conference on caste and kinship in South Asia at Harvard University, December 10–13, 1976. The comments of Nur Yalman, Louis Dumont, and S. J. Tambiah were particularly useful in preparing the final draft but, of course, I remain responsible for the views presented here.

2. I am aware of the conflicting viewpoints of the authors referred to in this paragraph (see Barnett, Fruzzetti, and Östör 1976 and 1977; Marriott 1976c).

3. Compare this with the Bengali contrast between the *bhog deha* of animals, a body that sustains only, and the *karma deha* of human beings, a body that is subject to moral responsibility (Davis 1976:16, n. 23).

4. For a review of Hindu medical speculations on these matters see Dasgupta (1932:302–319).

5. The blood (*rakta*) from which the material body is formed is a complicated substance, and my informants, like Yalman's (1967:139), easily find themselves holding apparently contradictory positions. One may be told in one breath that all members of one's lineage (*bhaubund*), that is, agnates and their wives, are related by blood, while a mother's sister's daughter is not a blood relative (*raktaca natevaik*). If one then asks if it is permissable to marry one's mother's sister's daughter, however, one will be told in the next breath that such a marriage is not permissable because the girl's blood and that of one's mother and, therefore, of oneself are the same. It is for this reason, among others, that I have argued elsewhere (Carter 1974a, 1975) that we are dealing here with a segmentary system in which *blood* means different things in different contexts.

6. The relative immunity of children to pollution is described in considerable detail for another region of India in Harper (1964:155, 158–160, 164, 190).

7. For accounts of the initiation of *sannyasins* see Bharati (1961:151–155), Stevenson (1920:422–423), and Kane (1941:953–962). Their funerals are described in Dubois (1906:538–541), Stevenson (1920:153, 200–201), and Kane (1953: 229–231). Harper (1964:167) and Kane (1953:230) note the restrictions on the observance of death pollution for and by *sannyasins.*

8. On the Varkari Sampradaya and *bhakti* in Maharashtra see Ranade (1933) and Deleury (1960).

9. Kane notes that blind, deaf, impotent, or otherwise handicapped actors may be denied those *sańskar* that confer full personhood (1941:297–299, 430–431).

10. Compare this with Srinivas (1952).

11. A similar pot is used to represent ancestors in annual memorial sacrifices.

12. Here I quote my informants, but their views are partially confirmed by Kane, who notes that only *paramahamsa sannyasins* are prevalent in modern India (1953:230) and that these are regarded by many authorities as "beyond the pairs of dharma and adharma, truth and falsehood, purity and impurity" (1941:939).

13. See the references to Harper and Kane in note 7 above.

14. See the references to Kane in note 12 above.

6. From *Kanyā* to *Mātā*

1. This essay, presenting a segment of the effort required to consider a kinship system as a cultural system composed of a language of certain fundamental categories and principles, takes clues from both Louis Dumont's work and David Schneider's. Simultaneously, a natural inclination toward the indigenous-view approach, which McKim Marriott follows in a distinct way of his own, is evident. However, my analytical stance is my own, and I am unconditionally responsible for what I do here, particularly since I do not claim to have followed approaches of any one of these three anthropologists in any complete manner. However, their individually disparate yet selectively overlapping procedures and insights remain attractive signposts to me for such explorations.

During its presentation as a draft at the Harvard University workshop (December 1976), I received comments on aspects of this paper from several participants, particularly Professors Schneider, Yalman, Madan, and Vatuk, and a subsequent written communication from Lina Fruzzetti and Ákos Östör. While without attributing any shortcomings of this paper to these colleagues, I remain most grateful to all of them for their helpful comments.

This essay (along with those segments that could be subsequently written) was conceived in general terms at the Institute for Advanced Study, Princeton, during 1974–1975. My 1974 trip to my field, supported by the Center for Advanced Study, University of Virginia, and a 1976 trip, supported by the American Philosophical Society and the University of Virginia, helped me greatly in checking further how people link norms to practices on the one hand and to textual constructs on the other. I was aided in writing this paper by the Small Grants Committee at the University of Virginia. I acknowledge and appreciate help from all these sources.

2. These data also help me extend a discussion (Khare 1975) that was couched in terms of embedded affinity and consanguineal ethos. The latter phrases were employed to convey a quality of cultural thought that, it was proposed, pervades the northern system of kinship terminology. It was an attempt to show how kin terms as communicators of a cultural system undergo masking or unmasking, precision or imprecision, and transformation or substantiation around some distinctions of consanguinity and affinity. As I had observed then (1975:260), "the 'internal' cultural conception enters as a significant factor for ordering both the logic and sentiment of systemic relations," it is now my aim to see what happens when the internal cultural conception is predominantly found to express itself

along the orders of systemic and contextual constructs of *dharma* and *karma*. I shall also continue to support, though more indirectly, the argument that "the northern notion of affinity is actually . . . far more revealing about the system and about its 'consanguineal ethos' " (Khare 1975:259). Thus also is the *kanyā-sūhāgin-mātā* axis of symbolic transformation selected for this discussion.

A general point made before (Khare 1975:254), and as given below provides us with our conceptual point of departure: "The Hindu intellect . . . seems to be more centrally interested in 'converting' one moral category into the other rather than simply keeping the two in perpetual opposition without proposing systemic modes of transformation between them."

3. There is no easy and accurate translation available for the English term *kinship* in Hindi. *Sagé sambandhī* versus *nātédār* is one of several popularly used pairs to cover consanguineal and affinal sets of relatives. The verb *lagnā* is most widely used in referring to and ascertaining who is related to whom and how; but there is no noun from the same root. The point of a processual (or transformational) conception of kinship is significant. Accordingly, my gloss of kinship, for the present, is "being properly related."

4. Schneider's (1976) formulation behind this term agrees with my analytical assignment for derived key constructs within the Indian system. He notes: "The system of symbols and meanings cut across the system of norms, or, stated differently, a given galaxy is dispersed among a number of different institutions. Further, any given institution is intersected by a series of galaxies just as any given galaxy is intersected by a series of institutions" (1976:210).

In the Hindu conception primary constructs, that is, those coming from *sṛuti* and/or *smṛti* (and often upheld by contextual *sadācāra* and *siśtācāra*), yield derived key constructs by an overlap between themselves and contextual classifiers. Here only the primal is the most genuine and the purest, therefore most authoritative within the cultural system (cf. Lingat 1973:15) to offer directions. The Hindu *dharma* is an archetype-guided system, emphasizing the roles of derived key constructs for connecting ideas to action. However, depending on the context at hand, the derived key constructs can either move closer to or away from the primary construct; sometimes they may even overlap. However, ideally a derived key construct like *kanyā* or *satī* is always reducible to *nārī* and the latter to the cosmic female principle.

5. The reference here is to *dṛṣta* (seen) and *adṛṣta* (unseen) distinctions of the Hindu system. (For the relevance of this distinction in the food system, see Khare 1976a, 1976b). Kane (1941:437–438) succinctly summarizes this in the context of marriage as he notes how "a seen (*dṛṣta*) or easily perceptible reason for a rule stated in the sacred texts" is only "recommendatory" (for example, as in marrying a girl who has visible defects), while "if there is an unseen (*adṛṣta*) reason for a rule," such a rule becomes "obligatory" (as in marrying a *sagotra* or *sapravara* girl). We thus notice how the invisible cultural reasons in general acquire a greater value over those visible in the scheme of Hindu distinctions. For example, *karma* is always a partially visible (as an activity) and invisible (as an ethical cosmic) construction. However, the more the *adṛṣta* dimensions stand behind a *karma* rule or a principle, the more culturally powerful it is held to be, and it will also be normatively more subscribed to, explicitly or implicitly, among the twice born.

6. As Kane (1941:444) points out, these are: *gaurī* (a girl of eight); *rohiṇī* (a girl of nine); *kanyā* (a girl of ten); and *rajasvalā* (a girl over ten). Note how the last is distinguished by implied menstruation. For another scheme see Prabhu (1963:181), where *bālā* covers the first sixteen years of a girl. Also, notice how Apte (1965:333) mentions four meanings of this term: "an unmarried girl or daughter," "a girl ten years old," "a virgin, maiden," and "a woman in general." In the field I encountered the first and third as the strongest usages; the second was known to few but was not in social usage; and the last was least known except under a metaphorical usage.

7. As a part of the Hindi-Sanskrit lexicon, *saubhāgyavātī* takes after the idea of *saughāgya,* which, besides being the auspicious state of wifehood, refers in general to what Apte (1965:1001) variously calls good fortune or luck, blessedness and auspiciousness, and grace, charm, beauty, and grandeur. However, more importantly, note his reference to that "fortunateness" that consists in "a man's and woman's securing the favor and firm devotion of each other." As a jural and ritual classifier, it fundamentally opposes wifehood to widowhood. An unhappily married woman thus remains a full *sūhāgin.* Other terms closely related to the above are *sadhwā* (opposite of *vidhwā*) and *subhagā.* (For usage of the latter see, for example, Prabhu 1963:169.)

8. This phrase obviously refers to the mythological Savitri who faced Yama to seek the return of the life of her dead husband, Satyavana. Today women employ it in different contexts with meanings ranging from idealistic to joking and even sarcastic. For example, *Woh apné ko barī satī sāvitrī samajhtee hai* (She is not what she claims to be). In such a usage, there is sarcasm and even an implied admission of jealousy against a woman who is especially devoted to her husband.

9. In an earlier draft I invented and employed the *jananī/mātā* complex to draw attention to the differences between the birth giving and other cultural formulations on *mātā* within the Hindu scheme. The distinction itself is amply recognized within the system by a number of popular as well as textual terms. For example, compare *mātā* and *dhāya,* and *sagī* and *sautélī mā* in popular usage, and textual lexicon *janyétrī* or *janma dātrī* or *janitrī* or *janittva* (Apte 1965:446) against *mā* or *mātā* or *jananī* or *matrikā* (Apte 1965:755). Nevertheless it is not quite the same as I previously proposed. Internally, it is more precisely a distinction of the contents of *dharma* rather than of nature versus culture. Both *sagī* and *sautélī* mothers enter the *dharma* of motherhood, but there is no *dharmika* reason for the second remaining mother inferior to the first. *Mātā* is thus used here as a catch-all *dharma* construct, removing the necessity to employ the *jananī/mātā* phrase, but without ignoring the *sagī/sautélī* distinction. The latter scheme is important because within the Hindu cultural system it occupies a prominent place—as much for proving that the birth-giving mother is the true mother as opposed to the stepmothers and foster mothers as for the converse, where the latter (*dharma mātā*), though not biologically related to the child, can prove themselves to be superior to the birth-giving one. There is a tension here in favor of being a better mother. Some other sociologically significant terms for mother are: *jayā* (see Manu IX:8), *ambā* (one who rears [children's] limbs), *susṛusū* (one who nurses and looks after the son) and *jananī* (the principal cause of son's birth); see Prabhu (1963:253).

10. In the cosmic egg (as in *hiraṇyagarbha;* see Manu in Bühler (1886:2–14, including footnotes) a moral construction of sexual principles is latent. In normal

bodies (as in *nara* and *narī*) it is pervasive (its absence, either contrived or by birth—*janma-jāt,* or in function, is anomalous; for example, compare the social and ceremonial positions of the people who are *hijrā; napuṃsaka* and *bāñjha*). In mythological domains sexual principles are highly transformational—sometimes problematic (as with *jīva* or *ātman*) and sometimes auxiliary or secondary (as with Nārāyaṇa, the prime creator; note how in Manu's law codes the necessity of sexual differentiation between creatures is positioned only after the opening thirty-one verses). For a range of interplaying mythologic relations, see O'Flaherty (1973), particularly 255–286 for data. Such a transformation, given its implications for cultural definitions of *genesis* and *incest* (see Leach 1974, 1976:71–75), must especially attract our attention. Apart from explaining such examples as a "mythological inconsistency" (Leach 1976:74), they communicate something about the way a problem is conceived and handled by the people themselves. That they are not merely mythologic (cf. Leach 1976:69–70) but a cultural verity that explains and supports the customary social practices is crucial to remember. The mythical, as being a crucial powerhouse for cultural signification, has had a telling social reality for the common Hindu. It continues to be so for the majority.

11. While no detailed consideration can be undertaken here of such vital aspects of *dāna,* we may note how practising *dāna* is pervasively considered to yield *vṛiddhi* (increment). One popular line a pleased receiver of *dāna* utters today is: *betā! dina dūne rāta caugunė baṛhō* (Son! [may your fortunes] double by day and quadruple by night). Ideas of addition and multiplication are obvious here; multiplication inheres addition. Subtraction and division run counter to this logic, where one whole broken in parts yields only fractions, not similar wholes. However, the idea of genetic replication is agreeable, where one whole leads to many wholes like the previous one, for it again implies addition and multiplication. A marriage symbolically anticipates this transformational logic, which a *sūhāgin* fulfills by becoming a *jananī.* A progeny is in fact called *vṛiddhi* to one's family.

12. Let us be clear that *sapiṇda* literally means "possessed of" or sharing same or similar *piṇda,* where the latter is an obsequial rice ball. "Shared particles" might be an anthropologically convenient but internally a strange metaphorical gloss for *sapiṇda,* one smacking of scientism, particularly since *piṇda* always basically means a lump, ball, or globe (see Apte 1965:617).

13. One could be greatly tempted to recall and employ the principle of consubstantiality here, particularly since it makes sense in a discussion of filiation (see Pitt-Rivers 1973). However, the problems in translating the Western idea of substantiality into an Indian one are still enormous; the logical relation of coexistence (*Compact Edition of the Oxford English Dictionary,* 1971, p. 3385) is comparatively problem free.

14. According to some of my informants, 63 vividly shows a state of *sahgamana.* "Persons of opposite sex face each other to reproduce, and as they do so they, under *dharma,* enhance their value as 63 does in relation to 36, though the digits involved are the same. It also shows how a *bhāi/bahén* (36) relationship is just the total opposite of a *patī/patnī* (63) relationship." These remarks of an informant were carried further by another, when he observed that the increment (as in 63) also occurs when "a devotee comes face to face with God; when he does

not and his mundane existence signifies only 36." This relationship of intrinsic increase, which is symbolized in this case by 63, is generally much more valued within the cultural system.

15. On a comparative basis, one could conjecture whether the Anglo-Saxon idea of affinity, where ideally the children can neither add to nor subtract from nor transform the basic two-individual (husband-wife) relationship, and where the individuality of both is separately sufficient, necessary, and secure, offers a contrasting example. Based on the strength of the jural and politicoeconomic Individual, the West forges the idea of affinity in a distinctly different way than does the Hindu system. This conceptual difference is critical to remember before freely applying the prevalent anthropological concept of affinity to a non-Western society like India.

16. Given the extraordinary cultural depth the constructs like *piṇda* and *srāddha* have for the Indian system, they must offer us a major access to the nature of language that the Hindu kinship system insists on. *Srāddha,* as will be discovered, is a highly generic cultural construction for the Hindu cosmology. It is a basic paradigm on which various observances, including kinship and affinal usages, are handled as variations on a theme. It is deeply guided by the *dharma* of both a sacrifice and a gift and of the seen and the unseen.

7. Widowhood among "Untouchable" Chuhras

1. The word *untouchable* is put in quotation marks here to remind the reader of two things: first, that untouchability was officially abolished by the Constitution of India (1950), and second, that the term *untouchable* is not the translation of a term used by the people themselves. The term seems to have been used first by the Maharaja of Baroda in some hearings before the Depressed Classes Mission of Bombay in 1909 (Galanter 1972:298). The term used by Western Hindi speakers and by the people of Khalapur for the lowest category of caste groups was *ashudd* (unclean). The four higher classes equated with the *varnas* of Sanskrit religious writings—the Brahmans, Kshatriya, Vaishya, and Shudras—were considered to be *shudd* (clean). The term will appear without quotation marks throughout the remainder of this essay.

I owe thanks to Sylvia Vatuk and Nancy Edwards, who read through this version of the paper and made some helpful suggestions, and to the editors and other members of the 1976 Harvard seminar as well.

2. Khalapur was one of a number of villages in India studied as part of the Cornell India Program, directed by Morris F. Opler of Cornell University. Study of Khalapur went on from 1953 to 1956; it was financed by the Ford Foundation. Members of the study team included anthropologists, economists, a political scientist, a psychologist, and a linguist. The project resulted in scores of published articles, several dissertations, and books. A more or less complete bibliography of publications from the Khalapur study is in Kolenda (1982). The author was a postdoctoral fellow doing ethnography in Khalapur from 1954 to 1956. I continue to be grateful to Cornell University for the opportunity to do my first field work in India in Khalapur.

3. Sylvia Vatuk (1981: personal communication) has pointed out that the term usually used among people of the Meerut area is that "the four *gotras* should not 'match' " (*milnā,* in Hindi). She believes that it is the *sapiṇda* rule that prohibits

marriage with cousins. This may be true for some groups in Uttar Pradesh. I never heard the *sapiṇda* rule cited in Khalapur by either high- or low-caste informants. However, the four-*gotra* rule does have the effect of prohibiting marriage between all four types of cousins. One's father's brother's children have the same *gotra* as Ego (*gotras* being taken patrilineally). One's father's sister's child would belong to a different *gotra* from Ego, but that child could not marry Ego, because Ego would have the same *gotra* as that child's mother. Similarly, mother's sister's child could not be married because both individuals would have mothers with the same *gotra,* and mother's brother's child could not marry Ego because Ego's mother would have the same *gotra* as that child.

4. *Havans* refer to offerings made to deities and spirits through the medium of fire; bits of food are sprinkled into the fire or poured onto the fire, as in the case of *ghee* (clarified butter) and are thus brought to the deity or spirit. *Puja* refers to offerings of flowers (*phul*) and other things such as coconuts and bananas made to a deity or spirit.

5. The word *dowry* has certain connotations in the European context that are not quite correct in this context––essentially the idea that the bride's parents provide the newly married couple with an endowment, wealth, or property, giving them a sound financial basis for a family. In this context, on the other hand, a sizable sum of money is given by the bride's people to the groom's father. This money may well be used by the groom's father to clear debts or to provide a dowry for one of the groom's sisters.

6. Vatuk (1981: personal communication) asked what the rationale was for this prejudice. While this might be investigated much further, there was some belief among villagers of the region that husbands and wives are lucky or unlucky, both to each other and to the husband's joint family. While usually it was a wife who was considered to have brought bad luck upon her husband and her husband's natal household when she moved into it, nevertheless, there seemed also to be a feeling that a man had "killed" his first wife through his being unlucky. Thus, one would be entrusting an innocent girl to a man suspected of being unlucky, unlucky enough that his first wife died, in marrying a virgin to a widower.

Conclusion

1. We are indebted to David Schneider for his commentary on an earlier draft of this chapter.

2. Cf. Dumont (1980), where he reiterates this criticism of our 1976 essays and reaffirms his approach to kinship without any additional arguments that might resolve the inconsistency we noted.

3. Here we refer the reader to our earlier formulation of the project in Barnett, Fruzzetti, and Östör (1976, 1977). This volume, like all our work since then, should be seen as a step toward the fulfillment of the promise formulated there in more polemical terms. The following argument is adopted from 1976:627.

References

Concepts of Person: Fifteen Years Later*

ABU LALI, S. 1988. Rape in India: An Empirical Picture. In *Women in Indian Society*, ed. R. Ghadially. New Delhi: Sage Publications.

ANANT, S. 1986. *Women at Work in India: A Bibliography*. New Delhi: Sage Publications.

ARCHER, G. 1984. *Songs for the Bride: Wedding Rites of Rural India*. New York: Columbia University Press.

AWASTY, I. 1982. *Rural Women of India: A Socio-Economic Profile of Jammu Women*. New Delhi: D. K. Publishers.

BABB, L. A. 1988. Indigenous Feminism in a Modern Hindu Sect. In *Women in Indian Society*, ed. R. Ghadially. New Delhi: Sage Publications.

BANERJEE, N. 1985.. *Women Workers in the Unorganized Sector: The Calcutta Experience*. London: Sangam Books Ltd.,

BARNETT, S. 1976. Coconuts and Gold. *Contributions to Indian Sociology* (N. S.) 10: 133–56.

BARNETT, S., L. FRUZZETTI, and Á. ÖSTÖR. 1976. Hierarchy purified. *Journal of Asian Studies* 35: 627–46.

——— 1977. On a comparative sociology of India: A Reply to Marriott. *Journal of Asian Studies* 36: 599–601.

BORTHWICK, M. 1984. *The Changing Role of Women in Bengal*. Princeton: Princeton University Press.

CAPLAN, P. 1985. *Class and Gender in India: Women and their Organizations in a South Indian City*. London: Tavistock Publications.

CARRITHERS, M., S. COLLINS, and S. LUKES, eds. 1985. *The Category of the Person*. Cambridge: Cambridge University Press.

CARTER, A. T. 1988. Does Culture Matter? The Case of the Demographic Transition. *Historical Methods*.

CHAKI-SIRCAR, M. 1984. *Feminism in a Traditional Society: Women of the Manipur Valley*. New Delhi: Vikas Publishing House.

CUSTER, P. 1986. Women's Role in the Tebhaga Movement. *Manushi* 6(2): 28–33.

DANDEKAR, H. 1986. Indian Women's Development: Four Lenses. *South Asia Bulletins,* (1), Spring: 25–29.

DAS, V. 1982. *Structure and Cognition: Aspects of Hindu Caste and Ritual*. New Delhi: Oxford University Press.

CUSTER, P. 1986. Women's Role in the Tebhaga Movement. *Manushi* 6(2): 28–33.
DANDEKAR, H. 1986. Indian Women's Development: Four Lenses. *South Asia Bulletins,* (1), Spring: 25–29.
DAS, V. 1982. *Structure and Cognition: Aspects of Hindu Caste and Ritual.* New Delhi: Oxford University Press.
DANIEL, E. V. 1984. *Fluid Signs: Being a Person the Tamil Way*. Berkeley: University of California Press.
DHRUVARAJAN, V. 1988. *Hindu Women and the Power of Ideology*. South Hadley MA: Bergin & Garvey.
DIRKS, N. B. 1987. *The Hollow Crown: Ethnohistory of an Indian Kingdom*. Cambridge: Cambridge University Press.
——— 1989. The Original Caste: power, history, and hierarchy in South Asia. *Contributions to Indian Sociology* (N. S.) 23: 59–77.
DUBE, L., E. LEACOCK, and S. ARDENER, eds. 1986. *Visibility and Power: Essays on Women in Society and Development*. New Delhi: Oxford University Press.
DUMONT, L. 1962. The conception of kingship in ancient India. *Contributions to Indian Sociology* 6: 48–77.
——— 1975. Terminology and Prestations Revisited. *Contributions to Indian Sociology* (N. S.) 9: 197–215.
——— 1980. New Introduction to *Homo Hierarchicus*. Chicago: University of Chicago Press.
——— 1983. *Affinity as Value*. Chicago: Chicago University Press.
FRUZZETTI, L. 1981. Purer than Pure, or the Ritualization of Women's Domain. *Journal of the Indian Anthropological Society* 16: 11–18.
——— 1982. *The Gift of the Virgin*. New Brunswick NJ: Rutgers University Press.
FRUZZETTI, L., and Á. ÖSTÖR. 1976a. Is there a Structure to North Indian Kinship Terminology? *Contributions to Indian Sociology* (N. S.) 10: 63–95.
——— 1976b. Seed and Earth: A Cultural Analysis of Kinship in a Bengali Town. *Contributions to Indian Sociology* (N. S.) 10: 97–132.
——— 1984. *Kinship and Ritual in Bengal: Anthropological Essays.* New Delhi: South Asian Publisher Pvt. Ltd.
GHADIALLY, R., ed. 1988. *Women in Indian Society*. New Delhi: Sage Publications.
GOOD, A. 1982. The actor and the act: categories of prestation in South India. *Man* (N. S.) 17: 23–41.
GRAY, J. 1980. Hypergamy, Kinship, and Caste among the Chattris of Nepal. *Contributions to Indian Sociology* (N. S.) 14: 1–34.
INDEN, R. 1976. *Marriage and Rank in Bengali culture*. Berkeley: University of California Press.
INDEN, R., and R. W. NICHOLAS. 1977. *Kinship in Bengali culture*. Chicago: Chicago University Press.
JAIN, D., and N. BANERJEE, eds. 1985. *Tyranny of the Household*. New Delhi: Shakti Books.
JUNG, A. 1987. *Unveiling India: A Woman's Journey*. New Delhi: Penguin Books.
KAIMAL, P., and D. JONES. 1984. Women in the Arts. In *Women and Work in India*, eds. J. Lebra, J. Paulson, and J. Everett. New Delhi: Promilla and Co.
KHAN, M. S., and R. ROY. 1984. Death Dowry. *Indian Journal of Social Work* 45: 303–307.

KISHWAR, M. 1986. Dowry: To Ensure Her Happiness or to Disinherit Her? *Manushi* 6(4): 2–13.

KISHWAR, M., and R. VANITA, eds. 1984. *In Search of Answers: Indian Women's Voices from Manushi*. London: Zed Books.

KOLENDA, P. 1984. Woman as Tribute, Woman as Flower. *American Ethnologist* 11: 98–117.

——— 1986. Caste in India Since Independence. In *Social and Economic Development in India*, eds. Dilip Basu and Richard Sisson, 106–128. New Delhi: Sage Publications.

——— 1987a. Living the Levirate: the Mating of an Untouchable Chuhra Widow. In *Dimensions of Social Life: Essays in Honor of David G. Mandelbaum*, ed. P. Hockings, 45–68. Berlin, New York, Amsterdam: Mouton de Gruyer.

——— 1987b. *Regional Differences in Family Structure in India*. Jaipur, India: Rawat Publishers.

——— 1989. The Joint-Family Household in Rural Rajasthan: Ecological, Cultural and Demographic Conditions for its Occurrence. In *Society from the Inside Out: Anthropological Perspectives on the South Asian Household*, eds. John N. Gray and David J. Mearns, 55–106. New Delhi: Sage Publications.

In press. Siblings in North, Central, and South India: A Comparison. In *Siblingship in South Asia*, ed. Charles W. Nukolid.

KOLENDA, P., ed. 1988. *Cultural Constructions of 'Woman.'* Salem WI: Sheffield Publishers.

KRYGIER, J. 1982. Caste and Female Pollution. In *Women in India and Nepal*, ed. Michael Allen and S. N. Mukherjee, 76–104. Canberra: Australian National University.

LEBRA, J., J. PAULSON, and J. EVERETT. 1984. *Women and Work in India: Continuity and Change*. New Delhi: Promila.

LEBRA-CHAPMAN, J. 1986. *The Rani of Jhansi: A Study of Female Heroism in India.* Honolulu: University of Hawaii Press.

LESSINGER, J. 1986. Work and Modesty: The Dilemma of Women Market Traders in South India. *Feminist Studies* 12(3): 581–600.

LIDDLE, J., and J. RAMA. 1986. *Daughters of Independence: Gender, Caste and Class in India*. London: Zed Books Ltd.

MADAN, T. N. 1985. Concerning the categories *subha* and *suddha* in Hindu culture: An exploratory essay. In *Purity* and *auspiciousness in Indian society*, eds. Frédérique Marglin and John Carman, 11–29. Leiden: E. J. Brill.

——— 1987a. *Non-Renunciaton: Themes and Interpretations of Hindu Culture.* New Delhi: Oxford University Press.

——— 1987b. Secularism in its place. *Journal of Asian Studies* 46(4): 747–60.

——— 1989. *Family and Kinship: A Study of the Pandits of Rural Kashmir.* New Delhi: Oxford University Press.

MADAN, T. N., ed. 1982. *Way of Life: King, Householder, Renouncer*. New Delhi: Vikas, Paris: Maison des Sciences de l'Homme.

MADAN, T. N., and A. BETEILLE, eds. 1975. *Encounter and Experience: Personal Accounts of Fieldwork*. New Delhi: Vikas, Honolulu: University of Hawaii Press.

MANN, K. 1987. *Tribal Women in a Changing Society*. New Delhi: Mittahl.

MARGLIN, F. A. 1985a. *Wives of the god-king: The rituals of the Devadasis of Puri*. New Delhi: Oxford University Press.

——— 1985b. Types of oppositions in Hindu culture. In *Purity and auspiciousness in Indian society*, ed. F. A. Marglin and John Carman, 65–83. Leiden: E. J. Brill.

MARRIOTT, M. 1976a. Hindu transactions: Diversity without dualism. In *Transaction and meaning*, ed. Bruce Kapferer, 109–42. Philadelphia: Institute for the Study of Human Issues.

——— 1976b. Interpreting Indian society: a monistic alternative to Dumont's dualism. *Journal of Asian Studies* 36: 189–95.

——— 1989. Constructing an Indian ethnosociology. *Contributions to Indian Sociology* (N. S.) 23: 1–39.

MARRIOTT, M., ed. 1990. *India Through Hindu Categories*. New Delhi/Newbury Park/London: Sage Publications.

MARRIOTT, M., and R. B. INDEN. 1974. Caste systems. *Encyclopaedia Britannica*, 15th ed., 3: 982–91.

——— 1977. Toward an ethnosociology of South Asian caste systems. In *The new wind*, ed. Kenneth David, 227–38. The Hague: Mouton.

MIES, MARIA. 1983. *The Lace Makers of Narsapur: Indian Housewives Produce for the World Market*. London: Zed Press.

——— 1986. *Indian Women in Subsistence and Agriculture Labor*. Geneva: International Labor Office.

MILNER, M. 1988. Status relations in South Asian marriage alliance: Towards a general theory. *Contributions to Indian Sociology* (N. S.) 22 (2).

MISRA, T. 1986. Feminism in a Traditional Society? *Economic and Political Weekly* 21(43): 54–56.

MUKHERJEE, P. 1983. The Image of Women in Hinduism. *Women's International Forum* 6(4): 379.

NANDY, A. 1988. Women versus Womanliness in India: An Essay in Social and Political Psychology. In *Women in Indian Society*, R. Ghadially, 69–80. New Delhi: Sage Publications.

ÖSTÖR, A. 1984. *Culture and Power: Legend, Ritual, Bazaar, and Rebellion in a Bengali Society*. New Delhi/Beverly Hills/London: Sage Publications.

ÖSTÖR, Á., L. FRUZZETTI, and S. BARNETT. 1982. *Concepts of Person: Kinship, Caste, and Marriage in India*. Cambridge: Harvard University Press.

PARRY, J. 1979. *Caste and Kinship in Kangra*. London: Routledge and Kegan Paul.

——— 1980. Ghosts, greed and sin: the occupational identity of the Benares funeral priests. *Man* (N. S.) 15: 88–111.

——— 1986. The gift, the Indian gift and the 'Indian gift.' *Man* (N. S.) 21: 453–73.

PAUL, M. C. 1986. *Dowry and Position of Women in India: A Study of Delhi Metropolis*. New Delhi: Inter Indian Publishers.

RAHEJA, G. G. 1988a. India: Caste, Kingship, and Dominance Reconsidered. *Annual Review of Anthropology* 17: 497–522.

——— 1988b. *The Poison in the Gift: Ritual, Prestation, and the Dominant Caste in a North Indian Village*. Chicago: University of Chicago Press.

——— 1989. Centrality, mutuality and hierarchy: shifting aspects of intercaste relationships in north India. *Contributions to Indian Sociology* (N. S.) 23: 79–101.

RAO, V. V. P., and V. N. RAO. 1988. Sex Role Attitudes of College Students in India. In *Women in Indian Society*, ed. R. Ghadially, 109–123. New Delhi: Sage Publications.

SARASWATI, B. N. 1977. *Brahmanic Ritual Traditions*. Simla: Indian Institute of Advanced Study.

SCHEFFLER, H. 1980. Kin Classification and Social Structure in North India. *Contributions to Indian Sociology* (N. S.) 14: 131–68.

SRINIVAS, M. N. 1984. *Some Reflections on Dowry*. New Delhi: Oxford University Press.

STUTCHBURY, E. L. 1982.Blood, Fire, and Meditation: Human Sacrifice and Widow Burning in Nineteenth Century India. In *Women in India and Nepal*, ed. Michael Allen and S. N. Mukherjee, 21–75. Canberra: Australian National University.

VATUK, S. 1969. A Structural Analysis of Hindi Kinship Terminology. *Contributions to Indian Sociology* (N. S.) 3: 94–115.

——— 1975. Gifts and Affines in North India. *Contributions to Indian Sociology* (N. S.) 9: 155–96.

——— 1982. Purdah Revisited: A Comparison of Hindu and Interpretations of the Cultural Meaning of Purdah in South Asia. In *Separate Worlds: Studies of Purdah in South Asia*, ed. H. Papanek and G. Minault, 54–78. Columbia MO: South Asia Books.

——— 1987. Authority, Power and Autonomy in the Life Cycle of the North Indian Woman. In *Dimensions of Social Life*, ed. P. Hockings, 23–44. Berlin: Mouton de Gruyter.

——— 1990. 'To be a Burden on Others': Dependency Anxiety among the Elderly in India. In *Divine Passions: The Social Construction of Emotion in India*, O. M. Lynch, 64–88. Berkeley and Los Angeles: University of California Press.

——— In press. The Cultural Construction of Shared Identity: A South Indian Muslim Family History. *Social Analysis*.

VISHWANATH, L. S. 1987. Women's Development through Voluntary Effort: Some Issues and Approaches. *Indian Journal of Social Work* 47(3).

WADLEY, S. S. 1975. Power in the Structure of Karimpur Religion. *University of Chicago Studies in Anthropology: Series in Social, Cultural and Linguistic Anthropology*, No. 2. Chicago: Department of Anthropology, University of Chicago.

WADLEY, S. S., and D. JACOBSON. 1987. *Women in India: Two Perspectives*. Delhi: Manohar Publications.

WULFF, D. M. 1985. Image and Roles of Women in Bengali Vaisnava padavali kirtan. In *Women, Religion and Social Change*, ed. Yvonne Yazbeck Haddad and Ellison Banks Findly, 217–245. Albany: State University of New York Press.

References

Introduction

BARNETT, S. 1976. Coconuts and gold. *Contributions to Indian Sociology* n.s. 10:133–156.

BARNETT, S., L. FRUZZETTI, and Á. ÖSTÖR. 1976. Hierarchy purified. *Journal of Asian Studies* 35:627–646.

——— 1977. On a comparative sociology of India. *Journal of Asian Studies* 35:599–601.

BARNETT, S., and M. SILVERMAN. 1979. *Ideology and everyday life.* Ann Arbor: University of Michigan Press.

FRUZZETTI, L. 1979. Muslim rituals: the household rites vs. the public festivals in rural India. In *Indian Muslim rituals,* ed. Imtiaz Ahmed. New Delhi: Vikas.

——— 1981. Purer than pure, or the ritualization of women's domain. *Journal of the Indian Anthropological Association.*

——— 1982. *The gift of a virgin: women, marriage, and ritual in Bengal.* New Brunswick, N.J.: Rutgers University Press.

——— n.d. Food and worship: analysis of Hindu and Muslim birth rituals. In press; Fruzzetti and Östör.

FRUZZETTI, L., and Á. ÖSTÖR. 1976a. Is there a structure to North Indian kinship terminology? *Contributions to Indian Sociology* n.s. 10:63–95.

——— 1967b. Seed and earth: a cultural analysis of kinship in a Bengali town. *Contributions to Indian Sociology* n.s. 10:97–132.

——— n.d. *Ritual and kinship in Bengal* (forthcoming collection of previously published papers).

KOLENDA, P. 1969. Region, caste, and family structure. In *Structure and change in Indian society,* ed. M. Singer and B. S. Cohn. New York: Viking Fund Publications in Anthropology.

——— 1976. Seven kinds of hierarchy in Homo Hierarchicus. *Journal of Asian Studies* 35:581–596.

——— 1978. *Caste in contemporary India.* Menlo Park, Calif.: Benjamin-Cummings Publishing Co.

MAYBURY-LEWIS, D. 1965. Prescriptive marriage systems. *Southwestern Journal of Anthropology* 21:207–230.

——— ed. 1979. *Dialectical societies: the Gê and Bororo of central Brazil.* Cambridge, Mass.: Harvard University Press.

ÖSTÖR., Á. 1979. *Puja in society.* Monograph No. 18. Lucknow, India: Ethnographic and Folk Culture Society.

——— 1980. *The play of the gods: locality, ideology, structure, and time in the festivals of a Bengali Town.* Chicago: University of Chicago Press.

——— n.d. *Deities, ritualists, merchants, and revolutionaries—toward the anthropology of a Bengali town* (forthcoming).

TAMBIAH, S. J. 1965. Kinship, fact and fiction in relation to the Kandayan Sinhalese. *Journal of the Royal Anthropological Institute* 95:131–173.

——— 1973. Dowry, bridewealth and the property rights of women in South Asia. In *Bridewealth and Dowry,* ed. J. Goody and S. J. Tambiah. Cambridge: Cambridge University Press.

VATUK, S. 1972. *Kinship and urbanization: white-collar migrants in north India.* Berkeley: University of California Press.

YALMAN, N. 1962a. On the purity of women in the castes of Ceylon and Malabar. *Journal of the Royal Anthropological Institute* 93:25–58.

——— 1962. The structure of Sinhalese kindred: a re-examination of the Dravidian terminology. *American Anthropologist* 64:548–73.

——— 1967. *Under the bo tree: studies in caste, kinship and marriage in the interior of Ceylon.* Berkeley: University of California Press.

1. The Cultural Construction of the Person in Bengal and Tamilnadu

DUMONT, L. 1957. Hierarchy and marriage alliance in south Indian kinship. Occasional Paper 12. London: Royal Anthropological Institute of Great Britain.

——— 1961. Marrriage in India: the present state of the question, part 1. *Contributions to Indian Sociology* 5:75–95.

——— 1964a. Marriage in India: the present state of the question, part 2. *Contributions to Indian Sociology* 7:77–98.

——— 1964b. A note on locality in relation to descent. *Contributions to Indian Sociology* 7:71–76.

——— 1966. Marriage in India: the present state of the question, part 3. *Contributions to Indian Sociology* 9:90–114.

——— 1970. *Homo Hierarchicus, the caste system and its implications.* London: Weidenfeld and Nicolson.

GEERTZ, C. 1974. Religion as a cultural system. In his *Interpretations of culture.* New York: Basic Books.

KAPADIA, K. M. 1947. *Hindu kinship.* Bombay: Popular Prakashan.

——— 1958. *Marriage and family in India.* Bombay: Oxford University Press.

KARVE, I. 1965. *Kinship organisation in India.* 2nd ed. Bombay: Asia Publishing House.

LUKÁCS, G. 1971. *History and class consciousness: studies in Marxist dialectics.* London: Merlin Press.

SCHNEIDER, D. M. 1968. *American kinship: a cultural account.* Englewood Cliffs, N.J.: Prentice-Hall.

——— 1972. What is kinship all about? In *Kinship studies in the Morgan centennial year,* ed. P. Reining. Washington, D.C.: Anthropological Society of Washington.

YALMAN, N. 1962. The structure of the Sinhalese kindred: a re-examination of the Dravidian terminology. *American Anthropologist* 64:548–573.

———. 1967. *Under the bo tree: studies in caste, kinship and marriage in the interior of Ceylon.* Berkeley: University of California Press.

2. Bad Blood in Bengal

DUMONT, L. 1957. *Hierarchy and marriage alliance in south Indian kinship.* Occasional Paper 12. London: Royal Anthropological Institute of Great Britain.

——— 1966. Marriage in India: the present state of the question, part 3. *Contributions to Indian Sociology* 9:90–114.

——— 1975. Terminology and prestations revisited. *Contributions to Indian Sociology* n.s. 9:197–216.

FRUZZETTI, L. 1982. *The gift of a virgin: women, marriage and ritual in Bengal.* New Brunswick, N.J.: Rutgers University Press.

FRUZZETTI, L., and Á. ÖSTÖR. 1976a. Is there a structure to north Indian kinship terminology? *Contributions to Indian Sociology.* n.s. 10:63–95.

——— 1976b. Seed and earth: a cultural analysis of kinship in a Bengali town. *Contributions to Indian Sociology.* n.s. 10:97–132.

FRUZZETTI, L., Á. ÖSTÖR., and S. BARNETT. 1976. The cultural construction of the person in Bengal and Tamil Nadu. *Contributions to Indian Sociology* n.s. 10:157–82.

INDEN, R., and R. NICHOLAS. 1977. *Kinship in Bengali culture.* Chicago: University of Chicago Press.

KAPADIA, K. M. 1947. *Hindu kinship.* Bombay: Popular Prakashan.

LÉVI-STRAUSS, C. 1973. *Totemism.* Hammondsworth: Penguin University Books. (First English publication 1963).

SCHNEIDER, D. M. 1970. What should be included in a vocabularly of kinship terms? Tokyo: *Proceedings of Eighth Congress of Anthropological and Ethnological Sciences,* pp. 88–90.

——— 1972. What is kinship all about? In *Kinship studies in the Morgan centennial year,* ed. P. Reining. Washington, D.C.: Anthropological Society of Washington.

VATUK, S. 1969. A structural analysis of Hindi kinship terminology: *Contributions to Indian Sociology* n.s. 3:94–115.

——— 1972. *Kinship and urbanization: white-collar migrants in North India.* Berkeley: University of California Press.

——— 1975. Gifts and affines in north India. *Contributions to Indian Sociology* n.s. 9, 2:155–196.

3. Forms of Address in the North Indian Family

BASSO, E. 1975. Kalapalo affinity: its cultural and social contexts. *American Ethnologist* 2:207–228.

BEAN, S. S. 1975. Referential and indexical meanings of *amma* in Kannada: mother, woman, goddess, pox, and help! *Journal of Anthropological Research* 31:313–330.

——— 1978. *Symbolic and pragmatic semantics: a Kannada system of address.* Chicago: University of Chicago Press.

BEARDSLEY, R. K., J. W. HALL, and R. E. WARD. 1959. *Village Japan.* Chicago: University of Chicago Press.

BECK, B. E. F. 1972. *Peasant society in Koṅku.* Vancouver: University of British Columbia Press.

BHARATI, A. 1963. Kinship term avoidance and substitution in north Indian middle class milieux. *Sociologus* 13:112–120.

BLOCH, M. 1971. The moral and tactical meaning of kinship terms. *Man* 6:79–87.

BROWN, R. W., and M. FORD. 1961. Address in American English. *Journal of Abnormal and Social Psychology* 62:375–385.

BUSCH, R. C. 1972. In-laws and out-laws: a discussion of affinal components of kinship. *Ethnology* 11:127–131.

CARTER, A. T. 1973. A comparative analysis of systems of kinship and marriage in South Asia. *Proceedings of the Royal Anthropological Institute of Great Britain and Ireland* 1973:29–54.

——— 1976. Household and demography: an Indian case. Unpublished paper presented to the annual meeting of the American Anthropological Association, Washington, D.C.

——— 1978. On the use and abuse of "kinship algebra"; kintype classification, categories of kinship relations, and address. Unpublished paper presented to the Tenth International Congress of Anthropological and Ethnological Sciences, New Delhi, India.

——— 1979. Children's usages of kin terms in Maharashtra, India: the acquisition of social deixis. Unpublished paper presented to the annual meeting of the American Anthropological Association, Cincinnati, Ohio.

CASSON, R. W. 1975. The semantics of kin term usage. *American Ethnologist* 2:229–238.

CASSON, R. W., and B. ÖZERTUĞ. 1974. Semantic structure and social structure in a central Anatolian village. *Anthropological Quarterly* 47:347–373.

——— 1976. Respect and address in a Turkish village: a quantitative sociolinguistic account. *American Ethnologist* 3:587–602.

CHATTERJEE, P. 1972. Familingual and familinear relationships: two patterns of control by the invoking of family roles. *American Anthropologist* 74:231–241.

CHAO, Y. R. 1956. Chinese terms of address. *Language* 32:217–241.

CONANT, F. 1961. Jarawa kin systems of reference and address: a componential comparison. *Anthropological Linguistics* 3:19–33.

DAS, V. 1976. Masks and faces: an essay on Punjabi kinship. *Contributions to Indian Sociology* n.s. 10:1–30.

DRUMMOND, L. 1978. The transatlantic nanny: notes on a comparative semiotics of the family in English-speaking societies. *American Ethnologist* 5:30–43.

DUMONT, L. 1962. Le vocabulaire de parenté dans l'Inde du nord. *L'Homme* 2:5–48.

——— 1966. Marriage in India: the present state of the question, part 3. *Contributions to Indian Sociology* 9:90–114.

——— 1975. Terminology and prestations revisited. *Contributions to Indian Sociology* n.s. 9:197–216.

EDER, J. F. 1975. Naming practices and the definition of affines among the Batak of the Philippines. *Ethnology* 14:59–70.

ERVIN-TRIPP, S. 1972. On sociolinguistic rules: alternation and co-occurence. In *Directions in sociolinguistics,* ed. J. J. Gumperz and D. Hymes. New York: Holt, Rinehart and Winston.

EVANS-PRITCHARD, E. E. 1948. Nuer modes of address. In *Language in culture and society,* ed. D. Hymes. New York: Harper and Row.

FISCHER, J. L. 1964. Words for self and others in some Japanese families. *American Anthropologist* 66:115–132.

FORTES, M. 1949. *The web of kinship among the Tallensi.* London: Oxford University Press.

——— 1969. *Kinship and the social order: the legacy of Lewis Henry Morgan.* Chicago: Aldine.

FRIEDRICH, P. 1966. Structural implications of Russian pronominal usage. In *Sociolinguistics,* ed. W. Bright. The Hague: Mouton.

FRUZZETTI, L., and Á. ÖSTÖR. 1976. Is there a structure to north Indian kinship terminology? *Contributions to Indian Sociology* n.s. 10:63–96.

GOODENOUGH, W. H. 1965a. Yankee kinship terminology: a problem in componential analysis. *American Anthropologist* 67:259–287.

——— 1965b. Personal names and modes of address in two Oceanic societies. In *Context and meaning in cultural anthropology,* ed. M. E. Spiro. New York: The Free Press.

HUNT, E. 1969. The meaning of kinship in San Juan: genealogical and social models. *Ethnology* 8:37–53.

INDEN, R., and R. NICHOLAS. 1977. *Kinship in Bengali culture.* Chicago: University of Chicago Press.

JAIN, D. 1969. Verbalization of respect in Hindi. *Anthropological Linguistics* 11:79–97.

KARVE, I. 1965. *Kinship organisation in India.* Bombay: Asia Publishing House.

KELKAR, A. 1962. Marathi kinship terms: a lexicographical study. *Transactions of the Linguistic Circle of Delhi* 1959–1960:1–22.

KHARE, R. S. 1975. Embedded affinity and consanguineal ethos. *Contributions to Indian Sociology* n.s. 9:245–261.

KITAOJI, H. 1971. The structure of the Japanese family. *American Anthropologist* 73:1036–1057.

KROEBER, A. L. 1909. Classificatory systems of relationship. *Journal of the Royal Anthropological Institute* 39:77–85.

LEAF, M. 1971. The Punjabi kinship terminology as a semantic system. *American Anthropologist* 73:545–554.

——— 1972. *Information and behavior in a Sikh village: social organization reconsidered.* Berkeley: University of California Press.

LEE, M. Y. 1976. The married woman's status and role as reflected in Japanese: an exploratory sociolinguistic study. *Signs* 1:991–999.

LOWIE, R. L. 1929. Relationship terms. *Encyclopaedia Britannica* 19:84–89.

MCCOY, J. 1970. Chinese kin terms of reference and address. In *Family and kinship in Chinese society,* ed. M. Freedman. Stanford: Stanford University Press.

MURDOCK, G. P. 1949. *Social structure.* New York: Macmillan.

NEEDHAM, R. 1966. Age, category and descent. *Bijdragen tot de taal-, land- en volkenkunde* 122:1–33. (Republished 1974 in *Remarks and inventions: skeptical essays about kinship.* London: Tavistock Publications).

POCOCK, D. 1972. *Kanbi and Patidar.* Oxford: Clarendon Press.

SCHEFFLER, H. W. 1977. On the "rule of uniform reciprocals" in systems of kin classification. *Anthropological Linguistics* 19:245–259.

——— 1980. Kin classification and social structure in North India. *Contributions to Indian Sociology* n.s. 14:131–168.

SCHNEIDER, D. M. 1955. Kinship terminology and the American kinship system. *American Anthropologist* 57:1194–1208.

——— 1968. *American kinship: a cultural account.* Englewood Cliffs, N.J.: Prentice-Hall.

——— 1969. Componential analysis: a state-of-the-art review. Unpublished paper presented to a symposium on Cognitive Studies and Artificial Intelligence Research, Chicago.

SERVICE, E. R. 1960. Sociocentric relationship terms and the Australian class system. In *Essays in the science of culture,* ed. G. E. Dole and R. L. Carneiro. New York: Crowell.

STIRRAT, R. L. 1977. Dravidian and non-Dravidian kinship terminologies in Sri Lanka. *Contributions to Indian Sociology* n.s. 11:271–293.

SWARTZ, M. J. 1960. Situational determinants of kinship terminology. *Southwestern Journal of Anthropology* 16:393–397.

TAX, S. 1955. Some problems of social organization. In *Social anthropology of North American tribes,* ed. Fred Eggan. 2nd ed. Chicago: University of Chicago Press.

TURNER, J. 1975. A formal semantic analysis of a Hindi kinship terminology. *Contributions to Indian Sociology* n.s. 9:263–292.

TYLER, S. A. 1965. Koya language morphology and patterns of kinship behavior. *American Anthropologist* 67:1428–1440.

——— 1966. Context and variation in Koya kinship terminology. *American Anthropologist* 68:693–707.

VAN DER VEEN, K. 1972. *I give thee my daughter.* Assen: van Gorcum.

VATUK, S. 1969a. A structural analysis of the Hindi kinship terminology. *Contributions to Indian Sociology* n.s. 3:94–115.

——— 1969b. Reference, address and fictive kinship in urban north India. *Ethnology* 8:255–272.

——— 1972. Kinship terminology in northern India. *American Anthropologist* 74:791–793.

——— 1975. Gifts and affines in north India. *Contributions to Indian Sociology* n.s. 9:155–196.

4. The Ideology of the Householder among the Kashmiri Pandits

BAMAZI, P. N. K. 1962. *A history of Kashmir.* Delhi: Metropolitan Books.

BÜHLER, G. 1964. *The laws of Manu.* Delhi: Motilal Banarasidass.

CHATTERJI, J. C. 1914. *Kashmir Shaivism.* Srinigar: The Research Department, Kashmir State.

DUMONT, L. 1957. For a sociology of India. *Contributions to Indian Sociology* 1:7–22.

——— 1960. World renunciation in Indian religion. *Contributions to Indian Sociology* 4:33–62.
——— 1966. A fundamental problem in the sociology of caste. *Contributions to Indian Sociology* 9:67–89.
——— 1970. *Homo Hierarchicus: the caste system and its implications.* London: Weidenfeld and Nicolson.
——— 1977. *From Mandeville to Marx: the genesis and triumph of economic ideology.* Chicago: University of Chicago Press.
GEERTZ, C. 1973. *The interpretation of culture.* New York: Basic Books.
MACDONELL, A. A. 1924. *A practical Sanskrit dictionary.* London: Macmillan.
MADAN, T. N. 1965. *Family and kinship: a study of the Pandits of rural Kashmir.* Bombay: Asia Publishing House.
——— 1972. Religious ideology in a plural society: the Muslims and Hindus of Kashmir. *Contributions to Indian Sociology* n.s. 6:106–141.
——— 1975a. Structural implications of marriage in north India: wife-givers and wife-takers among the Pandits of Kashmir. *Contributions to Indian Sociology* n.s. 9:217–243.
——— 1975b. On living intimately with strangers. In *Encounter and epxerience: personal accounts of fieldwork,* ed. A. Beteille and T. M. Madan. New Delhi: Vikas Publishing House.
MANUSMRITI. See Bühler, G.
MARRIOTT, M. 1977. Hindu transactions: diversity without dualism. In *Transaction and meaning: directions in the anthropology of exchange and symbolic behavior,* ed. B. Kapferer. Philadelphia: Institute for the Study of Human Issues.
MAYNE, J. D. 1953. *Treatise on Hindu law and usage,* by N. Chandrasekhara Aiyar. 11th ed. Madras: Higginbothams.
RADHAKRISHNAN, S. 1953. *The principal Upanisads.* London: George Allen and Unwin.
SCHNEIDER, D. M. 1968. *American kinship: a cultural account.* Englewood Cliffs, N.J.: Prentice-Hall.
——— 1976. Notes toward a theory of culture. In *Meaning in anthropology,* ed. K. Basso and H. Selby. Albuquerque: University of New Mexico Press.
SCHÜTZ, A. 1967. *Collected papers. I. the problems of social reality.* The Hague: Martinus Nijhoff.
——— 1976. *The phenomenology of the social world.* London: Heinemann Educational Books.
TAGORE, R. 1936. Gitanjali. In *Collected poems and plays.* London: Macmillan.
WEBER, M. 1947. *The theory of economic and social organization.* Glencoe, Ill.: The Free Press.

5. Hierarchy and the Concept of the Person in Western India

ALLCHIN, F. R. 1964. Trans., *Kavitavali of Tulsi Das* (with a critical introduction). London: George Allen and Unwin.
BARNETT, S. 1976. Coconuts and gold. *Contributions to Indian Sociology* n.s. 10:133–156.
BARNETT, S., L. FRUZZETTI, and Á. ÖSTÖR. 1976. Hierarchy purified: notes on Dumont and his critics. *Journal of Asian Studies* 35:627–646.

——— 1977. On a comparative sociology of India: a reply to Marriott. *Journal of Asian Studies* 36:599–601.

BASHAM, A. L. 1963. *The Wonder That Was India.* 2nd ed. New York: Hawthorn.

BATESON, G. 1971. The cybernetics of "self": a theory of alcoholism. *Psychiatry* 34:1–18.

BATESON, G., D. D. JACKSON, J. HALEY, and J. H. WEAKLAND. 1956. Toward a theory of schizophrenia. *Behavioral Science* 1:251–264.

BHARATI, A. 1961. *The ochre robe.* London: George Allen and Unwin.

BIARDEAU, M. 1965. *Ahamkāra,* the ego principle in the Upanishads. *Contributions to Indian Sociology* 8:62–84.

CARTER, A. T. 1971. Household partition in rural western Maharashtra. Paper read at the 1971 Annual Meeting of the American Anthropological Association, New York.

——— 1974a. A comparative analysis of systems of kinship and marriage in South Asia. 1973 Curl Prize Essay. *Proceedings of the Royal Anthropological Institute for 1973,* 29–54.

——— 1974b. *Elite politics in rural India.* Cambridge: Cambridge University Press.

——— 1975. Caste "boundaries" and the principle of kinship amity: a Maratha caste purana. *Contributions to Indian Sociology* n.s. 9:123–137.

CHATTERJEE, H. 1965. *Studies in some aspects of Hindu Samskaras in ancient India.* Calcutta: Sanskrit Pustak Bhandar.

DASGUPTA, S. 1932. A history of Indian philosophy, vol. 2. Cambridge: Cambridge University Press.

DAVIS, M. 1976. A philosophy of Hindu rank from rural West Bengal. *Journal of Asian Studies* 36:5–24.

DELEURY, G. A. 1960. *The cult of Vithoba.* Poona: Deccan College Postgraduate and Research Institute.

DIMOCK, E. C., JR. 1966. Doctrine and practice among Vaisnavas of Bengal. In *Krishna: myths, rites, and attitudes,* ed. M. Singer. Chicago: University of Chicago Press.

DUBOIS, ABBÉ J. A. 1909. *Hindu manners, customs and ceremonies.* Trans. with an introduction by H. K. Beauchamp. Oxford: Clarendon Press.

DUMONT, L. 1960. World renunciation in Indian religions. *Contributions to Indian Sociology* 4:33–62.

——— 1961. Caste, racism, and "stratification." *Contributions to Indian Sociology* 5:20–44.

——— 1965a. The modern conception of the individual: notes on its genesis. *Contributions to Indian Sociology* 8:13–61.

——— 1965b. The functional equivalents of the individual in caste society. *Contributions to Indian Sociology* 8:85–99.

——— 1970. *Homo Hierarchicus.* Trans. M. Sainsbury. Chicago: University of Chicago Press.

——— 1971. Religion, politics and society in the individualistic universe. *Proceedings of the Royal Anthropological Institute* 1970:31–41.

——— 1977. *From Mandeville to Marx: the Genesis and triumph of economic ideology.* Chicago: University of Chicago Press.

EDGERTON, F., trans. 1972. *The Bhagavad Gita.* 2nd ed. Cambridge, Mass.: Harvard University Press.

ELLISON, R. 1966. Hidden name and complex fate. In *Shadow and act.* New York: Signet Books.

FORTES, M. 1973. On the concept of the person among the Tallensi. In *La notion de personne en Afrique noire,* ed., G. Dieterlen. Paris: Editions du Centre National de la Recherche Scientifique.

FRUZZETTI, L., and Á. ÖSTÖR. 1976. Seed and earth: a cultural analysis of kinship in a Bengali town. *Contributions to Indian Sociology* n.s. 10:97–132.

FRUZZETTI, L., Á. ÖSTÖR., and S. BARNETT. 1976. The cultural construction of the person in Bengal and Tamil Nadu. *Contributions to Indian Sociology* n.s. 10:157–182.

GEERTZ, C. 1966. *Person, time, and conduct in Bali.* New Haven: Yale University Southeast Asia Studies, Cultural Report Series, No. 14.

GENNEP, A. VAN. 1960. *The rites of passage.* Trans. M. B. Vizedom and G. L. Caffee. Chicago: University of Chicago Press.

GENOVESE, E. D. 1976. *Roll, Jordan, roll: the world the slaves made.* New York: Random House.

GOFFMAN, E. 1959. *The presentation of self in everyday life.* New York: Random House.

——— 1961. *Asylums.* New York: Anchor Books.

——— 1963. *Stigma.* Englewood Cliffs, N.J.: Prentice-Hall.

——— 1967. *Interaction ritual.* New York: Anchor Books.

GOVERNMENT OF MAHARASHTRA. 1961. *Poona district gazetteer.* Bombay: Government Central Press.

HARPER, E. B. 1964. Ritual pollution as an integrator of caste and religion. *Journal of Asian Studies* 23:151–197.

HEESTERMAN, J. C. 1971. Priesthood and the Brahmin. *Contributions to Indian Sociology* n.s. 5:43–47.

INDEN, R. B. 1976. *Marriage and rank in Bengali culture.* Berkeley: University of California Press.

INDEN, R. B., and R. W. NICHOLAS. 1977. *Kinship in Bengali culture.* Chicago: University of Chicago Press.

KANE, P. V. 1941. *History of Dharmasastra,* vol. 2 parts 1 and 2. Poona: Bhandarkar Oriental Research Institute.

——— 1953. *History of Dharmasastra,* vol. 4. Poona: Bhandarkar Oriental Research Institute.

KEMPER, S. E. G. 1979. Sinhalese astrology, South Asian caste systems, and the notion of individuality. *Journal of Asian Studies* 38:477–497.

KHARE, R. S. 1976. *The Hindu hearth and home.* New Delhi: Vikas.

LAING, R. D. 1961. *Self and others.* London: Tavistock Publications.

MARRIOTT, M. 1966. The feast of love. In *Krishna: myths, rites, and attitudes,* ed. M. Singer. Chicago: University of Chicago Press.

——— 1976a. Hindu transactions: diversity without dualism. In *Transaction and meaning: directions in the anthropology of exchange and symbolic behavior,* ed. B. Kapferer. Philadelphia: Institute for the Study of Human Issues.

——— 1976b. An ethnosociological view. In *The new wind,* ed. K. David. The Hague: Mouton, World Anthropology.

——— 1976c. Interpreting Indian society: a monistic alternative to Dumont's dualism. *Journal of Asian Studies* 36:189–195.

MARRIOTT, M., and R. B. INDEN. 1978. Caste systems. *Encyclopaedia Britannica,* vol. 3, 982–991.

——— 1976. Toward an ethnosociology of South Asian caste systems. In *The new wind,* ed. K. David. The Hague: Mouton, World Anthropology.

MAUSS, M. 1938. Une catégorie de l'esprit humaine: la notion de personne, celle de moi. *Journal of the Royal Anthropological Institute* 68:263–282.

——— 1969. L'âme, le nom et la personne. In *Oeuvres,* vol. 2. Paris: Editions de Minuit. (First published 1929.)

MOLESWORTH, J. T., and G. T. CANDY. 1857. *A Dictionary, Marathi and English.* 2nd ed. Bombay: Bombay Education Society Press.

PANDEY, R. B. 1949. *Hindu samskaras.* Banaras: Vikrama Publications.

PANDEY, S. M., and N. ZIDE. 1966. Surdas and his Krishna-*bhakti.* In *Krishna: myths, rites, and attitudes,* ed. M. Singer. Chicago: University of Chicago Press.

PRADHAN, V. G., trans., and H. M. LAMBERT, ed. 1969. *Jnaneshvari,* vol. 2. London: George Allen and Unwin.

RANADE, R. D. 1933. *Mysticism in Maharashtra. History of Indian Philosophy,* vol. 7. Poona: Aryabhushan Press.

SINGER, M. 1966. The Radha-Krishna *bhajanas* of Madras City. In *Krishna: myths, rites and attitudes,* ed. M. Singer. Chicago: University of Chicago Press.

SRINIVAS, M. N. 1952. *Religion and society among the Coorgs of south India.* Bombay: Asian Publishing House.

STEELE, A. 1868. *The law and customs of Hindoo castes within the Dekhun provinces subject to the presidency of Bombay.* London: W. H. Allen and Co.

STEVENSON, S. 1920. *The rites of the twice-born.* London: Oxford University Press.

TELANG, K. T. 1961. *Gleanings from Maratha chronicles.* Bombay: P. C. Manaktala and Sons Ltd. (Published with *Rise of the Maratha power* by M. G. Ranade; first published 1892.)

VENKATESWARAN, T. K. 1966. Radha-Krishna *bhajanas* of South India. In *Krishna: myths, rites, and attitudes,* ed. M. Singer. Chicago: University of Chicago Press.

6. From *Kanyā* to *Mātā*

APTE, V. S. 1965. *The practical Sanskrit-English dictionary.* Delhi: Motilal Banarsidas.

BÜHLER, G. 1964. *The laws of Manu.* Delhi: Motilal Banarsidass. (First published 1886, by Oxford University Press, London.)

DUMONT, L. 1957a. Hierarchy and marriage alliance in south Indian kinship. Occasional Paper 12. *Royal Anthropological Institute of Great Britain and Ireland.*

——— 1957b. Kinship. *Contributions to Indian Sociology* 1.

——— 1966. Marriage in India: the present state of the question, part 3. *Contributions to Indian Sociology* 9:90–114.

——— 1975. Terminology and prestations revisited. *Contributions to Indian Sociology* n.s. 9:197–215.

KANE, P. V. 1941a. *History of Dharmasastra,* vol. 2, part 1. Poona: Bhandarkar Oriental Research Institute.

——— 1941b. *History of Dharmasastra,* vol. 2, part 2. Poona: Bhandarkar Oriental Research Institute.

——— 1953. *History of Dharmasastra,* vol. 4. Poona: Bhandarkar Oriental Research Institute.

KHARE, R. S. 1970. On hypergamy and progeny rank determination in northern India. *Man in India* 5:350–378.

——— 1972. Hierarchy and hypergamy: some interrelated aspects among the Kanya-Kubja Brahmans. *American Anthropologist* 74:611–628.

——— 1975a. "Embedded" Affinity and consanguineal "Ethos": two properties of the northern kinship system. *Contributions to Indian Sociology* n.s. 9:245–261.

——— 1975b. "Inside" apropos of "outside": some implications of a sociological debate. In *Main currents in Indian sociology,* ed. G. R. Gupta. Delhi: Vikas.

——— 1976a. *The Hindu hearth and home.* New Delhi: Vikas.

——— 1976b. *Culture and reality: essays on the Hindu system of managing foods.* Simla: Indian Institute of Advanced Study.

LEACH, E. R. 1974. *Claude Lévi-Strauss.* New York: Viking.

——— 1976. *Culture and communication: the logic by which symbols are connected.* London: Cambridge University Press.

LINGAT, R. 1973. *The classical law of India.* Trans. J. D. M. Derrett. Berkeley: University of California Press.

MADAN, T. N. 1975. Structural implications of marriage in north India: wife-givers and wife-takers among the Pandits of Kashmir. *Contributions to Indian Sociology* n.s. 9:216–243.

NEEDHAM, R. 1974. *Remarks and inventions: skeptical essays about kinship.* London: Tavistock Publications.

O'FLAHERTY, W. D. 1973. *Asceticism and eroticism in the mythology of Siva.* London: Oxford University Press.

PITT-RIVERS, J. 1973. The kith and kin. In *The character of kinship,* ed. J. Goody. London: Cambridge University Press.

PRABHU, P. H. 1963. *Hindu social organization.* 5th ed. Bombay: Popular Prakashan.

SCHNEIDER, D. M. 1968. *American kinship: a cultural account.* Englewood Cliffs, N.J.: Prentice-Hall.

——— 1972. What is kinship all about? In *Kinship Studies in the Morgan Centennial Year,* ed. P. Reining. Washington, D.C.: Anthropological Society of Washington.

——— 1976. Notes toward a theory of culture. In *Meaning in anthropology,* ed. K. Basso and H. Selby. New Mexico: University of New Mexico Press.

TAMBIAH, S. J. 1973. From varna to caste through mixed unions. In *The character of kinship,* ed. J. Goody. London: Cambridge University Press.

VATUK, S. 1969. A structural analysis of the Hindu kinship terminology. *Contributions to Indian Sociology* n.s. 3:94–115.

——— 1971. Trends in north Indian urban kinship: the "Matrilateral asymetry" hypothesis. *Southwestern Journal of Anthropology* 27:287–307.

——— 1972. Kinship terminology in northern India. *American Anthropologist* 74:791–793.

——— 1975. Gifts and affines in north India. *Contributions to Indian Sociology* n.s. 9:155–196.

ZAEHNER, R. C. 1969. *The Bhagavad-Gita.* Oxford: Oxford University Press.

7. Widowhood among "Untouchable" Chuhras

ABRAHAMS, R. G. 1973. Some aspects of levirate. In *The character of kinship,* ed. J. Goody. Cambridge: Cambridge University Press.

BARNETT, S. A. 1970. The structural position of a south Indian caste: Kontaikatti Velalar in Tamilnadu. Ph.D. diss. University of Chicago.

——— 1976. Coconuts and gold. *Contributions to Indian Sociology* 10:133–156.

BASHAM, A. L. 1954. *The wonder that was India.* New York: Grove Press.

BEALS, ALAN. 1962. *Gopalpur.* New York: Holt, Rinehart and Winston.

BECK, B. E. F. 1972. *Peasant society in Koṅku.* Vancouver: University of British Columbia.

BLUNT, E. A. H. 1969. *The caste system of northern India.* Delhi: S. Chand and Company. (First published 1931.)

BOHANNAN, P. 1966. *Social anthropology.* New York: Holt, Rinehart and Winston.

BRIGGS, G. 1920. *The Chamars.* London: Oxford University Press.

BÜHLER, G. 1969, trans., *The laws of Manu.* Oxford: Clarendon Press. (First published 1886.)

CARSTAIRS, G. M. 1957. *The twice-born.* London: Hogarth.

CHATTOPADHYAY, K. P. 1922. Levirate and kinship in India. *Man* 52, 25:36–41.

CHOCK, P. P. 1974. Time, nature and spirit: a symbolic analysis of Greek-American spiritual kinship. *American Ethnologist* 1:33–46.

COHN, B. S. 1955. The changing status of a depressed caste. In *Village India,* ed. M. Marriott. Chicago: University of Chicago Press.

CROOKE, W. 1907. *Natives of northern India.* London: Archibald Constable and Company.

DAVID, K. 1973. Until marriage do us part: a cultural account of Jaffna Tamil categories for kinsman. *Man* 8:521–535.

DRUMMOND, L. 1978. The transatlantic nanny: notes on a comparative semiotics of the family in English-speaking societies. *American Ethnologist* 5:30–43.

DUBE, S. C. 1955. *Indian village.* London: Routledge and Kegan Paul.

DUBOIS, ABBÉ J. A. 1906. *Hindu manners, customs and ceremonies,* trans. H. K. Beauchamp. Oxford: Oxford University Press.

DUMONT, L. 1957a. *Une sous-caste de l'Inde du sud.* Paris: Mouton.

——— 1957b. Hierarchy and marriage alliance in south Indian kinship. Occasional Paper 12. London: Royal Anthropological Institution.

——— 1964. Marriage in India: the present state of the question, part 2. *Contributions to Indian Sociology* 7:77–102.

——— 1966. Marriage in India: the present state of the question, part 3. *Contributions to Indian Sociology* 9:90–114.

——— 1970a. *Homo Hierarchicus.* Chicago: University of Chicago Press.

——— 1970b. The conception of kingship in ancient India. In *Religion, politics and history in India.* Paris: Mouton.

——— 1975. Terminology and prestations revisited. *Contributions to Indian Sociology* n.s. 9:197–215.

FORTES, M. 1949. *The web of kinship among the Tallensi.* London: Oxford University Press.

FRIEDL, E. 1964. Lagging emulation in post-peasant society. *American Anthropologist* 66:569–586.

FRUZZETTI, L., and Á. ÖSTÖR. 1976. Seed and earth: a cultural analysis of kinship in a Bengali town. *Contributions to Indian Sociology* n.s. 10:97–132.

FRUZZETTI, L., Á. ÖSTÖR, and S. BARNETT. 1976. The cultural construction of the person in Bengal and Tamil Nadu. *Contributions to Indian Sociology* n.s. 10:157–182.

FUCHS, S. 1960. *The Gond and Bhumia of eastern Mandla.* Bombay: Asia Publishing House.

GALANTER, M. 1972. The abolition of disabilities—untouchability and the law. In *The untouchables in contemporary India,* ed. J. M. Mahar. Tucson: University of Arizona Press.

GOUGH, E. K. 1956. Brahman kinship in a Tamil village. *American Anthropologist* 58:826–853.

——— 1960. Caste in a Tanjore village. In *Aspects of caste South India, Ceylon, and North-West Pakistan,* ed. E. R. Leach. Cambridge: Cambridge University Press.

HITCHCOCK, J. T. 1956. The Rajputs of Khalapur: a study of kinship, social stratification and politics. Ph.D. diss. Cornell University.

——— 1960. The martial tradition of the Rajputs. In *Traditional India,* ed. M. Singer. Chicago: University of Chicago Press.

HUTTON, J. H. 1963. *Caste in India.* London: Oxford University Press.

IBBETSON, D. C. J. 1903. Jats. *The census of India, 1901, ethnographic appendices.* Calcutta: Superintendent of Government Printing.

INDEN, R. B. 1976. *Marriage and rank in Bengali culture.* Berkeley: University of California Press.

INDEN, R. B., and R. W. NICHOLAS. 1977. *Kinship in Bengali culture.* Chicago: University of Chicago Press.

KANE, P. V. 1941. *History of Dharmasastra,* vol. 2, part 1. Poona: Bhandarkar Oriental Research Institute.

KAPADIA, K. M. 1947. *Hindu kinship.* Bombay: Popular Book Depot.

KARVE, I. 1953, 1965. *Kinship organisation in India.* Bombay: Asia Publishing House.

——— 1961. *Hindu society: an interpretation.* Poona: Deccan College.

KHARE, R. S. 1975. Embedded affinity and consanguineal ethos: two properties of the northern kinship system. *Contributions to Indian Sociology* 9:245–262.

KLUCKHOHN, F., and F. STRODTBECK. 1961. *Variations in value orientation.* New York: Row Peterson and Company.

KOLENDA, P. M. 1967. Regional differences in Indian family structure. In *Regions and regionalism in South Asian studies: an exploratory study,* ed. R. I. Crane. Monograph 5. Duke University Program in Comparative Studies in Southern Asia.

——— 1968. Region, caste and family structure: a comparative study of the Indian "joint" family. In *Structure and change in Indian society,* ed. M. Singer and B. Cohn. Chicago: Aldine.

——— 1978. *Caste in contemporary India.* Menlo Park, Calif.: Benjamin-Cummings.

——— 1982. *Caste, cult and hierarchy.* Delhi: Manohar.

LEWIS, O. 1958. *North Indian village.* Urbana: University of Illinois Press.

LYNCH, O. 1969. *Politics of untouchability.* New York: Columbia University Press.

MADAN, T. N. 1975. Structural implications of marriage in north India: wife-givers and wife-takers among the Pandits of Kashmir. *Contributions to Indian Sociology* 9:217–244.

MANDELBAUM, D. G. 1957. The family in India. In *Introduction to the civilization of India: changing dimensions of Indian society and culture.* Syllabus Division, University of Chicago Press, pp. 247–263. (Originally published in 1948 in *Southwestern Journal of Anthropology* 4:123–139).

MARRIOTT, M. 1955. Little communities in indigenous civilization. In *Village India.* Chicago: University of Chicago Press.

MAYER, A. 1960. *Caste and kinship in central India.* Berkeley: University of California Press.

MINTURN, L., and J. T. HITCHCOCK. 1966. *The Rajputs of Khalapur, India.* New York: John Wiley and Sons.

MOFFATT, M. 1979. *An untouchable community in south India: structure and consensus.* Princeton: Princeton University Press.

MURDOCK, G. P. 1949. *Social structure.* New York: McMillan.

——— 1950. *Africa.* New York: McGraw-Hill.

NAIK, T. B. 1956. *The Bhils.* Delhi: Bharatiya Adimjati Sevak Sangh.

O'MALLEY, L. S. S. 1932. *Indian caste customs.* Cambridge: Cambridge University Press.

PARSONS, T. 1951. *The social system.* Cambridge, Mass.: Harvard University Press.

RADCLIFFE-BROWN, A. R. 1950. Introduction. In *African systems of kinship and marriage,* ed. A. R. Radcliffe-Brown and D. Forde. London: Oxford University Press.

RAHEJA, G. 1981. Women in north Indian kinship. Unpublished paper read at the annual meeting of the Association for Asian Studies, Toronto, March 14, 1981.

SAHLINS, M. 1979. Individual experience and cultural order. Unpublished. (Cited by Schneider 1980.)

SCHNEIDER, D. M. 1968. *American kinship: a cultural account.* Englewood Cliffs, N.J.: Prentice-Hall.

——— 1972. What is kinship all about? In *Kinship studies in the Morgan centennial year,* ed. P. Reining. Washington, D.C.: The Anthropological Society of Washington.

——— 1980. Twelve years later. In *American kinship: a cultural account.* 2nd ed. Chicago: University of Chicago Press.

SCHNEIDER, D. M., and R. T. SMITH. 1973. *Class differences and sex roles in American kinship and family structure.* Englewood Cliffs, N.J.: Prentice-Hall.

SHAMASASTRY, R. 1967. *Kautilya's Arthasāstra.* Mysore: Mysore Printing and Publishing House. (First published 1915).

SINGH, I. 1944. *The Gondwana and the Gonds.* Lucknow: Universal Publishers.

SINGH, M. 1947. *The depressed classes.* Bombay: Hind Kitab.

SINGH, R. D. 1962. Family organization in a north India village: a study in culture change. Ph.D. diss. Cornell University.

SINHA, S. 1962. State formation and Rajput myth in tribal central India. *Man in India* 42:35–80.

SRINIVAS, M. N. 1966. *Social change in modern India.* Berkeley: University of California Press.

STEVENSON, M. S. 1930. *Without the pale.* London: Oxford University Press.

TURNER, J. 1975. A formal semantic analysis of kinship terminology. *Contributions to Indian Sociology* n.s. 9:263–292.

VATUK, S. 1969. A structural analysis of the Hindu kinship terminology. *Contributions to Indian Sociology* n.s. 3:94–115.

——— 1975. Gifts and affines in north India. *Contributions to Indian Sociology* n.s. 9:155–196.

——— 1980. The aging woman in India: self-perceptions and changing roles. In *Women in contemporary India and South Asia,* ed. A. de Souza. Delhi: Manohar.

YANAGISAKO, S. J. 1978a. Introduction to special section: American kinship. *American Ethnologist* 5:1–4.

——— 1978b. Variations in American kinship: implications for cultural analysis. *American Ethnologist* 5:15–29.

Conclusion

BARNETT, S., L. FRUZZETTI, and Á. ÖSTÖR. 1976. Hierarchy purified. *Journal of Asian Studies* 35:627–646.

——— 1977. On the comparative sociology of India: a reply to Marriott. *Journal of Asian Studies* 36:599–601.

BEAN, S. 1978. *Symbolic and pragmatic semantics.* Chicago: University of Chicago Press.

DUMONT, L. 1975. Terminology and prestations revisited. *Contributions to Indian Sociology* n.s. 9:197–215.

——— 1978. La communauté anthropologique et l'idéologie. *L'Homme* 18:83–110.

——— 1980. *Homo Hierarchicus,* preface to the complete English edition. Chicago: University of Chicago Press.

FOX, J. J., ed. 1980. *The flow of life: essays on eastern Indonesia.* Cambridge, Mass.: Harvard University Press.

FRUZZETTI, L. 1979. Review of Inden and Nicholas (1977). *American Anthropologist* 81:943.

FRUZZETTI, L., and Á. ÖSTÖR. n.d. *Ritual and kinship in Bengal: a collection of essays* (forthcoming).

INDEN, R. 1976. *Marriage and rank in Bengali culture.* Berkeley: University of California Press.

INDEN, R., and R. W. NICHOLAS. 1977. *Kinship in Bengali culture.* Chicago: University of Chicago Press.

MARRIOTT, M., and R. INDEN. 1976. Toward an ethnosociology of South Asian caste systems. In *The new wind,* ed. K. David. The Hauge: Mouton.

MARRIOTT, M. 1976a. An ethnosociological view. In *The new wind,* ed. K. David. The Hague: Mouton.

——— 1976b. Interpreting Indian society: a monistic alternative to Dumont's dualism. *Journal of Asian Studies* 36:189–195.

MAYBURY-LEWIS, D. 1979. *Dialectical societies: the Gẽ and Bororo of central Brazil.* Cambridge, Mass.: Harvard University Press.

MOFFATT, M. 1979. *An untouchable community in south India.* Princeton: Princeton University Press.

Index